Teaching Primary Humanities

Russell Grigg
Sioned Hughes

PEARSON

Harlow, England • London • New York • Boston • San Francisco • Toronto • Sydney • Auckland • Singapore • Hong Kong
Tokyo • Seoul • Taipei • New Delhi • Cape Town • São Paulo • Mexico City • Madrid • Amsterdam • Munich • Paris • Milan

Pearson Education Limited
Edinburgh Gate
Harlow
Essex CM20 2JE
England

and Associated Companies throughout the world

Visit us on the World Wide Web at:
www.pearson.com/uk

First published 2013
© Pearson Education Limited 2013

ISBN 978-1-4082-5134-8

British Library Cataloguing-in-Publication Data
A catalogue record for this book is available from the British Library

10 9 8 7 6 5 4 3 2 1
16 15 14 13 12

Typeset in 9.75/12 pt ITC Giovanni Std by 73
Printed by Ashford Colour Press Ltd., Gosport

Contents

> Think of tomorrow. The past can't be mended.
>
> (Confucius, *Analects*, 6th century BC)

The humanities, in some form or another, are well established in the curricula of many countries around the world, ranging from Australia to Sweden (Le Métais, 2003). However, over recent years, the status of the humanities subjects (history, geography and religious education) in primary and secondary schools in England has declined. There have been frequent reports about the weakening of pupils' knowledge and understanding as teachers lack subject expertise to engage and challenge learners. A recent review of the curriculum in England, chaired by Robin Alexander, suggests that children are leaving school with inadequate knowledge in the arts and humanities, having spent too many years 'tied to a desk' learning times tables (Curtis, 2009; Alexander, 2010). In geography, one in ten primary schools has abandoned teaching the subject despite its place as a compulsory national curriculum subject. In approximately half the primary schools visited by Ofsted, the English schools inspectorate, pupils in some classes were taught no geography at all (Ofsted, 2011b). The state of Religious Education (RE) in schools is also concerning. Many teachers are uncertain over what they are trying to achieve in the subject, and as a result there is a lack of well-structured teaching and learning (Ofsted, 2010). In Northern Ireland, the segregated educational system continues to cause concern in promoting the broader notion of RE (Fergus, 2011). The position of history in the primary school is also 'in the balance' (Ofsted, 2007) with too many pupils not challenged. The Better History group, a think tank of experienced history lecturers and teachers, are among those who call for a radical shake-up of the history curriculum in primary and secondary schools (Shepherd, 2011). The current review of the National Curriculum in England, launched by the Coalition government in 2011 and to be introduced in 2014, has a steer to strengthen the knowledge content of geography and history (see www.education.gov.uk/schools/teachingandlearning/curriculum).

These concerns should not undervalue the excellent contributions of professional bodies such as the Geographical and Historical Associations, and organisations such as the Culham Institute, an education charity that supports the teaching of RE through research, professional dialogue and resources (for instance see www.reonline.org.uk). Generally speaking, teachers are now better off than previous generations in terms of access to resources, planning documents, assessment tools and research to inform their practice. However, there is no doubt that primary teachers have been under pressure, suffering from 'initiative fatigue' over recent years. During the 1990s and early 2000s, the school timetable, particularly in England, has been dominated by literacy and numeracy with a relentless focus on 'standards' in these core areas. This has squeezed curriculum time and in many schools the humanities have been marginalised. Initial teacher training courses and opportunities for continuing professional development have also focused on literacy and numeracy with limited coverage in the humanities. One of the challenges for those supportive of primary humanities is overcoming the perception that these subjects are of secondary importance (Ofsted, 2007), lacking relevance in the modern world of technologies, science and material advancement.

Structure and Content

Each chapter of the book has three main features to promote engagement with the issues raised:

Tasks – these are directed activities to extend knowledge and understanding. They can be undertaken individually or in small groups.

Reflections – these are moments to pause and consider the implications of what is discussed.

Research Briefings – these are summaries of research pertinent to the points under discussion.

One of the challenges in writing this book is to ensure appropriate balance – between theory and practice, subjects, the phases of primary education and in meeting the needs of student and serving teachers at different stages of their careers. Where possible, the distinctiveness of the educational systems of England, Wales, Scotland and Northern Ireland needs is highlighted. For instance, Scotland has its *Curriculum for Excellence* rather than a National Curriculum, which operates elsewhere in the UK. The humanities are also organised in different ways: as social studies and religious and moral education in Scotland; as separate subjects for older pupils in England and Wales; as integrated themes in Northern Ireland. The Eurydice Network provides reliable information on each of the UK countries as well as other European education systems and policies: http://eacea.ec.europa.eu/education/eurydice/index_en.php.

Similar challenges are faced in describing the professional teaching standards and opportunities for continuing professional development. For the most up-to-date references, it is best to refer to the following official online sources:

England – the Department for Education: http://www.education.gov.uk/.

Wales – the Welsh Government: wales.gov.uk/legislation/subordinate/nonsi/educationwales/2009/3220099/?lang=en.

Scotland – the General Teaching Council for Scotland: www.gtcs.org.uk/standards/standard-full-registration.aspx.

Northern Ireland – Department of Education, Northern Ireland: www.deni.gov.uk/.

Chapter 1 provides a short history of the humanities, tracing their origins back to the ancient Greek interest in the human condition. In modern times, the humanities cover a broad range of studies. In the primary school, these often equate to history, geography and RE. More practical issues are discussed in Chapters 2 and 3 by considering the importance of planning and whether the humanities should be taught separately or through a cross-curricular approach. Chapter 4 focuses on the play-based curriculum for young children and their knowledge and understanding of their world. This needs to begin with the children's familiar experiences of home, school and local community. The potential of local study to excite, enthuse and engage learners of all ages is discussed in detail in Chapter 5. Pupils can pursue their own enquiries by raising questions, handling sources and undertaking fieldwork. In so doing they should acquire a sense of pride in their community. Heritage, whether personal, local or national, attracts major interest. Its appeal is discussed in Chapter 6, and the need for schools to make full use of museums, galleries and parks is made clear. Chapter 7 explores the role of the humanities in promoting pupils' awareness of Britain's diverse society, past and present. It also describes how the humanities can provide interesting contexts to meet the needs of different pupils. Chapters 8 and 9 take this further by showing how the humanities subjects are windows to a wider world. They should be at the forefront in promoting pupils' awareness of sustainability and global issues. Chapter 10 is concerned with the challenge of assessing progress in pupils' learning, while the final chapter highlights the need for teachers to continue their professional development in the humanities if their teaching is to remain sharp and current.

For too long, the humanities have been neglected and undervalued in both schools and initial teacher education. Ofsted (2011a) calls upon the Westminster government to ensure that there is sufficient subject-specific professional development to support primary teachers' work more effectively. Similar issues arise in primary geography with pupils experiencing too much variation in the quality of teaching (Ofsted, 2011b). Geography has suffered as a 'Cinderella' subject for decades – a survey by the Inspectorate in 1978 found much of geography school work was superficial (HMI, 1978). Finally, in RE the picture is equally alarming with teachers lacking confidence and knowledge to plan and teach high-quality lessons (Ofsted, 2010). Such reports indicate that the educational system is letting pupils down and is, frankly, in danger of promoting a kind of cultural amnesia. As the Humanities Association put it (www.hums.org.uk), what is needed is a dynamic curriculum that recognises the contribution of the humanities in providing the essential knowledge, concepts and skills that learners need to understand our world.

References

Alexander, R.J. (ed.) (2010), *Children, their World, their Education: final report and recommendations of the Cambridge Primary Review,* Abingdon: Routledge.

Curtis, P. (2009), 'Tests blamed for blighting children's lives', *The Guardian*, 20 February 2009.

Fergus, L. (2011), 'Open letter calls for school reform', *in Belfast Telegraph,* 7 September 2011.

HMI (1978), *Primary Education in England,* London: HMSO.

Le Metais, J. (2003), *International Trends in Primary Education, INCA Thematic Study 9,* London: Qualifications and Curriculum Authority.

Ofsted (2007), *History in the Balance,* London: Ofsted.

Ofsted (2010), *Transforming Religious Education*. London: Ofsted.

Ofsted (2011a), *History for All*, London: Ofsted.

Ofsted (2011b), *Geography – Learning to Make the World of Difference*, London: Ofsted.

Shepherd, J. (2011), 'History lessons are becoming a thing of the past', *The Guardian*, 20 January 2011.

Acknowledgements

We are grateful to the following for permission to reproduce copyright material:

Figures

Figure 1.3 from www.un.org/millenniumgoals; Figure 3.1 from Alexander, R.J. (ed) (2010) Children, their World, their Education: final report and recommendations of the Cambridge Primary Review, Abingdon, Routledge, p.274; Figure 3.2 from http://www.nicurriculum.org.uk/key_stages_1_and_2/areas_of_learning/the_world_around_us/, reproduced from: CCEA: When and how play is introduced in the Northern Ireland Curriculum 2008, © CCEA; Figure 4.1 from http://www.education.gov.uk/tickellreview, Tickell Review (2011), The Early Years: Foundations for life, health and learning – an independent report on the Early Years Foundation Stage to Her Majesty's Government, available at: www.education.gov.uk, Contains public sector information licensed under the Open Government Licence (OGL) v1.0. http://www.nationalarchives.gov.uk/doc/open-government-licence/; Figure 4.2 from CCEA (2008) pp.16 and 18, Learning through play at Key Stage 1, Belfast: CCEA, reproduced from: CCEA: World Around Us: GridGeography.pdf 2012, © CCEA; Figure 5.2 from Mia Grigg; Figure 5.6 from *Primary School Projects* Heinemann Educational Books (Waters, D. 1982) p.76, © Pearson Education Limited; Figure 5.7 from www.livingstreets.org.uk, Living Streets Scotland's Engaging Communities project was funded by Scottish Government; Figure 6.2 from sketch and photo by Mia Grigg; Figure 6.3 from www.culture.gov.uk/ukwhportal/map.htm, Contains public sector information licensed under the Open Government Licence (OGL) v1.0. http://www.nationalarchives.gov.uk/doc/open-government-licence/;Figure 6.4 from www.forestry.gov.uk/forestry/infd-7chcwe (Wood you believe poster, by the Forestry Commission England), Contains public sector information licensed under the Open Government Licence (OGL) v1.0. http://www.nationalarchives.gov.uk/doc/open-government-licence/; Figure 6.5 from www.nationalparks.gov.uk, Contains Ordnance Survey data © Crown copyright and database right 2011; Figure 7.2 from Statistical Bulletin, issued 28 July 2011: Baby names in England and Wales, 2010, Office for National Statistics licensed under the Open Government Licence v.1.0.; Figure 9.1 from Martin, F. and Owens, P. (2010), p.6, 'Children making sense of their place in the world' in Scoffham, S., ed., *Primary Geography Handbook*, Sheffield: Geographical Association; Figure 10.5 from DCSF (2008), p.87, Practice Guidance for the Early Years Foundation Stage, London: DCSF., Contains public sector information licensed under the Open Government Licence (OGL) v1.0. http://www.nationalarchives.gov.uk/doc/open-government-licence/; Figure 11.3 from www.lancsngfl.ac.uk/curriculum/, The Lancashire Grid for Learning, Fiona Revell – Lancashire County Council; Figure 11.5 from http://www.thomasmoreprimary.org.uk/pgf/doc/0002981tmp-O0-4lGeography2011-12.pdf

Tables

Table 2.1 adapted from *Teaching Religious Education*, Learning Matters (McCreery, E., Palmer, S., Voiels, V.) p.97, Reproduced by permission of SAGE Publications, London, Los Angeles, New Delhi and Singapore, from McCreery, E., Palmer, S., Voiels, V., Teaching Religious Education, Copyright (© Learning Matters, 2008); Table 2.2 from http://www.lcp.co.uk/primary-school/geography/geography-resource-files/, Bowden. D. and Copeland, P. (2001), LCP Geography Resource File – KS2, Lemington Spa: LCP; Table 4.2 adapted from *Teaching Humanities in Primary Schools*, Learning Matters (Hoodless, P., McCreery, E., Bowen, P., Bermingham, S. 2009) p.40, Reproduced by permission of SAGE Publications, London, Los Angeles, New Delhi and Singapore, from McCreery, E., Palmer, S., Voiels, V., Teaching Religious Education, Copyright (© Learning Matters, 2008); Table 4.5 adapted from 'What do five-year-olds know of the world? Geographical understanding and play in young children's early learning', *Geography*, 91(1), p.70 (Catling, S. 2006); Table 4.6 adapted from What do five-year-olds know of the world? Geographical understanding and play in young children's early learning, *Geography*, 91(1), 55–74 (Catling, S. 2006); Table 4.7 adapted from *Achieving QTS: Teaching Religious Education*, Learning Matters (McCreery, E., Palmer, S., Voiels, V.) p.92, Reproduced by permission of SAGE Publications, London, Los Angeles, New Delhi and Singapore, from McCreery, E., Palmer, S., Voiels, V., Teaching Religious Education, Copyright (© Learning Matters, 2008); Table 5.1 from www.cumbriagridfor-learning.org.uk, Work of the Learning Improvement Service, Cumbria County Council; Table 7.1 from www.statistics.gov.uk/babynames, Office for National Statistics licensed under the Open Government Licence v.1.0.; Table 7.4 adapted from *Reclaiming our Pasts*, Trentham Books (Claire, H. 1996) p.10, full acknowledgement to TRENTHAM BOOKS LTD; Table 9.1 adapted from Martin, F. and Owens, P. (2010), p.10, 'Children making sense of their place in the world' in Scoffham, S., ed., Primary Geography Handbook, Sheffield: Geographical Association; Table 9.4 adapted from *Teaching Religious Education*, Learning Matters (McCreery, E., Palmer, S., and Voiels, V. 2008) p.74, Reproduced by permission of SAGE Publications, London, Los Angeles, New Delhi and Singapore, from McCreery, E., Palmer, S., Voiels, V., Teaching Religious Education, Copyright (© Learning Matters, 2008); Table 9.6 from Talking about 'the last wilderness', *Primary Geography*, Spring (56), p.32 (Mackintosh, M. 2005); Table 10.3 adapted from Monitoring, Recording, Assessment and Reporting, *Primary History*, 57, p.36 (Lomas, T. 2011), Reproduced courtesy of The Historical Association; Table 10.4 from *Achieving QTS: Teaching Primary Geography*, Learning Matters. (Catling, S. and Willy, T. 2009) p.197, Reproduced by permission of SAGE Publications, London, Los Angeles, New Delhi and Singapore, from McCreery, E., Palmer, S., Voiels, V., Teaching Religious Education, Copyright (© Learning Matters, 2008); Table 10.5 from *Involvement of Teacher and Children Style: Insights from an International Study on Experiential Education*, Leuven University Press (Laevers, F. and Heylen, L. 2004); Table 11.1 from 'Models of continuing professional development: a framework for analysis', *Journal of In-Service Education*, 31(2), 235–250, (Kennedy, A. 2005), copyright © *Professional Development in Education*, reprinted by permission of Taylor & Francis Ltd, www.tandfonline.com, on behalf of *Professional Development in Education*; Table 11.2 adapted from *Reflective Teaching*, 3rd ed., Continuum (Pollard, A., Anderson, J., Maddock, M., Swaffield, S., Warin, J., and Warwick, P. 2008), © Pollard, A., Anderson, J., Maddock, M., Swaffield, S., Warin, J., and Warwick, P., 2008, Reflective Teaching, 3rd ed., by permission of Continuum, an imprint of Bloomsbury Publishing Plc.

Text

Poetry on pages 155–6 from *Wicked World*, Puffin (Zephaniah, B. 2000); Box on pages 183–4 adapted from Wide Horizons: The Children's Charter, *Primary Geographer* 20, pp.4–6 (Catling, S. 1995).

Photographs

(Key: L–left; R–right)

Alamy Images: World History Archive 4; **Russell Grigg:** 118; **HMSO:** ILEA (History in the Primary School, 1980) 102R, Plowden Report (DES,1967) 102L; **iStockphoto:** Duncan Walker 164; **Pearson Education Ltd:** The Illustrated London News Picture Library. Ingram Publishing. Alamy 241; **Sioned Hughes:** 86, 89, 92, 93, 218, 219, 242.

In some instances we have been unable to trace the owners of copyright material, and we would appreciate any information that would enable us to do so.

Author acknowledgements

We would like to thank all of those involved in the reviewing and editing process, particularly Dheeraj Chahal and Philippa Fiszzon. We are grateful to colleagues, students and children in many schools (particularly Ysgol Gymunedol Maenclochog/Maenclochog Community School), for their valuable contributions.

Dedication

*The book is dedicated to an inspirational teacher,
the late Olive Dyer, and to Mia and Tom –
for exploring the world with enthusiasm, laughter and mischief.*

1 The meaning, origins and contribution of the humanities

To know himself, a man must know the capabilities and performances of the human spirit; and the value of the humanities . . . is that it affords an unsurpassed source of light and stimulus.

(Matthew Arnold, 1822–1888, Chief Inspector of Schools; quoted by Conway, 2010: 49)

Learning objectives

By the end of this chapter you should be able to:

- define what is meant by the humanities;
- outline the origins and development of the humanities;
- recognise the contribution of the humanities in promoting positive values; and
- reflect upon the importance of history, geography and religious education in children's all-round development.

The meaning of the humanities

Put simply, the humanities explore human experience. This broad definition reflects the diverse studies of the humanities in the modern age. For instance, university students who follow a 'medical humanities' programme consider the therapeutic value of art, ethical issues associated with plagues in the past, and the influence of a family on a person's health and well-being (Evans and Finlay, 2001). Elsewhere, 'digital humanities' students might ask questions about economic, cultural and social challenges posed by ICT innovations such as e-books (Hockey, 2008). The huge scope of the humanities is well illustrated by the coverage within the

British Humanities Index, an online database of articles in over 370 internationally respected humanities journals and weekly magazines published in the English-speaking world. The major categories include: antiques, archaeology, architecture, art, cinema, current affairs, education, economics, environment, foreign affairs, gender studies, history, language, law, linguistics, literature, music, painting, philosophy, poetry, political science, religion and theatre. It is not surprising, then, that Adams (1976) referred to 'the humanities jungle' in trying to pin down the content of the humanities.

In subject terms, one way of looking at the humanities is to see how they are different from other branches of knowledge, such as the sciences. Those working within the humanities are not necessarily seeking a single correct answer and are more likely than scientists to accept ambiguities and various interpretations arising from beliefs, texts and practices. For Black (1975), what makes the humanities distinctive from the 'hard' sciences is that they are not concerned with 'neutralising' differences in pursuit of objective truth. He adds that students of the humanities want to go beyond *presenting* human perspectives by *critically* engaging with their subjects. The major building blocks for primary humanities covered in this book are shown in Figure 1.1.

Definitions of the Humanities

That group of subjects which is predominantly concerned with men and women in relation to their environment, their communities and their own self knowledge

(Schools Council, 1965: 14)

The 'humanities' includes history, possibly geography, the remnants of classical studies, some aspects of English and modern languages, religious education and so on

(Adams, 1976: 11)

Part of the primary curriculum that is concerned with individual human beings living and working in particular places and linked together with groups and societies, past and present

(Blyth, 1990: 1)

A collective term for a range of academic disciplines or fields, all of which draw upon a knowledge of the development, achievements, behaviour, organisation, or distribution of humanity

(Wallace, 2008: 132)

The study of the myriad ways in which people, from every period of history and from every corner of the globe, process and document the human experience

(Stanford University: https://humanexperience.stanford.edu/what)

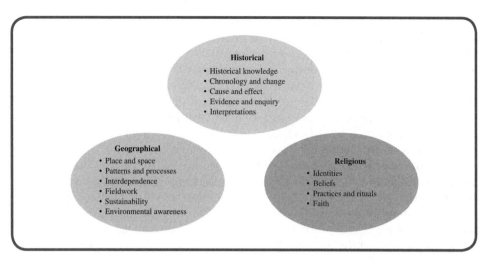

Figure 1.1 The major aspects of primary humanities covered in this book.

REFLECTION

- Consider the suggested definitions of the humanities in and try to create your own. Why is it so difficult to reach a commonly shared definition? Are there any features of the humanities that are widely agreed upon?

Ancient origins

The humanities have a long history. More than 2,500 years ago, the classical Greeks had a new conception of humanity and what the human mind was for: namely to reason, seek out patterns and, above all, ask questions (Kitto, 1951). Socrates (469–399 BC), one of the leading philosophers, proclaimed that 'the unexamined life is not worth living'. Socrates believed that by asking questions, listening to responses and then raising further questions (Socratic Method) teachers could reach the heart of what pupils believed. For Socrates, it was important for people to know *what* they were doing, *why* they were doing it and whether their actions were the *right* things to do. According to Hughes (2011: xix): 'We think the way we do, because Socrates thought the way he did.'

The study of history in Western civilisation began with the ancient Greeks. They produced the first historians, who asked such basic questions as 'Why did events happen when they did?' The word 'history' (from the Greek *historia*, meaning 'enquiry' or 'research') is derived from the writings of Herodotus (*c.* 484–425 BC). Considered 'the father of history', Herodotus was the first to document and analyse the causes of a war, the Persian War; 'Herodotus made it a rule for historians to explain the events they told' (Finlay, 1981: 158). Most significantly, he established the view that history should not favour one side or the other, since this would obscure truth (Warren, 1999). But it was another Athenian historian, Thucydides (*c.* 460–400 BC), who 'wrote true history' (Warren, 1999: 18). He probed beyond recollections of battles by scrupulously examining eyewitness accounts of military generals.

Geographical education in European experience also began with the ancient Greeks. Homer's *Odyssey* can be seen as the first travel book, composed in the eighth century BC. Greek librarian Eratosthenes (*c.* 276–196 BC) was the first to use the word 'geography' (literally 'writing about the earth') in his attempt to produce an accurate map of the world. He thought that the earth was a sphere and calculated (reasonably accurately) its circumference and the amount of habitable land. He also developed the concept of latitude. The Greek Strabo, writing in the first century AD, was the first to justify the usefulness of geography 'not only for politics and war, but also in giving knowledge of the heavens and of things on land and sea, animals, plants, fruits and of all that is to be seen in different regions' (quoted by Walford, 2001: 4).

The vibrant Athenian democracy involved debate and openness, whether in the assembly, market-place or the secondary 'schools' (from the Greek *skhole*, meaning 'a place of leisure'). These schools were aimed at the sons of wealthy citizens that had completed elementary schooling and had time on their hands to follow a course in liberal education – liberal in the sense that it was for free men, not slaves or servants, and was non-vocational in nature. They were run by a *paidagogos* (from which we derive pedagogy or the craft of teaching), or master teacher. He taught philosophy, politics, good manners and persuasive speaking (rhetoric) so that young men could become accomplished individuals, making good use of their leisure time (Finlay, 1981). The students learnt that traditions, beliefs and myths were not fixed doctrines to be handed on to the next generation but that they were to be questioned – this was nothing short of 'a revolution in education' (Finlay, 1972: 68).

Photo 1.1 Marcus Tullius Cicero. *Source:* © World History Archive/Alamy.

The Greek spirit of enquiry was given a practical edge by the Romans. The very word 'education' comes from the Roman home, for the Latin *educare* referred not to schooling but to how children were brought up and trained by their parents who 'drew out' their thinking (Bonner, 1977). The Romans generally appreciated that young children needed to read, write, count, weigh, measure and calculate. At a more advanced level, Roman statesman Marcus Tullius Cicero (106–43 BC) (see Photo 1.1) suggested a training programme for public speakers based on the 'studies of humanity' (*studia humanitatis*), which included *all* branches of learning. Cicero contrasted the 'humane and cultivated' life with the 'savage and barbarous', and a study of the humanities brought about the former. Castle (1961) suggests that the curriculum included Latin grammar, history, poetry, rhetoric, philosophy and music. These subjects prompted students to think clearly and judge critically. Our word 'critic' comes from the Greek *kritikos*, which originally applied to students who were critics of literature – the more able students became judges (*krites*) of literary quality (Bonner, 1977: 48–9).

The Greeks and Romans provided the blueprint for the education of the elite in Britain over the centuries. Classical writings were fused with Christian teaching to form the basis of the grammar and public school curricula through to the twentieth century. These schools aimed to provide learners with the intellectual skills and moral fibre expected of leaders. As Musgrave (1970: 254) observed: 'The British upper classes were convinced that a thorough grounding in the classics was the best training for a country's administrators, statesmen and military leaders.' The nineteenth-century Chief Inspector of Schools, Matthew Arnold, whose words open this chapter, advocated that children should be introduced to 'the best that has been thought and said'. Arnold demonstrated the classical humanist commitment to initiating children into the 'best' of cultural heritage. Michael Gove, education secretary, wants to reclaim Arnold's vision; for instance, he supported the sending of a free copy of the King James Bible to every state school in England, on the edition's 400th anniversary, so that they can access the best of Britian's cultural heritage. He also favours the virtues of a classical education, arguing that an 'audience would be gripped more profoundly by a passionate, hour-long lecture from a gifted thinker which ranged over poetry and politics than by cheap sensation and easy pleasures' (Shepherd, 2010; Vasagar, 2011).

The emergence of humanities in the curriculum

As separate subjects, history and geography first featured in the grammar school curriculum during the sixteenth century (Watson, 1909). Geography, along with the sciences and modern European languages, became important to the merchant and manufacturing middle classes. Since the earliest church schools of the post-Roman era, the education of the masses had focused on basic skills and religious instruction. History and geography became part of the first national curriculum for elementary schools introduced by the state in 1862. Even then, the substance of these early history and geography lessons focused largely on rote learning of kings, queens, battles, capes and bays, amounting to little more than 'adjuncts to biblical instruction' (Marsden, 2001: 33). Geography and nature study testified to the glories of God's creation, while history served moral purposes such as the need for obedience.

Religious Instruction (RI) was prominent on the school timetable through to the mid-twentieth century. In England and Wales, the 1944 Education Act conceptualised religious education (RE) as a combination of religious instruction and collective worship. It also gave local education authorities the option to establish a Standing Advisory Council on Religious Education (SACRE) to offer advice on teaching and resources in accordance with an agreed syllabus (Copley, 1997). This was strengthened by the 1988 Education Act, which required schools to reflect 'the fact that religious traditions in the UK are in the main Christian'. This tone remains stronger in Northern Ireland, where world faiths are not introduced until secondary schooling. The Education (Scotland) Act 1980 requires local authorities to provide religious observance in Scottish schools. RE and religious observance now form part of Scotland's *Curriculum for Excellence*, with schools and local authorities having the discretion to determine the content, frequency and location of religious observance. Similarly in England and Wales, every locally agreed syllabus sets out what is to be taught in schools although teachers' planning is also supported by national guidance materials (QCA, 2004; DCELLS, 2008) as discussed in Chapter 2.

The contribution of the humanities to children's education

The humanities enable people to make sense of the complex world in which they live. Without the lens of history, geographical awareness and an appreciation for religious beliefs, it is impossible to offer informed responses to such current affairs as: climate change, human rights violations, the war in Iraq, immigration, Islamophobia or the banking crisis. Historical, geographical and religious issues promote deep thinking by stimulating debate, questioning and reflection.

On a personal level, millions of adults gain satisfaction from the humanities. Local and family history are among the most popular hobbies, enabling people to reflect upon the experiences of their ancestors and their own identities. Many also recall 'private geographies' of their childhoods – the park they played in, their first home, the street, the 'days out' and the local characters and landmarks that gave their neighbourhood meaning. For thousands of years, religion has proven to be a matter of life and death – in the twenty-first century people continue to die prematurely because of inaccurate religious knowledge, intolerance and prejudice. Religion is still a powerful force in shaping our understanding of the world. Although the United Kingdom is becoming increasingly more secular, around half the population still follow a religion. Good religious education promotes pupils' personal well-being, including their understanding of why religion matters in the lives of other people. It should also challenge pupils to think about deep questions and consider whether religion is a force for good in the world. In one global survey 48 per cent of respondents said that 'religion provides the common values and ethical foundations that diverse societies need to thrive in the 21st century' whereas the other half (52 per cent) agreed that 'deeply held religious beliefs promote intolerance, exacerbate ethnic divisions, and impede social progress' (Ipsos, 2010).

The humanities contribute to the broad aims of education advocated by the highest-performing school systems in the world:

Economic – the education of pupils is expected to contribute to their own future economic well-being and that of the nation or region.

Cultural – the education of pupils is expected to introduce them to the best of their cultural heritage(s), so that they can contribute to its further development.

Social – the education of pupils is expected to enable them to participate in families, communities and the life of the nation.

Personal – the education of pupils is expected to promote the intellectual, spiritual, moral and physical development of individuals.

(DfE, 2011: 15)

Through the humanities, pupils learn to solve problems, ask questions, explore the diverse heritage of different cultures, gain insight into ethical and moral issues, develop informed opinions, read and write critically, construct stories, use technologies and reflect on their own identities. As Chapter 3 shows, the humanities promote literacy, numeracy and thinking skills, which are fundamental to twenty-first century life.

Values

Values are the fundamental convictions, beliefs and principles that guide behaviour. The National Forum for Values in Education and the Community in England identifies four areas of life in which values can be demonstrated (see Figure 1.2).

For some social commentators, the humanities subjects have lost their way in the twenty-first century, increasingly overshadowed by an emphasis on materialistic values, secularisation and the advance of technologies (Arroyo, 2002; Russo, 2005; Browne, 2008; Mayo and Nairn, 2009). The National Consumer Council suggests that the average 10-year-old has internalised between 300 and 400 brands – perhaps 20 times the number of birds in the wild that they could name (NCC, 2005: 2). The decline in children's well-being has been attributed to excessive advertising and marketing turning kids, from the age of two, into 'hyper-consumers' (Beder, 2009: 3). 'Retail therapy' and having money to buy things does not bring increased happiness, at least according to Richard Layard, one of the UK's leading economists. Layard (2006) points to the essential paradox that most people in the West strive for more income, and yet happiness is not on the increase. British children have been described as 'the least happy generation of the post-war era' (NCC, 2005: 2).

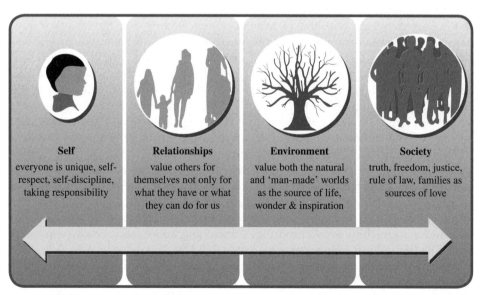

Self	Relationships	Environment	Society
everyone is unique, self-respect, self-discipline, taking responsibility	value others for themselves not only for what they have or what they can do for us	value both the natural and 'man-made' worlds as the source of life, wonder & inspiration	truth, freedom, justice, rule of law, families as sources of love

Figure 1.2 Core values in schools. *Source:* Based on The National Forum for Values in Education and the Community in England.

Many trace present-day concerns to the permissive 1960s – one leading writer declared that Christian Britain 'died' in the 1960s and has now reached 'the end of a long story' (Brown, 2001: 193). Christianity had traditionally offered a social cement that held communities together. The decline in religious marriage, Sunday observance, prayer and church membership, coupled with the rise of 24-hour shopping, and a general 'anything goes' attitude, has produced a very different generation today than that of the mid-twentieth century. In 2006, *The Good Childhood Inquiry* reported that 'the decline in religious and, more recently, secular belief in social obligation means there is less confidence in values such as generosity and fairness' (**www.childrenssociety.org. uk**; see also Layard, 2009).

Not everyone shares the view that Britain is in moral decline. Browne (2008: 4) points out that we are 'healthier, wealthier and wiser' (or better educated) than previous generations. Britain is now a more tolerant society with developments in human rights legislation, for instance relating to freedom of thought, conscience and religion. Moreover, research by the Young Foundation shows that although most people believe there was once a "golden age" of politeness, in some ways behaviour has improved over the last few generations (McVeigh, 2011). Guldberg (2009: 7) dismisses 'the childish panic about the next generation' and argues that the problem lies with adult society and the culture of fear that holds children back. Youngsters are generally optimistic about modern life. One poll by *RE Today*, on the eve of the millennium, found that children did not hanker after technology but wanted a more peaceful world in which people were treated fairly (Haigh, 1999).

In recent years there has been a renewed interest in values-based education where primary schools are encouraged to focus on direct teaching of values such as honesty, fairness and respect (Hawkes, 2003; Clutterbuck, 2008; Duckworth, 2009). In a climate of moral relativism, critics maintain that these fashionable values-led programmes have only produced children 'who know the slave trade was bad, but who are ignorant about how the right to vote was won in Britain' (Furedi, 2007: 5). Ideally, in this case, children need to learn both that eighteenth-century Britons were the world's leading transatlantic slave traders, and that in the nineteenth century Britain took the lead in a global campaign against slave-trading. Through such discussions, pupils begin to measure and counter bias, prejudice and stereotypes. The model set by teachers, in terms of openness to fresh ideas and alternative views, is of fundamental importance. But this does not mean 'sitting on the fence about anything controversial' or refusing to hold strong convictions (Watson and Thompson, 2007: 7). It is not simply about adopting a neutral position, but more a matter of demonstrating respect for the integrity of others.

The humanities are essential to the development of values. In history, social justice, ethics and moral courage can be promoted through the use of dilemmas such as whether or not to help an escaped slave in the 1840s (Claire, 2005), (see **www.history .ac.uk/resources/history-in-british-education/first-conference/claire-paper**). The Birmingham Agreed Syllabus for Religious Education (Birmingham City Council, 2007) is based on the teaching of 24 'dispositions', including: appreciating beauty, expressing joy, being fair and just, being courageous and confident, and living by rules (see **www. birmingham-asc.org.uk/overview.php**). Part of children's spiritual development is to question transient values associated with consumerism. Natural disasters, such as the Japanese tsunami in March 2011, serve as reminders of how flimsy our sophisticated world is, with billions of pounds of material goods swept away in a matter of minutes.

BOX 1.1 RESEARCH BRIEFING – CHILDREN'S VALUES

Theories of moral development suggest that young children move from making decisions based on self-interest, to taking into account what pleases others (conventional morality) and finally recognising that agreements can be changed or ignored when necessary. By the age of 11, children are capable of demonstrating empathy and altruistic behaviour, acting with a selfless concern for others. They can take value stances and positions on particular topics within the humanities, for instance relating to environmental issues. In one action research project, Owens (2004) asked Reception and Key Stage 1 children to draw anything in the school grounds that they themselves considered special and important. The drawings were classified and entered on a spreadsheet. She found that when teachers modelled values, the learning was more effective (see **www.geography .org.uk/eyprimary/primaryresearch**).

TASK

- With colleagues, construct an A–Z book of values and illustrate these with images drawn from the humanities that can be used for discussion (e.g. D to represent Democracy could include pictures ranging from the Acropolis to the Houses of Parliament).

Historical perspectives

Without the study of history, societies would be seriously disadvantaged – like driving a car without the use of a rear-view mirror. History provides individuals, families and nations with a sense of where they have come from and a context within which to understand contemporary affairs. Everything and everyone has a history. Books are now published on all kinds of topics, including: alcohol, bridges, buildings, death, divorce, education, empires, food, gardening, immigration, marriage, old age, sex, sport, and even a history of pee, entitled *Taking the Piss* (Hart-Davis and Troscianko, 2006).

However, well into the twentieth century, history teaching had tended to focus on the stories of 'white, Christian men'. Since the 1960s there has been growing recognition that the history curriculum should be more inclusive, reflecting the realities of the past and the development of a multicultural society. Chapter 7 discusses the emergence of Black, Asian and other perspectives on British history. Curriculum reforms throughout the UK have highlighted the need to introduce pupils to a range of historical perspectives including:

- the lives of women, men and children from different social, cultural, ethnic and religious backgrounds;
- stories from a range of human experience (e.g. economists, writers, musicians, football players, politicians, scientists, artists, ministers, miners, builders, explorers and doctors); and
- studies of local, national and international contexts.

Critics suggest that there is too much emphasis on 'multiple perspectives' in school history, leaving little time for teachers to develop a sense of narrative, particularly the unfolding story of Britain and its landmark events and personalities. Colley (2006) argues that pupils need to learn a standardised, chronological history of Britain. In 2005, David Cameron's favourite childhood book, Henrietta Marshall's patriotic *Our Island Story* (1905), was re-printed under the support of the Civitas think-tank and various national newspapers. The aim was to send a free copy to every primary school in the UK to raise awareness of Britain's culture. It is now available online at: **http:// digital.library.upenn.edu/women/marshall/england/england.html**.

Chronological awareness

There are continuing concerns that schools are neglecting to teach pupils a sense of chronology (Ofsted, 2007a). Nick Gibb, the schools minister in England, has called for an emphasis on 'facts, data and narrative' in history teaching (Garner and O'Grady, 2010). The importance of chronology, or ordered time, is that it provides a structure to enable historians to explore connections and sequences in the past. Historians seek to make links between events, analyse the decisions people made and the consequences of their actions. Timelines are a standard means of raising pupils' chronological awareness, and in the best practice they are interactive, highly visual tools, continually updated and personalised by the pupils. Initially, young children use common words relating to the passing of time, such as 'old', 'new', 'before', 'after' and 'years', for instance by comparing pictures of themselves as babies, toddlers and infants as part of a personal timeline. Phrases such as 'a long time ago' will have different meanings for young children but constant reference to landmark events in their lives and those adults around them, along with local applications (e.g. 'this was when our school was built'), will contribute to greater consistency in understanding.

Older pupils should begin to use specific historical labels such as 'Roman', 'Victorian' and 'twentieth century'. They should make connections between events and situations in different periods of history. Pupils should discuss the choice of dates and sources to support a class timeline that best characterise the periods and topics they investigate. For instance, groups of pupils studying the Victorians could be set the challenge of selecting five key events in the period and compare findings.

Research suggests that children remember more of what they are taught in history when they use timelines and other frameworks (Hodkinson, 2001). This is because they are more able to place, order, store and retrieve what they have learned. Well-structured discussions about old family photograph albums, museum artefacts and anniversaries contribute to pupils' understanding of change over time. Pluckrose (1991) suggests the use of time-boxes where teachers collect objects and pictures and sort them into shoe boxes according to criteria such as period (e.g. Victorian, 1960s), materials (e.g. paper, stone, plastic, metal), styles (e.g. house architecture) and technologies (e.g. pictures of flint axe head, medieval knife, 1900s car, credit card).

Historical evidence

For historians, the most important concept is evidence, which underpins all historical enquiries. Many teachers introduce the idea by referring to the work of detectives in seeking out clues in a particular investigation. One of the most popular and effective activities is to use 'evidence' bags in which groups of pupils are presented with different artefacts, from which they try to deduce as much as they can about the owner. Variations include the use of lost wallets, dustbins and suitcases from the attic. The intention is to develop understanding about the nature of evidence and how it should be handled. The idea can be extended to geographical (e.g. objects from different lands) and religious (e.g. items belonging to different faiths) contexts. The important point here is that pupils are *doing* history in the process of asking questions, making deductions and reaching informed conclusions.

Historians have access to a wide range of documentary, oral and visual evidence. Such evidence diminishes further back in time. Take the example of the written word. Since the nineteenth century, millions of books have appeared. During the eighteenth century, around 350,000 books were published. Between 1641 and 1700 the figure was 100,000; between 1475 and 1640 it dropped to about 30,000 (Black and MacRaild, 1997: 87). Evidence needs to be marshalled and evaluated against the questions that historians investigate. In the primary school, these lines of enquiry should have strong social angles, such as:

- Where and how did people live? (Homes.)
- What did people eat? Where did they get their food from? (Agriculture, Trade, Industry.)
- How was life different for rich/poor, or town/country dwellers? (Social class.)
- What did people do to keep themselves well? What did they do when they were ill? (Health.)
- How did people travel around? (Transport.)
- What did people believe, hope and fear? (Worship.)
- What kinds of technology did people have to make life easier? (Weapons, Inventions, Communication.)
- What did people do for entertainment and recreation? (Culture.)
- Who made the big decisions in people's lives? (Family, Institutions, Government.)
- How was life different/similar then, compared to now?

History is informed by archaeology, described as 'the history of our nation's waste disposal' or 'gardening upside down' (Robinson and Aston, 2002: 6). Teachers can trawl online newspaper databases to find examples of recent archaeological discoveries to engage pupils' interests, such as the largest coin hoard ever found in Britain (*The Observer*, 12 December 2010), Roman gladiator skeletons in York (*Daily Telegraph*, 18 December 2010) and the possible finger bone of the missing pilot Amelia Earhart, who as a castaway on a Pacific island was feared to have been eaten by crabs (*The Guardian*, 14 December 2010). In reality, archaeology is less thrilling than the media suggests. But its significance is illustrated by the fact that it is the only source of information for prehistory (before written records), which spans 99 per cent of the whole history of humankind (Renfrew and Bahn, 2004: 13). Corbishley (1994: 13) points out that archaeology can also give children a fundamental geographical experience because to understand place, reference must be made to its past. Visits to historical sites raise geographical questions such as:

- Why was this site chosen?
- Where is the nearest supply of water?
- How did the occupants use the water?
- How would the surrounding landscape have been used?
- Where did the building materials come from?
- Would the materials have been renewable?
- What sorts of pollution would there have been?
- What sorts of problems do large numbers of visitors to the site pose?
- How can sites be maintained for future generations?
- What could be done to keep them pleasant places to visit?

Advice on teaching archaeology is available from the Council for British Archaeology (**www.britarch.ac.uk**). English Heritage has produced a series of teachers' guides that show how archaeological evidence can be used by teachers across the curriculum.

Interpretations

Teaching materials should reflect how the past is interpreted in different ways. Historian E.H. Carr (1970) famously likened history to fishing, with historians 'catching' facts in the ocean of the past. The type of catch will depend upon where the historian chooses to fish, and the bait/tackle used. Historians can select facts to fit their perspectives. There is no shortage of events, themes or personalities to illustrate different historical interpretations. The National Portrait's *Heroes & Villains* (National Portrait Gallery, 2003) contains differing expert views on famous historical figures including: William Shakespeare, Henry VIII, Oliver Cromwell, Winston Churchill, David Lloyd George, Emmeline Pankhurst, Diana (Princess of Wales) and Margaret Thatcher.

Historians disagree for many reasons. Sometimes they hold different values and beliefs, pursue varying lines of investigation, or cannot agree on the significance of particular pieces of evidence. The legacy of the British Raj is seen in some quarters as destructive and 'evil' (Grasse and Rimbaud, 2007). Others highlight the positives of British rule, such as the introduction of parliamentary democracy, the rule of law and a modern social-economic system (Paxman, 2011). Although history itself does not change, the interpretation of history changes as new materials come to light.

Each year the National Archives release documents that have been declassified and made open to the public for the first time. For example, in 2010 it was revealed that the Nazis tried to infiltrate the Scout movement. Lord Baden-Powell, founder of the Boy Scouts, responded enthusiastically to a Nazi charm offensive that aimed to align his movement with the Hitler Youth in the lead-up to the Second World War. Secret files belonging to the intelligence service, MI5, revealed how Hitler Youth 'spyclists' surveyed Britain's bridges and rivers during pre-war cycle tours (Milmo, 2010).

More generally, historians, journalists and researchers pore over Cabinet papers in search of new insights into how the country was governed in the recent past. The result is the publication of 'revisionist' history in magazine articles, books and websites. Take, for instance, the accuracy of the catchy label 'Swinging Sixties'. In 1969, John Lennon agreed that the Cautious Sixties would have been a better description. In reality, Swinging London was actually limited to a small number of restaurants, shops and clubs where a handful of influential people met regularly and were photographed as a result (Marr, 2007). Arguably, for many ordinary people in the 1960s life in Britain was less about sex, drugs and rock 'n' roll, and more to do with 'bingo, Blackpool and Berni Inns' (Sandbrook, 2006: xxiv).

Geographical perspectives

There are many definitions of geography, most revolving around the study of places and people. The diversity of geographical content, covering a range of methodologies and spanning the physical and social sciences as well as the humanities, makes it difficult to summarise the essentials of geography. However, Bennetts (no date), identifies five main areas:

1. the physical and human environments and processes, at the Earth's surface;

2. relationships between people and environments;

3. the character of places;

4. the significance of location and spatial patterns, interactions and relationships; and

5. the relevance of place, space and environment for human welfare.

World leaders recognise that geography matters. As former UN Secretary-General Kofi Annan explained: 'I often find myself saying 'show me the maps.' For UN peacekeepers, maps provide clarity over possible border disputes and indicate terrain. However, Annan recognises that geography is more than pouring over maps. In international conflict, he adds, 'we should not forget that geographers are on the front lines, too' (Mapes, 2001). For instance, health workers benefit from demographic data generated by geographers.

Geographers share with historians a commitment to exploring. The enquiry approach in geography is characterised by the following methods: carrying out fieldwork; analysing data by sorting, sequencing, classifying or ranking trends; using atlases, maps and websites such as Google Earth; creating sketch maps that locate places and features; researching and debating issues linked to 'geography in the news'; and using a range of sources to understand places and processes.

Places

Places are social constructions as well as geographical entities. In other words, people attach significance to particular spaces by allocating place-names and attributing physical, human and environmental characteristics. People are constantly involved in what Cresswell (2004: 6) calls 'place-making activities' whether building home extensions, cleaning up beaches, establishing a new community garden, or organising neighbourhood watches. Nations project their own sense of place to the rest of the world through postage stamps, money, national stadia, tourist brochures and television adverts.

Children begin to acquire a sense of place the moment they start to crawl around as babies. Their direct sensory experiences develop as they explore indoor and outdoor environments. By the age of five, most children readily ask questions about where they live and the natural world. As Chapter 4 notes, their understanding of place can be developed through local visits, role play and the use of sources such as aerial photographs and large-scale maps. Practical activities such as digging and planting in a designated garden area, observing minibeasts and habitats, and running an outdoor market, raise pupils' awareness of their immediate surroundings.

Children have a natural interest in faraway places. De Blij (2005) draws on his own first experience of geography when as a boy his family left their home in Rotterdam during the Nazi fire-bombing of 1940. In their new countryside home, life continued to be a struggle. But De Blij found hope in his father's library, reading about tranquil worlds far away where food could be plucked from trees. He was excited by descriptions of active volcanoes, tropical storms and unfamiliar customs. The geography books almost literally gave De Blij a new lease on life. Children come into contact with the wider world on a daily basis, especially through the media, story books and holidays. For pupils to understand the relevance of geography, teachers should make full use of current news. A collection of newspaper headlines can stimulate much debate among pupils on issues such as floods, water shortages, famine, migrations of people, rising oil prices and fair trade.

The challenge for teachers is that distant places, particularly those from the 'Third World', are often reported upon only for negative reasons. By extension this can lead to a narrow, misinformed view of everyday life in these places. Wiegand (1992) recommends that teachers establish what attitudes children have towards a particular place at the start and end of a project. Images highlighting similarities with the children's own place are likely to lead to positive attitudes, whereas those that convey differences can produce negative responses (Martin, 2006). However, caution is still needed so that children do not see advanced materialistic societies as superior to non-Western cultures. Children need to build positive attitudes towards other people around the world by understanding what it is like to live in different places, how these compare to their own locality, and how places are linked together, for instance through trade. The concept of global interdependence is often introduced by re-tracing the trade route for a particular commodity, such as bananas or chocolate. This enables pupils to see how consumer choices affect individuals and environments around the world. It also increases their knowledge of the complexity of international trade.

Patterns and processes

Geographers make sense of the human and natural worlds by identifying patterns to help them predict what might happen in the future. Human patterns can be detected in the migration of people, the movement of goods and the development of settlements (villages, towns and cities). Decisions on where people live, shop, go for entertainment or on holiday, are shaped by factors such as the size, function and location of places. Pupils can explore what services are available for different ages and contrast these with other localities. In the natural world, weather and climate patterns can make a significant difference to the livelihood of farmers, the enjoyment of tourists, provision for transport, education and sport. The internet is a rich source of awesome weather images to stimulate children's interests, including tornadoes, lightning strikes, rainbows, dust storms, hurricanes, coastal fog, and glacial melts. Children can make simple equipment to measure rain (gauges), sunshine (temperature) and cloud cover (mirrors with grids marked on), visit interactive websites to describe places (e.g. **www.bbc.co.uk/schools/whatisweather**), study weather photographs and plan activities based on newspaper forecasts. The Met Office website provides forecasts, interactive games and lesson plans on topics such as weather around the world and tourism (**www.metoffice.gov.uk/education**).

The notion of climate, or the average rainfall and temperature for a place over a period of time, is more difficult for children to grasp. Martin (2006) suggests that children compare climates from around the world by using 'living graphs', which show average rainfall and sunshine for each month in the year for the chosen places, for instance London and Bangalore. Children are asked to discuss statement cards and match them to particular months and places. Examples of statements include: 'Still no sign of rain. My parents are worried about the crops' and 'I need an extra blanket at night now. It's getting cold'. In some cases, statements might apply to both locations. The key point is for children to build up a picture of variations in climate.

Environmental issues

Geographical education is particularly concerned with exploring environmental questions such as how natural resources can be sustained. In this regard, geography is a very forward-thinking subject. As Carter (1998: 10) notes, 'too much time is spent educating young people for yesterday and today, and far too little on educating them for tomorrow'. In England, the National Framework for Sustainable Schools seeks to promote pupils' understanding of sustainability through a selection of 'doorways', such as Food and Drink and Energy and water. It recommends a range of activities such as growing fresh vegetables in the school grounds or collecting rain water.

The idea of 'global footprints' can raise pupils' awareness of how people can damage or improve the environment. Ofsted (2008: 15–16) reports how, through practical activities (such as the use of a tray of sand and a shoe), Year 2 pupils are able to understand that this means 'leaving their mark on something'. They can suggest what aspects of the environment they would like to improve such as preventing trees being cut down or reducing litter on the local high street. Cities have huge ecological 'footprints' – to service Londoners, for instance, requires an area of land 120 times the size of the city, while air pollution from Chinese cities cuts crop production by a third (Allaby *et al.*, 2006: 102). The story *Belonging* by Jeannie Baker (Walker Books, 2004) cleverly introduces 'green' issues to young children as they view through a window the changing use of a garden and neighbourhood over the course of a generation. The author explains that the title of the book denotes that we belong to the land rather than the common view that land is owned by somebody.

Geographers investigate people's interaction with their surroundings (human geography), for instance through farming, construction and pollution. Publications and websites associated with bodies such as Oxfam, National Geographic and the Earth from the Air (**www.earthfromtheair.com**) show the dramatic changes to the planet brought by deforestation, natural phenomena such as earthquakes, volcanoes, tsunamis and global warming. The world is now 1.1 °F (17.2 °C) warmer than 100 years ago and there is clear evidence that many glaciers are retreating and polar ice caps shrinking (Allaby *et al.*, 2006).

Yet like history, geography is not a neutral subject. In a provocative blog, Austin (2011) asks, 'Why don't Americans believe in global warming?' Around two-thirds of Americans do not think climate change is a serious problem. Austin points out that America is one of the few places where you can turn on the television and catch a debate between mainstream figures about whether climate change is even real. Al Gore, former vice president, is not one of the sceptics. He quotes Mark Twain's words 'Denial ain't just a river in Egypt' and shows how the maps of the world would need to be redrawn if the inconvenient truth of climate change is ignored (Gore, 2006: 254). Climate change is not the only controversial subject that engages geographers. Geography raises many social and moral questions about land use, people's rights and the impact of government policies on the environment.

Adopting a geographical perspective means recognising the responsibilities of global citizenship including understanding the need to tackle poverty and injustice. The United Nations, Oxfam and other organisations provide a wealth of educational materials promoting global citizenship, a theme further discussed in Chapter 9. The UN Millennium Development Goals (see Figure 1.3), set for 2015, have a strong emphasis on tackling child poverty. But progress is slow. In 2005, an estimated 1.4 billion people were still living in extreme poverty (United Nations, 2010). The Department for International Development provides an overview of how the UK is contributing to meeting these goals.

Religious perspectives

Religious Education (RE) is more often than not set apart from the humanities. This reflects a philosophical difference, with roots dating back to Renaissance thinking when studies in humanity (Greek and Latin literature) emerged as separate from 'divinity' or religious studies. Blyth (1990) argues that RE is separate from the humanities because he sees the subject as challenging children to encounter *their* own reality, behaviour and beliefs, rather than what *others* do, think and believe, which he perceives is the scope of the humanities. However, religion is a basic part of human life – as

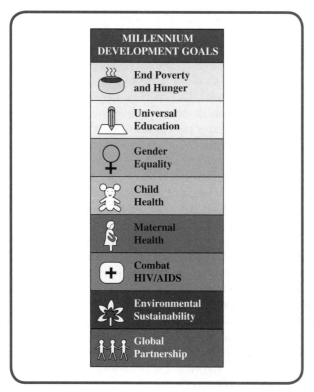

Figure 1.3 The UN's eight Millennium Development Goals for 2015. *Source:* www.un.org/millenniumgoals.

Gellman and Hartman (2002) point out, tribes in remote parts of the earth have food, shelter and language but they also have some form of religious (divine) belief that shapes their way of life. On a global scale religion is such a significant part of human experience – around eight in every ten people on the planet claim that religion matters to them, whether through rituals, prayers or as a means of identity. Religion and belief influence how people speak, act and think. It determines what they wear, eat, drink, and their choice of entertainment. It identifies individuals, families and communities.

That said, there is strong evidence that religious identity and commitment in the UK is less common now than in previous generations, especially among young people. Measuring religiosity includes factors such as regular attendance at places of worship, feelings of identifying with particular religious traditions or rituals, and personal beliefs and practices such as prayer. Many people attend church only at times of ritual, such as baptisms, weddings and funerals, or at times of personal crisis. They are described by Davie (1995: 94) as 'believing without belonging'. There are also large numbers of people who no longer identify with any religion and can be described as neither believing nor belonging.

Hence teachers face significant challenges in conveying to children the relevance, joy and value of religion in everyday life. They can point to the contribution of faith groups in bringing communities together and offering a wide range of services including Sunday schools, book clubs, toddler groups, counselling and environmental projects. In some communities, especially ethnic minority groups, there is also a strong sense of spiritual identity manifested in music, carnival and dance. African-Caribbean Pentacostalists and British Muslims are examples of growing faith groups (Bradley, 2007). The UK has a well-established religious heritage that continues to shape national identity, for instance in terms of its landmarks, holidays and customs.

Effective RE introduces pupils to a variety of perspectives in a respectful and open way, without seeking to promote religious over non-religious alternatives, or vice versa. Pupils should learn to respect different cultures and religious traditions, without accepting them uncritically (Eaude, 2008). One of the aims of RE is to equip pupils with the tools to make their own choices in life in an informed and critical way. One point that all religions have in common is that we are here for a reason and that human life has a purpose. In a sense, religions invite people to take a spiritual journey to find out the meaning of life. For Hindus, it is about finding release from the cycle of being reborn over and over again. For Buddhists, the desired destination is a state of being or enlightenment. Muslims hope on the Day of Judgement to cross the bridge that leads to the garden of Paradise by doing the will of Allah while on earth. For Christians, it is about finding salvation and everlasting life. For Jews, the journey is a way of showing love of God by following his commandments.

Religion invariably features in the news in a negative light. In 2007, a Hindu woman was sacked for refusing to remove a nose stud signifying her religion (Sugden, 2007), while in 2009 a Christian hospital worker faced the same prospect if she did not remove her cross on the grounds that it might spread infection (Wilkes, 2009). Good practice in RE explores controversial issues – including media misrepresentations of religion (DCSF, 2009: 16). Muslims, in particular, suffer from a negative press. Words such as 'terrorist', fundamentalist' and 'fanatic' are more often associated with Muslims than any other religion. Violence has created the greatest challenge to Muslim identity this century (Rippin, 2012). Yet associating an entire group with the actions of some of its members is neither fair nor acceptable in a civilised society.

One of the dangers of discussing religious issues in the news is to ignore the positive influence of religion in people's lives. For instance, following the attempted stabbing of Stephen Timms, a Christian MP, by a young Muslim woman, Muslim children made a gift for the MP to 'heal the faith divide' – it was a picture of Joseph and Pharaoh: a story familiar to Christians (it is found at the end of the Book of Genesis), Muslims and Jews (Gimson, 2011). Christianity and Islam are often regarded as natural adversaries, but there are striking affinities between the faiths. Good RE encourages pupils to learn from different religions, beliefs, values and traditions while exploring their own beliefs and questions of meaning.

Learning from and about religion

The 1988 Education Act required local authorities in England and Wales to produce their own agreed syllabus for RE. There has been subsequent guidance (QCA, 2004) on content culminating in the popular phrase 'learning from and about religion'. Broadly speaking this corresponds to:

- learning *from* religion – pupils' own responses to the issues explored;
- learning *about* religion – religious beliefs, teachings, sources and practices.

Table 1.1 Big six religions that feature in most RE syllabuses in primary schools

Major religions	Summary
Christianity	Beliefs and practices that follow Jesus of Nazareth, seen as the sole son of God.
Judaism	Beliefs and practices of the Jews, derived from the teachings in the Hebrew Bible and centred on maintaining an agreement (covenant) with God.
Islam	Beliefs and practices based on the teachings of the prophet Muhammad and preserved in the Qur'an.
Hinduism	Beliefs and practices drawn from the scriptural authority of the Vedas and the caste/class system.
Sikhism	Traditions based largely on the moral and religious instructions from ten teachers (gurus) and the sacred book *Guru Granth Sahib*.
Buddhism	Ethical and philosophical religion based on the teaching of Siddhartha Gautama (the Buddha or 'Awakened One').

However, Erricker *et al.* (2011) point out that there have been different interpretations among local authorities, with some pursuing a more objective, intellectual and critical approach to RE while others favour a more positive view of religions as a force for good. The authors identify the characteristics of good RE, including: a focus on significant concepts; exploration of religious material; reflection and expression of pupils' own life experiences; encouragement for pupils to take a critical view of what they encounter in RE lessons. Ofsted (2007b) recommends that schools give pupils more opportunities to investigate religion to deepen their understanding, particularly relating to the core beliefs of Christianity. In practical terms, it calls upon schools to make greater use of fieldwork and visitors (Ofsted, 2010).

Faith or trust is central to religion: trust in God or gods, trust in a particular set of religious teachings, trust in traditions or religious leaders (see Table 1.1). For Buddhists, faith is necessary to find enlightenment. For Muslims, faith and works are inseparable. The relationship between faith and works has occupied the best minds in Christianity over the centuries. Those who say that faith is only necessary for salvation do not see that good works are the fruits of real faith, while those who argue that works alone matter do not recognise that salvation is God's gift and cannot be earned (Gellman and Hartman, 2002). The difference between faith and belief is well illustrated in the story of Charles Blondin (1824–1897), who in 1859 crossed the Niagara Falls on a tight rope. When he arrived to loud applause on the other side, he asked who believed that he could return. The crowd nodded but no-one was willing to jump inside a wheelbarrow that Blondin wanted to push across, with the exception of his manager, Harry Colcord. Faith requires a step into the unknown, an expression of unconditional confidence and trust.

There is a danger that the guidance for teachers provided through the locally agreed syllabuses does not give sufficient attention to the diversity within each of the big six religions. For instance, Panjwani (2005) shows that Islam is often depicted without regard to its internal diversity and historicity. He points to the example of the varied architecture of mosques, beyond the dome and minaret. Schools also need to be mindful that there are likely to be other religious minorities within their locality, such as the Jehovah's Witnesses, Quakers and Mormons. Individual pupils may be brought up in faiths outside the 'mainstream' and teachers should be sensitive to their beliefs. It is good practice to contact the specific denominations to ascertain what they believe rather than what their critics claim; most have websites which set out their beliefs and practices.

Conclusion

The humanities are the least abstract of subjects and the most intimate in terms of humanity. They provide the stories that enrich life's experiences, the raw materials to persuade, inform and entertain, prompting the full range of emotions and thoughts. The disciplines of the humanities prompt students to think critically about the challenges that they face as individuals, as well as in society at large. They spark debate over why certain values are held and where those values came from. This is essential in order to understand why people act the way they do.

SUMMARY

- The humanities originated in ancient Greece, more than 2,500 years ago.

- The modern meaning of 'the humanities' applies to a broad study of human experience.

- In subject terms, 'primary humanities' is often equated with history, geography and religious education. Each of these offer unique ways of looking at the world.

- History focuses on people and events in the context of time.

- Geography is primarily concerned with places, people and the environment.

- Religious education involves learning from and about religion and beliefs.

- Although there are different perspectives within each of the humanities subjects, they share common values including a search for truth, empathy for others and respect for the environment.

References

Adams, A. (1976), *The Humanities Jungle*, London: Ward Lock Educational.

Allaby, M., Dauncey, G., Flannery, T., Kolbert, E., Lomborg, B., Lynas, M. and Pearce, F. (2006), *Fragile Earth*, London: Collins.

Arroyo (2002), *The Humanities in the Age of Technology*, Washington DC: Catholic University of America Press.

Austin, E.G. (2011), 'Why don't Americans believe in global warming?' *The Economist*, 8 February 2011.

Baker, J. (2004), *Belonging*, London: Walker Books.

Beder, S. (2009), *This Little Kiddy Went to Market*, London: Pluto Press.

Bennetts, T. (n.d.), 'Improving pupils' geographical understanding in the primary and lower secondary phases of the school curriculum', available at: **www.geography .org.uk**.

Birmingham City Council (2007), *The Birmingham Agreed Syllabus for Religious Education 2007*, available at: **www .birmingham-asc.org.uk/agreedsyl1.php**.

Black, M. (1975), 'Some Tasks for the Humanities' in Niblett, W.R. (ed.), *The Sciences, the Humanities and the Technological Threat*, London: University of London Press.

Black, J. and MacRaild, D.M. (1997), *Studying History*, London: Macmillan.

Blyth, A. (1990), *Making the Grade for Primary Humanities*, Milton Keynes: Open University Press.

Bonner, S.F. (1977), *Education in Ancient Rome*, London: Methuen & Co.

Bradley, I. (2007), *Believing in Britain*, London: I.B. Tauris & Co.

Brown, C. (2001), *The Death of Christian Britain*, London: Routledge.

Browne, A. (2008), 'Has there been a decline in values in British society?', Joseph Rowntree Foundation, available at: **www.jrf.org.uk.**

Carr, E.H. (1970), *What is History?* London: Penguin.

Carter, R. (ed.) (1998), *Handbook of Primary Geography*, Sheffield: Geographical Association.

Castle, E.B. (1961), *Ancient Education and Today*, London: Penguin.

Claire, H. (2005), 'You did the best you can: history, citizenship and moral dilemmas' in Osler, A. (ed.) *Teachers, Human Rights and Diversity*, Stoke on Trent: Trentham Books.

Clutterbuck, P. (2008), *Values: A Programme for Primary Students: A Programme for Primary Schools*, Carmarthen: Crown House.

Colley, L. (2006), 'What are British values?, *The Guardian*, 17 May 2006.

Conway, D. (2010), Liberal Education and the National Curriculum, London: Civitas.

Copley, T. (1997), *Teaching Religion*, Exeter: University of Exeter Press.

Corbishley, M. (1994), *Archaeology in the National Curriculum*, London: English Heritage.

Cresswell, T. (2004), *Place. A Short Introduction*, Oxford: Blackwell.

Davie, G. (1995), *Religion in Britain since 1945. Believing without Belonging*, Oxford: Blackwell.

DCELLS (2008), *National exemplar framework for religious education for 3 to 19-year-olds in Wales*, Cardiff: Welsh Assembly Government.

DCSF (2009), *Religious education in English schools: Non-statutory guidance 2009*, Nottingham: DCSF.

De Blij, H. (2005), *Why Geography Matters?* Oxford: Oxford University Press.

DfE (2011), *Framework for the National Curriculum*, London: DfE.

Duckworth, J. (2009), *The Little Book of Values: Educating Children to Become Thinking, Responsible and Caring Citizens*, Carmarthen: Crown House.

Eaude, T. (2008), *Children's Spiritual, Moral, Social and Cultural Development*, Exeter: Learning Matters.

Erricker, C., Lowndes, J., and Bellchambers, E. (2011), *Primary Religious Education – A New Approach*, Abingdon: Routledge.

Evans, M. and Finlay, I.G. (eds) (2001), *Medical Humanities*, London: BMJ Books.

Finlay, M.I. (1972), *Aspects of Antiquity*, London: Pelican.

Finlay, M.I. (ed.) (1981), *The Legacy of Greece*, Oxford: Clarendon Press.

Furedi, F. (2007), 'Introduction: Politics, Politics, Politics!' in Wheelan, R. (ed.) *Corruption of the Curriculum*, London: Civitas, 1–10.

Garner, R. and O'Grady, S. (2010), 'Schools Minister: children are deprived of knowledge', *The Independent*, 2 July 2010.

Gellman, M. and Hartman, T. (2002), *Religion for Dummies*, New York: Wiley Publishing.

Gimson, A. (2011), 'After the stabbing of Stephen Timms, a gift to heal the faith divide', *The Telegraph*, 26 February 2011.

Gore, A. (2006), *An Inconvenient Truth*, London: Bloomsbury.

Grasse, S. and Rimbaud, P. (2007), *Evil Empire: 101 Ways England Ruined the World*, Philadelphia, Quirk Books.

Guldberg, H. (2009), *Reclaiming Childhood*, London: Routledge.

Haigh, G. (1999), 'Awe and wonder; values', in TES Magazine, 26 November 1999, available at: **www.tes.co.uk/article.aspx?storycode=305803**

Hart-Davis, A. and Troscianko, E. (2006), *Taking the Piss*, Stroud: The Chalford Press.

Hawkes, N. (2003), *How to Inspire and Develop Positive Values in Your Classroom* LDA Cambridge.

Hockey, S. (2008), 'The History of Humanities Computing' in Schreibman, S., Siemens, R. and Unsworth, J. (eds), *A Companion to Digital Humanities*, Oxford: Wiley Blackwell, 3–19.

Hodkinson, A. (2001), 'Enhancing temporal cognition in the primary school', *Primary History*, 28: 11–14.

Hughes, B. (2011), *The Hemlock Cup: Socrates, Athens and the Search for the Good Life,* London: Vintage.

Ipsos (2010), The Munk Debates: Blair and Hitchens. Is Religion a Force of Good in the World? Toronto: Ipsos.

Kitto, H.D.F. (1951), *The Greeks*, London: Pelican.

Layard, R. (2006), *Happiness. Lessons from a New Science*, London: Penguin.

Layard, R. (2009), *A Good Childhood*, London: Penguin.

Lpsos (2010), The Munk Debates: Blair and Hitchens. Is Religion a Force of Good in the World? Toronto: Ipsos

Mapes, J. (2001), 'Changing World Needs Geographers, Says UN Head', *National Geographic News*, 8 March 2001, available at: **http://news.nationalgeographic.com/news/2001/03/0308_annan.html**.

Marr, A. (2007), *A History of Modern Britain*, Oxford: MacMillan.

Marsden, W.E. (2001), The School Textbook, London: Woburn Press.

Martin, F. (2006), *Teaching Geography in Primary Schools*, Cambridge: Chris Kington Publishing.

Mayo, E. and Nairn, A. (2009), *Consumer Kids*, London: Constable & Robinson.

McVeigh, T. (2011), 'Rude Britannia is a myth, says report into English manners', *The Observer*, 9 October 2011.

Milmo, C. (2010), 'Operation Dib-dib-dib: how Nazis tried to infiltrate the Boy Scouts', *The Independent*, 8 March 2010.

Musgrave, P.W. (1970), *Sociology, History and Education*, London: Methuen & Co.

National Consumer Council (2005), *Shopping Generation*, London: NCC.

National Portrait Gallery (2003), *Heroes and Villains*, London: National Portrait Gallery.

Ofsted (2007a), *History in the balance*, London: Ofsted.

Ofsted (2007b), *Making sense of religion*, London: Ofsted.

Ofsted (2008), *Geography in schools – changing practice*, London: Ofsted.

Ofsted (2010), *Transforming religious education*, London: Ofsted.

Owens, P. (2004), 'Researching the development of children's environmental values in the early school years' in Special Publication No.1 – *Researching Primary Geography, Register of Research in Primary Geography*, 2004, 64–76.

Panjwani, F. (2005), 'Agreed syllabi and un-agreed values: religious education and missed opportunities for fostering social cohesion' in *British Journal of Educational Studies*, 53(3), 375–393.

Paxman, J. (2011), *Empire: What Ruling the World Did to the British*, London: Viking.

Pluckrose, H. (1991), *Children Learning History*, Oxford: Blackwell.

QCA (2004), *The Non-Statutory Framework for RE*, London: QCA.

Renfrew, C. and Bahn, P. (2004), 4th edn, *Archaeology: Theories, Methods and Practice*, London: Thames & Hudson.

Robinson, T. and Aston, M. (2002), *Archaeology is Rubbish*, London: Channel4 Books.

Russo, J.P. (2005), *The Future Without a Past*, Missouri: University of Missouri Press.

Rippin, A. (2012), 4th edn, *Muslims*, London: Routledge.

Sandbrook, D. (2006), White Heat, London: Abacus.

Schools Council (1965), Working *Paper 2. Raising the School Leaving Age: A cooperative programme of research and development*, London: HMSO.

Shepherd, J. (2010), 'Profile: Michael Gove', *The Guardian*, 12 May 2010.

Sugden, J. (2007), 'Woman sacked for wearing Hindu nose stud', *The Times*, 17 September 2007.

United Nations (2010), *The Millennium Development Goals Report*, New York: UN.

Vasagar, J. (2011), 'Michael Gove to send copy of King James Bible to all English schools', *The Guardian*, 25 November 2011.

Walford, R. (2001), *Geography in British Schools 1850–2000*, London: Woburn Press.

Wallace, S. (2008), *Oxford Dictionary of Education*, Oxford: Oxford University Press.

Warren, J. (1999), *History and Historians*, London: Hodder & Stoughton.

Watson, F. (1909), *The Beginnings of the Teaching of Modern Subjects in England*, Wakefield: S.R. Publishers Ltd.

Watson, B. and Thompson, P. (2007), *The Effective Teaching of Religious Education*, Harlow: Pearson.

Wiegand, P. (1992), *Places in the Primary School*, London: Falmer Press.

Wilkes, D. (2009), 'Hospital worker told she'll be sacked if she keeps wearing crucifix because 'it might spread infection', *Daily Mail*, 25 May 2009.

Useful Websites

The Humanities Association sets out to to provide an independent forum for debate about major issues in all aspects of Humanities education: **www.hums.org.uk**.

The Geographical Association seeks to further geographical knowledge and understanding through education. Among its resources is the *Primary Geographer* magazine: **www.geography.org.uk**.

The Historical Association sees itself as the Voice for History, promoting the study, teaching and enjoyment of the subject. It provides many teaching resources including *Primary History*: **www.history.org.uk**.

The RE Handbook provides a resource for teachers wishing to develop their subject and professional knowledge in the teaching of religion in primary and secondary schools in England: **http://re-handbook.org.uk**.

CHAPTER 2

Planning and preparing to meet curriculum requirements

We must plan carefully to ensure that every child gains the maximum from our teaching.

(Barnes, 2007: 183)

Schools sustain their excellence by continually seeking to improve teaching and learning.

(Ofsted, 2008: 45)

Learning objectives

By the end of this chapter you should be able to:

- identify the links between planning, teaching, learning, monitoring and assessment;
- explain the differences between long-, medium- and short-term planning;
- reflect upon the need to be selective when preparing resources; and
- recognise the importance of planning lessons that address subject-specific knowledge, skills and understanding in order to ensure the delivery of a broad and balanced curriculum.

The purpose of planning

In education, planning is the process of thinking and developing ideas that lead to the production of plans that serve as guides for teachers and other practitioners (Hayes 2007). The word 'guide' is a reminder of the need to adopt a flexible approach that will allow for the unexpected. Planning should not constrain teachers and prevent them from responding to the unexpected and turning these experiences into learning opportunities. Much of children's learning occurs spontaneously – their natural inquis-itiveness should not be stifled by regimental planning. In the Early Years, there needs to be a balance between teacher-directed tasks (where the teacher guides the learning) and child-initiated activities, where the children select what they want to do according to their own interests and abilities.

Planning is important for a number of reasons. It provides a clear focus and purpose for learning. It supports teachers when reflecting on their own practice and enables them to make the most of time available. Systematic planning and lively teaching are important for effective learning (Ofsted, 2002a).

Planning operates at different levels and within a range of contexts. Long-term plans provide an overview for teaching during a child's time in school. These can include whole-school curriculum maps setting out the topics for study within each year group, how the National Curriculum is covered and the time allocated for each subject and area of learning. Long-term plans can also include transitional arrangements or bridg-ing units from one phase of education to the next, or themes, festivals and visits to be covered during the year. Medium-term plans cover the details of the programme for a particular year group, including relevant activities, resources and assessment opportu-nities. Many schools derive their short-term planning directly from these and do not write separate lesson or session plans. Irrespective of the format or approach to plan-ning, it is essential that teachers are clear about their learning objectives or intended learning outcomes and have in place the necessary organisational and assessment strategies for these to be achieved.

Over recent years, throughout the UK schools have benefited from guidance on plan-ning at local and national level. Particularly in England, there has been the introduction of non-statutory national strategies and schemes of work published by the Qualification and Curriculum Authority (QCA). However, Ofsted found that in too many schools the QCA schemes of work were being adopted without particular thought to the needs of the school (Ofsted, 2002b). Moreover, few subject leaders/coordinators used the plan-ning guidance booklets that accompany the schemes. Critics have also claimed that the QCA schemes of work were too prescriptive and creativity was stifled to the detriment of humanities teaching. According to Turner-Bisset (2005), they removed the need for teacher decision-making and critical thinking and created an alternative curriculum. While these schemes had their faults, nonetheless they provided a framework of support, particularly for those student and serving teachers who lacked confidence in planning the humanities subjects. They offered key questions, clear objectives and subject-specific vocabulary to structure lessons.

The cycle of planning

Planning can be viewed as a cyclical process (see Figure 2.1). Good teaching and learn-ing require detailed planning. Good planning, in turn, depends upon how well chil-dren's learning is assessed and how well the teaching is evaluated. Only by taking these factors into account can one hope to develop and improve the quality of teaching.

Planning is not a fixed and sterile exercise but should be seen as a flexible, organic and creative process – described by the Geographical Association as 'curriculum-making'. This is the creative act of interpreting a curriculum specification and turning it into a coherent scheme of work. This then needs to be resourced and developed into lesson experiences. It is a creative act that lies at the heart of good teaching (Scoffham, 2010: 132).

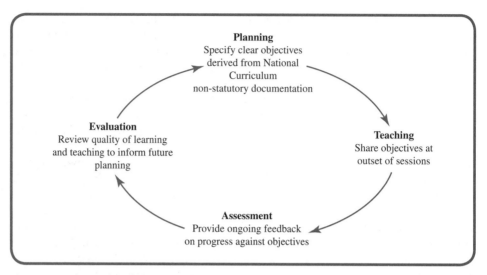

Figure 2.1 The cycle of planning (behaviourist, objectives-led model).

Although schools follow different planning formats, they share common features. The planning process is usually described as including three stages: long-term, medium-term and short-term (see Figure 2.2). Hoodless *et al.* (2009) use the analogy of a tree to illustrate links in the planning process. Medium-term plans are represented by branches that connect to the trunk (long-term plan, i.e. the National Curriculum), which links to roots (legislation). The teacher is unable to create individual lesson activities (twigs) without the branches, trunk and roots.

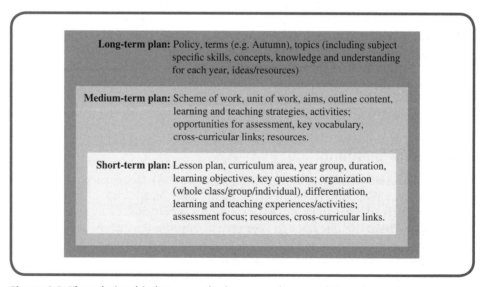

Figure 2.2 The relationship between the long-, medium- and short-term plans.

Long-term planning – national curricula and frameworks

Long-term plans should be based around the requirements of the respective curriculum frameworks. They should guide teachers in planning for progression in content and skills over a period of time. They should also give an overview of what is covered over an entire key stage. It is through long-term plans that schools identify their aims for all subjects or areas of experience, mapping out topics to be taught through the year and to whom. These long-term plans are usually reviewed once a year or every other year to update them in line with any national changes, for instance the Foundation Stage in England and the revised National Curriculum orders, and the Foundation Phase in Wales. The purpose of long-term planning is to set out how the school interprets national requirements and guidelines, for example relating to the National Curriculum. In framing their long-term plans, many schools in England will pay close attention to the principles embodied in *Every Child Matters* (DfES, 2004) and the 2020 *Children and Young People's Workforce Strategy* (DCSF, 2008) with their emphasis upon a collaborative approach among professionals to planning, intervention and assessment. Early Years practitioners throughout the UK also refer to the respective guidelines for planning learning for young children, such as those relating to the Foundation Stage (England and Northern Ireland) and Foundation Phase (Wales). Schools in Northern Ireland are expected to follow the Revised Northern Ireland Curriculum – Primary (CCEA, 2007), where the curriculum is set out in six areas of learning:

- Language and Literacy;
- Maths and Numeracy;
- The Arts;
- The World Around Us;
- Personal Development and Mutual Understanding; and
- Physical Education.

Although the areas of learning are noted separately, teachers should, where appropriate, integrate learning across the six areas to make relevant connections for children. Teachers have considerable flexibility to select within the learning areas those aspects they view as appropriate to the ability and interests of their pupils. The Area of Learning, 'World Around Us' (CCEA, 2007: 2) combines aspects of geography, history and science and technology with an emphasis on children having opportunities to explore, investigate and think about their world – past, present and future. Where possible, 'The World Around Us' can be taught through cross-curricular topics and linked to the other areas of the curriculum. In Scotland, schools are expected to address the aims of *Curriculum for Excellence* by providing a coherent, more flexible and enriched curriculum. It sets out to enable each child to be:

- a successful learner;
- a confident individual;

- a responsible citizen; and
- an effective contributor.

Source: www.ltscotland.org.uk/curriculumforexcellence/curriculumoverview/index.asp.

Geography and history are placed within 'social studies'. Pupils' experiences and outcomes have been organised into:

- People, past events and societies;
- People, place and environment; and
- People in society, economy and business.

TASK

- Collect examples of schemes of work for history, geography and RE. What structural features do they have in common and which formats do you find most useful?

Requirements for Religious Education (RE)

The teaching of RE in schools throughout the UK is compulsory, although parents have the historic right to withdraw their children from lessons. Whole-school planning for RE should consider the particular status and character of the school. In England and Wales, in voluntary aided and foundation schools with a religious character, RE is taught in keeping with the school's trust deeds. Locally agreed syllabuses set out the content for study in maintained schools. Schools can draw upon national guidance such as *Religious education in English schools: Non-statutory guidance 2010* (DCSF, 2010) or the *National Exemplar Framework for Religious Education for 3 to 19-year-olds in Wales* (DCELLS, 2008).

In Scottish schools, teachers are expected to take account of the religious and cultural diversity within their own local communities, whilst recognising the unique role of Christianity within the story of Scotland. Using the Bible as a foundation, it is hoped that pupils will develop a knowledge and understanding of Christian beliefs and practices and an ability to relate Christian morals to their own lives (Scottish Executive, 2006). In Scotland, RE is one of the eight core curriculum areas within *Curriculum for Excellence* in non-denominational schools and in Roman Catholic Schools. The Core Syllabus of Religious Education in Ireland (drawn up in consultation with the main Christian denominations) focuses on three learning objectives which are 'The Revelation of God', 'Christian Church' and 'Morality' (CCEA, 2007). Integrated primary schools in Northern Ireland represent both Protestant and Catholic traditions and were established as part of the peace and reconciliation process. Pupils are encouraged to understand, respect and celebrate all backgrounds. Integrated schools are obliged to deliver the Northern Ireland Curriculum, but where there are significant numbers from a particular faith, schools are required to meet these needs by preparing children for sacramental and liturgical participation; for instance, Roman Catholic children would be prepared for their First Holy Communion and Confirmation. World faiths, other than Christianity, are not taught until the secondary phase of education.

When planning for RE, schools should provide opportunities for pupils to experience and learn about religion in their school, community, country and globally. In England, the *Religious education guidance in primary schools* recommends that schools should prioritise teaching of Christianity and five other religions such as Islam, Judaism, Buddhism, Hinduism and Sikhism. It also recommends that pupils should study other religious traditions such as the Baha'i faith, Jainism, and Zoroastrianism, and secular beliefs such as humanism and atheism. In Wales, schools should provide opportunities for pupils to develop the three interrelated core skills – 'Engaging with fundamental questions', 'Exploring religious beliefs, teachings and practice(s)' and 'Expressing personal responses' through a breadth of religious education contexts, for instance 'The World', 'Human Experience' and 'Search for Meaning' (DCELLS, 2011).

The planning for a school within a strong Muslim community is shown in Table 2.1 and makes use of the old QCA scheme of work for RE. The school states that at Key Stage 1

Table 2.1 Long-term planning for RE

	Autumn 1	Autumn 2	Spring 1	Spring 2	Summer 1	Summer 2
Reception	Me and my family	Happy times	No RE	New life	Homes	No RE
Year 1	Family celebrations	Expressing joy	Who was Mohammed?	New beginnings	No RE	Belonging
Year 2	Who was Jesus?	How do Christians celebrate? Christmas?	Caring for the world	Stories from Islam	Who lives around here?	The Church
Year 3	Stories from Christianity	Celebrating Shabbat	At home with a Jewish family	Easter customs	The Qu'ran	At home with a Muslim family
Year 4	Journeys	Introducing the Bible	The Mosque	Being a Christian	Religion in our area	Caring for others
Year 5	Pilgrimage in Islam	The meaning of Christmas	Stories from Jewish Judaism	The meaning of Easter	Living as a Muslim	Creation
Year 6	Questions and answers	Christmas around the world	The Synagogue	Rules and responsibility	Ideas about God	Growing up in religion

Source: Adapted from McCreery *et al.* (2008: 97).

pupils should learn about Islam and at least one other religion, while Key Stage 2 pupils should learn about Islam and at least two other religions. It can be seen from the planning that themes are revisited as the children go through the school, building on their previous learning. This allows for progression and development and ensures that their RE curriculum has coherence across their primary experience. Further examples of long-term plans for RE can be seen on the following website: **www.birmingham-asc.org.uk/ resourcing.php**.

REFLECTION

- Reflect on the differences for RE provision across England, Wales, Scotland and Northern Ireland. Do you agree with the Irish model of postponing world faiths other than Christianity until secondary schooling?

Medium-term plans

Medium-term plans are working documents for the teacher or team of teachers to use and amend. They cover a shorter period of time, sometimes a term, half a term or sometimes one week, and are used, for example, in literacy where the subject is taught every day. Medium-term plans set out the body of the topic to be taught:

Geography – 'A local environmental issue' (Year 5);

RE – 'Ideas about God' (Year 6); or

History – 'What was it like for children in the Second World War?' (Year 4).

The format of medium-term plans will vary from school to school. However, the common features include: learning objectives, key questions, learning and teaching strategies, curriculum references, and opportunities for assessment (Table 2.2). The most important aspect of medium-term planning is the setting of appropriate yet challenging objectives. These are derived from the National Curriculum for each subject to be taught and also from exemplary materials produced by local authorities or national bodies. Objectives can focus on knowledge, skills or children's understanding of important concepts in that subject. These objectives are also important in assessing what the children have learned.

Table 2.2 shows an example of a geography unit of work, which is based on an enquiry approach or planner that focuses on key questions leading the activities. The unit has been designed to be easily adapted for any local issue, such as the effect of a hypermarket on a town centre or should the high street be closed to traffic, or the construction of a leisure centre. Each key question can be the starting point for discussion, written work or practical tasks. Continuity and progression should be shown between activities and between key questions. Consideration should be given to the way the activities build on the knowledge and understanding previously gained. The potential to develop key skills should be noted within the activities, with due consideration

Table 2.2 Medium-term plan for Geography

Lesson	Key ideas and enquiry questions	Learning objectives – children should learn . . .	Teaching and learning suggestions	Learning outcomes – children can . . .	Assessment for Learning
Lesson 1	What is the issue?	• about the nature of the issue to be investigated • to develop speaking and listening skills through interviews	• identify a local issue • compile enquiry questions • gather opinions	• understand the nature of the issue	• discussion and observation
Lesson 2	Fieldwork – visit the site	• to locate features on a map • to record field observations • to see effects on environment and people	• visit the site	• recognise features on a map • understand the nature of the issue	• observation and discussion
Lesson 3	A visiting speaker	• how to question outside speakers to summarise the views of others	• discuss with visiting speaker	• show that they have learnt more about the issue • summarise the speaker's views	• newspaper report (communication skill)
Lesson 4	How will the local area be changed?	• to use maps at a variety of scales • to identify key natural and human features • to communicate findings in different ways	• talk about how the issue will affect sectors of community and the environment	• begin to understand how natural and human features in area may affect the issue	• presentation of work
Lesson 5	What are the interest groups involved in the issue?	• how people affect their environment • that different people hold different views about an issue	• design a questionnaire and decide how it is to be carried out	• understand the views of different people about the issue • understand who is likely to gain or lose from the issue	• questioning

(Continued)

Table 2.2 (*Continued*)

Lesson	Key ideas and enquiry questions	Learning objectives – children should learn . . .	Teaching and learning suggestions	Learning outcomes – children can . . .	Assessment for Learning
Lesson 6	How might the issue be resolved?	• how and why different people seek to manage and sustain their environment • how to analyse and present their findings	• collate information gained from questionnaires • present findings • make a display	• present findings appropriately • suggest ways in which the issue might be resolved	• choice of method
Lesson 7	How did the issue arise?	• to use secondary evidence to compare before and after	• look at visual images of the area in the past • look for change • identify one key environmental problem	• identify changes arising from the issue	• poster
Lessons 8–9	Why is this an issue?	• about recent and proposed changes in locality • about a particular issue arising from the way land is used	• design a poster • plan and prepare presentation to a stimulated public meeting	• summarise and categorise the range of views involved	• presentation
Lesson 10	Is the development sustainable?	• how and why people seek to manage and sustain their environment • how to disseminate ideas	• talk about dissemination of findings • write letters to media, developers, planning department	• express and justify their own views on the issue	• participation

Source: LCP File (2001).

to the fact that it should be used to enhance and improve the delivery of the subject. Assessment should focus on the knowledge, understanding and skills to be developed. Evidence of achievement can be demonstrated through written, oral or practical forms, such as reports, maps and presentations.

Short-term plans

The final part of the planning process is to prepare short-term plans. These should ensure that the class will receive a balance of activities appropriate to their needs.

Lesson or session planning formats will vary according to the age group, course requirements and school contexts. Most teachers working within the 3 to 11 age range will use weekly overviews, which note objectives or key questions, summaries of the session content, group activities, resources, the role of additional adults and assessment opportunities. Common elements to lesson plans are outlined in Table 2.3.

As noted in Chapter 4, pupils themselves should be actively involved in the planning process to encourage independence and ownership of their learning. This can be achieved when they:

- suggest topics to study;
- select questions to explore;
- contribute ideas to how the classroom is set up;
- make the resources for the lesson;
- suggest possible activities;

Table 2.3	What does a lesson plan need to do?
Objectives	Set out the learning intentions for the children, i.e. *what* the children will learn.
Learning experiences/ activities	Show how the learning will be achieved, i.e. *what* activities you will provide for the children. Show a detailed pathway through the lesson, including time management, i.e. *how* you provide a structure for the learning experiences.
Teacher's role	Show the actions that will be taken by the teacher to ensure that learning takes place, i.e. *what* you will do.
Resources	Indicate the materials and equipment that will be needed for the whole session, i.e. *what* you will need for yourself and for the children.
Assessment indicators	Show at what point in the session particular learning objectives are being explored, i.e. *when* the children will be doing the learning. Show what evidence you will be looking for from the children and how you will gather that evidence, i.e. *how* you will know that learning has occurred.

- decide who will distribute and collect resources; and
- suggest how they might show what they have learnt in the lesson.

This should not be limited to young children. Older pupils should discuss and negotiate learning objectives, activities and resources and be fully involved in the assessment process.

Probably the most significant development in our understanding of geographical learning in the last 15 years has been the increasing recognition of the importance of the geographies that children themselves bring to the classroom (Cooper *et al.*, 2006). Catling (2003) proposed the '3Es' (enabling, enhancing and empowering) for initiating children into an enquiry approach. Developments such as child-initiated activities, which are embedded in Wales's Foundation Phase and particular schemes such as the Geographical Association's 'Young Geographers' (**www.geography.org .uk/projects/younggeographers**) and 'Making Geography Happen (**http://geography .org.uk/projects/makinggeographyhappen**) show the potential of empowering pupils to make decisions and take ownership of their learning.

Pupils should be challenged to reflect on their own beliefs and be encouraged to respect other points of view. When planning religious education teachers should also consider the developmental stage of the pupils and their capacity to engage with complex ideas. Time for reflection and discussion in depth is very important for effective learning and teaching in religious and moral education.

TASK

- Study the example of a short-term plan in Table 2.4. How does the lesson plan compare with short-term planning approaches you have used?

BOX 2.1 RESEARCH BRIEFING – PLANNING

Research indicates that the most effective planning models focus on promoting active learning, such as the 'Plan, Do and Review' model, which has guided the very successful 'High/Scope' approaches in Early Years' classrooms (Vogel, 2001). This has been extended by Watkins *et al.* (2007), who offer a 'Plan, Do, Review, Learn and Apply' multiple cycle for all ages. In history, this might involve teachers planning opportunities for pupils to collect sources (Do), identifying points of view (Review), synthesising ideas (Learn) and making sense of another situation (Apply). Brophy and Good (1986) stressed that effective teachers demanded productive engagement with the task, prepared well, and matched tasks to the abilities of the children. Effective lessons are based around a clear structure, common understanding of the purpose behind the lesson and stimulating introductions and strong conclusions.

Table 2.4 A lesson plan for Key Stage 2 History: Second World War

Curriculum area: History (Second World War)   **Year group:** 4   **Duration:** 1 hour

Date:

Context: 2nd lesson on topic (1st lesson introduced concept of evacuees and timeline).

Learning objectives:

- to describe the evacuee experiences locally;
- to ask relevant questions about the past;
- to distinguish between facts and opinions.

Key questions

- What can you recall about evacuees during the Second World War?
- How can we find out about evacuees locally?
- How do these sources compare?

Organisation – Whole Class/Group/Individual Mainly group work.

Differentiation

- Use of key vocabulary lists;
- *Support Staff*: classroom assistant to support child A and B in recording.

(Mixed ability groups)

Activity structure

Introduction   (10 mins)

- Recap on previous lesson, noting when the war happened (refer to timeline).
- Stimulate interest by showing a selection of new images relating to evacuees and model questioning (range and relevance).
- Give examples of facts and opinions.
- Refer to support available including question prompt cards and wall display.
- Share learning objectives.

Lesson development   (40 mins)
Children work in groups investigating their sources. Each group to complete a two-column grid with the headings: 'What key things does this source tell us about the war?'; 'What would we like to know more about?'

Group A – photographs of evacuees
Group B – newspaper story of evacuees
Group C – online resource (viewed in support room):
www.bbc.co.uk/history/interactive/animations/wwtwo_movies_evacuees/index_ embed.shtml
Group D – audio recordings of evacuee memories

Discussions focus on evacuee experiences and teasing out facts and opinions. Groups to discuss the quality of their questions using wall-display criteria.

(Continued)

Table 2.4 (*Continued*)

Extension (if necessary)

Further sources available for study include logbook extracts and school register – identify facts and opinions from these (read guidance on completing a school logbook).

Pause for thought: How do we know which sources to believe if they tell us different things?

Conclusion   (10 mins)

Review progress by asking spokesperson for each group to:

- each give one fact and one opinion about evacuees;

- propose their 'red hot' (most interesting) questions; and

- explain homework (to select one of the questions from the class to find out more about).

Assessment

- Focus on progress against learning objectives and include self assessment – how well have you done? Complete 'How well can you. . .?' grid (describe what it was like for evacuees / give facts and opinions/ask an interesting question).

Resources

Photographs, audio recordings, local newspaper headlines, logbook extracts, website, question prompt cards, wall display, timeline.

Cross-curricular links

Geography; Literacy; ICT.

Preparing, selecting and critically evaluating resources for planning

The preparation of resources, equipment and the general learning environment has a direct bearing on the successful outcomes of lessons. Purposeful learning is unlikely when pupils are presented with worksheets of low-level challenge, colouring-in exercises and a diet of paper and pencil activities. Boredom, inattention and indiscipline can follow. Resources should therefore be well presented, inspiring, relevant to the learning objectives and appropriate to the ages and abilities of the pupils. Planning and preparation should take into account the amount of time needed to master lesson content, which may vary from two to four times as much for pupils with learning difficulties (Slavin, 1987). Planning for varying learning objectives according to the needs of pupils is one suggested strategy. Preparation also needs to consider how learning is to be monitored and recorded, for example through direct observations, questioning, field notes or quizzes.

The rise in the number of teaching assistants in schools over recent years has increased planning demands on teachers, although their contribution in supporting learners is often invaluable. Their role has also changed from 'domestic helper' to assistant teacher, and their effective deployment calls for clarity of expectations, good training and close working relationships. Ofsted (2002a) reports that few schools monitor the time that individual pupils, particularly those of low ability or with special educational needs, spend with assistants rather than teachers.

Teachers can gain immediate access to a wide range of resources to support the planning of units and lessons in the humanities. Although the Internet is an obvious first point of reference, resources such as books, posters and poetry for the humanities can be found in publisher catalogues such as Scholastic, Pearson and Heinemann. Artefacts can be borrowed from museums, or bought from junk shops and market stalls. Maps are available from Ordnance Survey, local council planning departments and tourist boards. Leaflets, anniversary packs and brochures are often published by the Post Office, British Rail, banks and other organisations. Parents and grandparents can usually be relied upon to support class projects with photographs and other memorabilia.

The Internet

While the Internet provides extensive learning and teaching materials, pupils (and teachers) need to be able to select and critically evaluate resources (see Table 2.5). Major research of Internet use by 9 to 19-year-olds reports that 92 per cent have access at school, 75 per cent at home and 19 per cent in their bedrooms. Around 30 per cent of all pupils have received no lessons on using the Internet (Livingstone and Bober, 2005). The skills of effective research, understanding risks and evaluating the worth of online sources are not well developed. Choosing the most appropriate information is a bit like 'trying to get a sip of water from a fire hydrant' (McGuire *et al.*, 2000: 44). Within Internet environments, many readers are frustrated when they do not receive immediate answers to their searches, resulting in the adoption of a 'snatch and grab philosophy . . . not apparent in print text environments' (Sutherland-Smith, 2002: 664). Developing a good search strategy involves being clear about what is needed, where to look and how best to find the information. Particular features narrow searches by criteria such as images, maps, news and video. It is possible to view material with geographical, historical or religious themes on sites such as **www.primaryresources .co.uk** and **www.bbc.co.uk/schools/websites/4_11/site/geography.shtml**.

One of the problems when copying and pasting images from the Internet is that the embedded hyperlink can also be copied. This can cause difficulties if the original web page changes and the accompanying text is no longer appropriate for children. To avoid this scenario, Woods (2010) advocates the simple rule of right-clicking on the picture and then 'Save Picture As' rather than copy and paste.

Most search engines look for each word, regardless of whether it is part of a phrase or not and of how far apart the words appear in the document. But there are options to conduct an 'exact phrase search' using quotation marks or the advanced search facility available in most search engines. Other ways of narrowing searches include the use of plus ('+') and minus ('−') signs. By placing a plus sign in front of a word, the search focuses on pages that contain the exact word, while entering a minus sign excludes the term. More advanced tools include Boolean operators (AND, OR, NOT), named after Irish mathematician George Boole, which functions as follows:

Question: I need information about President Obama

Boolean logic: OR

Table 2.5 Selecting and critically evaluating resources to support planning from the Internet

Do's	Don'ts
• Legitimate online research involves repetitive and continuous searching, filtering and citing of articles – much more than 10 seconds.	• Do not use the information gained from 10 seconds of online research using Google and copy-pasting links to Wikipedia.
• Decide if the topic is 'Hard research' (objective research, facts, figures, statistics and measurable evidence) or 'Soft research' (opinion-based, cultural and more subjective).	• Do not research a topic without any consideration given to the type of research you hope to achieve.
• Use different search engines and keywords by narrowing and deepening your search.	• Do not rely on searches such as Wikipedia and Internet Public Library.
• Bookmark and stockpile possible good content.	• Do not leave a possible good site before bookmarking, 'favourite'.
• Filter and validate the content (author/source/date of publication) and use Google 'link:' feature to see the backlinks for a page.	• Do not depend on commercial websites and do not be swayed by ranting, overstating, overly-positive commentary.
• Do amend any resource to address the learning objectives of your lessons/session to ensure that they correspond with the short-/medium-/long-term plans – for instance, delete some of the slides or use a few seconds of the video clip.	• Do not use the resources immediately in your lessons without considering issues such as 'appropriate and relevant' – is this the best resource for teaching this particular aspect of History/ Geography or RE?

Source: Based on www.studygs.net/research.htm.

Search: President OR Obama

Return: all items containing either President or Obama.

Question: I'm interested in who believes in God

Boolean logic: AND

Search: belief AND God

Return: all items containing belief and God.

Question: I'm interested in Glasgow, but not football

Boolean logic: NOT

Search: Glasgow NOT football

Return: all items referring to Glasgow but not football.

There are useful general guides available to help maximise Internet searching (Dolowitz *et al.*, 2008), along with introductions to the Internet such as: **www.Internet101.org**. Providing clear guidance on e-safety is particularly important in an age when around one in three children report that they receive 'nasty comments' via email, Internet messaging, chat rooms or through virtual worlds (Simmons and Hawkins, 2009). Such guidance should also extend to adults, so that photographs or comments about children comply with professional codes of conduct and school or local authority expectations; for instance, it would be inappropriate for a student teacher, learning support assistant or teacher to publish photographs of children, say on a school visit or during a residential stay, on the Internet without the permission of parents and the headteacher. The rise of social networking sites such as Facebook, Friends Reunited and MySpace, has led to occasional reports of inappropriate publication of school-related materials. Pages and photographs can be copied, mirrored on another site or cached by a search engine – this means that even if the original is removed, it could still be traced elsewhere.

There is a danger that teachers can too readily rely on the Internet to acquire free resources without considering carefully their fitness for purpose. Ultimately, the value of resources depends upon the teacher's imagination, pedagogical knowledge and technical skill; despite considerable criticism, PowerPoint, for instance, can prove a powerful learning tool (Lightfoot: 2011; Lauridsen, 2009).

The preparation of high-quality resources can make a real difference to the quality of learning and teaching. Table 2.6 offers a checklist of possible resources for the humanities. Specific sources will be required for particular topics, such as local study covered in Chapter 5, while Chapter 8 discusses further the selection of resources for

Table 2.6 A checklist of useful resources when planning for the humanities

Written sources	ICT resources – hardware and software
Documents, census returns, diaries, maps, articles, books, stories, letters, newspapers, brochures, flyers, inventories, notes, street directories.	Digital camera/video, flip cameras, mp3, i-pods, i-pads, digital microscope, microphone, talking books, DVDs/video/TV programmes, internet, websites.
People	**Visual resources**
Visitors to class – wardens/guides, religious people; oral history – interviews; questionnaires – e.g. current issues in the local area (wardens, education officer – heritage/national parks, etc.).	Picture books, comics, maps, satellite images, pictures, photographs, aerial photographs, postcards, greeting cards, paintings, posters, artefacts, buildings, photo packs, globes, atlases.

teaching the wider world. Plenty of time needs to be allocated to the finding and organisation of resources such as photographs, written material, ICT material, eyewitness accounts and artefacts. It is also helpful first to seek advice from the humanities leader or coordinator, who may have invested time and energy in collating resources for each unit. Contacting parents, carers and the wider community can result in 'new' resources being introduced into the school. Care must be taken, however, to list all the items and return them to their rightful owners. Other useful sources of teaching materials include the local teachers' centre, library or museum, many of which provide loan services. Asking family and friends and visiting local antique fairs or junk shops, although time consuming, can be very rewarding. These can be used for whole-class lessons or they can be rotated around groups to ensure that all children have one or two opportunities to do some first-hand learning.

Subject-specific skills, concepts, knowledge and understanding

Over recent years there has been a strong focus on promoting skills and making connections between subject areas as discussed in Chapter 3. However, there is also a need for teachers to retain in their planning and delivery a focus on subject specific matters if pupils are to be equipped with the knowledge and understanding to handle complex issues – for instance, 'the Creation' in RE, 'climate change' in Geography or 'nationalism' in History (Table 2.7).

Two of the most important generic concepts in the humanities subjects are time and place. Table 2.8 shows an example of how to develop these two main concepts focusing on geography and history.

Teachers' subject knowledge and their professional judgements are at the heart of successful planning to meet pupils' needs (Owens, 2010). The Rose Review (2009) points out that although learning might be organised in 'Areas of Learning', teachers should have the freedom to plan both within and across these 'Areas'. Alexander (2010) stresses the importance of teacher's subject knowledge and argues for sufficient training and resources to enable educational entitlement for all – seen as access for all pupils to the highest quality of teaching and learning. As Chapter 11 concludes, professional development is critical to ensuring that such high quality is retained. The Geographical Association recognises the need for teachers to be confident in their subject knowledge in order to teach it well and make sound links across the curriculum. To this end, there are a number of teacher support mechanisms in place such as the Geography Champions scheme.

One of the dangers of discussing planning is that it is seen in isolation from the teaching and assessment process. Moreover, it should not discount the importance of responding to children's interests and ideas. Planning is a means to an end – namely to motivate pupils by providing stimulating, relevant and enjoyable activities. While identifying and sharing with children clear learning objectives or intentions for a lesson is important, teachers should expect some learning to occur outside the initial planning (Kerry, 2011).

Table 2.7 Subject-specific skills within the humanities

History	Religious Education	Geography
Chronology – use timelines to sequence events.	Identifying and developing an understanding of ultimate questions and ethical issues.	Locating places, environments and patterns; identifying and locating places, using atlases and maps.
Use appropriate key words to estimate, measure and describe the passage of time.	Values, listening with empathy and working with others – personal and interpersonal skills.	Mapping skills/ fieldwork – follow directions, estimate and calculate distances.
Historical knowledge and understanding – identify differences between ways of life at different times; understand why people did things, what caused specific events and consequences of those events.	Enquiry and investigation of the nature of religion, its beliefs, teachings and ways of life, sources, practices and forms of expression.	Identify and describe spatial patterns of places and environments and how they are connected.
Interpretations of history – identify the ways in which the past is represented and interpreted; distinguish between fact and opinion, giving some evidence / knowledge-based reasons for this.	Reflecting and responding to personal and others' perceptions and experiences.	Identify similarities and differences, compare and contrast places and environments.
Historical enquiry – ask and answer questions; plan the investigative approach to be used; use a range of sources.	Exploring and respecting faith in the community.	Investigating a geographical issue, e.g. Why does it flood?
Change and continuity.	Develop an understanding of the influence of beliefs, values and traditions on individuals, communities, society and cultures.	Geographical enquiry, e.g. microclimate – predict, measure, collect and record data and draw conclusions.

Table 2.8 Key Stage 2: Place and Time

Place (Geography)	Change Over Time (History)
• How place influences the nature of life. • Ways in which people, plants and animals depend on the features and materials in places and how they adapt to their environment. • Positive and negative effects of natural and human events upon a place over time. • Features of – and variations in – places, including physical, human, climatic, vegetation and animal life.	• How change is a feature of the human and natural world and may have consequences for our lives and the world around us. • The effects of positive and negative changes globally and how we can contribute to some of these changes. • Ways in which change occurs over both short and long periods of time in the physical and natural world.

Source: Adapted from Northern Ireland Curriculum, KS2: The World Around Us, CCEA (2007).

SUMMARY

- It is important to understand the links between planning, teaching, learning, monitoring and assessment.

- Planning operates at three connected levels: long term, medium term and short term. Long-term plans should provide an overview of how the humanities are organised in the school and be updated regularly in accordance with national, local or school policy changes. Medium-term plans or schemes of work should tie closely to National Curriculum and non-statutory guidance. Short-term plans drill down to the details of what is taught, how, when and how the learning is assessed.

- Resources should be well presented and selected to stimulate interest. They should support the achievement of learning objectives. While the Internet has already transformed teachers' planning of lessons and preparation of resources, online material needs to be carefully considered for its appropriateness.

- There is a need to address subject-specific knowledge, skills and understanding when planning lessons in order to ensure the delivery of a broad and balanced curriculum.

References

Alexander, R.J. (ed.) (2010), *Children, their World, their Education*, London: Routledge.

Barnes, J. (2007), *Cross-Curricular Learning 3–14*, London: Sage Publications Limited.

Bowden, D. and Copeland, P. (2001), *LCP Geography Resource File – KS2*, Lemington Spa: LCP, available at www.lcp.co.uk/primary-school/geography/geography-resource-files.

Brophy, J. and Good, T. (1986), *'Teacher behaviour and student achievements'*, in Wittrock, M.C., (ed), Handbook of Research on Teaching, New York: Macmillan, 328–275.

Catling, S. (2003), 'Curriculum contested: Primary geography and social justice', *Geography*, 88 (3), 164–210.

CCEA (2007), *Northern Ireland Curriculum Primary*, Belfast: CCEA, available at: www.nicurriculum.org.uk/docs/key_stages_1_and_2/northern_ireland_curriculum_primary.pdf.

Cooper, H., Rowley, C. and Asquith, S. (2006), *Geography 3–11: A Guide for Teachers*, London: Fulton.

DCELLS (2008), *National Exemplar for Religious Education for 3 to 19-year-olds in Wales*, Cardiff: Welsh Assembly Government.

DCELLS (2011), *Religious Education: Guidance for Key Stages 2 and 3 – Key messages for planning learning and teaching*, Cardiff: Welsh Assembly Government.

DCSF (2008), *2020 Children and Young People's Workforce Strategy*, Nottingham: DCSF.

DCSF (2010), *Religious education in English Schools: Non-statutory guidance 2010*, Nottingham: DCSF.

DfES (2004), *Every Child Matters: Change for Children*, London: DfES.

Dolowitz, D., Buckler, S. and Sweeney, F. (2008), *Researching Online*, Basingstoke: Palgrave Macmillan.

Hayes, D. (2007), *Joyful Teaching and Learning in the Primary School*, Exeter: Learning Matters.

Hoodless, P., McCreey, E., Bowen, P., Bermingham, S. (2009), *Achieving QTS: Teaching Humanities in Primary Schools*, Exeter: Learning Matters.

Kerry, T. (2011), *Cross-Curricular Teaching in the Primary School (Planning and Facilitating Imaginative Lessons)* London: Routledge.

Lauridsen, O. (2009), *Learning Styles and PowerPoint: A new and exciting approach*, London: Microsoft Office. (http://innovativeteachertoolkit.com/documents/additional/PowerPoint_and_Learning_Styles.pdf.)

Lightfoot, L. (2011), 'Are your pupils bored by the whiteboard?' in *Tespro*, 16 December, 2011, 4–9.

Livingstone, S. and Bober, M. (2005), *UK Children Go Online: Final Report of Key Project Findings*, London: London School of Economics and Political Science.

McCreery, E., Palmer, S., and Voiels, V. (2008), *Teaching Religious Education*, Exeter: Learning Matters.

McGuire, M., Stilborne, L., McAdams, M. and Hyatt, L. (2000), *The Internet Handbook for Writers, Researchers and Journalists*, New York: Guilford Press.

Owens, P. (2010), 'Re-making the curriculum', *Primary Geographer 72*, 8–9.

Ofsted (2002a), *Teaching Assistants in Primary Schools: An Evaluation of the Quality and Impact of their Work*, London: Ofsted.

Ofsted (2002b), *Good teaching, effective departments*, London: Ofsted.

Ofsted (2008), *Curriculum Innovation in Schools*, London: Ofsted.

Rose, J. (2009), *Final Report: Independent Review of the Primary Curriculum*, DCSF, available at: www.education.gov.uk/publications/eOrderingDownload/Primary_curriculum_Report.pdf.

Scoffham, S. (2010), *Primary Geography Handbook (Revised Edition)*, Sheffield: Geographical Association.

Scottish Executive (2006), *The Equality Act 2006: Guidance for Schools*, Edinburgh: Scottish Executive.

Scottish Government (2009), *A Curriculum for Excellence: Building the Curriculum 4 – Skills for learning, skills for life and skills for work*, Edinburgh: Scottish Government.

Simmons, C. and Hawkins, C. (2009), *Teaching ICT*, London: Sage.

Slavin, R. (1987), 'Ability grouping and student achievement in elementary schools. A best-evidence synthesis', *Review of Educational Research*, 57, 293–336.

Sutherland-Smith, W. (2002), 'Weaving the literacy web: Changes in reading from page to screen', *Reading Teacher*, 57: 7, 662–669.

Turner-Bisset, R. (2005), *Creative Teaching History in the Primary Classroom,* London: David Fulton Publishers.

Vogel, N. (2001), *Making the Most of Plan-Do-Review*, Ypsilanti, MI: High/Scope Press.

Woods, S. (2010), *The Essential Guide to Using ICT Creatively in the Primary Classroom*, Harlow: Pearson.

Watkins, C., Carnell, E. and Lodge, C. (2007), *Effective Learning in Classrooms*, London: Sage.

Useful Websites

Further examples of long-term plans for RE can be seen at: www.birmingham-asc.org.uk/resourcing.php.

The Geographical Association's 'Young Geographers' and 'Making Geography Happen' at: www.geography.org.uk/projects/younggeographers; www.geography.org.uk/making geographyhappen.

The old QCA schemes of work are available at: http://webarchive.nationalarchives.gov.uk/20090608182316/standards.dfes.gov.uk/schemes3/.

Cross-curricular learning and teaching in the humanities

One thing stands out in all the most successful schools . . . they opt for an approach towards education which rests on traditional subject disciplines.

(Michael Gove, Education Secretary, 2009)

Throughout our discussion of curriculum we stress children's learning does not fit into subjects.

(DES 1967a: 203)

Learning objectives

By the end of this chapter you should be able to:

- define the cross-curricular approach and explain its rationale in the humanities;
- critically reflect upon the longstanding debates associated with cross-curricular teaching;
- identify the major considerations when planning cross-curricular activities; and
- describe the contribution of the humanities in promoting pupils' literacy, numeracy, ICT and thinking skills.

Subject teaching versus cross-curricular studies

Cross-curricular work, once popular in primary schools during the 1960s and 1970s, is back in fashion . . . at least among many educationalists (Barnes, 2007; Rowley and Cooper, 2009; Kerry, 2011). This popularity is reflected in numerous curriculum models and publications. For instance, the 'Creative Learning Journey' is replete with topic wheels linked to 'essential skills and areas of learning' rather than 'disjointed discrete subjects' (**www.creativelearningjourney.org.uk**) while the Hamilton Trust charity favours a topic-based curriculum to engage pupils in and out of school (**www. hamiltonplay.org.uk**). However, there are also high-profile critics of the drift away from subject teaching towards cross-curricular studies. Furedi (2007) is among those alarmed by the downgrading of traditional geography, history and other academic subjects. This is an international trend. For instance, former Australian Prime Minister John Howard claimed that traditional subjects such as English, history and geography had been displaced by 'incomprehensible drudge' in the form of 'Studies of Society and the Environment' (Beder, 2009: 131).

In England, Michael Gove's claim that the best schools organise the curriculum along subject lines is dubious. For instance, Ofsted (2009: 17) reports that outstanding schools (in the most socially deprived areas) do not follow a particular mode of planning:

> Some organise pupils by ability in the core subjects; others do not. Some cover many of the subjects through themes; others invest a lot of time in the creative curriculum and can demonstrate benefits in writing and other forms of expression.

Nonetheless, Gove's view does illustrate the importance of understanding clearly the rationale behind cross-curricular work and the need to justify its potential to improve pupils' learning in the humanities.

What is meant by a cross-curricular approach?

'Cross-curricular' is a term used to describe knowledge, activities, skills or initiatives that are applied across the curriculum and not confined to one subject (Barnes, 2007; Wallace, 2009). The approach is often used interchangeably with topics and themes, although these are not synonymous terms (see Table 3.1). While topic work is rooted in the notion of applying skills in a range of contexts, Fisher (2002: 53) points out that such links are often engineered by the teacher rather than the class, leaving 'topics as incomprehensible to children as subject divisions are'. She reminds us that topics are the vehicle of learning and not the purpose of it. Good cross-curricular teaching enables pupils to pull together knowledge from different areas and apply this to everyday life.

The Cambridge Primary Review provides an excellent overview of the debates surrounding subjects and the respective role of knowledge and skills in the curriculum. It explores misconceptions about how the curriculum is organised and reminds readers of the historical insults that have been plied against those who support subjects and those who condemn them. The Review points out that a subject can 'mean anything we want it to mean' – the team suggest that what matters is not so much curriculum labels but what is taught and how. They add, 'a subject is not of itself old-fashioned just because subjects have been used as an organising device for over a century. If, as enacted in the classroom, a subject is irrelevant, it is the teacher who makes it so' (Alexander, 2010: 246).

Research makes it clear that the most important factors in successful learning are the quality of teaching and relationships between teachers and students (Hattie, 2009).

Table 3.1 Key terms associated with curriculum organisation

Term	Meaning and content
Themes	Teaching is organised around thematic units such as 'Homes', designed to explore connections between areas of learning.
Topic work	An approach to learning that draws upon 'children's concerns and involves them in the planning, executing and reflecting upon negotiated learning experiences' (Tann, 1988: 4).
Projects	Pieces of work produced by individuals or groups (Waters, 1982).
Areas of learning or experience	Means of organising the curriculum according to broad areas, rather than discrete subjects. For the humanities, DES (1985) suggested 'human and social' and more recently the Independent Review of the Primary Curriculum (DCSF, 2009) recommended 'historical, geographical and social understanding'. The model is particularly popular in Northern Ireland and Scotland.
Subjects, disciplines or domains	Subjects or disciplines are often defined by their methodologies or content, including their distinctive ways of thinking, vocabulary and symbolism. Domains are described as essential knowledge, skill, disposition and enquiry such as 'place and time' and 'faith and beliefs' (Alexander and Flutter, 2009).

International evidence suggests that the most successful schools do not structure the curriculum around subjects (McCulloch, 2011). Good thematic teaching does not lead to a neglect of the 'basics'. The highest-performing school systems, as in Korea, Canada and Singapore, adopt 'a rigorous thematic approach, while continuing to value and develop strong teacher subject knowledge' (McCulloch, 2011: 27).

Rationale

There is a tendency to see subject teaching and cross-curricular activity as polar opposites rather than complementary (DCSF, 2008). Those new to the profession need to be aware of the rationale behind cross-curricular teaching if they wish to become well-informed, reflective practitioners (see Table 3.2).

TASK

- Discuss with experienced colleagues their views of cross-curricular learning and teaching in the humanities. Do they have any evidence that such an approach makes a difference for pupils? What challenges have they faced?

Table 3.2 Arguments for and against cross-curricular learning

For	Against
Learning occurs in 'real' and relevant contexts.	Lacks coherence and depth.
Fits in with notions of 'holistic', 'natural' and 'experiential' learning; in keeping with children's cognitive development and view of the world.	Challenging to ensure progression and assessment of subject skills.
Makes curriculum more manageable.	Can become repetitive and links between subjects may be tenuous.
Opportunities for a more creative curriculum, tailored to the interests and needs of pupils.	Theme-based work is not always properly marked and comments are not subject-specific enough.

Theories of learning and knowledge

The traditional subject-based curriculum largely rests on an objectivist (behaviourist) view of learning where teachers adopt an instructional role in transmitting prescribed, essential knowledge, which exists 'out there' independent of the minds of individuals. In contrast, the cross-curricular approach is based on a socio-cultural theory of learning. This suggests that pupils learn and create their own knowledge by talking, working together, sharing ideas, asking questions and making connections across subject boundaries. Learning is also framed by cultural factors. For instance, East Asian students often comment that they prefer didactic teaching and rote learning to critical thinking, and see teachers as unchallengeable authorities (Jarvis *et al.*, 1998). Chinese educators see the value of memorising techniques to aid the acquisition of knowledge and understanding. What is often missing from such debate is an understanding of what is meant by 'essential subject knowledge', who selects what is considered worthy of sharing, which knowledge is omitted from the curriculum and the kinds of knowledge that learners encounter and need to process. Moreover, there is a tendency to assume that connections between prior knowledge and new experiences are best made through a cross-curricular approach.

There is no shortage of alarmist stories regarding children and young people's lack of knowledge in the humanities. One in three primary children are reported to think Winston Churchill was the first man on the moon while, even more disturbingly, around one in four adults thought that he was a fictional character who had more to do with a television advert for Churchill insurance (Moult, 2008). There are similar concerns over children's inadequate geographical knowledge (Ofsted, 2008) and the replacement of knowledge with morality connected to global citizenship (Standish, 2007). There are also concerns over a decline in Christian knowledge.

Dr John Sentamu, the Archbishop of York, regretted that 30 per cent of children in one survey thought Easter was to celebrate the birthday of the Easter Bunny (*The Daily Telegraph*, 4 April 2010). Public outcries over children's ignorance of basic factual knowledge in the humanities are not new nor are they confined to Britain. But rarely are the underlying assumptions implied by these concerns seriously questioned. Nonetheless, Michael Gove has announced that under the revised National Curriculum (to be introduced in 2014) pupils in England will be expected to learn about specific countries, cities, continents, rivers and oceans. In history, they will be expected to know key dates, periods and historical figures, including Churchill, Queen Elizabeth, Gladstone, Disraeli, Florence Nightingale and Horatio Nelson (Paton, 2011).

One of the problems here is that subject knowledge is too readily equated with factual content: the dates of historical battles, the location of cities and names of religious festivals. However, in addition to such propositional knowledge, subjects also include other forms of knowing: conditional (knowing when and why), procedural (knowing how), as well as private and public forms – for instance how individual historians and geographers make sense of knowledge in their respective fields. The Expert Panel appointed to review the National Curriculum in England sees socially refined knowledge as: 'concepts, facts, processes, language, narratives and conventions of each subject' (DfE, 2011: 11). Trainee and serving teachers should reflect upon questions associated with the nature and value of knowledge:

- What knowledge is worthy of sharing?
- What do the pupils already know?
- Which pupils know what?
- What do *I/they* know about this subject?
- Where can we find out more?
- What 'facts' are appropriate for this age?
- When transmitting knowledge which bits shall I leave out? Why?
- How shall I present this information?
- How far shall I let the pupils find out for themselves?
- Is this knowledge 'absolute' and fully agreed upon or is it contestable?
- How do I know this is true?
- Where has this knowledge come from?
- Why do pupils need to know this?
- What difference might this knowledge make?
- How can we add to this knowledge?

REFLECTION

- During your next teaching experience, consider the questions posed above.

Different types of knowledge change at different speeds; hence technological knowledge moves more rapidly than religious knowledge. The dawning of the information age (since the 1980s) has undoubtedly shaped the knowledge discourse. Instant access to Google and other systems present learners with more than 11.5 billion web pages, and the challenge for teachers and pupils alike is how to manage such 'information noise' (Holmes and Gardner, 2006). The amount of information is estimated to double approximately every seven years (Hayes, 2006). This is often used to justify a focus on developing transferable thinking skills so that pupils can adapt to change rather that spend too much time on acquiring information that has a short lifespan. However, as the Cambridge Primary Review points out, to tell children at the start of their school lives that 'Google and a mobile phone will do the trick is a travesty of what knowing and understanding ought to be about' (Alexander, 2010: 247). It is 'irresponsible' to limit pupils' horizons to the skills of accessing information without challenging them to engage with the knowledge, pose questions and evaluate what they find.

It would be a misrepresentation of subjects to limit their scope to propositional knowledge. The innovative Schools Council's *Place, Time and Society 8-13: Curriculum Planning in History, Geography and Social Science* (Blyth *et al.*, 1976: 32) viewed subject disciplines as 'resources' meaning the 'accumulative achievements' (e.g. sources, personal experiences, methods and skills) of the subjects rather than 'a body of content that must be absorbed'. The Schools Council wanted to preserve the wide and stimulating range of knowledge, skills and perspectives offered by each discipline so that they were not 'elbowed out . . . if merged into some synthetic and perhaps shapeless whole'. That said, the authors were not against integrated study. Rather, they called upon teachers to know how historians, geographers and social scientists worked. In this regard, the teachers were to act as mediators between the subjects and learners.

For social constructivists, knowledge results from individuals interacting with each other and with the environment they live in (Gredler, 1997). Learning is seen as a social process rather than taking place within an individual. Historians and geographers *create* knowledge by asking questions, interpreting sources, sharing ideas and making comparisons (see Table 3.3). Erricker *et al.* (2011: 76) illustrate a constructivist approach in religious education through a Living Difference project tied to the Hampshire Agreed Syllabus, in which children are 'involved', 'receptive' and 'don't worry about what they say'. Pupils are reported to latch onto ideas better because the focus is no longer on factual content but key concepts: 'They can focus on Hindu ideas about reincarnation, not what happens at a Hindu burial' (Erricker *et al.*, 2011: 77).

Social constructivism has been criticised in recent years by those keen to see the reinstatement of knowledge and a return to academic disciplines (Young, 2007). The argument runs that there is too much emphasis on competencies and skills. Writing in the context of geography education, Young (2007: 181) believes that schools exist to give pupils 'access to the powerful knowledge that most of them will not have the opportunity to acquire at home.' Lambert (2011) suggests that developments such as 'Thinking Skills', 'Learning to Learn' and 'Building Learning Power' adopt a deficit view of the learner to the detriment of their geography education:

This is an attack on young people as 'knowers'. It is also an attack on subjects such as geography. Even when subjects are not dismissed entirely, or replaced by a thematic

Table 3.3 Socio-constructivist approach to the humanities	
Subject	**Socio-constructivist elements**
History	• Discussing prior knowledge and experiences (e.g. 'What do we know about . . .?'). • Selecting and making sense of first-hand sources (e.g. pictures, maps, buildings, people, documents). • Carrying out historical investigations. • Comparing interpretations of the past. • Deciding on means of recording and communicating findings. • Emphasis on links with archaeological discoveries.
Geography	• Seeking out patterns, making links and comparing similarities and differences. • Selecting aspects of place that interest pupils, recalling and discussing previous experiences. • Role-play areas (e.g. setting up a travel agency, post office or passport office). • Opportunities for pupils to explore, play and travel in a variety of places, building on children's or young people's geographies. • Asking geographical questions.
Religious Education	• Focusing on *how* people believe as well as what they believe. • Seeking to promote an awareness of self and the wider world. • Knowledge is interpretative and transformative rather than pre-determined (e.g. pupils are encouraged to interpret biblical stories in the light of their own experiences).

or skills-led programme, the subjects are distorted by the softer therapeutic aims of the 'emotionally literate school'

(Lambert, 2011: 128)

The constructivist pedagogy has a strong influence in primary humanities (Littledyke and Huxford, 1998; Martin, 2006). However, good teachers need to demonstrate what Shulman (1987) famously called 'Pedagogical Content Knowledge' (PCK). This refers to teachers' ability to translate subject matter for teaching purposes through the use of analogies, examples, explanations and demonstrations. Although there are conceptual difficulties with PCK – for instance in terms of seeing knowledge as static and under-valuing the importance of teachers' beliefs in shaping knowledge – nonetheless PCK is a neat way of bridging subject expertise with teaching practice. More recently, the

Expert Panel reviewing the National Curriculum in England pointed out that schools need to make time for teaching knowledge and the development of skills:

> The two elements are not, however, equally significant at every age. In particular, developmental aspects and basic skills are more crucial for young children, while appropriate understanding of more differentiated subject knowledge, concepts and skills becomes more important for older pupils.

(DfE, 2011: 12)

BOX 3.1 RESEARCH BRIEFING – TO INTEGRATE OR NOT

Research on the cross-curricular approach presents mixed findings. Research in the late 1980s and early 1990s argued that the outcomes of an integrated model were less effective teaching (Alexander et al., 1992) although this has been contested (Campbell and Little, 1989). Kerry (2011) suggests that integration brings deeper learning than separate subject teaching. Greenwood's (2007) survey of geography teaching in Northern Irish primary schools found that only 7 per cent of 1,328 topics were taught in a subject-based, stand-alone way, with 91 per cent of teachers positive about cross-curricular teaching of geography. The Scottish inspectorate reports that thematic and topic work motivates pupils and enables them to take a more active part in their learning, for example by deciding aspects to study (HMIe, 2007). However, these 'soft' gains are very difficult to measure and are often based on informal observations. Knight (1993: 134–5) suggests that more successful outcomes occur when teachers pair subjects together, with one as a main focal point – 'more is not always better'. More recent research suggests that many outstanding English primary schools and international school systems do not structure learning around traditional subject disciplines (McCulloch, 2011).

The historical and ideological context for cross-curricular work

Since schooling began under the auspices of the medieval Church, the curriculum has been organized along subject lines with an emphasis on reading, writing, arithmetic (English and mathematics) and religious instruction. When taught, history and geography reinforced patriotic values, preserved British cultural heritage and amounted to an 'education for followship' – working-class pupils schooled to respect their betters (Gordon and Lawton, 1978:79). The utilitarian aim was to produce (cheaply and efficiently) literate, numerate, god-fearing and deferential citizens. For much of the nineteenth and early twentieth century, the curriculum model was shaped by an ideology that valued basic skills, academic subjects, knowledge of Great Britain, tradition, Christian values and moral education. The great Victorian advances in science, engineering and geography were driven by the pursuit of knowledge. Schools crammed pupils with as much information as they could and tested this with drill-and-practice assessments. In such a content-driven curriculum inevitably a hierarchy of subjects developed and this has remained essentially the same since Victorian times (Aldrich, 1996). To use a football analogy, English and mathematics have always been in the Premier League, RE has been gradually relegated to the First Division while history and geography have generally performed in the lower leagues. However, the striking feature of the primary curriculum spanning three centuries is its remarkable continuity in how knowledge has been classified and presented (Table 3.4).

There are longstanding criticisms of a subject-based curriculum in the primary school. For instance, in the 1930s alternative approaches such as the 'project method' were recommended in which children specified what they wanted to know, asked questions and devised ways of finding out. Textbooks suggested projects on 'shops', 'workers' and 'our town' for the primary school, including activities such as model making, local walks and creating picture maps (Hume, 1938). The Hadow Report (Board of Education, 1931) famously declared that 'the curriculum is to be thought of in terms of activity and experience rather than of knowledge to be acquired and facts to be stored' (1931:93).

Similar sentiments were expressed during the heady 1960s. *Primary Education in Scotland* (Scottish Education Department, 1965) pointed out that the acquisition of knowledge was no longer as important as fostering intellectual curiosity and independent learning. It believed that the curriculum was meaningful only if it was integrated and not thought of in terms of discrete subjects (Darling, 2003). In England and Wales, the Plowden and Gittins Reports (DES, 1967a; DES 1967b) provided official endorsement for a curriculum in which knowledge was organised around themes such as autumn, water or transport, to which subject matter could be added as and when necessary to illuminate the theme. The approach was seen as an antidote to the generally formal, dull and didactic teaching of the 1950s. A typical textbook referred to the new emphasis on 'enquiry, activity, discovery and communication' (Howson, 1969: vii), the breaking down of teacher isolation and the re-drawing of the curriculum resulting in the emergence of areas such as social studies.

Progressive education, a phrase first used in 1839, was closely associated with promoting children's individuality, growth, creativity, expression and imagination. Many had the impression that the Plowden Report saw subjects as contrived ways of viewing the world (Riley and Prentice, 1999). However, while it rejected organizing the timetable according to subjects in the education of young children, it saw the value of subject teaching with older juniors and called for the presence of specialist subject coordinators ('consultants') in primary schools. Members of the Plowden Committee were split over the question of RE because of their personal beliefs. A minority held that RE should not feature in the curriculum in a society that was increasingly rejecting the 'sanction of supernatural revelation' (DES, 1967a: 493). They advocated an alternative programme in moral or ethical education. Others wanted RE to influence the entire curriculum. Between these extremes, the majority called for a review of provision drawing upon research into what religious subject matter was relevant to children's interests, experiences and intellectual powers. Research (Goldman, 1965; Loukes, 1965) had suggested that pupils were confused by the transmission of biblical knowledge acquired in lessons. Rather, they needed opportunities to engage with everyday problems perceived to be relevant as a way of approaching religion.

Table 3.4 Overview of primary curriculum change in England, 1905–2010

Board of Education (1905)	DES (1959)	DES (1967)	HMI (1980)	Education Reform Act (1988)	Independent Review (2009)
English	Language Handwriting	English	English	English	English, communication and languages
Arithmetic	Mathematics	Mathematics	Mathematics	Mathematics	Mathematical understanding
Religious Instruction (RI)	Religion	RE	RE	RE*	RE
History	History	History	History and social studies	History	Historical, geographical and social understanding
Geography	Geography	Geography	Geography	Geography	
Nature study	Natural science	Science	Science	Science	Scientific and technological understanding
Physical Training (PT)	Physical Education (PE)	PE	PE including dance and games	PE	Understanding physical development, health and well-being
Art and craft (boys)	Art, craft and needlework	Art and craft	Art and craft	Art	Understanding the arts
Needlework (girls)				Design Technology (included Information Technology)	ICT capability
Music	Music	Music	Music and drama	Music	
		Foreign language	Foreign language	Welsh (for schools in Wales)	

Note: * The Education Reform Act (1988) established a Basic Curriculum of Religious Education and the National Curriculum.

Sources: Schools Council (1983), Schools Council Working Paper 75. Primary practice, London: Methuen; for Education Reform Act (1988) see http://www.legislation.gov.uk/; DCSF (2009), Independent Review of the Primary Curriculum: Final Report, Nottingham: DCSF

Critics of Plowden were concerned over the development of a 'magpie curriculum' that lacked coherence, structure and rigour (Bantock, 1971). Fears were expressed that a 'hit-and-miss' approach provided children with too much choice, avoiding areas of learning that they found challenging, thereby failing to develop perseverance and fundamental subject-specific skills. The 'demonisation' of education in the 1960s, as Tomlinson (2005: 22) puts it, has carried through to the twenty-first century. In 2004, David Bell, Chief Inspector of Schools, described much of the teaching in the 1960s as 'plain crackers' with 'too many incoherent or non-existing curriculums' and too many 'soft-centred beliefs that children would learn if you left them to it' (cited by Tomlinson, 2005: 22). While projects were often well planned and evaluated, it was less clear how they built on prior learning (Mallett, 2002). Even supporters of topic work, such as Tann (1988), acknowledged that there was a need for a clear rationale, close monitoring of children's achievements and good classroom management.

The National Curriculum was introduced in England and Wales in 1988 to establish an entitlement for all pupils, although its subject-based nature was never fully explained. Alternative curriculum models, such as 'areas of experience' advocated by Her Majesty's Inspectors during the 1980s, were ignored (Lawton and Chitty, 1988). Gaps between the subjects were supposed to be covered through a combination of cross-curricular themes, dimensions and skills. Among these was environmental education, education for citizenship and education for life in a multicultural society. Commentators were quick to flag up other themes such as media education (Webb, 1996), personal and social education, the European dimension and gender issues (Verma, 1994). The reality facing many primary schools was that they had little time to develop such themes, despite recognising their value, once they had given attention to the core and foundation subjects. As Ashcroft and Palacio (1995: 7) point out, these cross-curricular themes and dimensions were not well covered in the planning stage and consequently became peripheral when the curriculum was implemented.

Various ideological influences have shaped the development of the primary curriculum. The 'elementary' tradition was based on communicating essential knowledge while 'progressives' championed pupils' self-expression and curriculum innovation. A 'developmental' ideology focused on meeting the needs of children at different stages of growth. Alexander (1995) points out that these ideologies do not come in single file, one after another, but compete and interact. They remain powerful forces in the twenty-first-century curriculum discourse. Politically, a subject-based curriculum is often associated with a conservative outlook that advocates 'academic' standards, regular testing and an emphasis on memory, practice and rote. It frowns upon liberal relativism ('truth is what you make it'), pupil participation in the curriculum, group work and discovery approaches.

REFLECTION

- Which of the ideologies in Table 3.5 prevails most in the classroom/school environment that you are familiar with? Have you experienced differences between individual teachers and schools? Which of the ideologies are you comfortable with? How and when is it possible to combine aspects of these views during a school day?

Table 3.5 Elementary and progressive ideologies

Area	Elementary	Progressive/post-modern
Values	Control, discipline, measured performance	Pupil autonomy, creative and critical thinking
Outcomes	Academic standards	Pupils' well-being
Curriculum	Organised around subjects	Themes, projects, children's interests and ideas
Role of teacher	Teacher as instructor	Teacher as facilitator
Role of the learner	Passive recipient of received wisdom	Active, constructing their own knowledge
Methodology	Transmission of culture (didactic, formal, whole class)	Child centred (individual, discovery, exploration, enquiry)
Assessment	Assessment *of* learning (examinations, grades, setting)	Assessment *for* learning (self and peer review, focus on how to improve)
Learning environment	Structured, set resources provided	Open, negotiable, interactive
Learning emphasis	Knowledge, cognitive development	Skills, social and emotional development

The content of the curriculum in England has recently been reviewed, borne out of concern that it is too overcrowded. Many schools have struggled to meet the National Curriculum's aim to provide a broad and balanced curriculum in the context of a results-driven, attainment-obsessed agenda. According to the Cambridge Primary Review (Alexander and Flutter, 2009: 22): 'The most conspicuous casualties are the arts, the humanities and the kinds of learning in all subjects which require time for talking, problem-solving and the extended exploration of ideas.' The Review suggests an alternative model based on a more locally determined curriculum (30 per cent), in which the humanities feature in several 'domains' such as 'place and time' and 'faith and belief', similar to previous approaches in the 1970s (Blyth *et al.*,1976). The Cambridge Primary Review's eight suggested domains (Figure 3.1) are described as starting points for curriculum planning. They are not seen as named slots on a time-table or 'an invitation for low-grade topic work in which thematic serendipity counts for more than knowledge and skills' (Alexander, 2010: 266). These domains oper-ate beyond the traditional subject boundaries of primary history and geography to include the social sciences, such as archaeology.

Another curriculum review, chaired by Sir Jim Rose (DCSF, 2008), advocated six areas of learning and essential skills for life. Again this has echoes of a model recom-mended by Her Majesty's Inspectors during the 1980s (Lawton and Chitty, 1988). Rose argues for a national curriculum to be based on a combination of areas of

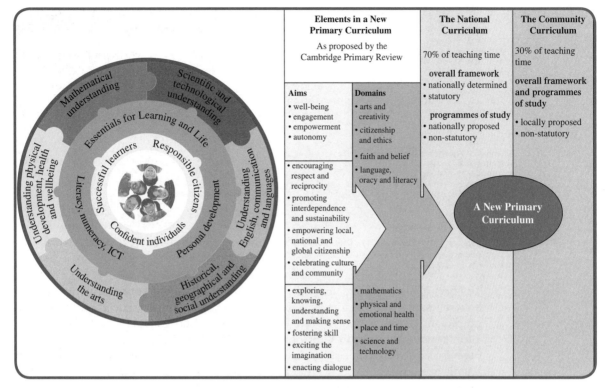

Figure 3.1 Primary curriculum models advocated by the Independent Primary Review and the Cambridge Primary Review. *Sources*: DCSF, 2009: 46; Alexander, 2010:274.

learning with traditional subjects. This has had its critics in the humanities field. The Humanities Association (HUMS) points to the potential for: 'fragmentation and further decline', dismissing the 'historical, geographical and social understanding' areas of learning as a pruned version of National Curriculum history and geography.

In the light of such concerns, the coalition government declared its plans to return the National Curriculum to its original purpose. The report by the Expert Panel appointed to review the National Curriculum recommends the retention of subjects and a clear focus on essential knowledge (DfE, 2011). It suggests that while subjects should remain statutory, schools should have a greater say in determining the specific content along the lines of the Cambridge Primary Review's local curriculum model.

Westminster's current subject-centred policy is not mirrored elsewhere in the UK (see table 3.6). In Scotland, one of the aspirations of Curriculum for Excellence is the promotion of interdisciplinary learning 'taking learning out of 'silos' to establish better connectivity in learning' (Smuga, 2008:11). The social studies experiences and outcomes have been structured under the three main headings:

- people, past events and societies;
- people, place and environment; and
- people in society, economy and business.

(Scottish Executive, 2006)

Table 3.6 Humanities across the primary curricula of the United Kingdom

England	Wales	Scotland	Northern Ireland
Understanding of the world (0–5)	Knowledge and understanding of the world (3–7)	Social studies (3–18)	The World Around Us (4–16)
History, Geography (5–11)	History, Geography (7–11)		
RE	RE (3–11)	Religious and moral education	RE (4–16)

Sources: Tickell Review (2011), DfEE (2000), DCELLS (2008), Scottish Executive (2006), CCEA (2007). See also respective government websites.

Teachers are expected to use this framework to highlight connections across and between subject boundaries covering historical, geographical, social, political, economic and business contexts. In Wales, 'there are no constraints relating to time allocations or the organization of subjects' (DCELLS, 2008: 7). Schools are free to organise the curriculum as they see appropriate. The emphasis in Welsh schools is on a skills-based National Curriculum at Key Stage 2 that builds upon the play-based and integrated Foundation Phase (3 to 7).

To teach history, geography and religious education well, teachers need to understand the nature of these subjects *before* planning any cross-curricular links. Ofsted (2008) reports the following example where geography was used as a context but which resulted in little geographical learning:

> As part of a themed week, pupils had attended an inter-school Olympics where they competed as and represented an allocated country, Pakistan. During the rest of the week they were involved in activities and lessons linked to Pakistan. The pupils thoroughly enjoyed the opportunities offered: they designed Asian-style clothes, made carpets using traditional designs and learnt about Muslim weddings, mosaics and mendhi patterns. However, pupils rarely explicitly studied the geography of Pakistan. Only in the Year 3 class was the opportunity taken to integrate the work into their geography topic of 'weather around the world'. Overall, despite studying a country in depth over the week, most pupils learnt very little about its geography.

(Ofsted, 2008: 17–18)

Planning

Cross-curricular planning can take various forms, including:

- pairing subjects or aspects such as history and geography or local study;
- connecting subjects through generic skills such as communication, thinking or numeracy;

- using a common theme as a basis for integration, such as 'food';
- building on shared concepts, such as interdependence, place, movement and energy, and change over time, as per the Northern Ireland model;
- an investigative approach based on a key question, such as 'What is it like to live in our community?' and
- planned teaching around a shared resource, for example following a visit, story or visiting speaker.

Good cross-curricular teaching requires secure knowledge and understanding of each subject, just as a good cook needs knowledge of the nutritional and aesthetic value of the different foodstuffs when preparing a meal. The philosophy behind cross-curricular work is to draw upon pupils' interests and avoid overly prescriptive plans. Outstanding schools are confident enough to 'customise' the statutory curriculum (Ofsted, 2002; Ofsted, 2009). Thompson suggests that topics should be thought of as a thread through which subjects are held together, like beads on a necklace (**www. keystagehistory.co.uk**). Some of the beads (i.e. subject contributions) will be bigger than others. But what matters is how they are threaded to ensure that there is a logical sequence for pupils. Hence a topic such as 'Going to the Seaside' could focus mainly on geography, then move to history and other areas such as drama.

One of the dangers of the cross-curricular approach is planning by word association. Laurie (2011) cites the example of how a theme such as 'water' could lead to choosing stories such as Charles Kingsley's *Water Babies* and *Noah's Ark*, geography work on the water cycle and a study of Victorian laundry work – the mere fact that they have links to water misses the true meaning of cross-curricular learning. In order to ensure breadth and balance, long-term plans should map out clearly how pupils will have opportunities to access their curriculum entitlement over the school year. In addition to the general planning considerations highlighted in Chapter 2, there are particular pointers for cross-curricular planning.

Principles for planning cross-curricular work include the following:

- Audit pupils' existing experience and knowledge against the curriculum requirements;
- Frame the study with key questions;
- Draw upon pupils' ideas, questions and interests;
- Choose a topic or theme that covers two or three main subject contributions but with one lead subject to provide focus;
- Map out the intended learning outcomes in terms of the essential knowledge, skills and concepts to be addressed;
- Avoid being overly ambitious – never force links between subjects; and
- Always include opportunities to develop communication, thinking, numeracy and ICT skills.

There are a number of questions to consider when choosing a theme, for instance:

- What are the anticipated learning outcomes?
- How well does this topic lend itself to a cross-curricular approach?
- Is this theme likely to stimulate and sustain pupils' interests?

- How relevant and significant is this theme to children's lives?
- How does the proposed content align with the curriculum requirements and
- How is progression in knowledge and skills assured?

Certain themes have strong potential for the humanities such as Myself, Homes, Family, Places and Time. But some themes naturally lend themselves to one humanities subject and not another. Transport, for instance, has clear geographical and historical potential in exploring its impact on the environment (e.g. the building of roads, trade routes, exports and imports) and developments through the ages (e.g. the impact of the railways in the 1840s, the bicycle craze of the 1890s or the motor car in the twentieth century). But the religious dimension should not be forced or contrived, for instance by telling the story of Jesus riding on a donkey.

In some cases teachers demonstrate considerable creativity in making subject links. For example, in a class topic on 'bridges' one teacher explored the idea of bridges and barriers in human relationships while in another class topic on 'time', pupils were asked to identify on personal timelines events that occurred only once (e.g. starting school) and events that were repeated (e.g. birthdays). This enabled the teacher to explore notions of linear and cyclical time and how it relates to Buddhism (Bastide, 1992: 60). Effective cross-curricular learning often arises from combining less obvious areas, such as science and history. For example, history can illuminate the ethical challenges faced by great scientists in their respective ages.

The humanities and skills across the curriculum

The skills of literacy, numeracy, information and communications technology and thinking have a high profile throughout the United Kingdom. These are among the essential skills for 'learning, work and life', as expressed in Scotland's *Curriculum for Excellence*. When the humanities are well taught, they make a significant contribution to developing these skills. They offer stimulating contexts for story-making, calculating, measuring, drawing, debating, exchanging information, listening, presenting ideas and interpreting visual cues.

Literacies

The humanities provide motivating opportunities for pupils to develop a wider range of 'literacies' beyond reading and writing:

Physical literacy – for example: reading aspects of the physical environment during fieldwork; developing self-confidence and physical competence through activities such as orienteering, Forest schools, trails and local history walks.

Visual literacy (or graphicacy) – for instance through visits to galleries, parks and museums, pupils can develop skills in interpreting paintings, religious artefacts, maps and films.

Religious literacy – for example, by challenging prejudice and gaining the skills and knowledge 'to engage in an informed and confident way with faith communities'.

(DCLG, 2008: 33)

Emotional literacy – developing empathy and managing personal feelings through listening to others; working in groups; sharing ideas; reflecting, and persevering at tasks.

E-literacy – searching, selecting, planning, evaluating and publishing activities.

Reading and writing skills can be developed as pupils interact with sources (see Table 3.7). These include:

- people (curators, librarians, local historians, politicians, ministers, wardens);
- places (archives, galleries, museums, Citizen's Advice Bureau, town halls), and media (magazines, CD-ROMs, websites, encyclopedias, databases).

Table 3.7 Examples of promoting reading and writing through the humanities

Skill	Possible activities
Writing	<ul><li>Identifying key points using highlighter pens or post-it notes.</li><li>Deleting irrelevant parts of texts.</li><li>Compiling lists.</li><li>Producing tables, diagrams, flow charts and mind maps.</li><li>Writing summaries (e.g. 'Five things everyone should know about Islam').</li><li>Writing historical, geographical or religious stories, reports, diaries, reflective journals, posters, postcards from around the UK/world, newspapers, museum signs, artefact labels, instructions, travel guides and brochures.</li><li>Producing displays (e.g. for a market stall).</li><li>Writing thank you letters/emails following visits.</li></ul>
Reading for information	<ul><li>Chronological texts – organised around a sequence of time (e.g. biographies, autobiographies, newspaper reports, eyewitness accounts).</li><li>Non-chronological texts – read from different starting points (e.g. websites, leaflets, maps, atlases, posters).</li></ul>
Undertaking research	<ul><li>Exploring previous knowledge (e.g. through mind maps).</li><li>Asking questions about photographs, artefacts, stories.</li><li>Devising questionnaires for interviewing elderly ones.</li><li>Finding, sorting and deducing information from a variety of sources (e.g. Internet, email, documents).</li><li>Comparing and evaluating sources (e.g. detecting bias, sorting facts and opinions by using different coloured pens).</li><li>Comparing ways of researching (e.g. Internet and library reference books).</li><li>Reaching informed conclusions.</li><li>Presenting findings in a variety of ways, such as:<ul><li>visual – posters, web pages, leaflets, board games;</li><li>aural – radio/TV programmes, drama, role play;</li><li>written – diary extracts, fact files, information books for younger children.</li></ul></li></ul>

Stories

Stories are essential to humanities teaching. They stimulate thought and satisfy the full range of human emotions. Stories of different kinds (such as myths and legends, parables, biographies, fiction and eyewitness accounts) can form an excellent springboard for cross-curricular work in history, geography and RE (Boyes, 1997; Nicholson, 1996; Shaw, 1999). Teachers can draw upon local folklore, as well as stories from around the world and from different cultures, to extend pupils' awareness of diverse lifestyles.

Popular follow-up activities to story-telling include:

- writing captions for different pictures in a story;
- arranging pictures in the correct sequence;
- writing a story from the viewpoint of a character;
- discussing the feelings and motives of characters;
- writing letters or cards from one character to another;
- story circles – one pupil begins a tale and stops after a few sentences. The next pupil picks up the story thread and continues it, then stops . . . and so on; and
- telling different versions of the same story; reconstructing a story using sentences from different parts.

Before telling a story, Turner-Bisset (2005) suggests asking children to fold a piece of A4 paper into eight by folding it in half lengthways and then crossways. They then unfold it and, as the story is told, they draw a picture of a scene from the story in each of the eight squares. This aids any subsequent written work.

In history, there are stories for every period to engage young minds in a range of social, moral and spiritual issues. The Second World War is particularly well covered through the likes of Michael Foreman's *War Boy* (Pavilion, 2006), Michael Morpurgo's *Friend or Foe* (Egmont, 2007) and Nina Bawden's classic *Carrie's War* (Puffin, 1973). In RE, children's own life stories are an important starting point in highlighting shared experiences, 'special' events and concepts of belonging and community. Stories can be drawn from the six major faiths to help pupils gain greater understanding and insight into how different people make sense of their worlds. For instance, stories of a great flood can be found in many cultures. Pupils can compare and contrast the popular story of Noah with other stories such as the Hindu story of Manu and the Babylonian *Epic of Gilgamesh*. In geography, children are quick to talk about places they know, their homes, streets, schools, where they have been on holiday, all of which are stories about places. Classic stories such as *The Jolly Postman* (Ahlberg and Ahlberg, 1986) are an ideal introduction to geographical terms, locations and maps. Stories also lead to discussions about faraway places experiencing conditions very different from most children's lives, such as earthquakes, volcanoes and tropical storms. Care should be taken with stories that convey simplistic, unbalanced and distorted images from parts of the world; for example, depictions of Africa as no more than a land of mud-huts, starving children and extreme poverty.

Reading, writing, speaking and listening are the main language skills, but the humanities offer contexts for other forms of communication through interpreting films and images, symbols, numbers and body language. In particular, drama is an excellent means of exploring historical, geographical and religious issues. For instance, the story of *Oliver Twist* lends itself to the following ideas:

Mime – children identify with a character and portray the body language in a scene such as when Oliver first meets Fagin;

Freeze frame – groups are assigned a particular scene to enact and then freeze for others to comment upon such as Oliver asking for more;

Speaking thoughts – individuals 'voice over' the thoughts of characters performing before them;

Conscience alley: two large groups are formed and asked to adopt one 'side' of a particular argument or viewpoint, for instance should the Artful Dodger steal an apple? A character from the story then walks between the two groups, stopping to seek advice from individuals acting as a conscience;

Hot-seating – an individual character is cross-examined by others;

Alternative view – ask individual pupils to narrate a scene from different perspectives, for example Fagin, Nancy, Bill Sykes; and

Judge and jury – set up a 'court room' to cross-examine witnesses and allocate roles such as prosecutor, defence lawyer, eyewitness, reporter, jury, judge, audience.

Numeracy skills

Numeracy is confidence and competence in handling numbers and measures in a range of contexts beyond mathematics lessons (see Table 3.8). For example, there

Table 3.8 Numeracy and Primary humanities	
Subject	**Numeracy skills**
History	• timelines, family trees and date charts; • analyse statistics such as population figures; • measuring, estimating and calculating during visits to historical sites; and • interpreting historical sources such as railway timetables, household inventories and accounts.
Geography	• exploring direction, distances and scale; • measuring, gathering, recording and analysing data in fieldwork; • presenting findings through bar charts, graphs, tables, pie diagrams; and • determining locations when using plans, maps and globes.
Religious Education	• exploring traditional units of measurement in holy books (e.g. cubits); • researching the religious significance of numbers (e.g. 40 nights, 7 days, trinity); • exploring shapes, patterns, symmetry and construction techniques within places of worship; and • problem-solving in real-life contexts (e.g. arranging a religious service).

are many activities involving classifying and sequencing natural objects in the school grounds that draw upon mathematical thinking. River studies, shopping surveys and the use of historical sources, such as census returns, require the focus and precision provided by the application of numeracy skills. Pupils' understanding of how historical and religious buildings function can be enhanced through estimating and measuring the size of rooms, and reflecting upon their relative size, shape and dimensions. Real-life contexts should be used to promote pupils' application of number skills. In geography, pupils can be provided with a supply of travel brochures to plan a family holiday with an allocated budget. A lesson on poverty in a developing country might include allocating pupils a sum of money (a monthly wage) to spend, along with a list of things to pay for, such as water, food, transport and clothes. Through such activities, pupils begin to recognise the challenges faced by many families to eke out a living.

ICT

One aspect of ICT that has grown at an astonishing rate is e-learning, defined as 'online access to learning resources, anywhere and anytime' (Holmes and Gardner, 2006: 14). Pupils have immediate access to online libraries, galleries, archives, museums, satellite images and maps. The use of multimedia, including the use of text, images, tables, sounds and animations, can also enhance knowledge and understanding in the humanities. Pupils' chronological awareness, for instance, can be promoted through online timelines (Leask and Meadows, 2000). Webquests provide opportunities for pupils to find, synthesise and analyse information. For instance, a webquest on Judaism might include:

Introduction – invites pupils to become a chief editor of a newspaper.

Task – to prepare a supplement to inform readers about the culture, religion and current affairs in Israel.

Process – pupils work as small groups of journalists to produce a report on an aspect of Israel.

Resources – such as websites, for example **www.bbc.co.uk/religion/religions/judaism**.

Evaluation – before submitting report, each group submits 'Important things I have learned'.

Conclusion – organise an event to launch the newspaper.

Source: **www.webquestuk.org.uk**.

Increasingly, pupils and teachers can access geographical information systems. For instance, through *Infomapper* pupils learn about the relief and geography of localities by studying aerial photographs (case studies can be viewed at **www.segfl.org.uk**). Software applications enable pupils to store, retrieve and process information quickly. Paintings, artefacts and photographs can be explored on the interactive whiteboard and 'de-constructed' through class discussions using a graphic pen. Here, websites such as the National Portrait Gallery, the British Film Institute and the National Archives' Learning Curve provide a rich seam of source material. Pupils can also embark on a number of 'virtual tours' of historic and religious buildings; for example, they can explore places of national religious significance such as Westminster Abbey, Canterbury Cathedral and St David's Cathedral (**www.request.org.uk**).

It is also important for pupils to develop critical e-reading habits and 'digital fluency' in locating and evaluating accurate information online (Bartlett and Miller, 2011). Child-friendly search engines, which develop questioning skills, include:

www.askkids.com.

http://kids.yahoo.com.

www.topmarks.co.uk.

http://dibdabdoo.com.

http://primaryschoolict.com.

Pupils need to evaluate whether ICT improves the speed and quality of their work, engages their interest and how their understanding has deepened. ICT certainly presents challenges: the cut-and-paste, uncritical mentality of a generation that has moved away from pen and paper towards editing tools and the 'new' language of text messaging. Moreover, young people are increasingly active in the world of social media – one survey suggests that one in four children aged between eight and eleven has set up their own social media profile (Guldberg, 2009: 122). With over 400 million users, Facebook would represent the third most populated country in the world. Its 'inhabitants' use technologies in three main ways:

Communication – for example social networking (Facebook, Linkedin, My Space), blogging (Twitter);

Collaboration – for example wikis, conferencing (e.g. Skype) and social documents (e.g. Google Docs); and

Multimedia – for example photographs (e.g. Flickr), video (e.g. YouTube), and virtual worlds (e.g. World of Warcraft).

Richardson (2006) shows how web-based digital photography such as Flickr can be used creatively by young children to capture field visits, visiting speakers and special projects.

There are many case studies of good practice in the use of ICT within primary humanities. For instance, Wegerif (2010) refers to the development of inter-faith dialogues by email designed to counter religious and racial tensions. Primary schools in Leicester were twinned with schools in Sussex and each child was paired with an email friend of a contrasting religious and/or cultural background from the partner school. The exchange included residential visits and weekly emails.

REFLECTION

- The Rose Review's recommendation for primary schools to teach social media, including the use of Twitter, blogs, webcams and podcasts, has been controversial (Paton, 2009). How might social media enhance pupils' understanding in the humanities?

Thinking skills

Over recent years the growth in thinking skills literature is a response to concern that schools are not doing enough to promote creativity and independent thought (Leat, 2001; Dean, 2002; Wallace, 2003; Lewis, 2009). The focus is on 'knowing *how* to learn', as well as knowing what to learn as teachers seek to 'uncover' learning rather than cover content (Jackson, 2002). The importance of developing a whole-school 'thinking culture' and a clear framework for thinking skills has been established (McGuinness, 1999; Higgins and Baumfield, 2001). Progression in thinking skills is characterised when pupils move from tangible to abstract thoughts, from personal views to more general comments (seeing the big picture) and by working from familiar to new contexts (see Figure 3.2).

Children's geographical thinking is based on how they locate themselves, and then see others, in space. It is also about their sense of belonging and their view of their immediate family and locality. They move from seeing the world in egocentric terms, to locating significant landmarks in their immediate environment and beginning to handle abstract concepts. By the age of four, many children can negotiate their way around a basic map, identifying simple symbols. Historical thinking begins when babies distinguish between past and present – when they recognise a familiar face they are drawing upon previous memories. Two-year-olds are able to reproduce a sequence of three events, indicating that they are sequencing first, next and last. By five, children are able to order a series of photographs of themselves. They also have an understanding of 'oldness' as being different from the present. Seven-year-olds speculate over the length of an event as they begin to come to terms with duration, which is more challenging than the order of when things occurred. Understanding 'historical time' is tied up with some understanding of personal, clock and calendar time (Robson, 2006).

Reasoning is the basis of all intelligent conversation. Rational thinkers recognise the importance of developing and presenting *balanced* arguments or lines of thought (the word reason derives from the Latin *ratio*, meaning balance). They know that in order to convince someone they need to have a good grasp of up-to-date, relevant evidence. This requires a willingness to probe beyond the surface, to 'read between the lines' and to avoid jumping too readily to conclusions. One of the major aims in teaching the humanities is to develop this sense of logical, balanced and critical thinking. For instance, Catling (2002) shows how in geography lessons pupils can develop reasoning skills through:

- drawing sketch maps to show key features of the locality or the distribution of specific features such as houses;
- drawing diagrams to show the sequence and relationship in river and coastal processes;
- drawing a series of pictures to show changes in an area over time; and
- using a set of photographs of different scenes and sorting them by particular features.

Critical thinking involves asking questions about historical events, religious practices and different lands. Pupils might generate questions relating to a news headline,

Thinking, Problem Solving and Decision Making

Show deeper geographical understanding of issues within The World Around Us by thinking critically and flexibly, solving problems and making informed decisions.	**FROM** **By the end of Year 4 pupils can:**	**TO** **By the end of Year 7 pupils can:**
Memory and Understanding	Sort and classify photos of and information about features/activities in their locality, for example, buildings, modes of transport or jobs. Identify similarities and differences between features of their own locality and those of other places, for example, clothes, homes and weather. Recognise patterns made by physical/human features in the environment, for example, seasonal change in school grounds or features of the town/countryside. Sequence pictures/information to demonstrate understanding of some geographical processes, for example, the journey of a letter or change in the local area. Use basic terms to describe geographical features, patterns, processes and changes, for example, river, stream, hill, slope.	Sort and classify photos of information about a range of places, for example, landscape features, buildings, etc. Identify similarities and differences between a range of features and places, offering explanations, for example, weather, house type, building materials. Begin to relate cause and effect in relation to spatial patterns of physical and human features, for example, high rainfall in upland areas of NI or settlement along the banks of the Nile. Order and sequence information to explain geographical processes, for example, the making of a product, changes in the course of a river. Use more precise geographical vocabulary to describe geographical features, patterns, processes and changes, for example, valley, source, mouth or erosion.
Developing a line of reasoning	Make simple predictions, for example, what would it be like to live in a hotter/colder country? Using maps: • Draw familiar objects/features in the classroom from a bird's-eye view. • Follow/give directions for a route on a large scale map, using left/right directions, for example, a journey through the school grounds. • Draw simple story/picture maps to locate significant features in relation to a story, for example, Little Red Riding Hood's journey through the forest, or a personal journey, for example, going to school. • Interpret information from a range of maps, for example, use of colour, relative size of places on globe/world map etc.	Investigate a geographical issue from different viewpoints, for example, the siting of a new bypass/shopping centre. Identify the pros and cons of each, make and justify a decision. Using maps: • Use a plan of the school grounds for orienteering and fieldwork activities; • Use appropriate maps for different purposes, for example, local maps, country maps; • Follow/give directions for routes on maps using 8 compass directions, for example, orienteering in a local forest; • Draw and use maps at a variety of scales, using 4-figure grid references to identify and locate features; • Interpret information from a range of maps, including OS maps, using, for example, standard symbols, use of colour etc.
Making Decisions and Solving Problems	Explore possible solutions to a local problem, for example, litter around the school. Examine evidence and opinions from a range of sources, for example, results of shopping survey, questionnaires.	Examine evidence and opinions from a range of sources, distinguish between fact and opinion, for example, researching information about life in another country. Make predictions about geographical change, for example, how might the local area look in 20 years time?

Figure 3.2 Progression in thinking skills within the geographical component of the World Around Us, Northern Ireland Curriculum. *Source*: www.nicurriculum.org.uk/key_stages_1_and_2/areas_of_learning/the_world_around_us.

poem, story, picture or museum artefact. They should learn to ask different kinds of questions (who? what? where? why? how? when?) and choose the most appropriate questions for their investigations. Critical thinking requires sifting facts from opinions, testing the accuracy of what is said, taking apart ideas (analysis), putting points together (synthesis) and judging whether something is plausible, preferable or worthy (evaluation). Critical thinkers weigh up the value of evidence, for instance the reliability of what people say, and reflect upon what has been learned in one context to develop more abstract understanding.

Creative thinking in the humanities involves considering alternative ways of seeing the world. Counterfactual approaches are popular in which the question 'What if . . . ?' is frequently asked. In history, for example, one leading historian asks: 'What if there had been no American War of Independence? What if Hitler had invaded Britain? What if Kennedy had lived?' (Ferguson, 2000). Not all historians are keen to embrace this 'virtual' approach, dismissing it in no uncertain terms as 'unhistorical shit' and little more than 'a parlour game' (see discussion by Black, 2008: 5, a supporter of counterfactualism). In geography, the 'What if' (we do nothing) scenario has been applied to such issues as global warming, waste disposal and rainforest destruction (Morris, 2007; Dorion, 2007; McIeish, 2007). The theme has been extended to religious education with titles such as *What if Nobody Forgave?* (McDonald, 2003), offering considerable scope for discussion.

SUMMARY

- The most important factor in successful primary humanities is the quality of teaching rather than whether the curriculum is organised around subjects or themes.

- Supporters of the cross-curricular approach say that it is the most appropriate way to organise the curriculum for young children. Critics are concerned about the dilution of subject knowledge. These views draw upon different learning theories and the relative value attributed to knowledge acquisition.

- The place of the humanities in the primary curriculum has been shaped by competing ideologies.

- Good cross-curricular planning requires secure knowledge and understanding of the distinctive contribution of history, geography and religious education.

- By their very nature, the humanities are subjects that call for creative and critical thinking. They also offer considerable scope for teachers to promote literacy, numeracy and ICT skills.

References

Ahlberg, J. and Ahlberg, A. (1986), *The Jolly Postman*, London: Puffin.

Aldrich, R. (1996), *Education for the Nation*, London: Institute of Education.

Alexander, R., Rose, A., and Woodhead, C. (1992), *Curriculum Organisation and Classroom Practice in Primary Schools: A Discussion Paper*, London: DES.

Alexander, R.J. (1995), *Versions of Primary Education*, London: Routledge.

Alexander, R.J. (2008), *Towards Dialogic Teaching: Rethinking Classroom Talk,* York: Dialogos.

Alexander, R.J. and Flutter, J. (2009), *Towards a New Primary Curriculum: a report from the Cambridge Primary Review. Part 1: Past and Present*, Cambridge: University of Cambridge Faculty of Education.

Alexander, R.J. (ed.) (2010), *Children, their World, their Education: final report and recommendations of the Cambridge Primary Review,* Abingdon: Routledge.

Ashcroft, K. and Palacio, D. (1995), *The Primary Teacher's Guide to the New National Curriculum*, Abingdon: Routledge.

Bantock, G. (1971), 'Discovery methods' in Cox, C.B., and Dyson, A.E. (eds),*The Black Papers on Education*, London: Davis-Poynter Ltd.

Barnes, J. (2007), *Cross-Curricular Learning 3–14*, London: Paul Chapman.

Bartlett, J. and Miller, C. (2011), *Truth, Lies and the Internet*, London: Demos.

Bastide, D. (ed.) (1992), *Good Practice in Primary Religious Education 4–11*, London: The Falmer Press.

Beder, S. (2009), *This Little Kiddy Went to Market*, London: Pluto Press.

Black, J. (2008), *What If?: Counterfactualism and the Problem of History*, London: The Social Affairs Unit.

Blyth, A., Cooper, K., Derricott, R., Elliott, G., Sumner, H., and Waplington, A. (1976), *Place, Time and Society 8–13: Curriculum Planning in History, Geography and Social Science*, Bristol: Schools Council.

Board of Education (1931), *The Primary School* (Hadow Report), London: HMSO, available at: www. educationengland.org.uk/documents/hadow1931.

Boyes, C. (1997), *Learning through story. History*, Dunstable: Folens.

Campbell, J. and Little, V. (eds) (1989), *Humanities in the Primary School*, Lewes: Falmer Press.

Catling, S. (2002), 'Thinking Geographically', Primary Geography, April 2002, 7–10.

CCEA (2007), *Northern Ireland Primary Curriculum*, Belfast: CCEA, available at: www.nicurriculum.org.uk/docs/key_stages_1_and_2/northern_ireland_curriculum_primary_pdf

Darling, J. (2003), 'Scottish Primary Education: Philosophy and Practice', in Bryce, T.G.K. and Humes, W.M. (eds), *Scottish Education*, Edinburgh: Edinburgh University Press, 7–36.

DCLG (2008), *Face to Face and Side by Side. A framework for partnership in our multi faith society*, DCLG: London.

DCELLS (2008), *Making the most of learning*, Cardiff: Welsh Assembly Government.

DCSF (2008), *Independent Review of the Primary Curriculum. Interim Report*, London: DCSF.

DCSF (2009), *Independent Review of the Primary Curriculum. Final Report,* page 47, London: DCSF.

Dean J. (2002), *Thinking Skills in Primary History*, Nuffield History Project.

DES (1967a), *Children and their Primary Schools: A Report of the Central Advisory Council for Education (England)* (Plowden Report), London: HMSO.

DES (1967b), *Primary Education in Wales. A Report of the Central Advisory Council for Education (Wales)* (Gittins Report), London: HMSO.

DES (1985), The curriculum from 5 to 16, London: HMSO.

DfE (2011), *The Framework for the National Curriculum. A report by the Expert Panel for the National Curriculum review,* London: Department for Education.

Dorion, C. (2007), *Waste Disposal (What If We Do Nothing?)*, London: Fanklin Watts.

Erricker, C., Lowndes, J., and Bellchambers, E. (2011), *Primary Religious Education – A New Approach*, Abingdon: Routledge.

Ferguson, N. (2000), *Virtual History: Alternatives and Counterfactuals,* New York: Basic Books.

Fisher, J. (2002), *Starting from the Child*, Maidenhead: Open University Press.

Furedi, F. (2007), 'Introduction: Politics, Politics, Politics!' in Wheelan, R. (ed.), *Corruption of the Curriculum*, London: Civitas, 1–10.

Goldman, R. (1965), *Readiness for Religion*, London: Routledge and Kegan Paul.

Gordon, P. and Lawton, D. (1978), *Curriculum Change in the Nineteenth and Twentieth Centuries*, Sevenoaks: Hodder & Stoughton.

Gove, M. (2009), *What is Education for? Speech by Michael Gove MP to the RSA*, 30 June 2009, available at: **www.thersa.org/events/video/archive/michael-gove-mp—29-june-2009.**

Gredler, M. E. (1997), *Learning and instruction: Theory into practice*, Upper Saddle River, NJ: Prentice-Hall.

Greenwood, R. (2007), 'Geography Teaching in Northern Ireland Primary Schools: A Survey of Content and Cross-curricularity' in *International Research in Geographical and Environmental Education,* Volume 16, Issue 4, 2007, 380–398.

Guldberg, H. (2009), *Reclaiming Childhood*, London: Routledge.

Hattie, J. (2009), *Visible Learning*, Abingdon: Routledge.

Hayes, D. (2006), *Primary education: the key concepts*, London: Routledge.

Higgins, S. and Baumfield, V. (2001), *Thinking Through the Primary Curriculum,* Cambridge: Chris Kington Publishing.

HMIe (2007), *Making effective use of curriculum flexibility in primary schools.*

Holmes, B. and Gardner, J. (2006), *E-Learning*, London: Sage.

Howson, G. (1969), *Children at school. Primary education in Britain today*, London: Heinemann.

Hume, E.G. (1938), *Learning and Teaching in the Infants' School*, London: Longman.

Jackson, E. (2002), 'Developing a thinking culture', Primary Geography, April 2002, 34–36.

Jarvis, P., Holford, J., and Griffin, C. (1998), *The Theory and Practice of Learning*, London: Kogan Page.

Kerry, T. (2011), *Cross-Curricular Teaching in the Primary School: Planning and Facilitating Imaginative Lessons*, Abingdon: Routledge.

Knight, P. (1993), *Primary Geography Primary History*, London: David Fulton.

Lambert, D. (2011), 'Reframing School Geography: A Capability Approach', in Butt, G. (ed.), Geography, Education and the Future, London: Continuum, 127–139.

Laurie (2011), 'Curriculum planning and preparation for cross curricular teaching' in Kerry, T. (ed.), *Cross-Curricular Teaching in the Primary School: Planning and Facilitating Imaginative Lessons*, Abingdon: Routledge, 125–141.

Lawton, D., Chitty, C., and Aldrich, R. (1988), *The National Curriculum*, London: Institute of Education.

Leask, M. and Meadows, J. (2000), (eds), *Teaching and Learning with ICT in the Primary School*, London: Routledge Falmer.

Leat, D. (2001), *Thinking Through Geography*, Cambridge: Chris Kington Publishing.

Lewis, E. (2009), *Thinking about Truth*, London: RMEP.

Littledyke, M., and Huxford, L. (1998), *Teaching the Primary Curriculum through Constructive Learning*, London: David Fulton.

Loukes, H. (1965), *New Ground in Christian Education*, London: SCM Press.

Mallett, M. (2002), *The English Primary English Encyclopedia*, London: David Fulton.

Martin, F. (2006), *Teaching Geography in Primary Schools*, Cambridge: Chris Kington Publishing.

McCulloch, J. (2011), *Subject to change: should primary schools structure learning around subjects or themes?*, Pearson Centre for Policy and Learning.

McDonald, C. (2003), *What If Nobody Forgave?: And Other Stories,* Boston: Skinner House Books.

McGuinness, C. (1999), *From Thinking Skills to Thinking Classrooms*, Nottingham: DfEE.

Morris, N. (2007), *Global Warming (What If We Do Nothing?)*, London: Fanklin Watts.

Moult, J. (2008), 'Winston Churchill . . . wasn't he the first man on the moon?' – and other classroom howlers', *Daily Mail*, 19 March 2008.

Mcleish, E. (2007), *Rainforest Destruction (What If We Do Nothing?),* London: Franklin Watts.

Nicholson, H.N. (1996), *Place in Story-Time: Geography Through Stories at Key Stages 1 and 2,* Sheffield: Geographical Association.

Ofsted (2002), *The curriculum in successful primary schools*, London: Ofsted.

Ofsted (2008), *Geography in schools: changing practice*, London: Ofsted.

Ofsted (2009), *Twenty outstanding primary schools. Excelling against the odds*, London: Ofsted.

Paton G. (2009), 'Twitter is put on new primary school curriculum', *The Daily Telegraph*, 20 January 2011.

Paton, G. (2011), 'National curriculum review: children to learn facts and figures in subject shake-up', *The Daily Telegraph*, 20 January 2011.

Richardson, W. (2006), *Blogs, Wikis and Podcasts*, Thousand Oaks: Corwin Press.

Riley, J. and Prentice, R. (1999) *The Curriculum for 7–11 Year Olds*, London: Paul Chapman.

Robson, S. (2006), *Developing Thinking & Understanding in Young Children*, London: Routledge.

Rowley, C. and Cooper, H. (2009), *Cross-Curricular Approaches to Teaching and Learning*, London: Sage.

Scottish Executive (2006), *A curriculum for excellence. Building the curriculum 1,* Edinburgh: Scottish Executive.

Scottish Education Department (1965), *Primary Education in Scotland*, Edinburgh: SED.

Shaw, S.M. (1999), *Storytelling in Religious Education,* Birmingham: Religious Education Press.

Shulman, L.S. (1987), 'Knowledge and teaching: Foundations of the new reform', Harvard Educational Review, 57, 1–22.

Smuga, G. (2008), Area Event keynote presentation, 'Building the Curriculum Three', available at:

www.ltscotland.org.uk/curriculumforexcellence/events/eventreports/areaevents/georgesmuga.asp.

Standish, A. (2007), 'Geography Used To be About Maps', in Wheelan, R. (ed.), *Corruption of the Curriculum*, London: Civitas 28–57.

Tann, C.S. (1988), *Developing Topic Work in the Primary School*, London: David Fulton.

Tickell Review (2011), *Tickell Review of the Early Years Foundation Stage*, London: DfE, available at: **www.education.gov.uk/tickellreview.**

Tomlinson, S. (2005), *Education in a post-welfare society*, Maidenhead: Open University Press.

Turner-Bisset, R. (2005), *Creative Teaching in History*, London: David Fulton.

Verma, G.K. (1994), *Cross-curricular Contexts, Themes and Dimensions in Primary Schools (Cultural Diversity & the National Curriculum*, London: Routledge.

Wallace, B. (2003), Using History to Develop Thinking Skills at Key Stage 2, London: David Fulton.

Wallace, S. (2009), *Oxford Dictionary of Education*, Oxford: Oxford University Press.

Waters, D. (1982), *Primary School Projects*, London: Heinemann Educational Books.

Webb, R. (1996), *Cross-curricular Primary Practice: Taking a Leadership Role (Handbook for Students and Newly Qualified Teachers)*, London: Routledge.

Wegerif, R. (2010), *Mind Expanding*, Maidenhead: Open University Press.

Young, M. (2007), *Bringing Knowledge Back in: From Social Constructivism to Social Realism in the Sociology of Education*, Abingdon: Routledge.

Useful Websites

RE Online is a portal site, providing information for all those working and interested in Religious Education in England: **www.reonline.org.uk.**

Nuffield Primary History website provides advice on cross-curricular work: **http://www.history.org.uk/resources/primary.html.**

Staffordshire local authority website includes many RE materials and guidance: **http://education.staffordshire.gov.uk/Curriculum/Subjectareas/ReligiousEducation/.**

Education Scotland has a Learning across the curriculum section which includes literacy and numeracy: **http://www.educationscotland.gov.uk/learningteachingandassessment/curriculumareas/index.asp.**

4 Play-based provision in the Early Years

We do not stop playing because we grow old. We grow old because we stop playing.

(George Bernard Shaw; cited by CCEA, 2008: 5).

Learning objectives

By the end of this chapter you should be able to:

- appreciate the longstanding interest in play as a vehicle for children's learning;
- reflect upon the value of play in children's all-round development;
- identify the characteristics of good early years provision and the implications for the humanities;
- describe how children's understanding of time, place and community can be developed through different types of play; and
- recognise the importance of using a variety of resources and approaches to develop children's knowledge and understanding of the world.

Natural curiosity

Play is a universal characteristic of humans, cutting across time, culture and place. Natural curiosity has proved to be so important in the development of the human race – hence the discovery of new lands, inventions, artistic achievements and the rise of science and technologies. The enthusiasm for play prompted Dutch historian Johan Huizinga (1950) to describe the defining characteristic of our species as *homo ludens* ('man the player') rather than *homo sapiens* ('man the thinker'). This love for play extends beyond schooldays well into old age. People play golf, play on the computer, participate in role-play events (from amateur dramatics to rehearsing speeches or interviews) or explore new gadgets. Originally, the toy industry developed to meet the needs of adults rather than children. For young children, exploration is a natural activity. They want to find out about their environments and play is often the most appropriate means of doing so. When they explore, imagine and construct, children are doing the very things that the humanities value most highly.

This chapter acknowledges the longstanding interest in play and discusses the rationale behind its widely-held support for children's learning in the Early Years. By the term 'Early Years', this chapter follows the Scottish Executive's (2006) view that it applies to 'educational provision that is developmentally and culturally appropriate for young learners' (**www.scotland.gov.uk/Publications/2006/02/06145130/1**). This is not fudging the issue but reflects the variability of settings, ages and content.

The philosophy of Early Years provision

In the twenty-first century, the education of young children has been the subject of renewed interest on a global scale (Bertram and Pascal, 2002; BERA SIG, 2003). In many countries, such provision shares common aims. At a macro level, these include promoting social cohesion, national cultural identity and respect for diversity. But there is also widespread recognition that the uniqueness of each child has to be nurtured. This means that curriculum guidance for the Early Years is intended to be used flexibly to respond to different needs. Broadhead *et al.* (2010) point out the tensions that exist between a responsive philosophy, in which practitioners respond to the interests and choices of children, and a cultural transmission/directive approach, which sees learning as a matter of acquiring socially approved knowledge, whether organised in subjects or areas of learning.

Much of the underpinning Early Years' philosophy is rooted in a co-constructivist view of learning. Rather than a teacher passing on information directly to children, constructivism suggests that the learner is much more actively involved in a joint enterprise with the teacher of creating ('constructing') understanding. This aligns well with the ways of thinking that characterise those who work within the humanities field. History is probably the most overtly constructivist subject in the curriculum (Copeland, 1994). Historians 'make' history by selecting evidence from the past to answer their lines of enquiry. Similarly, constructivists see geographical knowledge and place understanding not as a set of preconceived truths but as personal constructs, shaped by experience.

In recent years, a consensus has emerged relating to what is considered to be effective Early Years provision or Developmentally Appropriate Practice (DAP) in the UK and the USA (Siraj-Blatchford, 1999). The key characteristics of DAP are:

- a balance between children's self-initiated learning and practitioner guidance;
- opportunities for children to make meaningful choices between activities offered;
- scope to explore through active involvement;
- a mix of small group, whole group and independent activities;
- play as a primary (but not the exclusive) medium for learning;
- adults that demonstrate, question, model, suggest alternatives and prompt reflection; and
- systematic observation of children's learning and behaviour.

(Scottish Executive, 2006: 3)

In particular, play has become the raison d'être of Early Years provision in many settings. There is now a burgeoning 'play' industry, covering areas such as sociology, psychology and pedagogy (Broadhead et al., 2010; Tassoni and Hucker, 2005; Wood and Attfield, 2005; Moyles, 2010). There are publications on outdoor play, risk assessment, play for children with special educational needs, playwork, playworkers and the management of play. Families and schools can seek guidance from play advisers, counsellors and therapists, while there are organisations devoted to the promotion of play in schools and the community, such as Play England, Play Wales, Play Scotland and Playboard, for Northern Ireland (see websites). Children attend all manner of play facilities, including adventure centres, soft play areas and water parks.

The longstanding association of play with childhood has produced an extensive body of literature devoted to its history, definition, and justification. Hurst and Joseph (1998: 54) identify three elements in play:

1. disposition – children's need to explore the world around them;
2. context – freedom to choose, initiate and direct; and
3. observable behaviour – derived from the stages of play that evolve during early childhood.

The need for a shared, concise definition is evident when reviewing the literature on play (Siraj-Blatchford et al., 2006). The exact origin of the word 'play' itself is unclear but may derive from the medieval Dutch word *pleien* meaning to 'dance, leap for joy, and rejoice'. Brock et al. (2009) point out that if play is equated with 'having fun', this lends itself to many interpretations and behaviours. Young children themselves distinguish between 'work' as something they must do, and 'play' as something they can do (Marshall, 1994). Research by Sanderson (2006) shows that tasks defined as work are evaluated by outcomes (ends) whereas play-based tasks are valued for their intrinsic worth (means). Johnston and Nahmad-Williams (2009) provide a very readable commentary on the language of play and specific terminology. What matters most is the quality of children's learning experiences and recognition that these should be challenging, relevant and enjoyable.

Play – a recurring theme in early childhood studies

The importance of play in young children's development has long been recognised and it has been generally easier to justify in the education of the under-fives than with older children. There are a number of useful overviews setting out the contribution of different theories and theorists, notably Piaget and Vygotsky's views on cognitive development (Pound, 2005; Nutbrown, 2008; Johnston and Nahmad-Williams, 2009). Historically, as Chapter 1 notes, schools were originally conceived by the ancient Greeks as places where children from the wealthy classes made the most of their recreational (play) time. They were to enjoy their learning. The Greek philosopher Plato recognised the educational value of play to the individual and community. He suggested that if young children were to become builders, they should play at building houses. It was the sixteenth-century Protestant work ethic in Western culture that separated what one does when young and what one does as an adult.

Present-day practice in the Early Years has been shaped by thinkers that over the centuries shared a 'romantic' view of childhood, which valued innocence, inquisitiveness and creativity. The overseas list includes: Jean Jacques Rousseau (1712–1778), Johann Heinrich Pestalozzi (1746–1827), Friedrich Froebel (1782–1852), John Dewey (1859–1952), Maria Montessori (1870–1952), Rudolf Steiner (1861–1925) and Loris Malaguzzi (1920–1994). The UK has also had its pioneers. Robert Owen (1771–1858) instructed his infant teachers at New Lanark to 'make their playfellows happy' and he ensured that the schoolroom was furnished 'with paintings, maps, natural objects from the gardens, fields and woods' (Whitbread, 1972: 10). David Stow (1793–1864), who formed the Glasgow Infant School Society in the 1820s, stressed understanding rather than memorizing, valued children's spontaneous play and made extensive use of the playground (Rusk, 1933). The English master Henry Cook (1886–1939) wrote *The Play Way, an Essay in Educational Method* (Cook, 1917), which proved to be controversial for a generation (Aldrich and Gordon, 1989). It includes remarkable images of children performing their own historical and religious plays, transforming spare pieces of land and conducting outdoor lectures on subjects such as railways. He wrote:

> Boys and girls are still penned in the stocks, twenty-five to sixty of them at a time, to be spoon-fed on the same subject by the same teacher … Let us regard our pupils as individuals, and train their innate power along its natural course of development, so that we have in education growth instead of manufacture, always encouraging rather than punishing, guiding rather than goading.

(Cook, 1917: 351–353)

Susan Isaacs (1885–1948) was among those who believed that children should be free to explore and experiment with the physical world. For Isaacs, the skill of the teacher was to meet this desire to explore by providing the materials, time and space so that children could answer their own questions about the world (Whitbread, 1972). Margaret McMillan (1860–1931), who was born in New York but worked and lived (with her sister Rachel) in the UK for much of her life, established the first open-air nursery school. The McMillan sisters viewed the outdoors as a place to learn, and not a place to have a break from learning (Johnston and Nahmad-Williams, 2009).

These pioneers have left a significant legacy in terms of a renewed emphasis upon outdoor learning, creativity and responding to the needs of individual children. Their influence is also seen in the multifaceted role of the practitioner working as a model, guide, facilitator, observer, friend, listener and reviewer.

TASK

- Choose a pioneer in Early Years education and find out more about why they valued play-based learning

The value of play

The all-round benefits of children playing regularly have been well reported (Bruce, 2001; Filer, 2008; Wood and Attfield, 2005; Moyles, 2006; Brock *et al.*, 2009). There is also a growing body of evidence relating to specific forms of play. For example, Bergen, (2002) shows that there is a strong relationship between high-quality pretend play and development of specific academic skills such as problem-solving, narrative recall and self-regulation. In summary, the main arguments are that through play children:

- are highly motivated to learn;
- develop the core skills of language, literacy and numeracy;
- develop wider knowledge, understanding and skills across all areas of learning and
- develop positive attitudes to learning, school life and their environment.

Guha (1996:2) has even argued the 'economic' case for play in school:

> Efficiency is enhanced because teachers have to spend less time to motivate children to learn because teaching is more effective as teachers achieve a better 'fit' between their instruction/explanation and the child's thinking.

Although play has acquired a hallowed status in some quarters, there remain questions about the exact relationship between play and learning (Scottish Executive, 2006). A review by the British Educational Research Association found that play is too often limited in frequency, duration and quality, with teachers and adults adopting a reactive 'watching and waiting' approach (BERA EYSIG 2003: 14). Moreover, Nutbrown (2008: 155) believe that 'many teachers struggle to 'fit' play into their pedagogical repertoire' and there are reports that practitioners do not always understand the purpose of play, when to intervene and how to evaluate its impact on learning. The extent to which young children are allowed free play and explore areas outside the learning objectives remains a dilemma for practitioners (Goouch, 2009).

Play is very much a social construct, framed within a society's cultural norms. Woodhead (1998) gives examples of countries where play is not highly valued – for instance, Bangladesh, Ethiopia, the Philippines and Central America. In many parts of Asia the emphasis on whole-class teaching and the authority of the teacher in Early Years settings reflects a strong Confucian tradition. The UK's more liberal approach values children's independence and autonomy, although the school timetable still reflects the historical division between playtime and lessons.

Provision of play and areas of learning

Play has a high profile in the provision for Early Years throughout the UK. In England, the Tickell Review (2011) acknowledges the importance of a child-led, play-based framework. It recommends that practitioners should focus on the characteristics of effective learning and assumes that play facilitates this (see Figure 4.1).

Since 2008, the play-based Foundation Phase has been established in Wales and there is a general belief among practitioners that children's skills are improving (Estyn, 2010). In Scotland, one of the key elements of transformational change advocated in the Early Years Framework (from birth to eight) is 'improving outcomes and children's quality of life through play' (Scottish Government, 2008: 5). In Northern Ireland, a child-focused Foundation Stage was introduced in 2007 and practitioners (including those at Key Stage 1) have received the clearest guidance on what, why, where, when, who and how to implement play across all areas of learning (see Figure 4.2).

Learning characteristics	How [name of child] learns
By playing and exploring • finding out and exploring • using what they know in their play • being willing to have a go	
Through active learning • being involved and concentrating • keeping on trying • enjoying achieving what they set out to do	
By creating and thinking critically • having their own ideas • using what they already know to learn new things • choosing ways to do things and finding new ways	

Figure 4.1 Characteristics of effective learning in the Early Years *Source*: Tickell Review, (2011: 79).

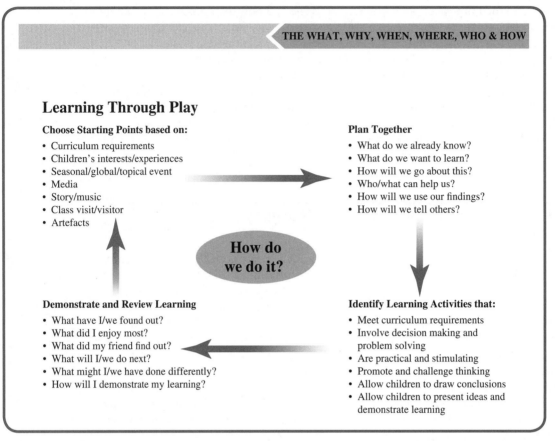

Figure 4.2 When and how play is introduced in the Northern Ireland curriculum. *Source:* CCEA, (2008:16, 18.)

Throughout the UK, Early Years provision is organised around areas of learning rather than discrete subjects (see Table 4.1). The foundations for historical, geographical and religious 'ways of thinking' can be developed across these areas of learning. Examples of more explicit links with the humanities are set out in Table 4.2.

Understanding the world

In England, the Tickell Review (2011) recommends that understanding the world should be built around three aspects:

1. people and communities (formerly time and communities);

2. the world (formerly place); and

3. technology.

These should be viewed in a concentric way, beginning with children's exploration of their own worlds and the people and things that matter to them; before moving to consider the inter-relationship of people and communities and of living and non-living things, together with the influence of time and place on the environment and tradition. The use of technology has been broadened to reflect the pace of change although

Table 4.1 Humanities and the areas of learning/curriculum areas in the Early Years

England: Foundation Stage (0–5)	Wales: Foundation Phase (3–7)	Northern Ireland: Foundation Stage (3–5)	Scotland: Curriculum for Excellence (3–18)
Prime areas:			
Communication and Language	Language, Literacy and Communication Skills	Language and Literacy	Languages
Personal, Social and Emotional Development and	Personal and Social Development, Well-Being and Cultural Diversity	Personal Development and Mutual Understanding	Health and Well-being
Physical Development	Physical Development Welsh Language Development	Physical Development and Movement	Religious and Moral Education
Specific areas:			
Literacy			
Mathematics	Mathematical development	Mathematics and Numeracy	Mathematics
Understanding the World	Knowledge and Understanding of the World	The World Around Us	Sciences Social Studies
Expressive Arts and Design	Creative Development	The Arts	Technologies
		Religious Education	Expressive Arts

Sources: Tickell Review (2011); DCELLS (2008); CCEA (2007); Scottish Government (2009).

Table 4.2 Humanities context within the Early Years curriculum

Intended Learning outcomes	Areas of Learning	Concepts and suggested activities
Understand that people have different views, cultures and beliefs that need to be treated with respect.	Personal, social and emotional development	Community – develop empathy and respect for people from different religious backgrounds.
Use talk to organise, sequence and clarify thinking, ideas, feelings and events.	Communication, language and literacy	Place – a visit to the beach – Where have I been? What did I see? What did I like/dislike about the beach?
Use everyday words to describe position.	Problem solving, reasoning and mathematics	Place – Where do I live? Where is the park?
Find out about the past and present events in their own lives, and in those of their families and other people they know.	Knowledge and understanding of the world	Time – invite a visitor to the classroom to talk about celebrations/toys in the past; explore artefacts; compare and contrast.
Show awareness of space, of themselves and others.	Physical development	Place – how do we travel from one place to another?
Use their imagination in art and design, music, dance, role-play and stories.	Expressive Arts and Design	Community – role-play different ways of life/ religious celebrations.

Source: Adapted from Hoodless, *et. al.,* (2009: 40).

debate continues over the appropriateness of information and communications technology in the Early Years (Brooker, 2003).

Time

Children's learning about the world and the key concepts of time, place and community begins with their own experiences (see Table 4.3). The responsibility of practitioners is to offer children the opportunity to share these experiences and explore those of others. Children's interests and views should be respected and built upon. This has given rise to the notion of a 'developmentally appropriate curriculum' (see Hurst and Joseph, 1998), rooted in the belief that young children's desire to know more, explore, question, think, create and communicate should not be stifled by a predetermined and approved body of knowledge to be learnt.

From their home visits and children's visits to the setting, practitioners observe children's growing awareness of time through daily routines such as mealtimes, and their response to the narrative structures of picture books and stories. Children might have extended this understanding through spending time with grandparents and other family members, and through religious and cultural activities (Thornton and Brunton, 2010). In addition, through the medium of film and television, young children are frequently exposed to 'time-related' events such as anniversaries.

The chronological aspects of children's understanding need to be enriched with a sense of what it was like to live in past times. By exploring their own histories and those from the recent past – within living memory – young children build up a picture of *then*, what people did that was so different from today. Their understanding of basic concepts (change over time, continuity, cause and evidence) is strengthened when they 'do' history by handling objects, interview people, visit local sites and watch films.

Place

Babies' understanding of place begins from the moment they explore the space around them. Although children's development is not uniform in all areas, by about eight

Table 4.3 Previous possible experiences of humanities

Geography (Place)	History (Time)	RE (Community)
• Local travel (e.g. to school, shops) and further afield (e.g. on holidays and visits). • Experiencing the weather. • Seeing the sky at night. • Experiencing their local environment. • Experiencing a different environment (e.g. seaside).	• Family photographs. • Family stories. • Talking to older relatives. • Seeing old buildings. • Thinking about past events. • Seeing old objects, pictures and books around the house.	• Attending a place of worship. • Attending family celebrations (e.g. wedding, baptism). • Hearing religious stories. • Celebrating festivals (e.g. Diwali; Thanksgiving, Christmas, etc).

months they begin to take a greater interest in the outdoors and start to take notice of the actions of others and what different objects do. By the age of three, most children enjoy playing with small world models. Government guidance suggests that between 30 and 50 months, children should be introduced to features in the setting and immediate environment, for instance by making visits to local shops (DCSF, 2008: 87–88). By the age of five, many children are able to describe where they live and features in the natural world, and talk about what they like and dislike. The age of instant communication means that very young children are exposed to places, people, issues and events from around the world. Hence Cooper *et al.* (2010) are among those who argue for the introduction of a global dimension in Early Years settings.

Communities

Children's sense of belonging to a community begins from birth. They develop close attachments to special people in their families and wider community of friends and neighbours. They may accompany parents to places of worship, join playgroups, clubs and societies and be part of a range of social networks. These experiences develop children's understanding of themselves and others. Gradually they move from becoming dependent members of communities to active contributors. Their membership of different communities changes in line with their stages of development. As babies learn to interact they are beginning to develop a sense of what is acceptable in their social and physical environments. Through play, three- to five-year- olds develop sharing and cooperating skills, express views by using new language and gain a better understanding of their place in the community; for instance by helping to set the table for lunch, tidying up resources or planting seeds in the playgroup garden. Many four-year-olds are beginning to show awareness of the differences between people in their community,

BOX 4.1 RESEARCH BRIEFING – KNOWLEDGE AND UNDERSTANDING OF THE WORLD

Research into nursery children's specific knowledge and understanding of time, place and community is relatively underdeveloped when compared to other areas of learning. Neuroscience shows that from birth, children construct their own world of time, change and sequence (Scott, 2005). Friedman (1991) found that four-year-olds are able to judge the relative recentness of 'target' events, one seven weeks and the other one week before testing. One significant geographical finding is that children as young as four are able to express sophisticated views on caring for the environment, including distant places such as tropical rainforests (Palmer and Birch, 2004). Stories, puppets and pictures have been used effectively by many practitioners and researchers to discuss moral and ethical issues with young children. But nursery children's spiritual and religious development is not so well researched (Radford, 1999). Research shows that teachers often confuse young children's spirituality, morality and religiosity (Pugh and Duffy, 2009).

such as age, size, colour and relationship. Children's transition from home to school or to a new phase of schooling, such as Key Stage 1, marks membership of a new or different community and needs to be managed sensitively. The making of 'biographical' materials, such as pictures of homes, is a good way of easing such transition.

Forms of play and the humanities

Effective practice in the Early Years includes a balance of teacher and child-led activities (see Table 4.4). It is a matter of professional judgement in deciding upon the nature and extent of adult intervention – the same activity could mean different degrees of adult input according to children's needs, interests and capabilities. However, planning needs to consider learning objectives, playful activities and teaching strategies, groupings, time (for adults to observe, interact and assess learning), allocated adult roles and opportunities for assessment. It cannot be assumed that all children know how to play (Shefatya, 1990). They need to learn how to use resources, relate to others and manage their emotions.

Providing good learning opportunities requires the following:

- setting up areas with stimulating resources, inside or outside;
- organising particular activities in specific bays;
- choosing the focus of the story to be read; and
- observing and spending time with particular children to encourage their learning in a specific direction.

There is much advice on the range of geographical activities that can be provided in a nursery environment (Conway *et al.*, 2008; Cooper, 2004; Hoodless, *et al.*, 2006; Martin and Owens, 2008). Young children need to develop their geographical knowledge and skills in a range of indoor and outdoor contexts (see Table 4.5).

Table 4.4 Examples of teacher-led and/or child-initiated activities

RE	Geography	History
• Looking at books about children of different faiths. • Designing invitations to celebrations. • Practising writing letters from other languages. • Recounting a visit to a place of worship.	• Drawing and labelling maps. • Describing places. • Reading and talking about maps. • Looking at books about faraway places. • Recording their visit using 'talking book'.	• Looking at old books. • Labelling a timeline. • Looking at books about past times. • Oral history • Interviewing people – using a digital microphone (easi-speak).

Table 4.5 Environmental contexts for geographical play		
Play environments	Context of geographical play	Examples of environments
Real environments	Places that are part of the 'normal' or adult environment, used by people of many ages and not necessarily intended for children's play or other use. They are sites that children may subvert or manipulate for play activities.	Rooms, gardens, playgrounds, parks, the beach, waste/derelict land, overgrown areas, woodlands, fields, paths/alleys, streets, shopping malls, garage plots, car parks, 'out-of-the-way' spaces in playgrounds and around buildings.
Miniature environments	Places designed for younger children to play in, adapted to younger children's sizes. Places created for play and games rather than for physical exercise.	Playgrounds, adventure play areas. Child-sized buildings, 'forts', walkways, playground street markings, with cars, pushchairs. Small-scale furniture: tables, chairs, cookers, cupboards, beds, and 'home' equipment such as cutlery, crockery, cooking utensils, model foods.
Toy environments	'Small-world' play equipment. These can be realistic and replicate the world children see or can be fanciful. Their role is to enable children to create their own 'real' and imagined places.	Model buildings, furniture, equipment, people, animals. Place/environment playmats, road layouts, buildings, street furniture, vehicles, people, trees, fences, domestic and farm animals, railway tracks and rolling stock.
Virtual environments	'Places' created using computer software for children. These might be based on TV or film animations or created to be explored, 'inhabited' or played within by children, and to which they might be able to add features from sets or icons.	Stimulated 'real' places, fantasy 'worlds'. Pictograms to move and position in extant 'worlds' or to create new places and scenes. Bee-bots, programmable toys.

Source: Adapted from Catling (2006: 70).

Children learn through sensory experiences, such as journeys they make with their families and physical exploration of places. They learn through the imitations of adult activities they observe. Table 4.6 outlines five aspects of play that support children's geographical, historical and religious learning.

Table 4.6 Five aspects of play

Aspects of play	Opportunities to support children's geographical, historical and religious learning	Geographical, historical and religious applications
1. **Sensory play**	Encounters and examinations of the environment through the senses (sight, touch, smell, sound, taste) and mobility.	• Feeling the texture of natural and built features. • Identifying different types of smell in the locality, and their source. • Discriminating different sounds locally and their sources. • Cooking/eating different foods from various parts of the world; and/or during religious festivals. • Talking about favourite and disliked places locally, elsewhere and from stories and television programmes.
2. **Exploratory play**	Movement about the environment to develop spatial awareness. Investigating places to find out what is there – in familiar and new places.	• In the outdoor area, journeys around road layouts and obstacles courses. • Journeys to the local playground or park, to shops, to local religious building, etc. • Talking about play areas, seeing what shops sell and asking why and to whom, buying resources for cooking. • Using a simple map to locate places in relation to each other in school and beyond.
3. **Imaginative play**	Role play used to begin to grasp ways that adults act in and use places, and what is in them.	• Use of free imaginative play in the 'home bay' set up a type of place (e.g. a shop). • Role-playing staff and customers on a bus journey • 'Being' people debating what to do with waste items. • Pretend play as children/ adults in their own and other communities locally and across the world – work, houses, leisure, worship. • Setting up a play building or tent for free-play activities (e.g. pirate ship).
4. **Representational play**	Model making, drawing and writing involved in activities in places – to recreate the places and extend the play.	• Using play mats to make journeys and identify routes and activities. • Using pictures, maps and aerial photographs to find objects/ features in and outside. • Making drawings of objects and features in and out of school. • Using tools, equipment and materials, to make models of local places.
5. **Fantasy play**	Creation of imagined places and environments, realistic or fantastical, which might be acted out, drawn or written about.	• Using play materials and toys to make buildings, sites, etc. for free play. • Using natural and artificial materials in the outdoor area to create features and places for imaginative play. • Role-play – historical events.

Source: Adapted from Catling (2006: 68).

Structured role-play

One view of structured play is where the adult sets the activity, resources and time. In practice, the degree of adult involvement varies and some prefer the High/Scope idea of 'shared control' (Johnston and Nahmad-Williams, 2009). Structured role-play gives children the opportunity to enter into and 'play' with knowledge they acquire through first-hand experience, books, television and other information from teachers (McCreery, *et al* 2008). Such play areas give children opportunities to consolidate their knowledge and perhaps more importantly to make sense of it in terms of their own understanding of the world. Structured play can manifest itself in small-world play where the children in effect act as 'god' as they manipulate characters, or role-play where they are a participant actor. Dolls' houses can be decorated for festivals. Cloth synagogues and other artefacts can be purchased from commercial suppliers such as Articles of Faith, and toys can be transformed into characters to be used in re-enactments of stories. Examples of ideas for structured play areas with a cultural and religious dimension are shown in Table 4.7.

It is important for children's social development for them to become actively involved in the setting up of play areas, even if it is only to decide what should go into the house after an initial lesson on growing up in a Muslim family. New items can be added or changed on a regular basis; for example, the moon will be changed as Eid approaches. During Eid a meal is laid out on the floor, as it is customary among many Muslims from the Indian sub-continent to sit on the floor to eat. Cutlery is not normally used. Some Muslims also have a special meal on Christmas day because they view Jesus (Isa) as a prophet.

It is sometimes appropriate for adults to enter the role-play, for instance as a postman/woman arriving with a recorded parcel; a neighbour asking for an inconveniently parked car to be moved; a washing-machine repair person or a visitor (family or friend). Alternatively, the creation of the space can be left entirely to the children, who have the freedom to respond to the day's story, whether fiction or non-fiction, as they desire. Adults should provide suitable props for play, for example baggy pants, tops and head scarves in a dressing-up box, a mat that could be used as a prayer rug, picture books, and a photograph of Mecca. A role-play area can be used in this way to explore other world religions.

Table 4.7 Ideas for structured play areas with a cultural/religious dimension

Shop – selling Muslim items (e.g. prayer mats, beads, Qu'rans, etc.).

Newsagents – selling seasonal cards, cards associated with rites of passage (e.g. birth, bar mitzvah, weddings, death, passing driving test); newspapers and magazines from different cultures.

Cake shop – shapes linked to the seasons, celebration cakes.

The Christmas story – crib with straw, crowns, soft toy animals, tea towels for shepherds, inn-keeper's registration book, passports.

A church (or other place of worship) – stained glass windows with the life of Jesus, lectern for Bible, bowl as font, hymn books, candlesticks, hymn numbers board, piece of cloth for a cape.

Source: McCreery (2008: 92).

Photo 4.1 A market day in Kenya – 'home corner'. *Source:* S. Hughes.

Independent play

Independent or free play is characterised by children choosing resources and activities themselves, often from a menu. Bruce (2004) refers to 'free-flow' play in which children move freely between indoor and outdoor areas although they are expected to follow rules. Areas of the school can be transformed into market places (Photo 4.1), homes near and far, shopping streets and old buildings, to develop young children's imaginative and independent play.

With People's homes often contain features that are distinctive of particular traditions. Items need to be selected carefully as some objects can be considered precious and it could cause offence to members of communities if their artefacts are not treated with respect. There is also a need to be sensitive when shrines are part of the home and not encourage children to use them for worship. It is best if the area that represents the shrine does not contain any specifically religious artefacts. Flowers and incense sticks might suffice (Hoodless, *et al.* 2009). Table 4.8 shows examples of possible religious features included in homes.

Outdoor play

Within the last generation or so, concerns have been raised about the lack of time children spend playing outdoors and the detrimental impact on their well-being. Hence across many countries there has been increasing governmental support for learning outside; for instance, Scotland's *Curriculum for Excellence through Outdoor Learning* (Scottish Government, 2010) and England's Council for Learning Outside the Classroom, set up in 2009 (**www.lotc.org.uk**). Estyn (2011), the Welsh inspectorate, reports that many schools and settings have invested considerable time, energy and money in improving provision for outdoor learning in the Foundation Phase. Young children's outdoor learning experiences were judged to be 'good' or 'better' in two-thirds of the sessions inspectors observed. Holden's (2011) research project

Table 4.8 Religious features in homes

A Christian home might contain:	• Images of Jesus • Receptacle for holy water • Bible • Rosary beads • Prayer Book • Children's versions of Bible stories • Palm Cross
A Hindu home might contain:	• Shrine with images of deities, flowers, incense sticks • Traditional Indian costume • Vegetarian food • Pictures of deities • Bhagavad Gita
A Muslim home might contain:	• Qu'ran • Prayer mat • Topi • Halal food • Images of Mecca • Head scarves • Calligraphy containing words from the Qu'ran

entitled *Children's Playground Games and Songs in the New Media Age*, shows that playground activities and games can have a profound effect on children's learning *(see* **http://projects.beyondtext.ac.uk/playgroundgames/index.php***)*. The research linked play with curriculum activities – the mapping of spaces and games in particular requiring history and geography skills.

Effective outdoor learning needs to be well organised and include a variety of stimuli such as:

- a creative area, for painting, rubbings, music-making, crafts and other such activities;

- a quiet area with seats and shelters, books and pictures;

- an environmental play area where there are a wide variety of resources including a sandpit and water tray, model vehicles and buildings, toy animals and people, path or road markings, mobile child-size buildings or building fronts painted on walls, wheeled vehicles, and similar play resources as well as ground to dig and a garden area to plant in, a wild area and natural objects to make things with; and

- an open space with equipment to do off-the-ground climbing, balancing, swinging, sliding, etc. activities, with small apparatus.

(Catling and Willy, 2009: 95)

Outdoor areas such as these largely reflect the Reggio Emilia approach to young children's learning in pre-school environments (Cadwell, 1997; Thornton and Brunton, 2010). These areas have much potential for the humanities, through investigations, exploring, making and building, enacting, small-toy play and the use of language. These activities are not exclusive to particular outdoor 'spaces'. Creativity can occur in any of them through imaginative role play or the use of laid-out apparatus, which might as readily be the source for explorations and investigations as might the wild area, a street scene or a set of photographs Catling and Willy (2009).

Children love caves, dens and places they can make into their own 'bases' in bushes or woods, in alcoves or under stairwells in or outside buildings (Tovey, 2007; White, 2008). While the nursery area may not provide opportunities, there may be a 'play hut', small-scale 'buildings' or tents that children can use as play spaces for imaginative games, or crates, boxes, frames and drapes for den-making activities (Cooper, 2004). These should be allowed to be the children's own 'secret places' (Dixon and Day, 2004). A variety of 'home' resources, such as furniture, crockery and cutlery and toys, can be provided for the children to use in their play hut or den, but they should decide what to use. Children can be encouraged to talk about their play and to take digital photographs of their special place and activities, though they may be reluctant to let adults into their world. Supervising adults can provide prompts and ideas to extend the children's own 'den' play. A photographic record can be maintained through the years and discussions held over how to care and improve the area. It can be a source for role-play, for storytelling and modelling ('Can you show me what it is like because I cannot go in there?'), or a context for talking about how it 'feels like home'.

The use of play implies that children have both the right and opportunities to make choices about their activities outdoors (and inside). These choices are influenced by available resources. Permanent features such as climbing frames and small-scale huts can be used regularly for environmentally orientated play. When provided with a variety of 'environmental' toys children have the chance to direct their own learning in relation to the event, place and environmental experiences they have had or imagine.

The playground area is the first place outside that offers a context for learning in the humanities. Children can design routes, practise mapping skills and play games that explore compass points. Children are often able to draw maps even before they can read or write and can use maps they have drawn to retell a journey or a storyline from their play. In the outdoor area, children could use sticks, stones and chalk to leave trails for each other to follow, using arrow shapes to point the way. Regular observations and discussions about the weather will enable children to appreciate the effects of the weather on daily life in different environments. As they progress, children will be able to set up experiments and carry out investigations, for example to gather data about wind and rainfall and then represent the results graphically through ICT.

As Chapter 5 notes, the locality is an excellent context for learning (Conway, et al., 2008; Milner, 1996; Salaman and Tutchell, 2005). Local visits help children gain a greater understanding of the natural and built environment. Through observing the work people do, discovering the different types of transport used locally and how buildings are used, children will begin to understand change within a locality and the way in which people's actions lead to a change in the environment. A well-organised visit to a local shop, park, place of worship or museum, offers children many authentic learning experiences (Photo 4.2).

Young children's observational and communication skills develop when they are encouraged to describe what they see along the street. Accompanying adults should focus on the children's view of the 'world', at their eye-level. A walk in the local area

Photo 4.2 Children visiting a local post office to post letters. *Source:* S. Hughes.

can be followed by sequencing the journey using photographs, expressing preferences for particular features of the environment and drawing a plan of the local area with symbols to represent particular features. Features can be noticed, including street names, service covers in the pavements, entrances to drives and gardens, fences and walls, seats and different surfaces.

Children can take digital photographs and/or video-clips to record selected features and views that they see, or record their comments and thoughts for use back in the nursery. During their walk they might talk about what they like or dislike, for example favourite places or the fact that people drop litter. Directional language can be encouraged when children turn corners; or it can be used to highlight where features are in the park, or to indicate features the children would like to see added to or removed from the street, the park and play area. Children should start with knowledge and understanding gained from visits in their locality when comparing and contrasting places such as the beach, town or country. Visits to contrasting places should allow children to develop their skills of enquiry, become competent in identifying and discussing geographical features and have first-hand experiences of a range of different environments.

Resources to promote knowledge and understanding of the world

There is a good range of resources available to Early Years practitioners to develop children's knowledge and understanding of the world. Bodies such as the British Association for Early Childhood Education provide general resources including posters, outdoor education materials and training packs (**www.early-education.org.uk**).

Commercial websites include **www.earlyyearsresources.co.uk**, which sells a wide range of items including books – for instance on famous historical people and events – inflatable globes, rain gauges, town jigsaws, eco dominoes, faith packs and festival resources. The Association of Play Industries is the lead trade body within the play sector and includes free online resources on creating play spaces, managing risk, designing playgrounds and involving the community (**www.api-play.org**). Local and national museums and galleries should also be consulted. Children should be taught how to care for resources, particularly those of sentimental value such as family heirlooms.

Stories

Using stories in various forms, such as picture books and eye-witness accounts, adds depth to learning experiences. Stories promote key vocabulary in the humanities and allow children to develop inferential, prediction and sequential skills. They add dimensions of time and place, offer contexts for promoting conceptual understanding, such as change, and introduce difficult issues at a safe distance. Stories can also help to provide opportunities for children to respond in awe and wonder to new materials. The learning context can be planned in a way that fires pupils' imaginations:

> Sarah was introducing the children in her Nursery to the Hindu Diwali story of Rama and Sita and their encounter with the demon Ravanna. As the children returned from afternoon play, they found the classroom in darkness, expect for a row of tiny lights at the front of the room. From somewhere in the dim light, some gentle Indian music was playing. The children began to speak in excited whispers as they settled themselves on the carpet. At the front of the room was a screen made out of a white sheet and beside this Sarah sat waiting for the children to settle.
>
> As they did, she began to tell a story, 'A long time ago in the land of India, lived a prince and his beautiful wife . . .' As the story began a light came on behind the screen and two shadow puppets began to dance across their stage. As Sarah told the story, hardly a sound could be heard, as the children listened and the story unfolded with only the tinkling music as accompaniment.
>
> *(Thomas, S., Maenclochog Community School)*

At the outset, it is important to create the appropriate environment for story-telling. In the classroom, it is common for younger children to be seated on the carpet while older ones may form a circle. Outdoor environments such as woodlands, parks, galleries and museums are also ideal settings for stories. Organisations such as English Heritage offer extensive services including professional story-tellers.

Stories like *Owl Babies* (Waddell and Benson, 1992) and the *Very Hungry Caterpillar* (Carle, 2002) can be used to enhance numerous curriculum areas, but in a historical sense they can be utilised to introduce very basic ideas about the passing of time, like night and day and yesterday and tomorrow. Myths, legends and fairy tales, although not based in historical fact, introduce children to skills like connecting cause and effect that can be expanded in later school years. Cox and Hughes (1998) explore the link between fiction and historical understanding in some detail. They stress that stories can act as a vehicle for historical understanding: the internal chronology and narrative form of a story provides children with support to order and recount the past. They argue that through exploring the beliefs and actions of characters in stories children can begin to appreciate the feelings and motivations of people and important historical process. Role-playing can be a good way to check to see if a child has understood the content and meaning of a story.

Stories can also help children understand the concept of old and new, and the influence of past events and characters. Through stories, songs and rhymes, children's sequencing skills of the passing of time are reinforced. Through listening to stories, examining photographs and asking and answering questions, children can learn about places that are further away, for instance *Kabo's Diary* (Dyer and Scurlock, 2002). This is an entertaining and colourful story about a young child called Kabo visiting his grandmother's home in Botswana. From story books children can develop their understanding of people that live faraway, the types of food produced, the different types of travel and transport and how to use atlases and globes to locate places.

Many teachers use artefacts, paintings, poems, passports, toys, puppets and natural objects to accompany stories. 'Story sacks' containing a variety of objects related to the story are also popular. Digital stories via the interactive whiteboard can also enhance sessions.

Visual sources

Visual sources such as pictures, photographs, paintings and postcards can also be a valuable resource when teaching humanities to young children. They can learn to sequence events in their day by using evidence from photographs, and by recording their ideas in pictures and booklets. Using photographs that they take themselves (both indoors and outdoors), children can progress to sequencing events in the week and for longer periods. 'Taking' a photograph or painting a picture is an active process and this creation lends itself to discussion about what the photographer or painter wanted to convey. The world of digital photography and computer software enables teachers to illustrate powerfully (for instance with reference to pictures of children themselves and the locality) how images can be cropped or distorted in some way. This is preparation for children beginning to understand interpretations.

Digital photography is an exciting means of supporting young children's enquiry skills. Photographs of earlier generations can provide a good stimulus for children to explore and ask questions about past times and events as well as also engaging parents'/carers' interest in the curriculum. Photographs might also contribute to a class museum of old/new household items or toys that children can handle and compare, while at the same time learning relevant vocabulary to describe the characteristics that identify artefacts from different periods of time. Children can also use photographs to sequence events of a religious celebration or worship. Aerial photographs of the locality will help children to begin to understand how different places relate to each other and how to use relevant geographical terms to describe particular features. Five-year-olds are capable of relating to an aerial photograph of their school area (Blades *et al.*, 2005).

Photo 4.3 Children create a jeep to go on a safari. *Source:* S. Hughes.

Construction activities

Construction activities can also be used to teach humanities in the Early Years. Having visited places in connection with the humanities, and noted their features, children can re-create them using a variety of construction materials. For instance, they could create places of worship with significant features; create vehicles for particular journeys (Photo 4.3) or construct a town. Children could create small world scenarios or record their experiences by drawing, painting, model-making or using appropriate computer software. Starting with the knowledge of their own home children might talk about where they live, make a model with construction equipment or draw the house, progressing to different types of transport, describing and recording their journey to school pictorially.

Visitors

A range of visitors can also help children understand the wider world around them. It is essential that they are well prepared to work with very young children. Such people might include: a religious minister talking about a coming celebration; a mum bringing in her newborn baby; a parent making some food with the children; a grandparent talking about when they were a visitor from another country (Photo 4.4) and a traffic warden talking about their work. As children develop knowledge about workplaces and roles of people in their locality, they will act out

Photo 4.4 Visitors from Lesotho talk to children about their village life.
Source: S. Hughes.

roles, be able to listen to visitors and question them about their roles, record what they find out and progress to carrying out a survey enquiring about the occupations other children would like when they grow up. Visitors might be asked to talk about their own childhood or school days with the children. This will enable children to develop their knowledge and understanding of ways of life in different times, to engage in two-way conversations as well as examine photographs and artefacts and listen to stories. This will help children interpret evidence and understand why people did things, why events happened and some of the consequences. These visitors' accounts can be compared with books, DVDs, museum displays and so on to help children understand that there are different ways of interpreting the past.

Technologies

Beyond computers, there is a wide range of technologies (such as television, radio, audio tapes, videos, 'programmable toys' such as Bee-Bot, mobile phones, CD-ROMs and digital cameras) that can motivate young children's interest in their own neighbourhood, the past, places and lifestyles of others. Research by Stephen and Plowman (2003) highlights the need for nurseries to broaden the focus of ICT from computers to other forms, including digital still and video cameras, mobile phones, electronic keyboards and toys. The case for ICT in the Early Years is not clear-cut (Alliance for Childhood, 2000). Critics maintain that there are social, cognitive and health risks associated with extensive use of ICT in the Early Years including: social isolation, potential repetitive strain injuries, constraints on physical exercise, creativity and communication skills, and – contrary to the claim of enthusiasts – reduced levels of motivation. Although ICT is not a panacea to the challenge of motivating children, it does offer considerable learning potential provided adults set good role models in their use (Morgan and Siraj-Blatchford, 2009). Moreover, ICT can support the development of positive dispositions such as perseverance, creativity and collaboration (O'Hara, 2008).

Most young children view technologies with a positive attitude and embrace the prospects of playing with them. Children are empowered when they choose to use technologies. During one research project, Evans and Fuller (1996, in Farrell 2005) placed toy phones into the role-play area and observed children from a distance. The researcher conversed with children when they picked up the phone, including asking questions relating to the research agenda. The children held the 'power' in this relationship, as the conversation was on their terms, free from obvious pressure or direction from adults, and they could end the interview when they wanted. Many young children arrive in nursery and reception classes with a growing awareness of mobile phones, high-definition television boxes and digital cameras. One in four six-year-olds have their own computers (Mayo and Nairn, 2009: 127). Structured play activities on themes such as the travel agents, the post office, the railway station, the market, the museum, the cinema and the bank, provide opportunities for children to use technologies in appropriate humanities contexts. Walkie-talkies, programmable toys and floor robots can be used to develop mapping skills and location knowledge outdoors. PowerPoint and interactive whiteboards can be effectively used by children in the Early Years to present a simple sequence of events, thereby promoting chronological understanding. Young children can also be taught to add image and sound files to personalise their stories (Barber *et al.*, 2007).

Conclusion

Although this chapter has focused on play, it is important to conclude by emphasising that this is not the only means by which young children learn about time, place and community. As Chapter 5 notes, visits to local places of interest enrich young children's understanding of their heritage, while visitors' diverse experiences add depth and meaning. Moreover, there are times when formal instruction is appropriate, for instance in communicating key safety information when exploring woodlands and other outdoor areas or setting out 'rules' before entering a place of worship, library or gallery.

SUMMARY

- It is important to understand the rationale behind the play-based philosophy that underpins the Early Years provision.

- Different forms of play and other activities promote young children's geographical, historical and religious learning.

- There is a good range of resources to support young children's understanding of the world around them. These include stories, visual sources, play-based equipment, museum and gallery resources, technologies and visitors. These should be carefully selected to meet the needs of children.

- Early Years practitioners use a variety of approaches to engage young learners' interest in the humanities.

References

Aldrich, R. and Gordon, P. (1989), *Dictionary of British Educationalists*, London: Woburn Press.

Alliance for Childhood (2000), *Fool's Gold: A Critical Look at Computers in Childhood*, available at: www.allianceforchildhood.net/projects/computers/computers_reports_fools_gold_download.htm.

Barber, D., Cooper, L., and Meeson, G. (2007), *Learning and Teaching with Interactive Whiteboards*, Exeter: Learning Matters.

Bergen, D. (2002), 'The Role of Pretend Play in Children's Cognitive Development', in Early Childhood Research and Practice, 4:1, available at: http://ecrp.uiuc.edu/v4n1/bergen.html.

Bertram, T. and Pascal, C. (2002), *Early Years Education: An International Perspective,* London: QCA.

Blades, M., Spencer, C., Plester, B. and Desmond, K. (2005), 'Young Children's Recognition and Representation of Urban Landscapes from Aerial Photographs and in Toy Play', in Allen, G. (ed.), *Human Spatial Memory*, London: Lawrence Erlbaum.

British Educational Research Association – Early Years Special Interest Group (BERA- SIG) (2003), *Early Years Research: Pedagogy, Curriculum and Adult Roles, Training and Professionalism*, available at: www.bera.ac.uk/pdfs/BERAEarlyYearsReview31May03.pdf.

Broadhead, C., Howard, J., and Wood, E. (2010), *Play and Learning in the Early Years: From Research to Practice*, London: Sage.

Brock, A., Dodds, S., Jarvis, P. and Olusoga, Y. (2009), *Perspectives on Play, Learning for Life*, Harlow: Pearson.

Brooker, L. (2003), 'Integrating New Technologies in UK Classrooms: Lessons for Teachers from Early Years Practitioners', in *Childhood Education*, 79: 5, 261–267.

Bruce, T. (2001), *Learning Through Play – Babies, Toddlers and the Foundation Years*, London: Hodder & Stoughton Education.

Bruce, T. (2004), *Developing Learning in Early Childhood*, London: Paul Chapman.

Burn, A (2011), *Children's Playground Games and Songs in the New Media Age*, 2009–11 Project Report, London: Centre for the Study of Children, Youth & Media.

Cadwell, L. (1997), *Bringing Reggio Emilia Home: Innovative Approach to Early Childhood Education*, London: Teachers' College Press.

Carle, E. (2002), *The Very Hungry Caterpillar*, London: Puffins Books.

Catling, S. (2006), 'What do five-year-olds know of the world? Geographical understanding and play in young children's early learning', *Geography*, 91(1), 55–74.

Catling, S. and Willy, T. (2009), *Achieving QTS. Teaching Primary Geography*, Exeter: Learning Matters.

CCEA (2007), *Northern Ireland Primary Curriculum*, Belfast: CCEA, available at: **www. nicurriculum.org.uk/docs/key_stages_1_and_2/ northern_ireland_curriculum_primary_pdf**.

CCEA (2008), *Learning through play at Key Stage 1*, Belfast: CCEA.

Conway, D., Pointon, P. and Greenwood, J. (2008), 'If the world is round, how come the piece I'm sitting on is flat?' Early Years geography', in Whitbread, D. and Coltman, P. (eds), *Teaching and Learning in the Early Years*, London: Routledge.

Cook, H. C. (1917), *The Play Way. An Essay in Educational Method*, London: Heinemann.

Cooper, L., Johnston, J., Rotchell, E. and Woolley, R. (2010), Knowledge and Understanding of the World, London: Continuum.

Cooper, H. (ed.) (2004), *Exploring Time and Place. Through Play*, London: David Fulton Publishers Ltd.

Copeland, T. (1994*), A Teacher's Guide to Using Castles*, London: English Heritage.

Cox, K. and Hughes, P. (1998), 'History and Children's Fiction' in Hoodless, P. (ed.) *History and English in the Primary Curriculum Exploiting the Links,* London: Routledge.

DCELLS (2008), *Knowledge and Understanding of the World – guidance to support the knowledge and understanding of the world area of learning in the Foundation Phase Framework for Children's Learning for 3 to 7-year-olds in Wales*, Cardiff: Welsh Assembly Government.

DCSF (2008), *Practice Guidance for Early Years Foundation Stage: Setting the Standards for Learning, Development and Care for Children from Birth to Five,* London: Department for Children, Schools and Families.

Dixon, J. and Day, S. (2004), 'Secret Places: 'You're too big to come in here', in Cooper, H. (ed.), *Exploring Time and Place Through Play*, London: David Fulton.

Dyer, O. and Scurlock, V. (2002), *Kabo's Diary*, Llandysul: Gwasg Gomer.

Estyn (2010), *Foundation Phase training and its impact on learning and teaching*, Cardiff: Estyn.

Estyn (2011), *Outdoor Learning – an evaluation of learning in the outdoors for children under five in the Foundation Phase*, Cardiff: Estyn.

Evans, P. and Fuller, M. (1996), 'Hello, who am I speaking to?' *Communicating with pre-school children in their educational research settings,* in Early Years, 17(1), 17–20.

Farrell, A. (2005), *Ethical Research with Children*, Maidenshead: Open University Press.

Filer, J. (2008), *Healthy, Active and Outside!: Running an Outdoor Programme in the Early Years*, Oxon: Routledge.

Friedman, W. J. (1991), 'The Development of Children's Memory for the Time of Past Events', in *Child Development*, 62: 139–155.

Goouch, K. (2009), 'Forging relationships in play', in Papatheodorou, T. and Moyles, J. (eds), *Learning Together in the Early Years*, London: Routledge, 139–151.

Guha, M. (1996), 'Play in School', in Blenkian, G., and Kelly, A. Early Childhood Education, London: Paul Chapman.

Hoodless, P., McCreery, E., Bowen, P., Bermingham, S. (2009), *Teaching Humanities in Primary Schools*, Exeter: Learning Matters.

Huizinga, J. (1950), *Homo Ludens,* Boston: Beacon Press.

Hurst, V. and Joseph, J. (1998), *Supporting Early Learning*, Buckingham: Open University Press.

Johnston, J. and Nahmad-Williams, L. (2009), Early *Childhood Studies: Principles and Practice*, Harlow: Pearson.

Martin, F. and Owens, P. (2008), *Caring for Our World: A Practical Guide to ESD Ages 4–8*, Sheffield: Geographical Association.

Marshall, H. (1994), 'Children's Understanding of Academic Tasks: Work, Play or Learning', in *Journal of Research in Childhood Education*, 9:1, 35–46.

Mayo, E. and Nairn, A. (2009), *Consumer Kids: How big business is grooming our children by profits*, London: Constable and Robinson.

McCreery, E., Palmer, S. and Voiels, V. (2008), *Achieving QTS: Teaching Religious Education: Primary and Early Years,* Exeter: Learning Matters.

Milner, A. (1996), *Geography Starts Here! Practical approaches with nursery and reception children*, Sheffield: Geographical Association.

Morgan, A. and Siraj-Blatchford, J. (2009), *Using ICT in the Early Years: Parents and Practitioners in Partnership*, London: Practical Pre-School Books.

Moyles, J. (2006), *The Excellence of Play*, Buckingham: Open University Press.

Moyles, J. (2010), *Thinking about Play: Developing a Reflective Approach*, Maidenhead: Open University Press.

Nutbrown, C. (2008), *Early Childhood Education; History, Philosophy and Experience*, London: Sage.

O'Hara, M. (2008), *Teaching 3–8*, London: Continuum.

Palmer, J. and Birch, J. (2004), *Geography in the Early Years*, London: Routledge.

Pound, L. (2005), *How Children Learn*, London: Step Forward.

Pugh, G. and Duffy, B. (2009), (eds), *Contemporary Issues in the Early Years*, London: Sage.

Radford, M. (1999), 'Spiritual development and religious education', in David, T. (ed.), *Young Children Learning*, London: Paul Chapman, 168–203.

Rusk, R. (1933), A History of Infant Education, London: University of London Press.

Salaman, A. and Tutchell, S. (2005), *Planning Education Visits for Early Years,* London: Paul Chapman Publishing.

Sanderson, L. E. (2006), 'Effects of Work and Play Signals on Task Evaluation', in *Journal of Applied Social Psychology*, 18:13, 1032–1048.

Scott, W. (2005), 'When we were very young: emerging historical awareness in the earliest years', *Primary History*, 39: 14–17.

Scottish Executive (2006), *Insight 28: Early Years Education: Perspectives from a review of the international literature*, Edinburgh: Scottish Executive, available at: **http://scotland.gov.uk/ Publications/2006/01/26094635/1.**

Scottish Government (2008), *The Early Years Framework*, Edinburgh: Scottish Government.

Scottish Government (2009), *A Curriculum for Excellence: Building the Curriculum 4, Skills for learning, skills for life and skills for work*, Edinburgh: Scottish Government.

Scottish Government (2010), *Curriculum for Excellence through Outdoor Learning,* Glasgow: Learning and Teaching Scotland

Siraj-Blatchford, I. (1999), 'Early Childhood Pedagogy: Practice, Principles and Research', in Mortimore, P., (ed.) *Understanding Pedagogy and its Impact on Learning*, London: Paul Chapman.

Siraj-Blatchford, I., Sylva, K., Laugharne, J., Milton, E., and Charles, F. (2006), *Monitoring and Evaluation of the Effective Implementation of the Foundation Phase Project Across Wales.*

Shefatya, L. (1990), 'Socio-economic status and ethnic different in socio dramatic play: theoretical and practical implications', in E. Klugman and S. Smilansky (eds), *Children's Play and Learning: perspectives and policy implications*, New York: Teachers College Press.

Stephen C. and Plowman L. (2003), *ICT in Pre-School: A 'Benign Addition'?* Dundee: Learning and Teaching Scotland **www.ltscotland.org.uk/edresources/ publications.asp?id=872**.

Tassoni, P. and Hucker, T. (2005), *Planning Play and the Early Years,* London: Heinemann.

Tickell Review (2011), *The Early Years: Foundations for life, health and learning – an independent report on the Early Years Foundation Stage to Her Majesty's Government*, available at: **www.education.gov.uk**.

Tovey, H. (2007), *Playing Outdoors: Spaces and Places, Risks and Challenge (Debating Play),* Maidenhead: OUP.

Thornton, L. and Brunton, P. (2010), *Bringing in the Reggio Approach to Your Early Years Practice*, London: Routledge.

Waddell, M. and Benson, P. (1992), *Owl Babies*, London: Walker Books.

Whitbread, N. (1972), The Evolution of the Nursery-Infant School; A History of Infant and Nursery Education in Britain, 1800-1970, London: Routledge & Kay Paul.

White, J. (2008), *Playing and Learning Outdoors,* London: Routledge.

Woodhead M. (1998), 'Quality in Early Childhood Programmes – a contextually appropriate approach (1)', *International Journal of Early Years Education*, 6, 1, 5–17.

Wood, E. and Attfield, J. (2005), *Play, Learning and the Early Childhood Curriculum*, London: Sage.

Useful Websites

The British Association for Early Childhood Education was set up in 1923 and is the leading national voluntary organisation for Early Years practitioners: **www.early-education.org.uk**.

Learning through Landscapes aims to develop children's outdoor education. The Scottish equivalent is Grounds for Learning and in Wales it is LTL Cymru: **www.ltl.org.uk**.

Play England, Play Wales and Play Scotland are devoted to promoting children's play: **www.playengland.org.uk**; **www.playwales.org.uk**; **www.playscotland.org**; **www.playboard.org**.

Exploring the locality

When children spend time in the great outdoors, getting muddy, getting wet, getting stung by nettles, they learn important lessons – what hurts, what is slippery, what you can trip over or fall from.

(Peter Cornall, 2010, Head of Leisure Safety at RoSPA)

Exploring localness involves looking at how people express and experience their differences from others, and what they share with people.

(Smith, 1994: 10)

Learning objectives

By the end of this chapter you should be able to:

- define and evaluate local study in the primary school;
- describe possible historical, geographical and religious starting-points to local study;
- identify the kinds of questions, sources and approaches to consider when planning a local study; and
- reflect on the potential of a street study to promote children's enquiry skills.

What is the locality?

For many teachers, the locality equates to the area around the school, often associated with the expression 'our square mile' and normally containing the homes of the majority of pupils in the school (DCELLS, 2008a: 13). In a strict geographical sense, the locality has been defined as having a radius of less than 2 kilometres (1.2 miles)

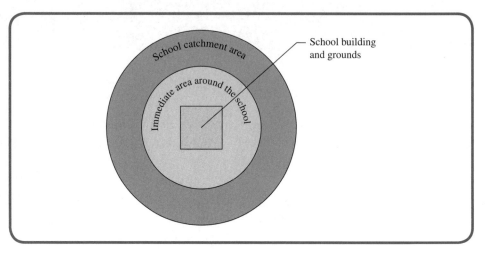

Figure 5.1 Possible scales of local study in the primary school.

and, in the case of urbanised areas, probably containing no more than 10,000 residents (Day, 2006). The locality can be seen as three separate areas covering the school buildings and grounds, the immediate vicinity around the school and the wider neighbourhood (see Figure 5.1). Milner *et al.* (2004) add that teachers should consider more distant features, such as hills, church towers and factories, if they contribute to the character of the locality. The locality can be revisited continually through different geographical 'focal lenses' as children deepen their local knowledge and experience (Catling and Willy, 2009).

Geographically speaking then, the parameters of local study should be limited to a village or part of a town rather than extend to a city or region. Historically, 'local' has proven to be an organic unit reflecting changes in the way in which a community has organised itself. The 'parish' (originally derived from classical Greek, 'neighbour' or 'near house') was the smallest defined area of local government in rural areas served by the church. In England, the parish church dominated village life and remains the oldest building in most localities. For centuries, the church served not only to mark the rites of passage (christenings, weddings and funerals) but also the only means of accessing information about the outside world. Public notices continue to be posted in church porches. Although the parish boundary defined administrative matters, such as the operation of workhouses and schools, it did not restrict movement of people in and out of the parish. Hence there is a strong argument for pupils to consider historical communities in relation to others rather than in isolation (Hey, 1998). Local historians focus on the stories of individual villages and towns, particularly those of 'ordinary people in ordinary places' (Lewis, 1989: 8). The scope of local history is considerable, as demonstrated by the many events that feature as part of the Historical Association's Local and Community History Month (**www.history.org.uk/events**).

Clifford and King (2006: x) point out that locality needs to be defined from within. They see the neighbourhood, the housing estate, the village, the suburb and the street as areas that have a sense of belonging – definable by those who live, work and play there. They argue that when things are looked at on a larger scale, sensitivity is lost and abstractions begin – people become 'the public', fields become 'sites' and woods are viewed as 'natural resources'.

A sense of belonging involves individuals 'identifying with a particular place, taking pride in it and having faith in the capacity of local institutions to act fairly and openly' (DCSF, 2010: 3). Exploring localities is not only about physical features such as churches, castles and parks. It is also a spiritual journey in recognising the emotional investment in places and spaces. Visitors to monasteries and abbeys, such as Mount Grace Priory (north Yorkshire) and Tintern (Monmouthshire), can feel spiritually renewed when they reflect on the silence, solitude and simplicity of monastic life. In some cases, it motivates individuals to simplify their lifestyles in the bustling modern age and has captured the public's imagination with television programmes such as *The Monastery*, *The Retreat* and *The Convent* (Jamison, 2006). In every locality there will be places considered sacred or holy because they imbue a special feeling in people. Historically, these include ancient stone circles such as Avebury (Wiltshire) and Glastonbury Tor (Somerset), which continue to attract New-Age devotees. There are also landscapes that are regarded for their 'spiritual' nature such as the Lake District, Snowdonia and the Giant's Causeway (County Antrim). In many local areas there are holy wells as testified by place and street names such as 'Holywell' (north Wales), Wells (Somerset) and Well Street. In the Middle Ages holy wells were dressed with flowers on their saint's day. This ancient custom is still celebrated in places such as the Peak District.

REFLECTION

- Think about your own area and where you would find a quiet, sacred place to meditate. How might you encourage children to do the same, for instance in a busy, urban school setting?

Contrasting localities

From a geographical perspective, localities should be chosen to allow similarities and contrasts to be drawn between places – for instance, in terms of climate (hot or cold countries), location (rural or urban), and wealth (economically advantaged or less well developed). Within the UK, contrasts might include a seaside town and a suburb, or an inner-city community and a rural village. By establishing links with a school elsewhere in the UK and overseas, pupils can extend their understanding of national and global issues. Scoffham (2002), for instance, illustrates how comparisons can be drawn between a local street and Mengles Road, a side street in Dindigul, a town in southern India. The street's small textile and fabric workshops, school, training institute, church and international hotel contribute to the character of the area. The thriving street life includes many street vendors and weavers working on the roadside. But Scoffham points out that, as in England, there is a distinct pattern to the day. In the quiet of the early morning, refuse is cleared away, children arrive at school and traffic builds up as lorries, taxis and bicycles make their way through the town. Peace returns later in the day as the heat intensifies.

The value of local study

The value of local study in children's education has long been recognised (see Photos 5.1–2). The Hadow Report (1931: 102) highlighted the contribution of visits to local places of interest to children's progress in history, geography and nature study. HMI (1959: 291) reinforced this view, even suggesting the need for a second follow-up visit to sites such as woods, ponds and museums, in order to consolidate learning. Projects in the 1970s and 1980s showed how the locality is an ideal context for the development of pupils' motivation, confidence and skills, for instance in collecting data, experimenting, mapping, and examining documents (Harris, 1971; Blyth *et al.*, 1976; Lines and Bolwell, 1971; ILEA, 1980; Pinnell, 1986; Boyle, 1987). The potential of local study and outdoor learning in general has been flagged up through the recent curriculum reviews across the UK. Scotland's *Curriculum for Excellence* (Scottish Executive, 2005), the Northern Ireland Curriculum (DENI, 2006), the Foundation Phase in Wales (DCELLS, 2008b) and the Foundation Stage in England (DfES, 2007) all highlight learning gains associated with local study, particularly for young children.

Literacy, numeracy and ICT skills

The locality provides a powerful stimulus for developing learners' skills in literacy, numeracy, and information and communications technology (ICT). Pupils might

Photos 5.1–2 For many years local study has developed children's mathematical skills (such as measurement, scale and estimation), as shown by these photographs of a children's weather station in the 1960s and a street investigation of the 1980s.
Sources: DES, (1967); ILEA, (1980: 2).

write letters to the local newspaper to express their views on a particular issue such as the closure of a shop, produce labels for a museum exhibition, or compile a guide-book for a local place of worship. Mathematical skills can also be fostered through a wide range of local contexts including visits to shops, historical sites, graveyards, woodlands and farms. Pupils can undertake traffic and other surveys gaining skills in handling data using graphs, charts and diagrams. They can practise measuring and calculating skills using first-hand sources such as census returns. Photographs of different shapes in the environment can be taken, analysed and shared. Pupils can also search out evidence for numbers in the local environment, ranging from bus stops to milestones. Pupils can practise numeracy skills when making timelines of local events. Problem-solving challenges can be set such as working out areas, angles, heights and volumes associated with particular buildings.

Pupils' speaking and listening skills can be promoted through local investigations. Debates can centre on local environmental issues, such as land redevelopment. Children can adopt the role of local reporters covering current issues and make presentations in public meetings and 'televised' debates using digital video cameras. By regularly interviewing local residents, pupils learn to ask questions, listen carefully, show patience, manage equipment and begin to see that there are different perspectives on life. This is not only beneficial to children – as Howarth (1998) points out, 'two-way learning' occurs between interviewer and interviewee. It brings generations together.

Local study offers much scope for developing pupils' skills in ICT. There are a number of software packages that introduce computer mapping and geographical information systems. The Ordnance Survey OpenData is part of the drive to increase innovation, and support the government's 'Making Public Data Public' initiative (**www.ordnancesurvey.co.uk/oswebsite/products/os-opendata.html**).

In walking around the area, pupils can use digital cameras to record their experiences. They can use their images to produce real or 'interactive' postcards, describing the best features of their locality, to send to another school. Databases can be created to log findings and evaluate sources. For instance, Peter Higginbotham's first-rate website on workhouses (**www.workhouses.org.uk**), replete with 5,000 images, 1,800 maps and 2,500 web pages, is a rich source for local study. The transcribed census returns can easily be transferred to Microsoft Excel and used by pupils to investigate the ages of 'inmates', mapping their birthplaces using online tools and comparing former occupations. They may deduce that some occupations were common to localities, such as lace makers in Tiverton (Devon), cotton-stocking knitters in Mansfield (Nottingham) and ironworkers in Merthyr Tydfil (Glamorgan). Groups of pupils can 'adopt' a different family from a workhouse and set their own questions for others to consider. Ethical issues relating to social exclusion (why were children separated from their parents in the workhouse, and why were workhouses so dreaded?) and 'handicapped' people (idiots, imbeciles, lunatics) provide material for good personal and social education.

Good local study should include frequent outdoor learning. First-hand experiences such as observing, measuring, photographing and interviewing bring the humanities to life. Such active learning has widespread support in the UK curriculum and publishers have been quick to highlight the all-round benefits of learning outdoors (Knight, 2009; Bilton, 2010). The Westminster government acknowledges the value of outdoor learning through its manifesto for *Learning Outside the Classroom* (LOtC), which pledges support for all pupils to have 'regular, continuous and progressive LOtC experiences' (DfES, 2006).

BOX 5.1 RESEARCH BRIEFING – OUTDOOR LEARNING

The emotional, physical and cognitive benefits associated with working within the 'real' environment have been extensively researched (Rickinson, 2001; Fien *et al.*, 2001; Rickinson *et al.*, 2004; Dillon *et al.*, 2005). For example, the National School Grounds Survey (*Learning through Landscapes* 2003), reports that of 700 schools surveyed 65 per cent believed that school grounds improvements had increased overall attitudes to learning while 73 per cent identified considerable improvements in behaviour, as well as a significant reduction (64 per cent) in bullying. Academic gains were also noted (see **www.lotc.org.uk/Resources/Research**). Specifically, fieldwork has a positive impact on children's long-term memory because the experiences outside are markedly different, and therefore easier to recall, from everyday classroom life.

Challenges

A recent survey by Ofsted (2008a: 5) attributed limited fieldwork opportunities to concerns over health and safety, lack of curriculum time, a shortage of staff expertise and insufficient finance. Geographically, the locality needs to be compared to other localities, a wider region and the country as a whole. For instance, if a class is studying a car factory in the locality, they could investigate where in the UK the parts come from and which countries receive the finished cars. Many first-hand historical sources are not available in a format that is readily accessible to young children, although county record offices and libraries have produced some excellent materials for schools. For instance, the Hampshire Record Office provides educational packs, online sources and videos on titles such as 'The Home Front in Hampshire', 'A 1930s Infant School' and 'Studying Local History: a guide to useful sources' (**www3.hants.gov.uk**).

The organisation of visits and fieldwork requires careful planning, including due regard to risk assessment. School and local authorities should have clear guidelines about taking children out of school. If visiting a park or garden, for instance, discarded syringes and hypodermic needles are a particular hazard because of the risk of transmission of disease. Practical provision for hand washing needs to be available, for instance through the use of alcohol gels or other hand sanitizers. Parents should be informed of appropriate clothing and footwear, along with the use of sun creams where necessary. Society's excessive risk aversion has prompted schemes such as Go4it (**www.hti.org.uk/products/go4it**) to award schools that develop a risk-positive climate, so that a 'cotton-wool' generation of children learn to manage risks and enjoy the occasional cartwheel or game of conkers. Such activities and experiences, which previous generations of children enjoyed, are now seen as troubling or dangerous (Gill, 2007).

Historical starting points

The school building itself is often a good starting point for local history. Investigations can begin by establishing a timeline drawing upon interviews with ex-pupils, and studying old photographs and plans. Victorian and Edwardian schools often have punishment ledgers and logbooks or diaries, available in the county record office or the school itself. By walking around the school searching out architectural clues from the past, children can develop skills of deduction and inference. They can raise questions about the location of the school and how the area has changed by examining Ordnance Survey maps.

Every school is situated in a locality with its own 'curiosities' or unusual sites of historical interest (Timpson, 1989; Hannigan, 2006). Many fascinating examples are cited by Ashley (2005), such as the 20 regimental badges carved on the downland chalk in Fovant (Wiltshire) to commemorate the soldiers who died in the First World War. In some cases, the regeneration of areas has led to the rediscovery of objects and buildings that hitherto had been ignored.

Place names

The obvious historical starting point for local study is the name of the school, street, village or town. The UK has some intriguing place names including: Lower Slaughter, No place, Pity Me, Sandwich, Great Snoring, Blubberhouses, Bishops Itchington, Piddlehinton and Ugley. Many of the oldest names derived from rural features: trees, streams, gardens, dwellings by rivers. In Gaelic, for instance, *derry* means 'oakwood', *carraig* means 'rock', and *tully* or *knock* means 'hill'. Even the industrial heartland of Birmingham is softened by 'the farm of Beornmund's people'. However, over a period of 1,000 years or so, spellings change and it is not possible to be certain about the meaning of a place – 'Birch Wood' may have meant that only one birch tree was present rather than many.

The influence of Christianity can be traced in place-names. Children can explore the prevalence of *Llan* (Wales), *kirk* (Scotland), *kil* (Ireland) and *Church* or *minster* using Ordnance Survey maps. Less obvious are place names that contain *stow* (Old English), which meant 'meeting place' – frequently these were religious gatherings. Bristol was once *Brycg Stow*, meaning 'the place of assembly by the bridge'. Morwenstow (Cornwall) is named after Morwenna, a local female saint. Other place names are linked to the names of ecclesiastics (priests, monks, canons, bishops, abbots and nuns), or monasteries, religious houses and crosses (Cameron, 1996). Local reference libraries are likely to hold copies of guides on place names (e.g. Reaney, 1960; Gelling, 1997; Owen, 1998) and there are some excellent online sources. A project on names can extend to streets, public houses and other buildings, and utilise sources such as gravestones, trade directories and maps.

Customs

Local study should draw upon stories of events, characters and customs that have shaped the development of the area and illustrate significant themes in history. For instance, Granny Cousins was Poole's famous 'Knocker-up' who used a pole for tapping on upstairs bedroom windows to wake people for the start of the day. She would start at three o'clock in the morning, and was often seen later in the day sleeping around the town.

Such a story raises discussion points relating to the impact of the clock, described as the 'key invention of the Industrial Revolution' and the 'operating system of capitalism', on people's lives (Honoré, 2005: 22). It is the one object that makes everything else possible – such as meetings, deadlines and transport. Persuading early industrial workers to live by the clock was difficult. Punctuality became a priority and a celebrated Victorian virtue while slowness became a cardinal sin. In modern times, the cult of speed has been challenged by those who do not equate speed with quality of life. Many localities feature blue plaques to commemorate the contribution of individuals to 'human welfare or happiness', as advertised by the English Heritage scheme (started in 1867).

Many local customs have charitable origins associated with the distribution of food or drink to the poor. County reference libraries should hold sources on local and national folklore and customs (Owen, 1991; Day, 1998; Bennett, 2007; Ayto and Crofton, 2005). Some traditions are highly controversial in nature, such as the annual burning of the Pope at Lewes (Sussex). Others are in danger of being lost to future generations, such as the folk stories associated with the Fens of the East of England. However, in general, Round (2006) points out that many local authorities are taking an active interest in customs as a means of attracting tourists and celebrating community distinctiveness.

Geographical starting points

The geographical area from which children attend any particular school can vary considerably in nature and size. It is important for teachers to get to know the school's locality, given that many probably live outside it. To state an obvious but important point: going for regular walks around the neighbourhood can reveal many features that go unnoticed from the car.

School grounds

Every school can be seen as a 'little geography' (Carter, 1998: 213) in itself. Most Early Years practitioners will use the classrooms, school building and grounds as starting points for geography, as discussed further in Chapter 4. There is extensive guidance in making effective use of the school grounds (Harriman, 2008; Garick, 2009; Bilton, 2010). Pupils can undertake simple map-making activities, weather watches, land use surveys, direction games and follow sensory walks. The 'old' Qualifications and Curriculum Agency (2002) scheme based on improving the school grounds can be adapted for different ages and contexts (Years 1 to 6). For instance, a small-scale project might focus on improving one aspect of the school site such as putting in new plants and containers, or a more ambitious scheme, for example redesigning the school playground. These opportunities enable learners to work together in planning, developing and reviewing their ideas. They can apply mathematical skills by investigating costs and limitations of different plans.

Immediate neighbourhood

Moving from the school grounds, pupils should learn about their neighbourhood's physical, environmental and human features, such as the layout of streets, noise pollution and the kind of work people do. Appropriate fieldwork experiences include: mapping where children live, surveying how children travel to school, and identifying individual buildings on local photographs. It is critical that young children learn how to look around and pursue their own lines of enquiry relevant to their everyday lives (see Figure 5.2).

It can be rewarding to focus on a particular issue, such as the challenges facing wheelchair-users, parents with buggies or the partially sighted, when moving around a shopping precinct, rather than doing a general study of shops. Catling and Willy (2009) suggest a range of local problems to examine including:

- changes to local services such as the closure of a post office;
- examining conflicting views on issues such as parking; and
- exploring different people's use of local services such as leisure facilities.

Table 5.1 expands upon this and highlights the major aspects of local geography in the primary school. Pupils need to understand that adults do different kinds of work, to recognise different uses of land and to explain why buildings are located in the local area. By contrasting the locality with another of similar size in the UK, pupils can recognise

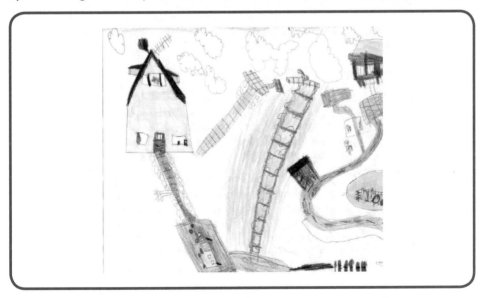

Figure 5.2 A journey from home to school by a six-year-old, passing the neighbour's horse, family cars, overgrown railway line, bollards, a busy road and park. *Source*: Mia Grigg.

Table 5.1 The major aspects of local geography in primary school

Settlement:	• variety and styles of homes • origin of the settlement • layout of the settlement • building and land use • growth and changes
Services:	• shops and services • public and private
Leisure:	• leisure, activities, facilities • parks, open spaces
Journeys:	• roads, paths in locality • linking to other places • buses, railways, air, boat • journeys people make • movement of goods • transport networks
Works:	• different types of work • industry, agriculture, retail • location of economic activities • why they are there • how they are changing
Land use:	• different types of land use • patterns of land use • competition for land • conflict over use
People moving:	• why do people move • where to, where from
Attitudes:	• likes and dislikes • changes desired • effects on people
Landscape:	• different types of relief features • variety of rocks and soil • water: streams/rivers, ponds/lakes • the effects of finding e.g. artefacts and minerals • types of fresh water supply
Weather:	• heat, sun/cloud, wind, precipitation
Environment:	• changes to the environment • effects of pollution • managing and restoring • protecting environments

Source: www.cumbriagridforlearning.org.uk

similarities and differences in physical features and lifestyles. Their knowledge of inter-dependence can be increased by exploring areas such as tourism, trade and employment.

Local study should promote geographical skills such as using maps, following routes and graphicacy (interpreting and representing relationships). As part of a Young Geographer's Project, one teacher worked with Year 5 pupils to produce a long 'jour-ney stick' style map with a series of photographs to which children added comments on their return to school. Photographs were taken of any features that interested the group (**www.geography.org.uk/projects/younggeographers/resources/stpeters**). By applying these skills in real-life contexts, pupils develop their locational knowledge and raise awareness of local issues, for example the challenge for park keepers to maintain a clean, interesting and attractive environment in different seasons.

In walking around the park, pupils should consider design features such as kiosks, performance space, paths, benches, statues and playground. They should record how these are being used. Pupils can produce a photographic log of features and later in the classroom arrange these, highlighting the location on a map, writing or describ-ing suitable captions. They can also use digital photographs to produce a timeline of their day, such as 'We passed this shop on the right at 9:30 am' or 'This is the door to the museum, which we entered at 10:00 am'. The photographs can be sorted into groups to introduce the basic concept of land use, for instance those showing homes, shops, places of worship and offices. Comparisons can be drawn using pictures such as 'holiday snaps', Google images or postcards, showing other settlements in Britain and around the world. Affective or emotional maps, where pupils record their feelings about a place, are a useful means of visually expressing pupils' responses to school and other local environments (Tanner, 2009). Their use also empowers children to consider what action is necessary to improve 'negative' places. Potter and Scoffham (2006) discuss a case study of a boy with autistic spectrum difficulties whose map of the school was almost entirely 'sad' aside from the school office 'where everyone just keeps smiling at me'; the pupil was able to relate the experiences that lay behind his feelings.

Religious starting points

From a religious perspective, local study enables pupils to increase their awareness of different religions, beliefs, values and traditions. This can be achieved through the following means:

- exploring children's sense of belonging as members of local groups and clubs;
- organising regular local walks, pointing out how the environment should be cared for;
- listening and responding to visitors from local and wider faith communities;
- arranging visits to different places of worship, and focusing on the impact these have in the local community;
- understanding the role of local religious leaders;
- considering the feelings of other people at home, in the local community and in different parts of the world;
- visiting old people's homes to promote the value of giving;

- investigating local acts of neighbourliness, for instance by scanning newspapers; and
- telling stories about saints and religious figures associated with local churches.

As McCreery *et al.* (2008) point out, visiting speakers do not need to be members of the clergy – the best visitors are often parents, grandparents or other teachers. Visitors should not be asked to pray with children and the teacher should, if necessary, reassure parents with different beliefs that the session is purely educational while respecting their right to withdraw their children from the lesson.

Places of worship

It is important for learners to recognise that there may be a range of different places of worship within their local community, as any perusal of a telephone directory will reveal.

In areas where there are one or two predominant religions, it is just as important for pupils to think about why this might be and how they can learn about other faiths. It is likely that any class visits to places of worship will occur outside times for worship and there is a danger that children see and recall their emptiness rather than their vibrancy; hence the importance of liaising closely with the respective faith representative who may be able to provide photographs, artefacts, sound recordings or other sources. In any event, teachers can access excellent online guidance on preparation and etiquette when visiting places of worship for the six major faiths. In some areas, faith trails have been set up to introduce walkers to the history, beliefs and key locations of different faiths. In Bolton this covers 16 places of worship within a nine-mile zone (see Figure 5.3). Primary school children can create their own local faith walks on a much smaller scale.

Churches are arranged with increasing degrees of holiness. The churchyard wall stood as a boundary and in medieval times those that passed inside it entered a protected area where criminals could not be arrested. The church itself is divided into particular areas.

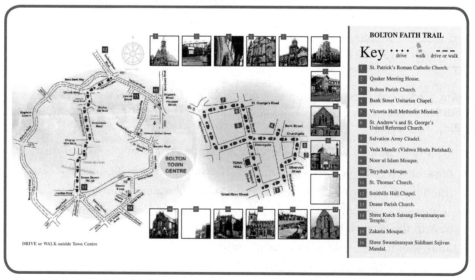

Figure 5.3 Bolton Faith Trail. *Source:* Bolton Interfaith Council www.boltoncommunity.co.uk/sei/s/911/f1.pdf.

The nave, the main body of the building, is where the congregation worships. Beyond this up a few steps lies the chancel, usually containing choir stalls. Next, the sanctuary is set aside for the priests and their attendants. This area is often separated from the chancel by an arch and altar rail. Within the sanctuary itself lies the altar. Behind this, in Roman Catholic churches, is the tabernacle – regarded as one of the most holy places. Some schools use churches and other places of worship to hold assemblies in an effort to convey the distinctive atmosphere of worship. Ofsted (2008b: 11) reports:

> In [one] school, in the face of some parental opposition, the headteacher felt it was extremely important to continue taking pupils each year to a mosque because simply being in that place contributed much to the pupils' understanding of Islam. It also helped to promote community cohesion.

Visits to churches and other places of worship can include on-site activities such as:

- looking for and labelling architectural features;
- noting language on tombstones;
- drawing sketch plans and elevations;
- estimating and measuring; and
- discussion on personal responses (e.g. how does the place make you feel?).

Following such experiences, pupils can devise questions for future visits. The following are examples of questions from nine and ten-year-olds who visited a mosque (Barnett *et al.*, 1987: 109):

Religious buildings	What do you call the building where you meet?
	How often is your building full?
Religious leaders	What do you call a leader in your religion?
	What does your work involve?
	Why did you become a religious leader?
Clothes and food	Do you wear special clothes at any time?
	Is there any food that you do not eat?
Special days	What are the names of your special festivals?
	What day do you normally meet?
Holy book	What is your holy book called?
	Who wrote it?
	How often do you read it?
	What language is it written in?
Prayers	Do you believe in one God?
	What is the name of your God?
	Do you have a special prayer?
	Do you teach children to pray?

Churches and other places of worship have a rich symbolism, conveyed for instance through numbers, colours and shapes. In Christendom, the cross is the major symbol, although historically it pre-dates Christianity – the ancient Egyptians had an ankh and the Indians a Swastika. Five, being the number of fingers on each hand and toes on each foot, clearly has had considerable significance since time immemorial; in Christian tradition '5' stands for the five wounds that Jesus suffered during his crucifixion while the number '7' represents perfection. Colours can have special meaning – green is the colour of life and growth while black symbolises sickness, death and mourning.

There are many time-markers within churches and churchyards that can help children develop a sense of chronology. Aside from gravestones, the time span covered by old trees can be recorded on timelines and compared with other 'natural' markers, such as the lifetime of bats and other wildlife. Prosser (1982) used a 600-year-old yew tree in a local churchyard as a 'living link' to the time of Henry V and the Battle of Agincourt – local archers participated and he speculated with the children as to whether the bows were made from the local yew. Church architectural features, such as wall paintings, windows and bell towers, also serve as discussion points.

Planning and managing a local study

Like any other unit of work, when planning a local study consideration should be given to intended learning outcomes, the allocation of resources, group organisation, assessment opportunities and health and safety matters. The schemes of work formerly provided by the DfES-run standards website (now hosted at the National Archives) include examples for local study. Excellent guidance is also available through some local authorities and professional bodies such as the Geographical Association. For instance, the Essex Grid for Learning includes support modules, for its Religious Education Agreed Syllabus, on 'The Local Anglican Parish Church' and 'Christianity in the local community' (**www.e-gfl.org**).

Principles for planning and managing local study are as follows:

- Start with familiar surroundings (i.e. the school and its grounds), moving 'outwards' to the surrounding streets and wider locality;
- Draw upon children's experiences (e.g. what they see on their way to school, where they shop, where they live, where they play games);
- Choose a focused rather than a broad subject (e.g. the High Street) rather than the whole village or town;
- Try to personalise local studies (e.g. by exploring what happened to a particular family in the past, or making use of local speakers to convey particular viewpoints);
- Frame the study with clear questions (e.g. What do we already know about the area? What is it famous for? What do we want to find out? What jobs do people do? What recreation is available? How has our locality changed? How is it different from . . . ? What might it be like in the future?);
- Involve the pupils in the planning, 'doing' (investigating) and reviewing stages;
- Take opportunities to compare and contrast the locality with other areas (e.g. by drawing upon pupils' holiday experiences);

- Acknowledge diversity within the locality (e.g. different viewpoints relating to a particular issue);
- Avoid stereotypes (e.g. teachers in our school during Victorian times were cruel and strict);
- Always set the local study in context (e.g. by considering the wider national picture);
- Identify and build upon key vocabulary (e.g. create glossaries, dictionaries and 'word walls');
- Use a range of stimulating sources including maps, artefacts, aerial photographs and memories;
- Emphasise the opportunities pupils have to add to our knowledge and understanding by undertaking unique research;
- Plan to develop enquiry skills including: observing, collecting, analysing sources, evaluating issues and synthesising information;
- Provide opportunities for first-hand visits to libraries, local museums and galleries;
- Build up a network of useful local contacts (e.g. librarians, curators, ministers, local historical society);
- Integrate information and communication technologies throughout the study (e.g. set up an ongoing database to record findings from surveys); and
- At the outset consider the intended 'product' outcomes (e.g. a school anniversary poster, a book about 'special people in our area', materials for a website or an exhibition at a local library).

Selecting the focus for local study will be influenced by curriculum requirements, staff expertise, the availability and accessibility of resources, time and the costs of planned visits. The locality offers so many possible content areas within the natural and human environments (see Figure 5.4). The natural environment, arising from the interaction of the earth's physical features and processes, creates diverse landscapes from dense woodlands to rocky seashores. The built environment is equally varied, from Victorian terraces to isolated farming communities. Other human environments result from social and cultural activities such as cooperative societies, Sunday schools and festivals.

Curriculum requirements

Local study is a common feature to the curricula throughout the UK, although teachers have considerable flexibility in choosing the content. The curriculum in England is under review at the time of writing, but the locality has been a longstanding feature of primary history, geography and religious education. In Wales, in Key Stage 2 history teachers can opt for a long-term study of changes in education or the history of a local castle or church, or a short-term study of one important event such as the effect of a war on the locality. In the Northern Ireland primary curriculum, the locality is integrated within four strands (interdependence, movement and energy, place and change over time) that make up the *World Around Us* (one of the seven areas of learning). In Scotland's *Curriculum for Excellence* (Scottish Executive, 2005), there is a strong local thread to social studies experiences and outcomes.

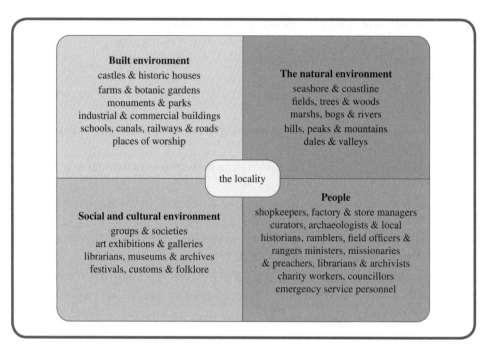

Figure 5.4 Dimensions of local study.

TASK

- Research the requirements for teaching about the locality in 'knowledge and understanding of the world' within the Early Years.

Enquiry-based learning

Local study is an ideal context for enquiry-based learning (EBL), which has a long tradition in the primary school under different guises such as 'discovery learning' (DES, 1967; Rowland, 1984). Although EBL is defined in different ways, the emphasis is on children asking questions, purposeful talk, working together, selecting and interpreting sources, outdoor learning and developing a line of enquiry. Successful EBL should not only develop pupils' local knowledge, thinking skills and respect for the environment, but also enable them to show responsibility, independence and an eagerness to find out more. The 'S' model (see Figure 5.5) highlights the key elements in good enquiry at all levels. A clear structure is necessary to make most effective use of time and resources. The skill of selecting carefully what information is needed should be taught from an early age. Discussion and modelling exercises can help learners choose the right questions to explore and frame a realistic line of enquiry within the time available. Hence a local study needs a sharp focus, building on what learners already know.

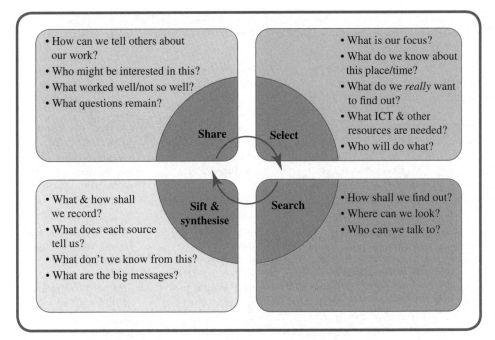

Figure 5.5 The S model – a simplified planning tool for local enquiries. *Source*: Russell Grigg.

Questions, sources and approaches – an example of exploring a street

A topic such as 'Our Street' offers a wealth of learning opportunities in the humanities (see Table 5.2) and has proven popular in the primary school for many years (Clear, 1987; Wood, 1994). Ideally, a chosen street would contain residential houses, a place of worship, public buildings and commercial premises, drawn from different periods of history. It should be easily accessible on foot during visits. The physical and social development of street life is well captured in Millard's beautifully illustrated *A Street Through Time* (Dorling Kindersley, 1998). Readers can see the importance of the river in the story, of a street spanning thousands of years, from supplying clean water and fresh fish for a camp of nomadic hunter-gatherers to bringing new trade to the village, then town and finally city.

For centuries, streets have attracted the interest of social observers – largely because they have witnessed the full range of human experience, including:

- cultural events (e.g. carnivals, musical performances and art exhibitions);
- political expressions (e.g. protests, riots and election campaigns);
- religious occasions (e.g. prayer meetings, preaching activities and Sunday school parades);
- social gatherings (e.g. parties and coffee mornings); and
- commercial activities (e.g. street markets and illicit activities such as drug deals).

Table 5.2 Possible learning opportunities in humanities for 'Our Street'

Historical	Geographical	Religious	Social
• Study change over time using a range of primary sources (e.g. census returns, old maps, photographs). • Interview elderly residents. • Explore the meaning behind street names, shop signs, plaques and signposts. • Investigate history of particular buildings. • Construct a timeline of the street. • Take photographs of historic street furniture and research their usefulness. • Read stories of famous people or landmarks in the street.	• Identify natural and physical features using Ordance Survey maps, fieldwork, aerial photographs. • Investigate the story of products sold by street traders and services. • Map the distribution of litter and litter bins. • Locate and chart the different kinds of buildings. • Chart the different materials used in builings. • Explore the pattern and layout of streets. • Photograph and compare different shop facscias. • Study local weather patterns. • Classify different kinds of streets in locality (main, intermediate and service roads). • Compare streets from around the world. • Conduct traffic surveys. • Map the street for land use. • Classify street furniture (e.g. those for drivers and pedestrians) for different services.	• Study sources such as religious artefacts and symbols in the street. • Devise a faith trail. • Visit places of worship on the street. • Reflect upon the messages behind street monuments such as war memorials. • Discuss how streets make people feel e.g. safe, fearful, angry, cool. • Explore the work of missionaries, 'Big Issue' and charities such as Oxfam to rescue people from the streets (e.g. street gangs).	• Debate issues affecting the school grounds and building. • Conduct surveys to gain insights into people 's views on social issues such as pedestrianisation. • Find out about the council's approach to sustainability (e.g. reduction of carbon footprint through cycle paths). • Compare the work of different street artists including the use of graffiti. • Organise a social event for the community. • Interview local councillors, charity workers and ministers about issues such as homelessness, vandalism and litter. • Pose questions for debate (e.g. Are street musicians a nuisance?).

Streets matter because they are not only places to live, work and shop, but they have a strong psychological hold on people's lives. The Catholic historian Paul Johnson (2004: 50) remembers, as a child of the 1930s, Primitive Methodists preaching on street corners and singing hymns, leaving him to ask: 'Were they really "primitive", something I associated with 'natives' in Africa, who wore paint (and) carried spears?' There are many local library publications that explain the origin and development of streets; for instance Leslie and Leslie's (2003) account of 100 streets in central Newcastle and Horton's (2002) thematic approach to street names in Liverpool.

Hitchcock and Shore's (2002) comprehensive study of London streets raises questions such as 'How did you find your way in a badly mapped London without formal addresses?' and 'Has the London cabbie changed at all?'

Fieldwork

The most effective studies of streets include regular fieldwork experiences. Children need to build up a picture of a street by taking photographs, interviewing residents, carrying out surveys and examining buildings. When children walk along a street it is important that they are encouraged to explore at different levels (see Figure 5.6). Looking above, they can take note of the height of houses, any chimneys, the shape and style of the windows and doors. At ground level children can also look out for inspection covers for fire hydrants, sewers and coal holes. The latter can be found

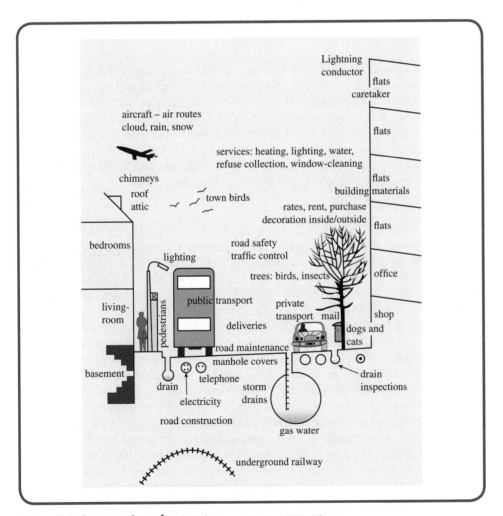

Figure 5.6 **Cross-section of a street.** *Source*: Waters, (1982: 76).

Photo 5.3 Composite collections of street signs. *Source:* R. Grigg.

in the pavements outside Victorian houses that had cellars under the road (Warren, 1978). The key point is for children is to see how such furnishings relate to people's lives. Hence coal was tipped through the coal-hole covers into cellars at a time when coal was a major source of household fuel. The covers were no more than a foot in diameter to prevent easy entry for a burglar. Street signs can be used as a basis for discussions over the management of traffic (see Photo 5.3). Street jewellery can be seen in many museums, such as the Black Country Living Museum, Blists Hill Victorian Town and Beamish, North of England Open Air Museum.

Sources

Any investigation of place requires an understanding of source material. For those teachers with a keen interest in local history, there are many first-rate guides (Stephens, 1994; Lord, 1999; Carter and Thompson, 2005; Andrews, 2007). There are also comprehensive guides to family history, which often has close associations with local study (Barratt, 2008). Sources can be difficult to trace, partial in nature and very time-consuming to collate. Many are not in a form accessible to young children, or require sophisticated re-working and interpretation. Put simply, primary sources need to be handled with care. Historical records were not intended for study in the classroom. Moreover, especially with the advent of the Internet, the indiscriminate collection of sources can leave the researcher overwhelmed. Nonetheless, sources – whether historical, geographical or religious in nature – form the backbone of local study. There are many sources related to a study of streets and the locality in general (see Table 5.3).

Nineteenth- and twentieth-century street scenes can be found for all towns and cities in published photographic histories. Teachers can access extensive online collections of old photographs, such as the evocative Victorian London street scenes of John Thompson (**www.victorianlondon.org**). Thompson described characters such as 'Cast-Iron Billy' who, for over 40 years, worked 14-hour shifts as an omnibus driver in the streets of London (Thompson, 1877). Local photographs are an excellent historical source, shedding light not only on the physical layout of streets but also on

Table 5.3 Notes on some of the main sources for a study of streets—most are available in county record offices or libraries

Sources	Contents
Maps	There are many different kinds of maps. Ordnance Survey maps show the development of the street and area since the nineteenth century, raising questions about changes in employment, origin of street names, disappearance of buildings and changes in land use. Earlier maps, including those of Christopher Saxton (1542–1611) and John Speed (1552–1629), show the layout of Tudor and Stuart towns.
Buildings	The buildings along a street can include shops, places of worship, schools, theatres and houses. Each will have its own historical and geographical context. Household records include inventories listing furniture and utensils. School records include logbooks, punishment ledgers and admission registers.
Illustrations	Photographs, most dating from the 1860s, often contain street images. They are very good for 'then' and 'now' discussions relating to changes in the street over time. Oblique photographs are taken at angles less than 90 degrees to the ground. They are taken by a photographer through the window of an aeroplane. They enable pupils to identify physical features while the front of buildings can still be seen. Aerial photographs are taken from immediately overhead, using a camera fixed to the underside of an aeroplane, pointing directly downwards at 90 degrees to the ground. Before the age of photography, prints and drawings were the main visual sources. More recently, films and videos have become available.
Transport records	The maintenance of roads produced many records such as those belonging to Turnpike Trusts, which were responsible for the upkeep and improvement of highways.
Travel writers' accounts	Early traveller accounts include Daniel Defoe's *A Tour Through the Whole Island of Great Britain* (1724–6). Local record offices may hold examples of diaries and journey descriptions.
Newspapers	Informative about events such as street markets, street parades, social events (e.g. races) and advertisements of local shops in street. Key source for news of the day, major events, local stories, prices, crime, births, marriages and deaths. Most libraries keep old newspapers on microfilm with some indexes depending on the newspaper and the library. The British Newspaper Library at Colindale, north London, is the major repository of British and Irish newspapers.
Street furniture	Furniture belonging to the street represents tangible links to the past. These items are also a means of developing spatial awareness by exploring their location in relation to buildings. Furniture such as red telephone boxes have become part of Britain's identity.
Trade directories	Identify property owners, names of shopkeepers, list of various tradesmen and brief descriptions of villages/towns such as times of street markets. Useful for comparing occupational change by using trade directories over a long period, such as 50 years.
Census returns	From 1841–1911, these provide details of people who lived in a street including age, gender, birthplace and occupation. Possible to trace who lived in street from one census to the next. Key source for a study of population statistics, trades/occupations, living conditions and demographics. Census records are closed for 100 years.

(Continued)

Table 5.3 (Continued)	
Sources	Contents
People's memories	Oral or spoken history provides valuable information about the lives of ordinary citizens, often neglected in standard histories. Older people may recollect street parties, particular traders and changes to shopping.
Court records	Petty session records include details of criminal prosecutions such as drunk and disorderly conduct in the street, or theft from a shop. The modern equivalent is the magistrates' court.
Postcards	First sent in 1870, postcards had become very popular by the 1920s, regarded as 'the phone call of the early part of the [twentieth] century' (Phillips, 2000: 13). Delivery was very quick, with up to five deliveries a day and it was not uncommon to find messages written at lunchtime to say that the writer would be home late for tea.

the human condition – for instance Scottish children are shown with bare feet and bent legs as a result of rickets (Smout, 1986). Newspapers and other contemporary journalist accounts provide a wealth of information about street life. Journalist Henry Mayhew recorded the diversity of poor street traders in *London Labour and the London Poor* (1851–62). He divided street people into six categories: sellers, buyers, finders, performers, working pedlars and labourers. Mayhew includes portraits of 'untouchables' such as scavengers, street sweepers and London nightmen who collected waste. He goes further than most by drawing outcasts from *beneath* the streets, such as the riverside mud larks, sewer ratcatchers and cesspool cleaners. Teachers can use extracts as a basis for discussions about moral issues such as poverty, charity and child labour (Volume 1 is available online at the University of Virginia Library's website, **etext.lib. virginia.edu/toc/modeng/public/MayLond.html**).

Social issues such as homelessness can be introduced through stories based on street life. For instance, Berlie Doherty's award-winning novel *The Street Child* (HarperCollins, 1995) is a fictionalised account of Jim Jarvis, the child that Dr Barnardo cited as the reason for opening his first home for children. The BBC has produced an audio pack to accompany the story (**www.bbc.co.uk/schoolradio/ english/streetchild.shtml**). These stories have resonance today. According to UN sources, there are approximately 150 million street children in the world. In terms of global citizenship, teachers can use resources produced by many charities, denominations and governments seeking to improve life for street children, such as UNESCO's Programme for the Education of Children in Need, which uses dance, music, sports, circus and art to 'rescue' children.

Libraries

There has been very little research in the UK on the impact of public libraries on pupils' learning. International evidence suggests pupils' reading attainment improves when there are close working relationships between librarians and teachers (Williams *et al.*, 2002).

These can take various forms including: electronic network links (such as a shared catalogue); book talks by public library staff at the school; homework alerts to the public library; referral of more complex reference questions from the school library; bulk loan of books and other resources from the public library. In the UK, innovative schemes have included storytellling librarians, who visited parks, housing estates and other community settings to share folk tales (Hill, 1973). More recently, the School Library Association advertises major events such as World Book Day, conferences and initiatives, such as the British Library's request in November 2011 for stories about playground games from the past (**www.sla.org.uk/index.php**). Pupils should also make regular and productive use of their class and school libraries. The Chartered Institute of Library and Information Professionals (CILIP) has produced helpful guidelines for primary school libraries (CILIP, 2002) covering the selection of resources, budgets, organisation, creating the right environment, teaching information literacy and judging success. In general, pupils need to exercise ownership of their library in terms of design, choice of books and how it operates (Bakewell, 2010).

For the humanities, many libraries hold local studies collections containing a range of primary or first-hand sources. These include: photographs, maps, census returns and newspapers (see Table 5.3). Birmingham holds one of the largest collection of nineteenth-century topographical photographs in the world – including the Francis Frith collection. Many local studies libraries also publish colourful and informative leaflets and newsletters.

County record offices/archives

Archives are collections of documents, manuscripts or other primary evidence, although the term is often used to describe the building in which they are housed. Many archives welcome young researchers if accompanied by an adult. There are strict rules relating to the handling of materials because they are often unique and irreplaceable. Archive sources such as census returns, maps and diaries can be an excellent springboard for geography, citizenship, mathematics and creative writing. The thrill of discovering something personal, such as an ancestor's school record, remains the greatest attraction of visiting archives. Most archives allow photocopying of records and in some cases visitors can take digital photographs of sources. Increasingly, source material is being made available online, for instance at the National Archives, which also offers comprehensive support materials for teachers and lists collections of archive material at local studies libraries (**www.nationalarchives.gov.uk/nra/default.asp**). The Scottish Archive Network includes an education microsite containing a guide to sources (**www.scan.org.uk/**). Kitching (1996) provides a concise and readable overview of archives while Coulston and Crawford (1995) focus on their educational potential. The ARCHON Directory includes contact details for record repositories in the UK (**www.nationalarchives.gov.uk/archon**).

Other repositories

The websites for the Royal Commission on Ancient and Historical Monuments in the UK include aerial photographs and other sources, along with guidance for teachers. Coflein (from the Welsh *cof*, 'memory', and *lein*, 'line'), is the online database for the National Monuments Record of Wales (NMRW), the national collection of information about the historic environment of Wales (**www.coflein.gov.uk**). Similar facilities are available for other parts of the UK. The Archaeology Data Service (ADS) supports research, learning and teaching with high-quality and dependable digital resources (**http://ads.ahds.ac.uk**). Its website includes an image bank covering the whole of the UK, from stone circles at Beaghmore (County Tyrone) to a Second World War pillar box overlooking Meadowsfoot Beach (Devon).

Street games, traffic and furniture

Exploring memories of street games is a rich source for local study. The street is one of the oldest play-places in the world – a source of perennial fun. The Opies (1969) found 2,500 names for street games played by children in England, Scotland and Wales during their research in the 1950s and 1960s. Teachers themselves, especially those over the age of 40, will recollect playing games on the streets or in the field without fear or restriction. As Kelleher (2007: 9) asks: 'Today's 8-year-old can dance, swim and may even speak a second language. But can they play hopscotch?' In reality, folklorists show that concerns about the decline of play are not new. In the nineteenth century, commentators blamed regimented national schools and the railways; in the twentieth century, it was the turn of the cinema, radio and gramophone; the twentieth-century scapegoats include comics, television and computer games (Bishop and Curtis, 2001). Many traditional games, rather than dying out, have been modified and relocated away from streets.

Able-bodied children and adults can take for granted the relative ease of moving around modern-day streets. Before the development of tarmac in the early twentieth century, roads constructed of limestone produced clouds of dust in the summer and ditches full of water in the winter (Reid, 2005). Prior to the development of gas (1803) and then electric street lighting, in most European towns and cities it was possible to hire linkboys, who would carry links (torches) to help pedestrians find their way around dark streets. In some communities they were nicknamed 'moon cursers' because they cursed the moonlight for damaging their trade. Wealthy families had their own footmen, who carried lanterns as they trotted alongside coaches, while one London tradesman taught his dog to carry a lantern in its mouth (Ekirch, 2005). In the absence of light, smells acted as invisible signposts – ranging from the fragrance of a honeysuckle bush to the stench of a dunghill – to aid individuals find their way around. A change of pavement level also alerted pedestrians to their location and it was common for individuals to use canes and staffs to feel the street ahead. Fanny Boscawen, an eighteenth-century aristocrat, developed a fear of going out at night when she was 'forced to walk gropingly like a blind man' (Ekirch, 2005: 134). Darkened streets in the pre-modern age were associated with thieves, murderers and evil spirits. Even in the daylight, streets could be dangerous places. Police and court records fascinate children, though teachers need to exercise some caution in selecting extracts, given the nature of some crimes; prostitution was a major street problem in many towns. In Bristol, police diaries described Victorian policemen walking on the beat encountering beggars, drunkards and rival football fans (Reid, 2005)!

Children's social skills can be promoted by arranging opportunities to interview elderly residents about their street memories. Teachers can also draw upon local biographies. Daiches (1957), a Scottish Jew, recalled his childhood streets in Edinburgh:

> A horse-drawn cart . . . the rattle of early morning milk-traps or the heavy clatter of vans drawing cases of Leitch's lemonade or Dunbar's mineral waters or sacks of coal along the uneven Melville Terrace. A chalk mark in the street brings back the girls playing 'peevers' on the Edinburgh pavements, or skipping to the traditional chants. And the traditional chanting of Hebrew prayers brings back the Meadows . . . and the old synagogue in Graham Street (pulled down over twenty years ago) with its mixed congregation of Yiddish-speaking immigrants and native-born Edinburgh Jews with their strong Edinburgh accent even in the singing of Hebrew hymns.
>
> *(Cited by Lownie, 2004: 188)*

Such memories open up powerful discussion points on social change, identities, and tradition. Buildings that have long vanished can be traced on local maps and plans.

Many streets will have monuments and statues to commemorate local landowners, generals, monarchs, writers and engineers (Darke, 1991). They also represent particular trades associated with the area, such as the Burton Cooper in Burton-on-Trent. Memorials can be powerful reminders of a troubled past, such as the street plaques and murals in Belfast (Viggiani, 2006; see **http://cain.ulst.ac.uk/viggiani/introduction.htm**). Few communities were unaffected by the two World Wars and the local war memorial is an important resource in addressing the question 'What are we remembering on Remembrance Day?' There are 36,000 First World War memorials in Britain alone, representing a 'massive and unprecedented outpouring of national grief' for the loss of a million or so men (Oliver, 2005: xi). These are the more prominent items of 'street furniture', but consideration should also be given to the more mundane structures such as post boxes, telephone kiosks and traffic lights. All of these determine the identity of a square, street or town. Nineteenth-century public water pumps were essential even though, as Warren (1978) points out, in some rural areas they could be a quarter of a mile away from houses, forcing some to use polluted river waste for cooking and washing. Van Effulen (2010) describes street furniture as the 'secret star of urban outdoor design', pointing out how benches, fountains and even rubbish bins make a significant contribution to the urban experience. Baglee and Morley (2006) have published a fascinating collection of 2,500 street signs that were common throughout Britain (see also **http://streetjewellery.com**). Where possible, it is important to look at the stories behind street furniture and consider the impact for residents today. A series of questions can be posed, such as: Why were traffic lights invented? What benefits have they brought? How do they work?

Street safety

Street safety should form an important aspect of a school's planning for personal, social and health education. The Pedestrians Association (now Living Streets) was instrumental in bringing about the introduction of the driving test, pedestrian crossings and 30 mph (48 kph) speed limits. Throughout the UK, Living Streets now supports community empowerment, which it describes as 'local people taking control and deciding what they need for their area, rather than accepting things as the way they are' (Living Streets Scotland, 2009: 9). The charity produces a range of resources

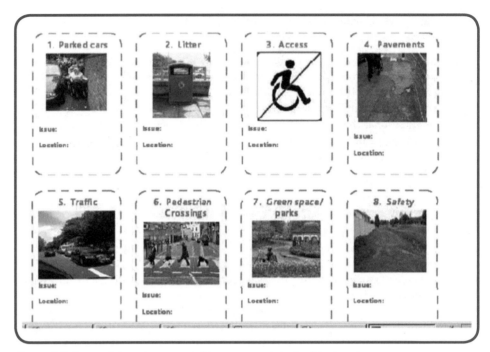

Figure 5.7 Potential environmental issues associated with streets. *Source*: Living Streets Scotland www.livingstreets.org.uk

to engage the community, including a toolkit to undertake an assessment of the local environment where main issues are identified (see Figure 5.7). Schools that have participated in street improvement projects have secured positive changes working alongside local councils.

A topic such as 'Our Street' illustrates the importance of making learning relevant, stimulating and enjoyable. Local study provides an ideal context for pupils to take increasing responsibility for their own learning. They can work with authentic materials, engage with real-life debates and focus on current 'live' issues.

Conclusion

One of the key dimensions to local study is focusing on what kind of *future* neighbourhood pupils would like to see. A futures perspective is critical to reframing the curriculum so that schools enable pupils to consider alternative futures, acknowledging cultural, economic, environmental and political influences. Several writers (Page, 2000; Hicks, 2001) highlight the 'missing' futures perspective in the curriculum and the right of pupils to explore their views on how they can contribute to making a just and sustainable future. The Transition Movement suggests that life without oil could be more enjoyable than people think and is committed to supporting local communities by moving away from dependency on fossil fuels, encouraging the growth of local food, sustainable homes and currency (**www.transitionnetwork.org**).

SUMMARY

- Local study has considerable educational potential as pupils engage with real environments.

- Begin local study by investigating the school and its grounds. Widen the study to the immediate area and neighbourhood.

- Contrast the locality to other areas in the UK and overseas.

- Historical experiences should include the stories behind local landmarks, events, customs and characters.

- Geographical experiences should focus on learning about the physical, environmental and human features of the locality.

- In religious education, pupils should learn about local places of worship and the impact these have on the community.

- In planning and managing a local study, teachers should have clear objectives in mind and consider carefully factors such as health and safety when taking pupils outdoors.

- Pupils should have opportunities to pursue lines of enquiry in their local study by visiting libraries, museums, galleries and archives.

- Topics such as 'Our Street' illustrate the kinds of questions, sources and approaches to local study. Pupils should gain first-hand experiences in developing fieldwork skills. They should learn how to interpret a range of written, oral and visual sources.

References

Andrews, J. (ed.) (2007), *Reader's Digest Local History Detective*, London: Reader's Digest Association.

Ashley, P. (2005), *Pastoral Peculiars*, London: English Heritage.

Ayto, J. and Crofton, I. (2005), *Brewer's Britain & Ireland*, London: Weidenfeld & Nicolson.

Baglee, C. and Morley, A. (2006), *The Art of Street Jewellery*, London: New Cavendish Books.

Bakewell, L. (2010), *Off the Shelf: How to Run a Successful Primary School Library and Promote Reading*, Stockport: Carel Press Ltd.

Barnett, V., Cole, O., and Erricker, C. (eds) (1987), *The Shap Handbook on World Religions in Education*, London: The Commission for Racial Equality.

Barratt, N. (2008), *Who Do You Think You Are?* London: HarperCollins.

Bennett, M. (2007), *Scottish Customs from the Cradle to the Grave*, Edinburgh: Birlinn (note spelling) Ltd.

Bilton, H. (2010), (3rd edn), *Outdoor Learning in the Early Years*, Abingdon: Routledge.

Bishop, J.C. and Curtis, M. (eds) (2001), *Play today in the primary school playground*, London: Open University Press.

Blyth, A. *et al.* (1976), *Place, Time and Society 8–13: Curriculum Planning in History, Geography and Social Science*, Bristol: Collins/ESL, Schools Council.

Boyle, B. (1987), *How Do We Know? Local Directories*, London: Collins Educational.

Cameron, K. (1996), *English Place Names*, London: Batsford.

Carter, R. (ed.) (1998), *Handbook of Primary Geography*, Sheffield: Geographical Association.

Carter, P. and Thompson, K. (2005), *Sources for Local Historians*, Chichester: Phillimore.

Catling, S. and Willy, T. (2009), *Achieving QTS. Teaching Primary Geography*, Exeter: Learning Matters.

CILIP (2002), *The Primary School Library Guidelines*, available at: **www.cilip.org.uk/Pages/default.aspx**.

Clear, K. (1987), *Investigating Local Streets and Shops*, Edinburgh: Nelson.

Clifford, S. and King, A. (2006), *England in Particular*, London: Hodder & Stoughton.

Coulston, I. and Crawford, A. (1995), *Archives in Education*, London: Public Record Office.

Daiches, D. (1957), *Two Worlds. An Edinburgh Jewish Childhood*, New York: Harcourt, Brace & Co.

Darke, J. (1991), *The MonumENt Guide to England and Wales*, London: Macdonald.

Day, B. (1998), *A Chronicle of Folk Customs*, London: Hamlyn.

Day, P. (2006), 'Transport Direct. Localities and their stops guidance', available at: **www.pti.org.uk/locality.htm**.

DCELLS (2008a), *Geography. Guidance for Key Stages 2 and 3*, Cardiff: Welsh Assembly Government.

DCELLS (2008b), *Framework for Children's Learning for 3 to 7-year-olds in Wales*, Cardiff: Welsh Assembly Government.

DCSF (2010), *Promoting community cohesion: the role of extended services*, Nottingham: DCSF.

DES (1967), *Children and their Primary Schools*: A Report of the Central Advisory Council for Education (England) (Plowden Report), London: HMSO.

Department of Education for Northern Ireland (DENI) (2006), *Outcomes of the Review of Pre-School Education for NI*, Belfast: DENI.

DfES (2006), *Learning Outside the Classroom Manifesto*, Nottingham: DfES.

DfES (2007), *Curriculum Guidance for the Foundation Stage*, London: DfES.

Dillon, J., Morris, M., O'Donnell, L., Rickinson, M. and Scott, W. (2005), *Engaging and Learning with the Outdoors,* Bath: Centre for Research in Environmental Education.

Doherty, B. (1995), *The Street Child,* London: HarperCollins.

Ekirch, A.R. (2005), *At Day's Close. A History of Nighttime*, London: Weidenfeld & Nicolson.

Fien, J., Scott W.A.H. and Tilbury, D. (2001), Education and Conservation: lessons from an evaluation, *Environmental Education Research* 7(4) 379–395.

Garick, R. (2009), *Playing Outdoors in the Early Years*, London: Continuum.

Gill, T. (2007), No Fear: *Growing Up in a Risk-averse Society*, London: Gulbenkian Foundation.

Gelling, M. (1997), *Signposts to the Past*, London: Phillimore.

Hadow Report (1931), *The Primary School*, London: HMSO.

Hannigan, D. (2006), *Eccentric Britain*, London: New Holland.

Harriman, H. (2008), *Outdoor Classroom: A Place to Learn,* Longwood: Red Robin Books.

Harris, M. (1971), *Environmental Studies*, London: Macmillan.

Hey, D. (1998), *The Oxford Companion to Local and Family History*, Oxford: Oxford University Press.

Hicks, D. (2001) *Citizenship for the Future: A practical classroom guide*, Godalming: World Wide Fund for Nature UK.

Hill, J. (1973), *Children Are People*, London: Hamish Hamilton.

Hitchcock, T. and Shore, H. (eds) (2002), *The Streets of London*, London: Rivers Oram Press.

HMI (1959), *Primary Education*, London: HMSO.

Honoré, C. (2005), *In Praise of Slow*, London: Orion.

Horton, S. (2002), *Street Names of the City of Liverpool*, Birkenhead: Countryvise Ltd.

Howarth, K. (1998), *Oral History: A Handbook,* Stroud: Sutton.

ILEA (1980), *History in the Primary School*, London: ILEA.

Jamison, C. (2006), *Finding Sanctuary: Monastic steps for Everyday Life*, London: Phoenix.

Johnson, P. (2004), The Vanished Landscape, London: Weidenfeld & Nicolson.

Kelleher, S. (2007), *The Games We Played*, London: English Heritage.

Kitching, C. (1996), *Archives the Very Essence of our Heritage*, Andover: Phillimore & Co.

Knight, S. (2009), *Forest Schools and Outdoor Learning in the Early Years*, London: Sage.

Learning through Landscapes (2003), *National School Grounds Survey,* Winchester, available at: http://www.ltl.org.uk/index.php

Leslie, J. and Leslie, J. (2003), *Down Our Streets: Newcastle's Street Names Explored*, Newcastle: Tyne Bridge Publishing.

Lewis, C. (1989), *Particular Places*, London: British Library.

Lines, C.J. and Bolwell, L.H. (1971), *Discovering Your Environment. History along Roads and Waterways*, London: Ginn & Company.

Living Streets Scotland (2009), *A Community Empowerment Toolkit*, Living Streets, available at: **www.livingstreets.org.uk/resources/**.

Lownie, R. (2004), *Auld Reekie. An Edinburgh Anthology*, London: Timewell Press.

Lord, E. (1999), *Investigating the Twentieth Century*, Stroud: Tempus.

McCreery, E., Palmer, S. and Voiels, V. (2008), *Achieving QTS. Teaching Religious Education*, Exeter: Learning Matters.

Millard, A. (1998), *A Street Through Time*, London: Dorling Kindersley

Milner, A., Jewson, T. and Scoffham, S. (2004), 'Using the School locality', in Scoffham, S., *Primary Geography Handbook*, Sheffield: Geography Association.

Ofsted (2008a), *Geography in schools: changing practice*, London: Ofsted.

Ofsted (2008b), *Learning Outside the Classroom*, London: Ofsted.

Oliver, N. (2005), *Not Forgotten*, London: Hodder & Stoughton.

Opie, P. and Opie, I. (1969), *The Lore and Language of Children*, Oxford: Oxford University Press.

Owen, T.M. (1991), *A Pocket Guide to the Customs and Traditions of Wales*, Cardiff: University of Wales Press.

Owen, H.W. (1998), *A Pocket Guide to the Place names of Wales*, Cardiff: University of Wales Press.

Page, J. (2000), *Reframing the Early Childhood Curriculum: Educational imperatives for the future*, London: Routledge Falmer.

Pinnell, P.M. (1986), *Village Heritage*, Stroud: Alan Sutton.

Phillips, T. (2000), *The Postcard Century*, London: Thames and Hudson.

Potter, C. and Scoffham, S. (2006), 'Emotional maps', *Primary Geography*, Summer 2006, 20–21.

Prosser, P. (1982), *The World on Your Doorstep*, London: McGraw-Hill.

QCA (2002), *Geography at key stages 1 and 2,* Unit 8: Improving the environment, London: QCA.

Reaney, P.H. (1960), *The Origin of English Place Names*, London: Routledge and Kegan Paul.

Reid, H. (2005), *Life in Victorian Bristol*, Bristol: Redcliffe.

Rickinson, M. (2001) 'Learners and Learning in Environmental Education: a critical review of the evidence', in *Environmental Education Research* 7 (3), 207–320.

Rickinson, M., Dillon, J., Teamey, K., Morris, M., Young Choi, M., Sanders, D., Benefieldet, P. (2004), *Review of research on outdoor learning*, Shrewsbury: Field Studies Council.

Round, S. (2006), *The English Year*, London: Penguin.

Rowland, S. (1984*), The Enquiring Classroom*, London: Falmer Press.

Scoffham, S. (2002) 'Streets Worldwide', in Primary Geographer, 46, 8–9.

Scottish Executive (2005), *Curriculum for Excellence: Social Studies experiences and outcomes*, Edinburgh: Scottish Executive.

Smith, M.K. (1994), *Local Education*, Buckingham: Open University Press.

Smout, T.C. (1986), *A Century of the Scottish People*, London: Fontana.

Stephens, W.B. (1994), *Sources for English Local History*, Frome: Phillimore.

Tanner, J. (2009), 'Special Places: Place attachment and children's happiness', Primary Geography, Spring 2009, 5–8.

Timpson, J. (1989), *Timpson's Towns of England and Wales. Oddities and Curiosities*, Norwich: Jarrold Colour Publications.

Thompson, J. (1877), *Victorian London Street Life in Historic Photographs*, London: Sampson Low, Marston, Searle & Rivington, republished by Dover (1994), London: Dover Books.

Van Effulen, C. (2010), *Street Furniture*, Salenstein, Switzerland: Braun.

Viggiani, E. (2006), 'Public Forms of Memorialisation to the Victims of the Northern Irish "Troubles" in the City of Belfast', MA Dissertation, available at: **http://cain.ulst .ac.uk/viggiani/introduction.htm**.

Warren, (1978), *Street Furniture*, Newton Abbot: David and Charles.

Waters, D. (1982), *Primary School Projects*, London: Heinemann Educational Books.

Williams, D., Coles, L., and Wavell, C. (2002), *Impact of School Library Services on achievement and learning in primary schools*, London: The Council for Museums, Archives and Libraries.

Wood, R. (1994), *A Victorian Street*, Hove: Wayland.

Useful Websites

The Westminster Government's Learning Outside the Classroom website: **www.lotc.org.uk**.

Examples of local authority guidance for planning local studies include Hertfordshire at: **www.thegrid.org.uk/ learning/geography/ks1–2/resources**; and Cumbria at: **http://www.succeedingwithscience.com/resource. php?id=28**.

The Geography British Isles project aims to collect geographically representative photographs and information for every square kilometre of Great Britain and Ireland: **www.geograph.org.uk**.

The British Association of Local History includes suggestions for schools: **www.balh.co.uk/education.php**.

English Heritage 'Engaging Places' supports learning through buildings and places and includes primary school street investigation projects: **www.engagingplaces.org .uk/home**.

'Heritage Explorer' is a special site area from English Heritage with images for learning and other resources for teachers, including interactive whiteboard activities: **www .heritageexplorer.org.uk/web/he/default.aspx**.

A list of websites on 'Using the Locality' in Northern Ireland is available at: **www.nicurriculum.org.uk/docs/ key_stages_1_and_2/areas_of_learning/the_world_ around_us/using_the_locality.pdf**.

6 Making the most of our inheritance

The familiar landmarks, public halls, old pubs and houses . . . define the character of our streets . . . Losing these, through neglect and decay, changes the way a town, city or village looks for ever, and squanders its most valuable assets.

(Thurley, 2002: 38)

Wherever I go, I also hear about people rolling up their sleeves and getting involved, not content just to let events pass them by . . . Volunteers give up their time to help with conservation projects, to protect wildlife and preserve our heritage.

(Craven 2010: 283–4)

Learning objectives

By the end of this chapter you should be able to:

- explain the meaning of heritage;
- describe the varied nature of the historic environment;
- evaluate the importance of heritage education;
- reflect on ways of introducing heritage issues to pupils; and
- assess the contribution of museum learning.

Heritage and the historic environment

In some quarters, the heritage industry has been characterised as little more than tea towels, trinkets and buttered crumpets in a National Trust café. But in its widest sense, heritage applies to what has been passed down from earlier generations (see Figure 6.1). It includes the physical environment of buildings and artefacts, the natural environment, the local park, river, canal or commons, cultural traditions

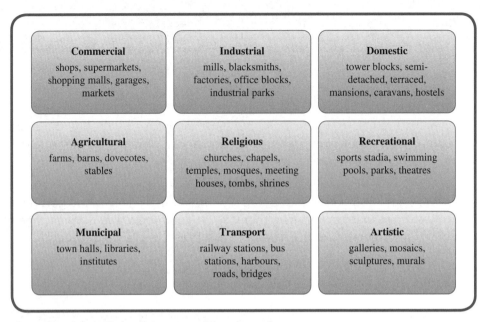

Figure 6.1 Our built heritage – possible categories.

and shared memories. Smith (2007: 1) argues that heritage is not only about the past or material things but also about people connecting with each other, 'making meaning in and for the present'. Family heirlooms, such as jewellery, watches, photographs, toys or household utensils, take on added significance when they are discussed, stories shared and feelings invoked. Such emotional investment is powerful in shaping not only how we see ourselves but also our relationships with others. Bourdillon (1994) prefers to use the term 'inheritances' rather than 'heritage' because this is seen as a more precise and helpful term for teachers. It reflects the inheritances of individuals, groups and families, as well as the more general shared inheritance of Britain.

Most people associate heritage with the historic environment. Officially this covers commercial and industrial buildings, historic houses, archaeological findings, country houses, gardens, townscapes and ecclesiastical buildings (House of Commons, 2006: 7). Houses are the most common form of building in history, 60 per cent of which were built before the twentieth century (Newman, 2001). This includes impressive town houses and 'set piece' country estates, originally built as displays of wealth and now in many cases major tourist attractions.

The UK has an extraordinary rich heritage considering its size. It has world-class museums and galleries, breathtaking landscapes and a wonderfully diverse built environment. Few schools are not within reach of heritage trails, folk museums, converted warehouses, old working farms, medieval churches, country parks or historic houses. It is claimed that the UK has the most varied built environment in the world – there are more interesting buildings per square mile here than anywhere else on the planet (Wilkinson and Ashley, 2006). Schools have a key role in raising children's awareness of their heritage, for instance by getting them involved in local conservation projects and taking advantage of the many excellent heritage services available.

Historic houses

The Historic Houses Association (HHA) represents 1,500 privately owned castles, houses and gardens throughout the UK. Around 300 of these are open to the general public and attract around 14 million visitors a year including 400,000 children and young people. The HHA has its own Learning Advisory Service with details of services such as costumed interpreters. There is a danger of children seeing country houses as a thing of the past, specifically pre-1914, when they started to decline with the passing of the resident servant. However, in many cases the present generation of owners have successfully shown that these remain living, vibrant homes. Chatsworth, Longleat and Woburn are three examples (Montgomery-Massingberd and Sykes, 2000). As well as homes for the rich, country houses were communities in which each estate employed dozens of workers – servants, gardeners, farm labourers, craftsmen and builders.

The UK's townscapes are composed of familiar buildings, such as schools, inns and town halls, which have been integral to everyday life in the past. Ordnance Survey maps are an excellent source to focus discussion about the location and prevalence of particular buildings, such as those designed for recreation. Pupils can use programmes such as Google street map when looking at their journey to school and they could even superimpose their own pictures. Photographs from local history publications and interviews with local residents are also essential sources to build up children's chronological awareness.

Castles

The Norman Conquest changed the UK landscape through the building of castles, cathedrals and abbeys. Around 2,000 castles or fortified residences were built in Britain between the eleventh and fifteenth centuries. The Normans also built more than 30 cathedrals and abbeys, of which St Albans, Durham and Norwich are the earliest. These expressed the Christian religion in a highly visual way. Unlike cathedrals, castles had more than one purpose. They served as defensive structures, comfortable homes for the elite, centres of regional administration and symbols of power and prestige. Fortresses such as the Tower of London represented the height of royal power, investment and domestic comforts. Others, such as Caerphilly castle, were pioneers in the latest military technology. The grandest castles were phenomenally expensive to build. The great tower at Dover, for example, absorbed between a quarter and a third of the king's annual budget (Morris, 2003: 60).

Castles are popular tourist attractions and are visited by thousands of school parties (see Figure 6.2). Teachers are well supported by the respective bodies charged with the care and preservation of castles. English Heritage has published excellent guidebooks and comprehensive educational resources for many of its castles. Cadw (the Welsh word for 'keep') is the organisation responsible for protecting the historic environment in Wales. It offers various services to schools including guided tours, interactive online resources, guidebooks and interpretation events.

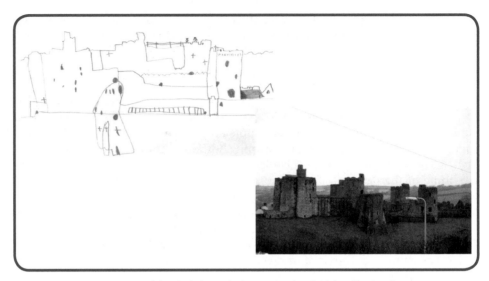

Figure 6.2 A seven-year-old's sketch and photograph of Kidwelly Castle (Carmarthenshire). *Source*: Mia Grigg

The National Grid for Learning Cymru includes online resources on castles and other aspects of Welsh heritage. Similarly, Historic Scotland cares for castles and provides learning resources including free publications, access to an online image bank and activity programmes for schools. The Northern Ireland Environmental Agency is responsible for protecting, conserving and promoting the country's natural environment and built heritage for the benefit of present and future generations. Its website includes informative castle guides (e.g. relating to Carrigfergus castle) and factsheets on subjects such as historic monuments of Down, wildlife gardening and natural heritage. The Ulster Architectural Heritage Society has also produced Key Stage 2 support materials for a study of castles in Ulster.

Pubs and inns

The story behind pub signs reveals a great deal about local and national heritage, including folklore, natural history, dialects, trades, industries, professions and sporting interests (Dunkling and Wright, 1987; Brandon, 2010). Pub sign-language originated during the Middle Ages, when most people were illiterate. Some names are popular in most parts of Britain and relate to national or international figures or events, such as the Duke of Wellington, the Queen Vic and Waterloo. Others are named after powerful local landowners or have links with important industries. Signs such as The Fleece, the Ram and the Woolpack remind us of the once prevalent woolen trade. Old pubs sometimes retain features such as mountain blocks to assist riders mounting a horse. Traditionally, inns differed from pubs because they offered accommodation. Today, 'inn' is often used by pubs as a punn – the old joke about Dew Drop Inn ('do drop in') has given rise to immitators such as Nip Inn, Dig Inn, Stagger Inn and Inn for a Penny. From the mid-seventeenth century, coaching inns were essential to Britain's transport system by offering fresh horses to stage and mail coaches, as well as a night's rest for travellers.

Industrial and commercial heritage

Many of the UK's oldest industrial buildings date back to the Industrial Revolution (*c*.1760–1840). These include mills, warehouses, canal locks, mines, towers, docks, piers and quaysides. In recent years, the subject of industrial heritage has been popularised by the efforts of Fred Dibnah (1938–2004), a former steeplejack from Bolton, whose achievements are commemorated by his own heritage centre. His biographer describes how Dibnah appealed to ordinary people by answering the most basic questions such as 'How the heck did they build that all that time ago?' and 'How did they manage to lift all that stone and wood up to such a great height?' (Hall, 2010: 6). Industry shaped the development of whole regions of the UK including: Cornwall's tin mining; cider-making in Somerset; brewing and pottery in Staffordshire; bobbin-making (cotton reels) in the Lake District; coal mining in south Wales and the north east of England; slate quarrying in north Wales; shipbuilding in Belfast; and whisky distilling in the Scottish highlands. There are excellent regional and national guides that explore such heritage (Bailey, 1982; Dibnah and Hall, 1999; Burton, 2002). There are also many industrial museums scattered throughout the UK, from one of the largest textile museums in the world at Armley Mills (Leeds) to the Irish Linen centre in Lisburn.

The UK's commercial heritage can be easily overlooked despite the material values that predominate in a consumer age. Many local banks, market halls and shops are steeped in history. On the national stage, the Bank of England, the Royal Mint and other financial institutions have excellent educational services. Similarly, major supermarket chains and household names such as Marks and Spencer, Tesco's and Sainsbury's have their own particular stories likely to engage pupils (Baren, 1997a; Baren 1997b). For example, teachers can access online sources and activities held at the Sainsbury Archive, which is part of the Museum in Docklands website (**www.museumindocklands.org.uk/English/Collections/CollectionsOnline/SainsburyArchive**). There are good opportunities here for teachers to develop pupils' financial skills. They can take advantage of current news, such as the 'credit crunch' or television series such as *'Turn Back Time: The High Street – 100 Years of British Life Through the Shop Window* (see also Wilkinson, 2010) as a means of making connections to retailing heritage. An obvious topic with young children is 'Our Shop' which opens up many opportunities for teachers to introduce concepts of historic change, continuity, values and fashion.

Maritime heritage

The British Isles possesses one of the most dramatic coastlines in the world comprising 6,289 islands. It is the third most populated island after Java in Indonesia and Honshu in Japan (Croker, 2009). No one in Britain lives more than 70 miles (113 kilometres) from the sea, and schools situated along the coastlines, from Cardigan Bay to the Wash, in particular should seek to raise children's awareness of their maritime heritage through local study. There are many aspects here that are fundamental to understanding particular communities: the fishing industry, the growth of seaside resorts, the creation of ports and harbours, smuggling, shipbuilding, quarrying, salt extraction, transport, defence, leisure and health (Gale, 2010). Networks such as the Coastal Communities Alliance provide online materials for the study of the past, present and future of seaside towns (**www.coastalcommunities.co.uk**). Footage from the BBC's popular television series *Coast* could illustrate many themes from Britain's 10,000 miles (16,000 kilometres) of coastline, including ground-breaking inventions, the stories of heroes and saints, villains and devils, and earth-shattering explosions (Somerville, 2006).

Similarly, schools in close proximity to a river should help learners appreciate its importance in shaping the locality. Rivers have been described as the secret routes to the nature, history and soul of the landscape (Rhys Jones, 2009). For many years a river study has been an integral feature of the geography curriculum at Key Stage 2 and teachers can benefit from considerable guidance and resources to conduct local river investigations (e.g. Edwards, 2006; Hibbert, 2005). Numerous local authorities provide online resources to support river studies. Typical fieldwork activities include surveying the rate of flow, measuring the river width and water depth, and using fresh water animals to determine water quality.

Sporting heritage

An important aspect of our national heritage is sporting traditions. The Victorians invented the rules and principles that underpin sport as we know it with the formation of bodies such as the Grand Caledonian Curling Club (1838), the Football Association (1863), the Rugby Football Union (1871) and the Gaelic Athletic Association (1884). Cycling became very popular in the 1890s, offering a liberating experience for women. Technological developments, such as the lawnmower and rollers, provided smooth playing surfaces and helped to promote sports like bowls, cricket, golf and lawn tennis. The growth of civilised sports corresponded with a decline in the more brutal pursuits such as cockfighting and prizefighting. The history of sport can be an excellent means of connecting with children's interests and a rich context for cross-curricular activities. Many premier league and championship football teams have excellent educational links to the community and proud traditions. These include Liverpool's 'Spion Kop' ('vantage point' in Afrikaans) association with the siege of Ladysmith in the Boer War. Manchester United's 'Busby Babes' (gifted young footballers, eight of whom died in a Munich air disaster in 1958) and Notts County, the world's oldest professional association football club, founded in 1862.

Religious heritage

The historic environment includes a wide range of ecclesiastical buildings, from imposing cathedrals and palaces to small chapels, church schools and monuments. Around 45 per cent of all Grade 1 (exceptional interest) listed buildings are places of worship – most of these are Church of England properties while others are Catholic parish churches, nonconformist chapels, Quaker meeting houses, synagogues, mosques, temples and gurdwaras. Many of the oldest buildings in communities are parish churches, of which an estimated 10 per cent are in need of urgent repair. Each one is unique, ranging from the tiny church at Bremilham (Wiltshire), which covers 12 square feet (3.6 square metres), located in a farmyard, to the huge Gothic church of St Mary Redcliffe in Bristol.

The decline in churches (since the 1960s, one church has closed each week) alongside the increase in the number of mosques (from seven in 1961 to 1,689 mosques in 2007) raises talking points for older pupils. Muslims now form the largest and most diverse religious minority in the UK, containing many smaller 'movements' and 'tendencies'. A number of organisations, such as the National Churches Trust, seek to stem the decline of Britain's church buildings. However, preserving church (and other historic) buildings is not a straightforward matter. In an increasingly secular society and in a climate of economic restraint, it is questioned whether this would be the most appropriate use of public funds. Edwards (2010) argues that this is to miss the community potential of these buildings, for instance serving as cafés, art galleries, mother and baby groups, and post offices, to supplement their role as places of worship.

A disappearing world?

One of the challenges for teachers is to convey to pupils the former vibrancy of religious life when visiting places of worship that are now attended by only a handful of worshippers. To begin with, churches should not be considered in isolation from the mostly anonymous parishioners that built, enlarged, decorated and maintained them. Local study of parish records and church architecture can shed light on the presence of the church in the life of the community. Even a cursory glance through nineteenth-century newspapers, school logbooks and charity reports will reveal the extent of voluntary good works, including the provision of free clothes and food for the poor, and the setting up of institutions such as ragged schools, almshouses and mission homes. The Victorian country parson created 'in and around his schools a form of community life completely unknown before in the countryside' (Tindall Hart, 1959: 48). The more conscientious parsons visited the sick, held evening schools, and chased up school absentees. In urban communities, local historians have shown the importance of the network of churches in addressing social problems and promoting the public good, such as Gorsky's (1999) study of charitable bodies in Bristol. The churches and chapels proved a focal point for social gatherings that brought communities together, the highlights of which were the tea parties, Sunday school outings, the Band of Hope and anniversary celebrations. Horn (1999: 245) points out: 'Preparations went on for months and it was an occasion for wearing new clothes, reciting specially learnt passages before parents and friends, listening to music and marching in procession through town or village'.

On such occasions young people could be steered away from the dangers of gambling, playing games on the Sabbath and drinking, towards more wholesome recreation such as walks, train journeys and embroidery. Ernest Haire remembered his Sunday experiences in the 1900s:

> We went to morning service and evening service and I went to Sunday school in between. People used to come to our house after church in the evening to have refreshments. Our friend brought music with them and we sang around the piano.
>
> *(Quoted by Arthur, 2006: 19)*

Not everyone recollects their religious heritage in a positive light. The Sabbath (originally Saturday) was strictly observed in many households, leaving children with no opportunities to play and socialise. Muir (1992: 88) argues that 'the church seems to have done its best to fill [people] with guilt and foreboding'.

The spiritual function of the parish was to cure (from Latin *cura* meaning to care) souls, baptism being of prime importance. The vestry minute books, held at the county record office, sometimes include details of allowances for the poor such as medicine, clothes or food. But there was also a darker side, which included recorded beatings of vagrants. The church courts also punished parishioners for a wide range of sins, including: drunkenness, swearing, playing games in the churchyard, washing clothes on the Sabbath, talking during sermons, and, most common of all, fornicating. The sermon was also the means of finding out about life beyond the village such as a public disaster. Above all, for many centuries prior to the Industrial Revolution, the parish provided everyday stability and routine. Yet some aspects of 'the world that we have lost' (Laslett, 2005) only serve to illustrate the progress that has been made in a less punitive age than previous generations.

REFLECTION

- To what extent do you think that religion still has a key role to play in a modern society?

Visual heritage

The UK's artistic heritage is wide ranging and includes the fine arts of painting, drawing and architecture, as well as the performing arts, such as dance, music and photography. Mullins (1983) points out that there are certain characteristics of British art. First, it is small in scale when compared to continental art, such as Florentine frescoes. This smallness is illustrated in the medieval missals, the Tudor and Stuart miniatures and eighteenth- and nineteenth-century watercolours. Second, he argues, British painters have been inflamed 'with a kind of xenophobic conservatism' (Mullins, 1983: 11). He explains that artists such as Hogarth, Constable and Reynolds were proud of being on an island set apart from mainland Europe, drawing upon their own traditions – particularly in literature – rather than the Greek-Roman Classical spirit, which predominated in Latin countries. Many of the best British painters were also poets and writers, such as Blake, Turner and Rossetti. Third, British artists have been strongly influenced by nature – Constable maintained that his art was to be 'found under every hedge and in every lane'. His *The Hay Wain* has been described as the 'Picture of Britain' (Brown, 2005: 158). It is, however, misleading to speak of one unifying tradition in British art. The distinctive contributions of Irish, Scottish and Welsh artists have been highlighted by many writers (Freeman, 2006). For instance, Peter Lord's striking three-volume visual history of Wales lays to rest the myth that the Welsh nation is devoid of a visual culture. Lord shows how the imaging of the country as a beautiful landscape has overshadowed the idea of Wales as home to communities with particular cultural characteristics (Lord, 1998–2003). Online collections and a plethora of guides to British paintings (e.g. Wood, 1999; Cowling, 2000) mean that teachers and pupils have ready access to major works of art.

Ten Paintings for Use with Pupils Studying the Victorians

1. Joseph Mallord William Turner's *Rain, Steam and Speed* (1844) – railways.
2. William MacDuff's *Shaftesbury* or *Lost and Found* (1862) – street children.
3. Ford Madox Brown's *The Last of England* (1855) – emigration.
4. Sir Luke Fildes, *Applicants for Admission to a Casual Ward* (1874) – poverty.
5. William Bell Scott, *Industry of the Tyne: Iron and Coal*, (*c.*1861) – industry and Empire.
6. Sir John Everett Millais, *The Blind Girl* (1856) – beggars, nature.
7. William Logsdail, *The Bank Royal Exchange, London* (1887) – street life.
8. Ford Madox Brown, *Work* (1852–65) – virtues of work.
9. Alfred Rankley, *The School Room* (1853) – dame school.
10. W. Powell Frith, *The Derby Day* (1858) – recreation, holidays.

The works of Pre-Raphaelites and social realists particularly illuminate major themes in the nineteenth century. It is important for pupils to learn about women artists, such as Mary Gow, Elizabeth Thompson and Kate Greenaway, as well as those from different regions of the UK.

Galleries

The UK is home to art galleries of international status, such as the National Portrait Gallery, National Gallery and Tate Britain. Many provide first-rate resources for teachers, including digital images, educational packs and posters. There are many publications describing how children's observational skills can be improved using paintings (Gittings, 2003; Blake, 2006). A project such as 'Take One Picture from the National Gallery' could be used by different ages. English Heritage (**www.heritageexplorer.uk**) suggests various teaching ideas including the use of reconstruction pictures that bring sites to life. Key questions to ask children when using visual sources include:

*   What are (paintings/photographs/sculptures) for?
*   Why was this (painting etc.) made? For whom?
*   What does the picture tell us about . . . the sitter? (Consider pose, expression and clothing.)
*   What do you notice first and why?
*   How does it make you feel?
*   Can we learn anything about relationships in the picture and
*   What is happening in . . . the background?

It is important to choose visual sources that tell stories. In religious education, paintings are a good source to use to tell biblical stories, events in the lives of the saints and moral tales. Although many images can be downloaded from the Internet, this cannot substitute for the experience of seeing the real thing in a gallery.

Photographs

Photographs provide an invaluable record of the past. In Scotland, these include the Museum of Scottish Country Life and SCOTLANDSIMAGES.COM (run by the National Archives of Scotland). Werner Kissling's recently published photographs of the Western Isles of Scotland, taken during the 1930s, record a way of life that has now all but disappeared. Kissling was once Hitler's secretary and died penniless in a Dumfries nursing home in 1988 (Russell, 2002; see also **http://futuremuseum. co.uk**). In Wales, the Gathering the Jewels website operated by the National Library of Wales includes relevant collections of photographers such as John Thomas (1838–1905). National Museums Northern Ireland hold more than half a million photographs, most from around 1880 (**www.nmni.com/home.aspx**). English Heritage has a large online photographic collection as part of its National Monuments Record. The ViewFinder website covers themes such as England's industrial heritage, women at work, and customs. Among the photographs are the works of Oxfordshire-based Henry Taunt, who photographed not only churches and country houses but also ordinary folk going about their business.

Specifically for schools, English Heritage operates a Heritage Explorer website with images arranged by theme and alphabetically, from abbeys to the Second World War, interactive games and teachers' notes arranged by phase and topic. The importance of photographers such as John Thomas, John Thompson and Henry Taunt is that they provide rare views of ordinary people at times when many were struggling to make ends meet. The UK's visual heritage is also well recorded by commercial companies such as Francis Frith (**www.francisfrith.com**) and the Hulton Archive (**www. gettyimages.co.uk/EditorialImages/Archival**).

World Heritage Sites

In 1972, the United Nations Educational, Scientific and Cultural Organization (UNESCO) adopted a Convention Concerning the Protection of World Cultural and Natural Heritage. This defines cultural and natural heritage sites of 'outstanding universal value for humanity from the point of view of history, art or science' (UNESCO, 1972: Articles 1–2, available at: **http://whc.unesco.org/en/ conventiontext**). The UK currently has 28 World Heritage sites (see Figure 6.3). These vary from the more famous sites such as Stonehenge, described as 'the world's oldest tourist attraction' (Addison, 2007: 104), to the Gough and Inaccessible islands, located in the south Atlantic. The most recent addition, in 2009, is the Pontcysllte Aqueduct and Canal in northeast Wales, which has the same status as the Great Wall of China.

Figure 6.3 Location of World Heritage Sites in the UK. *Source:* www.culture.gov.uk/ukwhportal/map.htm

> ### TASK
>
> • Select one of the World Heritage Sites in the UK and find out about how it is being preserved for future generations. What can children learn from this?

There are numerous museums and galleries linked to World Heritage sites, offering a range of excellent educational resources. For instance, the National Museums Liverpool provides resource bags, online images and teachers' notes to accompany visits, such as those focusing on the portrayal of Jesus at the Walker Art Gallery. They also have a strong emphasis on seeking to involve hard-to-reach and marginalised groups, who may face barriers to visiting our museums and galleries, such as looked-after children and those in hospital (**www.liverpoolmuseums.org.uk/learning/community**).

Natural heritage

The UK has an extraordinary concentration of natural beauty as illustrated in the many coffee-table style books produced by the Automobile Association, Reader's Digest and the BBC. Nature study was once a prominent part of the elementary school curriculum. For example, the Board of Education (1928: 220) reminded teachers that young children should frequently visit the school garden, if there was one, to follow seasonal changes and to keep a nature calendar to record observations. By the end of the Second World War, gardening and nature walks were well established in the primary curriculum (Board of Education, 1945). However, developments over the last 25 years or so have reduced opportunities for outdoor nature study. These have included:

- the attraction of indoor technologies (computers and television);
- parental fears over 'stranger danger';
- school concern over risks associated with arranging visits; and
- a narrow and restricted curriculum increasingly focused on the basics.

In his international bestseller *Last Child in the Woods*, Richard Louv (2005) laments the decline of natural history in the curriculum. He fears that children are suffering 'nature deficit disorder' – where they are not getting enough experience of the natural environment, resulting in physical, social and emotional damage. Notwithstanding the educational potential of the outdoors, a survey by Natural England reveals that fewer than 10 per cent of children regularly play in woodlands, countryside and parks. Less than one in four children is reported to visit a patch of nature near their home on a weekly basis (English Marketing, 2009: 5). Teachers can ask children to undertake a self-audit of how they use their time in a week.

Visits to woodlands, rivers and parks provide rich opportunities for teachers to develop pupils' skills in creative thinking, problem-solving, reasoning and communication. Beginning with the school grounds, pupils can rejuvenate areas by planting trees and managing allotments. They can work alongside education officers from national parks and other organisations in developing a sense of ownership and

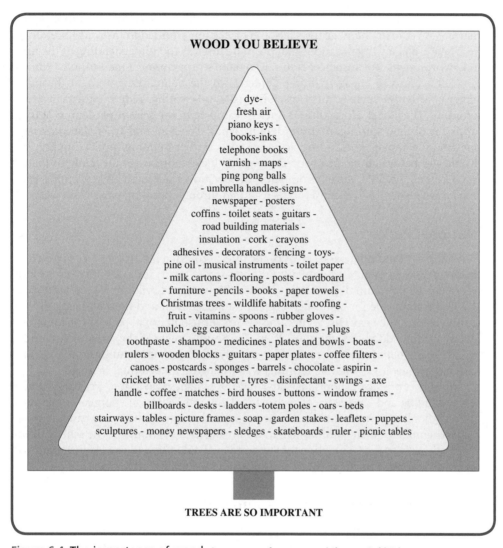

Figure 6.4 The importance of wood. *Source:* www.forestry.gov.uk/forestry/infd-7chcwe

respect, for example by designing and constructing new viewing benches. Teachers can benefit from a wide range of partnerships, including the Forestry Commission and Wildlife Trusts, many of which produce first-rate educational resources including activity booklets, CD-ROMs and posters (see Figure 6.4).

There is no doubt about the contribution of the natural environment to children's all-round education. Forest Schools, in particular, have attracted considerable support throughout England and Wales since the initiative was introduced in the mid-1990s. The impact on children's learning has included gains in confidence, social skills and language (O'Brien and Murray, 2006). Standing under a huge, ancient oak tree can be an intensely spiritual experience, knowing that it has seen at least 10 generations come and go. Trees have often served as meeting places and traditional boundaries, like Gloucestershire's Tortworth Chestnut, planted during the reign of King Egbert in

AD 800 (Stokes and Rodger, 2004). Trees have been likened to living museums, rich in narrative. Yet many heritage trees lack the protection afforded to historical buildings.

There are many organisations that promote interest and understanding of the natural environment. For instance, Natural England's programme 'One Million Children Outdoors' aims to engage children's interest in the natural environment through a range of activities, such as nut hunts, farm visits and creating wildlife gardens in school grounds. The Royal Horticultural Society campaigns for school gardening (**http:// apps.rhs.org.uk/schoolgardening/default.aspa**). The National Trust also runs regular school campaigns including activities such as den building, pond dipping, bug hunts and bat watching. Its properties provide ideal contexts for the study of themes such as food, wildlife, the environment, conservation and sustainability. Pupils' existing knowledge of such themes can be explored through mind maps or word webs.

National Parks

The UK has 15 national parks, areas of the finest protected landscapes (see Figure 6.5). Each one has its own National Park Authority (NPA) with responsibility for the conservation of the natural landscape, cultural heritage and wildlife. These authorities are also responsible for planning, recreation management and the well-being of local communities. The Peak District became the first British national park in 1951 and others were soon added through the 1950s. The South Downs is the most recent, added in 2010. The national parks each offer extensive learning opportunities in landscape, climate, archaeology, wildlife, farming, water, tourism and cultural heritage.

In the best practice, schools take advantage of schemes that aim to improve learners' understanding and experience of their natural environments. One popular programme is Eco-Schools, where schools are required to work through seven steps to gain the green-flag recognition of their commitment to improving the environment. The scheme is run internationally by the Foundation for Environmental Education (**www.fee-international. org**) and involves more than 32,000 schools and nine million students.

Field centres, nature reserves and sustainability centres

The Field Studies Council (FSC), established in 1943, runs centres throughout the UK. Its residential courses are designed to develop learners' personal confidence and social skills, environmental awareness, cultural appreciation, artistic development and physical well-being. Tutors can also offer outreach advice to schools on developing their own grounds for environmental activities. The FSC publishes a range of materials to support schools, including guidance on hedgerows, ponds, streams, gardening and exploring colour in the environment. Natural England also provides an interactive mapping website showing the location of nature reserves and country parks (**www.natureonthemap.org.uk**), and there are similar services elsewhere in the UK (e.g. **www.nnr-scotland.org.uk**). The Sustainability Centre in Hampshire offers primary schools themed days (e.g. 'Wood for Good', 'Farm Safari' and 'Herb Garden'), the teaching of bushcraft skills, and residential experiences (**www.sustainability-centre. org/index.php**). Similarly, in mid-Wales the Centre for Alternative Technology covers all aspects of green living and has a well-established education programme, including free online resources (**www.cat.org.uk**).

NATIONAL PARKS
Britain's breathing spaces

Cairngorms

Loch Lomond
and the Trossachs

Northumberland

North York Moors

Lake
District

Yorkshire Dales

Peak District

Snowdonia

Broads

Pembrokeshire
Coast

Brecon
Beacons

0 50 100 200
Kilometres
Contains Ordnance Survey data
© Crown copyright and database right 2011
© Cairngorms National Park Authority
© Scottish Government
© Exmoor National Park Authority

South Downs

Exmoor

New
Forest

Dartmoor

Figure 6.5 **The National Parks of Britain, 2011.** *Source:* www.nationalparks.gov.uk

Why does heritage matter?

Heritage is important for a number of reasons. At a personal, family and community level, heritage contributes to who we are – whether in the form of heirlooms passed from one generation to the next or landmarks that inject a sense of local pride. Heritage brings enormous pleasure to millions of UK residents and visitors from abroad. It satisfies wide-ranging and particular interests, including those held by the members of the Letter Box Study Group, the Battlefields Trust and the Fovant Badge Society. There is unsurpassing joy, awe and wonder to be derived from visiting historic buildings, national parks, palaces, cathedrals and museums. The British Museum, which opened in 1753 and is the world's first free museum, attracted 5.8 million visitors in 2010–11 – more than 5,000 people a day.

Heritage can bring major social and economic advantages. In some cases, heritage projects bring communities together and serve as a springboard for regeneration and economic prosperity. Heritage is a major part of the UK's economy. It covers tourism, publishing, media, museums, aspects of environmental protection and conservation. After financial services, heritage is the UK's biggest source of valuable export revenues. Although many of the leading museums and galleries do not charge an entry fee in the UK, visitors spend millions of pounds on shop goods, guided tours and special exhibitions.

There are significant environmental and social reasons why heritage matters. The process of restoring old buildings can reveal much about the wisdom of previous generations. There is now increasing application of old construction techniques and the use of sustainable building materials, such as timber framing, lime renders and mud. There are sound ecological reasons to reuse old buildings – many old houses have inherent energy-saving features such as thick walls and doors, small windows, good ventilation and well-insulated roofs (Luxton and Bevan, 2005). Restoring old buildings can bring psychological benefits to a community – people feel better if their important local buildings are cared for and well presented to visitors. The physical process of renovating an old building can be expensive and stressful, but it can also prove highly rewarding and exciting; there is always a chance of finding something that links the building to people who lived there long ago. Such was the experience when a small child's shoe was found in an attic during the renovation of a telegraph station on the northwest coast of Wales in 1991. The shoe was dated to around 1850, due to its machine stitching. It was the custom, if a child died, to place one of the shoes in the attic to keep the spirit close to the family (Davies, 2007). Heritage is particularly important during times of change because it provides a form of security, a visible point of reference, even a refuge (Cormack, 1978). Visiting an art gallery, rambling through a national park or sitting quietly in a place of worship, offers the individual respite and uplift during troubled times.

Heritage learning meets pupils' spiritual, moral, social and cultural needs. By visiting galleries, museums and national parks, pupils can be inspired by their surroundings – literally animated. They learn about what is socially acceptable behaviour and the kinds of ethical dilemmas associated with heritage and the environment. Most significantly, pupils develop their sense of identity by exploring family, local and national heritage, which defines their place in the world.

Teachers can use many approaches such as personal family experiences, stories, speakers and films to illustrate the importance of heritage. For instance, *The Patchwork Quilt* (Flournoy and Pinkney, 1987) conveys the importance of family ties and shared heritage. A little girl named Tanya helps her Grandma sew together a beautiful quilt from scraps collected from different family members. When the Grandma becomes ill, Tanya learns how to sew it herself and, with her mother's help, completes the quilt. Heritage is very much like a patchwork quilt – its size and something of its general appearance is known; but it is necessary to ensure that all the pieces that make up the whole fit together and there are not too many pieces that are alike (Jenkins, 1992).

English Heritage's magazine *Heritage Learning* is an excellent resource for all aspects of heritage. For instance, Issue 42 focuses on how we used to live, including teaching inside and outside the classroom, in castles, pastimes and pleasures, food and how people ate, and health and hygiene (**www.english-heritage.org.uk**).

Ten ways of introducing heritage to children

1. Discussing the idea of collecting – why people do this, what they collect, what happens to the collection.

2. Playing the 'Antiques Roadshow' (BBC1, from 1979), 'Cash in the Attic' (BBC1, from 2002) and similar games using items borrowed from families and friends. Pupils research realistic prices.

3. Asking children to think about antiques for the future. Hogben (2007) suggests 101 'lots' including: mobile phones (introduced in 1982); McDonald's toys (since (1996) and VHS videos (since 1976).

4. Sharing stories – whether personal recollections, historical fiction or biographical writing. A theme such as 'lost and found' works particularly well. For instance *Our House* (Rogers and Rogers, 1992) describes the different families that inhabited a house over two centuries, from the time it was built in the 1780s to the present day (1992). The old house is full of nooks and crannies, behind which a child's toy was hidden long ago and then found.

5. Inviting into the classroom an archaeologist to talk about a project.

6. Undertaking a heritage trail in the locality, photographing physical and natural landmarks of special value. Heritage 'on the doorstep' can focus on finding out more about famous local features or the names behind 'blue plaques'.

7. Asking groups of children to act as applicants and judges for the award of heritage lottery funding. They could produce a similar programme to the BBC series *Restoration* in deciding which buildings to save.

8. Visiting, sketching and photographing a listed building; finding out from the owner its needs.

9. Trawling newspapers to see examples of heritage in the news. For instance, erosion of the coastline, the closure of a parish church or loss of native species.

10. Using contemporary news, role-playing local council meetings based on real issues (e.g. to decide on whether an application to demolish an old building is passed in favour of building a new car park).

Museum learning

The Museums Association defines museums as 'institutions that collect, safeguard and make accessible artefacts and specimens, which they hold in trust for society' (**www.museumsassociation.org/home**). This definition includes galleries containing works of art. Neil MacGregor, Director of the British Museum, explains that the purpose of museums is 'telling history through things' (McGregor, 2010, xiii). His wonderful book tells the history of the world through 100 objects from the British Museum, spanning different times, cultures and continents. The final selection included a cooking pot, a golden galleon, a Stone Age tool and a credit card. Pupils can be encouraged to produce a more modest publication, such as the 10 most interesting things in their local museum. The three-part picture story *The Sandal* (Bradman and Dupasquier, 1999) is a subtle introduction to museums for young children. It shows how a sandal lost by a Roman child resurfaces in a modern museum. The contemporary child's shoe is also lost, only to appear in a museum of the future. A good overview of museum learning is provided by Culture 24, a comprehensive website providing information on museums, galleries, archives and libraries country-wide, current exhibitions, downloadable resources and online activities (**www.culture24.org.uk/home**).

The Museums Association estimates that there are around 2,500 museums in the UK. Of these, the Westminster government currently funds 21 museums and galleries in England, 13 of which are defined as 'national' by Act of Parliament. It also supports innovative educational and community projects based at museums and art galleries. Similar arrangements exist in other parts of the UK. For instance, Museums Galleries Scotland channels funding from the Scottish Executive to the sector and has over 350 member museums, from the Unst Boat Haven, dedicated to the maritime history of Shetland boats, to Glasgow's Police Museum, which traces the history of Britain's first police force. Many national and regional museums have online educational support materials. For instance, Learn with Museums is a major initiative to develop museum and archive education further across the East Midlands (**www.learnwithmuseums. org.uk**). Pupils can explore the story of shoes from around the world, using the collection at the Northampton Museum & Art Gallery or see video clips of a re-enacted Victorian farm at work.

Museums come in all shapes and sizes, including national museums, independent ones, those run by local authorities, universities, the National Trust (or National Trust for Scotland) and English Heritage properties. Museums cater for a diverse range of interests. Lovric (2007) has trawled the world for the most unusual museums, covering subjects such as spying, menstruation, madness, peanuts, sewers, funerals and cockroaches. Britain also has its fair share of curiosities, including the British Lawnmower Museum (Southport), the Morpeth Chantry Bagpipe Museum (Morpeth, Northumberland) and the Museum of Baked Beans (Davies, 2010). Many museums exhibit local industrial heritage; for instance, Stockport (Greater Manchester) has a hat-making museum, Honiton (Devon) is famous for its lace museum, while Llanberis (North Wales) has its slate museum. There are plenty of good general and specific guidebooks on museums and galleries (Fisher, 2005) but refurbishments, closures and relocations mean that online sources are often the most reliable reference for teachers. The magazine *Primary History* often includes relevant articles (see **www. primaryhistory.org**) while Talboys (2010) provides the most comprehensive guide, including planning and preparing for a visit, risk assessment, working on site, using a range of sources and follow-up activities.

The role of museums includes not only the conservation of artefacts but also their presentation and interpretation. The traditional 'Do not touch' signs are now less common in museums, replaced with the latest touch-screen technologies. Politically, museums have moved with 'nimble flexibility and creative fluidity' from authoritarian to egalitarian regimes (Hooper-Greenhill, 2007: 1). There is an increasing emphasis on interactivity, especially for schoolchildren. All museums have to select what they will represent and in so doing they are creating their own stories. The 'curriculum' resources of a typical museum include its paintings, artefacts, displays, exhibitions, models, texts, audio files, films and photographs. Research (Davies, 1999: 14) on visitor responses to museum experiences suggests that the most favourable occur when museums adhere to the following principles:

- use objects wherever possible even if 'telling a story';
- are people-orientated (rather than institutional orientated);
- focus on 'ordinary' people in their presentations (rather than the rich and famous);
- use oral history; and
- are thematic/analytical in their presentations rather than chronological/descriptive.

BOX 6.1 RESEARCH BRIEFING – CHILDREN AND MUSEUMS

Research on the impact of museums and galleries on children's learning is led by the Research Centre for Museums and Galleries (RCMG) at the University of Leicester. One of their surveys of more than 20,000 children and 936 teachers, reports that 90 per cent of Key Stage 2 pupils learnt something new after attending a museum. Moreover, there were gains through high levels of teacher satisfaction, high levels of teacher confidence in their pupils' learning and considerable enjoyment experienced by pupils of all ages (Hooper-Greenhill *et al.*, 2003). A second survey reports that teacher and pupil enthusiasm for museum visits is still high – 95 per cent of teachers thought that museums inspired pupils (Hooper-Greenhill *et al.*, 2006). Well-designed museum websites (e.g. http://tate.kids.org.uk) motivate pupils and promote positive attitudes (Charitonos, 2010).

Planning a museum visit, particularly if this involves an overnight stay, requires considerable preparation. Most museums offer the opportunity for preliminary visits in order to become familiar with the facilities and to discuss class needs. In setting up their own class or school museums, pupils should consider how they might obtain objects (loan services, junk shops, relatives, replicas from commercial companies), how to advertise the museum, how the collection is recorded, exhibited and stored, insurance issues, whether all objects will be handled, and how expertise from a local museum might help (Batho, 1994).

Using Artefacts

There are many ways that artefacts (objects made by humans) can be used to stimulate children's thoughts and feelings, including:

- Asking questions about an artefact's function, colour, shape, age, ownership, value (e.g. What was it made for? What does it look and feel like? How was it made? Is it well designed? What is it worth? Is it original?)

- Observational drawing – from different angles
- Produce written descriptions such as labels or text for information panels
- Produce audio or video recording describing the artefacts
- Sequencing similar objects
- Using Venn diagrams to note similarities (e.g. function)
- Play 'feely bag' games with mystery objects
- Role-play or storytelling based on artefacts
- Researching the life story of artefacts

PLANNING A MUSEUM VISIT

Location: Tel:

Museum officer contact: email:

Date of preliminary visit:

Date of planned class visit: Estimated time of arrival:

Means of transport: Contact:

Number of pupils: Year group(s):

Number of adults:

Names of other adults:

Intended learning outcomes:

1.

2.

Theme/topic:

PLANNING A MUSEUM VISIT (*CONTINUED*)

On-site activities:

Follow-up work:

Evaluation:

Permission slips from parents:	❏	Toilets	❏
Medical requirements of pupils:	❏	Lunch arrangements	❏
Risk assessment completed:	❏	Shop	❏
Deadlines for payments:	❏	Parking	❏
Deposit paid:	❏	Means of transport	❏
Receipts provided:	❏	Journey time	❏
Insurance checks (travel and health):	❏		
Arrangements for pupils with special needs:	❏		
Passports (if applicable):	❏		
Thank you card/email	❏		
Group leader:		Contact:	

Possible proforma for planning a museum visit. This can be adapted for use when visiting a place of worship or general fieldwork.

The stories behind the setting up and running of museums can raise pupils' appreciation for hard work, determination and vision. The concept of museums as places of learning and discovery for ordinary people can be attributed to Henry Cole (1808–1882). He was the key figure behind the Victoria and Albert and Science Museums. Cole was also associated with the first Christmas card, the first postage stamp, the

Public Record Office, the Great Exhibition, the South Kensington Museum and the Albert Hall. He viewed museums as 'antidotes to brutality and vice' (cited by Tait). The smooth operation of museums requires teamwork. The British Museum employs more than a thousand members of staff including: conservators, specialist curators, librarians and security guards. The setting of class or school museums can provide opportunities for pupils to cooperate and take an active interest in their local heritage.

Many museums offer loan services ('Museum in a box'), guided tours and visiting speakers. The larger museums will have dedicated education officers. They are likely to have teaching experience and can provide guidance on supporting pupils with different learning and physical needs. Increasingly, cultural organisations are under pressure to use their resources as a means of promoting social inclusion (DCMS, 2000), for instance by making some of these available online. Rather than being seen as add-ons, digital activities are expected to inform, amplify, support and develop an organisation's non-digital activities such as visiting programmes, exhibitions and outreach work for those that find it difficult to reach museums (DCMS, 2010: 12).

The importance of making the most of our heritage has been highlighted by John Curtis, keeper of the Department of the Middle East at the British Museum. He offers an international perspective in his dealings with museums from all over the world, even during the most difficult of circumstances; for instance, the British Museum was keen to publicise the looting of the National Museum of Iraq in 2003 by Iraqi insurgents, despite criticisms for getting involved in 'politics'. Curtis declared: 'We have to speak up for the museums and historical sites in Iraq because nobody else will. And one of the most important messages we can give is that we must never be complacent; we must never take our cultural heritage for granted' (Smith, 2006: 177).

SUMMARY

- Heritage is what has been passed down from earlier generations. This varies from personal heirlooms to world heritage sites.

- The historic environment includes houses, castles, pubs and inns, industrial and commercial sites, maritime heritage, sporting traditions, ecclesiastical buildings and works of art.

- The UK's natural heritage is very diverse and includes woodlands, rivers, beaches and mountains.

- Organisations such as English Heritage, the Forestry Commission and National Park Authorities provide many excellent resources for teachers.

- Heritage matters for many reasons, including the pleasure brought to many and its educational potential.

- Museums offer many exciting learning opportunities for pupils of all abilities and interests.

References

Addison, A.C. (2007), *Disappearing World*, London: Collins.

Bailey, B. (1982), *The Industrial Heritage of Britain*, London: Ebury Press.

Baren, M.E. (1997a), *How Household Names Began*, London: Michael O'Mara Books.

Baren, M.E. (1997b), *How It All Began Up the High Street*, London: Michael O'Mara Books.

Batho, G.. (ed.) (1994), *School Museums and Primary History*, London: Historical Association.

Blake, Q. (2006), Tell Me a Picture, London: Frances Lincoln Children's Books.

Board of Education (1928), *Handbook of Suggestions for Teachers*, London: Board of Education.

Board of Education (1945), *Handbook of Suggestions for Teachers*, London: Board of Education.

Bradman, T. and Dupasquier, P. (1999), *The Sandal*, London: Andersen Press Ltd.

Brown, D. A. (2005), 'The Nature of Our Looking', in Dimbleby, D., *A Picture of Britain*, London: Tate Publishing.

Brandon, D. (2010), *Discovering Pub Names and Signs*, Princes Risborough: Shire Publications.

Burton, A. (2002), *Daily Telegraph's Guide to Britain's Working Past*, London: Aurum Press.

Bourdillon, H. (ed.) (1994), *Teaching History*, London: Routledge.

Charitonos, K. (2010), 'Promoting positive attitudes in children towards museums and art: a case study of the use of Tate Kids in primary arts education', in: *Museums and the Web 2010: the International Conference for Culture and Heritage Online*, 13–17 April 2010, Denver, Colorado, USA.

Cormack, P. (1978), *Heritage in Danger*, London: Quartet Books.

Cowling, M. (2000), *Victorian Figurative Painting: Domestic Life and the Contemporary Social Scene*, London: Andreas Papadakis Publisher.

Craven, J. (2010), *John Craven's Countryfile Handbook*, London: BBC Books.

Croker, J. (2009), *8 out of 10 Brits: Intriguing and useless statistics about the world's 79th largest nation*, London: Random House Books.

Davies, S. (1999), 'Interpretation, Evaluation and Social History in Museums', in *Social History in Museum*, Vol. 24: pp. 1–18.

Davies, M. (2007), *Discovering Welsh Houses*, Cardiff: Graffeg.

Davies, H. (2010), *Behind the Scenes at the Museum of Baked Beans: My Search for Britain's Maddest Museums*, London: Virgin Books.

DCMS (2000), *Centres for social change: museums, galleries and archives for all: policy guidance on social inclusion for DCMS funded and local authority museums, galleries and archives in England*, London: DCMS.

DCMS (2010), *Encouraging Digital Access to Culture*, London: DCMS.

Dibnah, F. And Hall, D. (1999), *Fred Dibnah's Industrial Age: A Guide to Britain's Industrial Heritage – Where to Go and What to See*, London: BBC Books.

Dunkling, L. and Wright, G. (1987), *A Dictionary of Pub Names*, London: Routledge & Kegan Paul.

Edwards, A. (2010), 'The case for church buildings', *The Guardian*, 24 November 2010.

Edwards, N. (2006), *Rivers (Geography First)*, London: Wayland.

English Marketing (2009), *Report to Natural England on Childhood and Nature: A Survey on Changing Relationships with Nature Across Generations, Warboys*, Cambridgeshire: English Marketing.

Fisher, M. (2005), *Britain's Best Museums and Galleries*, London: Penguin.

Flournoy, V. and Pinkney, J. (1987), *The Patchwork Quilt*, London: Puffin.

Freeman, J. (2006), *British Art*, London: Southbank Publishing.

Gale, A. (2010), *Britain's Historic Coast*, London: NPI Media Group.

Gittings, C. (2003), *Portraits of Queen Elizabeth I: An Educational Resource Pack*, London, National Portrait Gallery.

Gorsky, M. (1999), *Patterns of Philanthropy: Charity and Society in Nineteenth-Century Bristol*, London: Royal Historical Society.

Hall, D. (2010), *Fred Dibnah's Buildings of Britiain*, London: Bantam Press.

Hart, A. Tindal (1959) *The Country Priest in English History*, London: Phoenix House.

Hibbert, C. (2005), *Investigating Rivers,* London: Evans Brothers.

Hogben, M. (2007), *101 Antiques of the Future*, London: New Holland.

Hooper-Greenhill, E., Dodd, J., Moussouri, T., Jones, C., Pickford, C., Herman, C., Morrison, M., Vincent, J., and Toon, R. (2003), *'Measuring the Outcomes and Impact of Learning in Museums, archives and Libraries'*, Leicester: RCMG.

Hooper-Greenhill, E. (2007), *Museums and Education*, Abingdon: Routledge.

Hooper-Greenhill, E., Dodd, J., Gibson, L., Phillips, M., Jones, C., and Sullivan, E. (2006), *What did you learn at the museum today? Second study*, University of Leicester.

Horn, P. (1999), *Pleasures and Pastimes in Victorian Britain*, Stroud: Alan Sutton.

House of Commons Culture, Media and Sport Committee (2006), *Protecting and Preserving our Heritage. Third Report*, London: House of Commons, available at: **www.publications.parliament.uk/pa/cm200506/cmselect/cmcumeds/cmcumeds.htm**.

Jenkins, G. (1992), *Getting Yesterday Right: Interpreting the Heritage of Wales*, Cardiff: University of Wales Press.

Laslett, P. (2005), *The World We Have Lost: Further Explored*, Abingdon: Routledge.

Lord, P. (2003), *The Visual Culture of Wales* (3 vols), Cardiff: University of Wales Press.

Louv, R. (2005), *Last Child in the Woods: Saving Our Children from Nature-Deficit Disorder*, London: Atlantic Books.

Lovric, I. (2007), *Cowgirls, Cockroaches and Celebrity Lingerie: The World's Most Unusual Museums*, London: Icon Books Ltd.

Luxton, C. and Bevan, S. (2005), *Restored to Glory*, London: BBC Books.

McGregor, N. (2010), *A History of the World in 100 Objects*, London: Allen Lane.

Montgomery-Massingberd, H. and Sykes, C.S. (2000), *Great Houses of England and Wales*, London: Laurence King.

Morris, M. (2003), *Castle: A History of the Buildings that Shaped Medieval Britain*, London: Channel4 Books.

Muir, R. (1992), *The Villages of England*, London: Thames and Hudson.

Mullins, E. (1983), *The Arts of Britain*, Oxford: Phaidon.

Newman, R. (2001), *The Historical Archaeology of Britain c. 1540–1900*, Stroud: Sutton.

O'Brien, L. and Murray, R. (2006), *A Marvellous Opportunity to Learn*, Farnham: Surrey.

Rhys Jones, G. (2009), *Rivers: A Voyage into the Heart of Britain*, London: Hodder & Stoughton.

Rogers, P. and Rogers, E. (1992), *Our House*, London: Walker Books.

Russell, M. (2002), *A Different Country*, Edinburgh: Scottish Arts Council.

Smith, L. (2006), *Uses of Heritage*, Abingdon: Routledge.

Smith, R. (2007), *The Museum*, London: BBC Books.

Somerville, C. (2006), *Coast*, St Helens: BBC Books.

Stokes, J. and Rodger, D. (2004), *The Heritage Trees of Britain and Northern Ireland*, London: Constable.

Talboys, G.K. (2010), *Using Museums as an Educational Resource*, Farnham: Ashgate.

Thurley, S. (2002), *Radio Times*, 13–19 July 2002, p. 38.

Wilkinson, P. and Ashley, P. (2006), *The English Buildings Book*, Swindon: English Heritage.

Wilkinson, P. (2010), *Turn Back Time: The High Street – 100 Years of British Life Through the Shop Window*, London: Quercus.

Wood, C. (1999), *Victorian Paiting*, London: Weidenfeld & Nicolson.

Useful Websites

The National Archives has award-winning resources for students and teachers. Its Education Service leads the field: **www.nationalarchives.gov.uk**.

The British Museum has excellent education programmes and resources: **www.britishmuseum.org/learning.aspx**.

The British Library learning website includes a wide range of cross-curricular resources: **www.bl.uk/learning/index.html**.

The Royal Commission on the Ancient and Historical Monuments has many resources including online: **www.rcahms.gov.uk**.

The English Heritage learning website has many resources including its free journal *Heritage Learning*: **www.english-heritage.org.uk**.

Heritage Explorer includes images by theme for schools, as well as interactive games and teachers' notes: **www.heritage-explorer.org.uk**.

Museums4Schools operates in the West Midlands: **http://museums4schools.org**.

Worcestershire local authority has produced a digital palette containing case studies of children's work in relation to themes such as landscapes, buildings and movement with the intention to hold 20,000 copyright free images: **www.digitalpalette.org.uk/flash/digipal_intro.swf**.

Art Galleries UK provides a list of the most famous galleries by county: **www.artgalleries.co.uk/Famous_Art_Galleries.htm**.

The Historic Houses Association supports Britain's privately-owned historic houses, castles and gardens: **www.hha.org.uk**.

The 'Show Me' website provides museum, gallery and heritage resources for children and teachers: **www.show.me.uk**.

The National Trust website has a section on conservation, heritage and learning: **www.nationaltrust.org.uk/main**.

National Museums Scotland has comprehensive programmes for schools and online support materials: **www.nms.ac.uk/learning.aspx**.

Historic Scotland provides information on how the Scottish environment is protected and includes resources such as an image bank: **www.historic-scotland.gov.uk/index.htm**.

SCOTLANDSIMAGES.COM is a picture library taken from Scotland's national collections: **www.scotlandsimages.com/default.aspx**.

The National Galleries of Scotland website has many resources including a frieze to enable children to identify key figures in Scottish history: **www.nationalgalleries.org/education/activity/6:253**.

The National Grid for Learning Cymru Wales has many resources, including a Castles of Wales microsite: **www.ngfl-cymru.org.uk/castles_of_wales**.

Cadw is the historic environment service of the Welsh Assembly Government and includes 'learning and discovery' materials: **www.cadw.wales.gov.uk**.

Gathering the Jewels, hosted by the National Library of Wales, has over 30,000 sources on Welsh life: **http://www.gtj.org.uk/**.

The Northern Ireland Environment Agency website has materials for teachers and pupils: **www.ni-environment.gov.uk**.

Who do we think we are?
Developing an inclusive humanities curriculum

The British are not a single tribe, or a single religion, and we don't come from a single place. But we are building a home where we are all able to be who we want to be, yet still be British. That is what we do: we take, we adapt and we move forward.

(Benjamin Zephaniah, 2006: 5)

Learning objectives

By the end of this chapter you should be able to:

- reflect upon what it means to be British and how the humanities promote a sense of identity;
- recognise that Britain has a rich multicultural heritage;
- reflect upon whether Britain is a tolerant country and engage critically with the challenges associated with multicultural education; and
- recognise the contribution of the humanities in meeting the diverse needs and interests of learners.

What does it mean to be British?

Debate about British identity has been high on the academic and political agenda over recent years (Logue, 2000; Devine and Logue, 2002; Kumar, 2003, Ward, 2004). Bernard Crick, who was charged by the Westminster government to define Britishness, saw it in political and legal terms – signifying allegiance to laws, government and broad moral and political concepts such as tolerance and freedom of speech (Crick Report, 1998). However, Britishness means different things to different people.

Former Conservative Prime Minister John Major, in the context of concerns about Britain losing its identity within the European Union, predicted:

> Fifty years on from now Britain will still be the country of long shadows on county grounds, warm beer, invincible green suburbs, dog lovers and pools fillers and – as George Orwell said 'old maids bicycling to holy communion through the morning mist.

(Quoted by Paxman, 1999: 142)

The speech was delivered on the eve of St George's Day in 1993 and conveys an idyllic, quaint and narrow view of English (albeit presented as British) identity. In contrast, Birmingham-born Rastafarian poet Benjamin Zephaniah recognises the 'melting pot' of Britishness, Britain's multicultural heritage and the shifting nature of British identity.

The British

Take some Picts, Celts and Silures
And let them settle,
Then overrun them with Roman conquerors.

Remove the Romans after approximately 400 years
Add lots of Norman French to some
Angles, Saxons, Jutes and Vikings, then stir vigorously.

Mix some hot Chileans, cool Jamaicans, Dominicans,
Trinidadians and Bajans with some Ethiopians, Chinese,
Vietnamese and Sudanese.

Then take a blend of Somalians, Sri Lankans, Nigerians
And Pakistanis,
Combine with some Guyanese
And turn up the heat.

Sprinkle some fresh Indians, Malaysians, Bosnians,
Iraqis and Bangladeshis together with some
Afghans, Spanish, Turkish, Kurdish, Japanese
And Palestinians
Then add to the melting pot.

Leave the ingredients to simmer.
As they mix and blend allow their languages to flourish
Binding them together with English.

Allow time to be cool.

Add some unity, understanding, and respect for the future,
Serve with justice
And enjoy.

Note: All the ingredients are equally important. Treating one ingredient better than another will leave a bitter unpleasant taste.

Warning: An unequal spread of justice will damage the people and cause pain. Give justice and equality to all.

Benjamin Zephaniah, Wicked World *(Puffin, 2000)*

REFLECTION

- What talking points for children arise from Zephaniah's poem?

Over recent years the question of identity has been sharpened against a background of such atrocities as the London (7/7) bombings of 2005. The attack's ringleader, Muktar Said Ibrahim, worked as a learning mentor in a Leeds primary school. Prime Minister David Cameron called for 'a clear sense of shared national identity' in the context of addressing ongoing concerns about radicalisation and Islamic extremism. The prime minister wants immigrants to be educated in 'a common culture and curriculum' (**www.number10.gov.uk/news/pms-speech-at-munich-security-conference**). Although much-criticised, 'Life in the United Kingdom' tests were introduced for immigrants in 2005, with questions based on the government's manual *Life in the United Kingdom: A Journey to Citizenship* (Home Office, 2007). Following the recommendations of the Crick Report (1998), citizenship became a statutory subject in England's secondary curriculum in 2002 and optional within the primary school. In Scotland, informed and responsible citizenship is one of the national priorities underpinning *Curriculum for Excellence*.

There is widespread political and popular support for schools to promote understanding of British heritage and to cultivate values such as respect for the law, tolerance and equality of opportunity – although these are not uniquely British values. According to a recent survey of 643 primary and secondary teachers, 72 per cent believe promoting 'British values' is part of their role in school (Barker, 2008). Traditionally, these have been White, Anglo-Saxon, Protestant (WASP) values imposed on all 'newcomers'. This chapter explores the role of primary schools in promoting a sense of British identity within the context of the humanities. Is this still relevant in a post-imperial, globalised and diverse British society? If so, what is the contribution of the humanities in developing pupils' understanding of Britishness?

The curricula afford opportunities for pupils to learn about the different countries that make up the UK. Unfortunately, these are not taken up well. For instance, Ofsted (2007) reports that in history lessons in English schools, pupils rarely learn about Scotland, Wales and Ireland, or major European and world themes. In Wales, one of the challenges is to address the fashion of denigrating 'the other' – particularly the English (Phillips, 2000: 159). On the other hand, it seems that pupils in English schools often misrepresent or omit Wales when drawing maps of Britain (Wiegand, 2006; Chave, 2011).

The relationship between the respective national identities of English, Scottish, Welsh and Irish (the 'home countries') and a wider British identity is complex and has attracted longstanding interest. In the *English People*, George Orwell (1947) refers to the English, capacity for gentleness, suspicion of foreigners, and enjoyment of football. The majority of English, Scots and Welsh do not consider themselves as British, only a majority of Ulster Protestants do (Kumar, 2003). Historically, Irish, Welsh and Scottish (Celtic) identities can be seen as a reaction *against* the dominant English identity. David Starkey argues that it is impossible to teach Britishness because 'a British nation doesn't exist . . . we are made up of four nations which constitute a marketplace of identities.' (**http://news.bbc.co.uk/1/hi/education/7040137.stm**).

That said, research (CRE, 2005) shows that despite the diversity of Britain's population, there are some common views about Britishness including: the idea of an 'island nation', distinctive topographical features (e.g. Scottish highlands, Welsh valleys and rolling hills), a pride in scientific and cultural achievement and shared values such as 'fair play'. The question of Britishness is discussed as part of the citizenship curriculum in English secondary schools. Ofsted (2011) highlights good practice when teachers encourage students to reflect on their own immediate heritage, and also broaden this to include the experiences of previous generations. Older pupils in the primary school should engage in discussions about national identities because this can improve their understanding of the challenges facing their own communities and wider contemporary society in addressing bias and intolerance. Knowles and Ridley (2006) report on successful projects in Cumbria; for example, Year 4 pupils explored a selection of photographs of British children from a range of different cultures and ethnicities. The children's common perceptions and stereotypical responses included the following:

- All white children are from Britain;
- The Black child must be poor and come from Africa;
- The parents of the Chinese child must be receptionists (they had seen Chinese hotel workers whilst on holiday); and
- The ginger-haired child must be Scottish.

(Knowles and Ridley, 2006: 7)

From these starting points, pupils explored whether the way someone looks or dresses is a good indicator of where they live. They questioned the idea of British national dress and the difficulty of agreeing on what this might look like. Follow-up sessions involved the pupils drawing a picture of what a British person might look like (to establish a baseline to show their understanding of multicultural Britain) and 'circle time' discussions of their differences. The pupils also returned to the original photo set and matched these to job titles that they thought the children might do when they were older. They were also asked to discuss which of the pictured children they most liked, looked the most honest, friendly and threatening. Finally, the pupils drew another picture of what a British person might look like, and many included elements of diversity in their second drawings. Such activities challenge pupils to justify their views and reflect on their own perceptions:

- You can't tell if someone is nice from a picture;
- Just because someone has got white skin you can't tell they're English; and
- You don't know who will be who from a picture.

Another project in north Wales involves Welsh- speaking boys from disadvantaged backgrounds exploring their perceptions of their own identity through the creation of superhero characters. Working in partnership with professional artists and designers, boys imagine how a Welsh superhero would look if he was brought up in the same community as them. The completed stories or web-comics contribute to a national discussion on language and identity (see **www.engagingwales.org/projects**).

The teaching of patriotism and loyalty to the state are well established in many countries, including the United States, France and Australia. In American elementary schools, the vast majority of pupils salute the flag and pledge their allegiance to the country. But patriotism poses dangers. When the Japanese airforce attacked Pearl Harbour in 1945, around 150,000 Japanese Americans including children were herded up and placed in concentration camps. Chinese traders made signs saying that they were Chinese rather than Japanese. One Japanese dealer advertised her wares with a cloud and the expression 'fashions by the yard'. This was interpreted by the American intelligence as a secret code, with the cloud representing an aerial attack, 'fashions' with the 'f' removed sounded like 'actions' while 'by the yard' was interpreted as a code for the naval yard of Pearl Harbour. The irony was that the dealer sold fabric that was in high demand for use as black-out curtains (BBC Radio 4, Random Edition Pearl Harbour, 7 December 2011).

Schools in England and Wales once celebrated Empire Day (24 May 1904–1958) in which children were reminded of the glories of the British Empire. Its collapse led to a reassessment of identity. Hayward and Freeman (1919), just after the First World War, called for a renewed emphasis on the nation's great poets, musicians, artists, religious teachers and scientists, to be manifested in separate celebrations days for Shakespeare, the League of Nations and Democracy. St George's Day is effectively a non-event when compared to St David's or St Patrick's Day, the American Fourth of July, the French Bastille Day or Australia Day, all of which are demonstrations of national unity. Howard (2011) suggests that St George himself is to blame, a Syrian-born Roman who is patron to many countries. He mischievously adds that St George should be replaced by the East Anglian nun-queen St Sexburga to revitalise England's pathetic national day. The Fifth of November, the anniversary of the Gunpowder Plot of 1605, is probably the nearest England has to a national celebration. The story (or stories) of this failed attempt to blow up Parliament is one of the best examples of how pupils can learn about evidence, interpretation ('Was Guy Fawkes set up?') and how the past is reconstructed by 'winners'.

Spiritual identities

Rather than focus on the civic dimension of being British, several writers have looked for the religious and spiritual aspects, arguing that Britain is not a secular state but a matter of overlapping spiritual identities (Jenkins, 1975; Bradley, 2007). Less than 10 per cent of people now attend places of worship in the UK each week. But this is not necessarily an indicator of religiosity or the lack of it. Measuring religion involves cognitive, social and behavioural aspects. Church attendance, for example, has become much more informal, irregular and dispersed in the post-war period. Moreover, other practices, such as reading religious literature, prayer, donations and community activity are all essential elements within any serious religious practice. The complexity of religion was understood by Thomas Cranmer as he drafted the Book of Common Prayer 'by thought, word and dede' (Spencer, 2009).

Bradley (2007: 59) maintains that the parish church in particular remains 'a visible embodiment of British identity'. He draws upon a wide range of 'spiritual treasures' to support his view, including myths and legends, national landmarks such as Stonehenge and Westminster Abbey, the long-running popular BBC television programme *Songs of Praise* and the Union Jack. But while the Union Jack is seen by many as a force for unity, tolerance and inclusion (Groom, 2006), some Catholics (especially in Ulster) see it as offensive, representing Unionist and Loyalist sectarianism, and reinforcing what they see as 'the British occupancy of Ireland' (Ewart *et al.*, 2004). In Northern Ireland, the issue of national identity is tied very closely to religious identity. A BBC survey in 2007, *State of Minds: the Children*, reported that many Catholic and Protestant children tended to live parallel and separate lives though there were signs that a shared Northern Irish identity was emerging (**http://news.bbc.co.uk/1/hi/northern_ireland/6761765.stm**).

REFLECTION

- What does Britain mean to you? Do you think there is such a concept as Britishness and, if so, should it be taught in school?

Great Britain, the British Isles and the UK

It is possible for teachers, let *a*lone pupils, to get confused about the meaning of the terms Great Britain, the British Isles and the UK (see Figure 7.1). It is more reprehensible, however, for teachers to substitute England for Britain. The nasty English habit of using the terms English and British interchangeably', dates back to the sixteenth century (Kumar, 2003). Historiography over recent years has sought to address Anglocentric views of Britain. For example, Norman Davies' 1,200-page *The Isles* (MacMillan, 1999) is among the best attempts to examine the complexity of the notion of 'Britain' and 'Britishness' over the last 2,000 years.

Approaches in the Early Years

Before reflecting upon questions of national identity, young children need to explore their own identities through themes such as 'Who am I?', 'All about me', 'Ourselves' or 'Babies'. Simple starting points can include sitting in a circle sharing names and basic personal information (birthdays, likes/dislikes, pets, names of siblings).

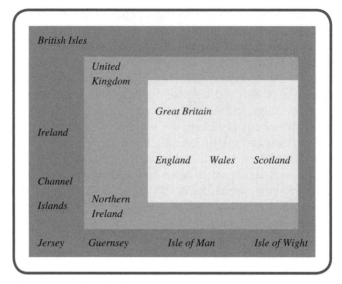

Figure 7.1 What is 'the UK'?

Fundamental concepts of change and continuity can be reinforced through the construction of personal timelines in which pupils sequence and discuss pictures of themselves and others. Here, there are many stories that explore personal feelings, such as Anthony Browne's *Changes* (Walker, 1997), which looks at the reaction of a boy awaiting the return of his parents from hospital with their new baby.

Names

The most obvious sign of identity is a person's name. When abandoned children were admitted to London's Foundling Hospital (now a museum) they were given a 'clean break' from their past by the assigning of new names. A display board in the museum is a poignant reminder – the first boy was baptised Thomas Coram and the first girl Eunice Coram, named after two of the founders (Pugh, 2007). Names often have strong religious and cultural associations. In Hinduism, names give information about the caste system, social position and occupation of the owner. Indian leader Mahatma Gandhi (1869–1948) began to change attitudes to the caste system and many Hindus have since dropped the use of a caste name. Among the top baby names for 2010 are the biblical names of Thomas (sixth), Joshua (eighth) and Jacob (twelfth). Islamic influence is also strong – Mohammed and Muhammad combined represent the fourth most popular boys' name in the UK. Care is needed when pronouncing names. In some cases shortening the name can change the meaning and can cause offence. For instance, the name Abdullah means 'servant of Allah', whereas if shortened to 'Abdul' it means 'servant' or 'slave' (Muslim Council of Britain, 2007).

The National Statistics website provides details of names through history for each decade back to 1904, examples of which are included in Table 7.1 and Figure 7.2. It also includes regional variations. These lists can provide a lead into family history and discussions about change, continuity, popularity and celebrity.

Figure 7.2 Word clouds for the 100 most popular names for boys and girls in England and Wales in 2010. The size of a name represents how many times that name was given, rather than the rank of that name. *Source:* Office for National Statistics.

Young children can be asked questions such as 'How did you get your name?' and 'What does it mean?'. This could lead to making connections between the people they know today and religious traditions: 'Are there others who share your name?' 'Who were they?' 'What did they do?' Children should be encouraged to see how everyone belongs to the human family.

The exploration of personal names can be extended to consider the meaning of nicknames and surnames (Freeman, 1994; Dunkling, 1998), although guessing the meaning of surnames is a dangerous game because they have changed considerably over time. The significance of names in the humanities should not be underestimated. One professor of geography has developed a database that tracks almost 50 million people in Britain via their surnames. The names are then matched to postcodes, to build up a picture of immigrant social mobility. The trend is one of immigrants moving from inner-city areas to suburbs. In London, for instance, there are now high concentrations of Sri Lankans in the south (New Malden, Mitcham), Sikhs in the west (Southall, Hounslow), Hindu Indians in the north-west (Wembley, Harrow) and Greek Cypriots in the north (Southgate, Palmers Green). Contrary to common stereotypes, the data suggests that many members of immigrant communities live in relatively prestigious neighbourhoods (Doward and Pemberton, 2011).

Exploring children's identities involves making connections to where they were born, their family, friendships and the place where they live. Children develop close affiliations to places, as most adults will recall from childhood experiences. 'Place attachment' contributes significantly to children's self-esteem and emerging identities

Table 7.1 Top baby names in England and Wales, 1904–2010

RANK	1904	1924	1944	1964	1984	2010
1	WILLIAM	JOHN	JOHN	DAVID	CHRISTOPHER	OLIVER
2	JOHN	WILLIAM	DAVID	PAUL	JAMES	JACK
3	GEORGE	GEORGE	MICHAEL	ANDREW	DAVID	HARRY
4	THOMAS	JAMES	PETER	MARK	DANIEL	ALFIE
5	ARTHUR	THOMAS	ROBERT	JOHN	MICHAEL	CHARLIE
6	JAMES	RONALD	ANTHONY	MICHAEL	MATTHEW	THOMAS
7	CHARLES	KENNETH	BRIAN	STEPHEN	ANDREW	WILLIAM
8	FREDERICK	ROBERT	ALAN	IAN	RICHARD	JOSHUA
9	ALBERT	ARTHUR	WILLIAM	ROBERT	PAUL	GEORGE
10	ERNEST	FREDERICK	JAMES	RICHARD	MARK	JAMES

RANK	1904	1924	1944	1964	1984	2010
1	MARY	MARGARET	MARGARET	SUSAN	SARAH	OLIVIA
2	FLORENCE	MARY	PATRICIA	JULIE	LAURA	SOPHIE
3	DORIS	JOAN	CHRISTINE	KAREN	GEMMA	EMILY
4	EDITH	JOYCE	MARY	JACQUELINE	EMMA	LILLY
5	DOROTHY	DOROTHY	JEAN	DEBORAH	REBECCA	AMELIA
6	ANNIE	KATHLEEN	ANN	TRACEY	CLAIRE	JESSICA
7	MARGARET	DORIS	SUSAN	JANE	VICTORIA	RUBY
8	ALICE	IRENE	JANET	HELEN	SAMANTHA	CHLOE
9	ELIZABETH	ELIZABETH	MAUREEN	DIANE	RACHEL	GRACE
10	ELSIE	EILEEN	BARBARA	SHARON	AMY	EVIE

Source: http://www.ons.gov.uk/ons/search/index.html?newquery=baby+names.

(Martin, 2006). It also involves discussion about their interests, religious beliefs and wider cultural experiences. The Northern Ireland Curriculum suggests a number of pertinent questions and activities for teachers to consider:

- What makes me, *me*?
- Can my identity change?
- How does diversity in our classroom measure up?

- What does identity mean to you?
- What's the diversity temperature in our school?
- What does diversity look like where you live?

Nursery children can work alongside carers and parents to make identity books containing photographs, drawings and first words, which form the basis of a welcome 'package' to school, reflecting their respective cultural backgrounds. Once young children have explored questions about themselves and their peers, they can begin to consider bigger issues relating to local, regional and national identities. They can also investigate the responsibilities associated with being a global citizen, discussed further in Chapter 8.

Young children and national identity

Teachers in the Early Years can draw upon a range of approaches and resources to explore with young children the history and significance of national symbols, landmarks, legends and myths. They can discuss the stories of national figures using multimedia resources. For instance, the National Grid for Learning Cymru website has online materials relating to the story of St David (**www.ngfl-cymru.org.uk/vtc/ngfl/2007-08/saintdavid/ds_english/index.html**). Scotland's Learning and Teaching website includes an animated story of St Andrew, the story of the Saltire and an interactive map showing how primary schools celebrate the day (**www.ltscotland.org.uk/scotland-sculture/standrewsday/index.asp**). Visits to museums, galleries and parks provide further opportunities for young children to make connections between their local heritage and the 'big' stories, for example by discussing statutes of famous people, war memorials and other landmarks. To introduce young children to national and global contexts, role play areas can be set up such as the opening of a new 'supermarket', where they can consider local produce, products 'made in Britain' and those from around the world. Similar learning opportunities might be presented through the operation of a travel agency or garden centre. Events such as the Olympics (2012), royal weddings and jubilees afford opportunities to celebrate British identity (photo 7.1)

BOX 7.1 RESEARCH BRIEFING – CHILDREN AND NATIONAL IDENTITY

Wiegand (1992) highlights that children's understanding of places such as countries is the result of a complex relationship between cognitive and affective domains. Five- and six-year-olds tend to identify with the local town, although by the age of seven they identify their national flag, aspects of dress and other national symbols (Barrett and Buchanan-Barrow 2002). This national identity does typically increase in importance through the course of middle childhood. Moreover, there is a strong correlation between children's geographical knowledge of the UK and their national identity (Barrett and Davey, 2001). Children develop a national affinity, having moved from a family focus to wider peer and community groups. Barrett (2005) found that the development of national identifications varied according to children's geographical location. Moreover, Catling (2009) points ▶

BOX 7.1 *(CONTINUED)*

out that children in some countries, such as Japan and Turkey, develop a stronger national identity at an earlier age than those from the UK. Carington and Short (1995) found that children appear to be relatively uninterested in the question of 'being British' and that children's responses that carry a potentially racist overtone are rare. However, Pierson (2002) reports that young children begin to show bias against other children different to themselves from as early as two unless they gain accurate information and see positive role models.

Photo 7.1 Child with face painted in Union Jack colours. (*Picture source*: Union Jack Girl © Still Pictures/Duncan Walker; **www.geographyteachingtoday.org.uk/ks3-resources/resource/who-do-we-think-we-are/what-is-britishness.**)

Working with older pupils

Teachers need to ensure that older pupils move beyond stereotypical and archaic impressions. Estyn (2001), the Welsh inspectorate, criticizes displays in Welsh schools for having too many pictures of sheep, daffodils and red dragon flags, thereby failing to promote a modern, exciting and accurate view of Wales.

Pupils can select and discuss appropriate images from the Internet, newspapers or magazines that they think represents their country well. Hence, for England, pictures might include: double-decker buses, tea, village cricket, Elgar, Shakespeare, the Queen, fish and chips, brass bands, crosswords, gardening and country churches. Groups can discuss their choices and whether there are any 'missing' images. Homework could include asking parents and grandparents for their one defining national image. These can be displayed alongside a map of Britain and 'published' in different forms, such as a calendar or poster. Pupils can also work in creating English, Scottish, Welsh, Irish or British cultural boxes. They can discuss what objects should be selected and the challenge of representing the diversity of culture – urban, rural, traditional and contemporary, musical, religious, linguistic and artistic. This can be extended to considering boxes from around the world, mindful of the need to avoid stereotypes. This can be achieved by basing the contents on what might be typically purchased, say in a local market.

From a geographical perspective, Catling (2009) suggests activities to promote older children's thinking about Britain. These include:

- using a map of the British Isles, asking pupils to locate places they think they know or places teachers think they should know;
- asking groups to produce a poster map for a particular purpose (e.g. car journey around the UK);
- asking pupils to design their own UK postcards for tourists;
- asking pupils to write their postal addresses from school/home to national, continental or global levels to introduce the idea of so-called 'nested hierarchies'; and
- asking small groups to choose symbols associated with Britain or to draw/write what comes to mind when they hear the words 'Britain' or 'British'.

Pupils' geographical knowledge and skills can be developed through 'migration mapping' by marking on a world map the places where pupils, parents/guardians/carers and grandparents were born. The map can be used as a basis for discussion of 'pull and push' factors behind migration. Local investigations can focus on the impact of different cultures evidenced in the diversity of shops and restaurants, place names and landmarks. By establishing links with a school from a contrasting locality, through organisations such as the Schools Linking Network, pupils can compare characteristics of different places. Local statistics, for example on ethnic background, religion and household types, are available from government websites (e.g. **www.neighbourhood.statistics.gov/uk**) and can form the basis for comparative investigations.

Multicultural heritage and education

By its very nature Britain has always been a multicultural society. A walk around Blackstock Road in London's Finsbury Park reveals an Irish pub, Indian newsagents, a Greek-Cypriot delicatessen, a halal butcher, West Indian businesses, a Chinse take-away, a Lebanese flower shop, a Jewish-run ironmongers, an Italian restaurant and a Spanish-run off-licence – as Merriman (1994: ix) suggests, 'all historians of immigration should use their boots'. According to *The Atlas of True Names* (Kalimedia Publishing, 2008) the word 'Britain' is probably derived from a combination of the

Greek word *prettanoi*, meaning tattooed people, and the Celtic word *brit*, meaning light coloured or speckled; hence Great Britain meant 'Great Land of the Tattooed'. Britain has been shaped by waves of invaders and migrants (e.g. Romans, Angles, Saxons, Vikings and Normans) each adding to its diverse cultural mix. The name England itself is derived from the invading Angles. The first recorded refugees date back to the arrival of twelfth-century Armenian merchants that fled persecution in the Ottoman Empire. Africans were among the Roman troops that defended Hadrian's Wall in the third century AD (Fryer, 1984). Asians also have a long history in Britain, dating back to the 1600s with the arrival of Indian domestics and sailors (Visram, 2002).

Black Britain

There is no shortage of informative accounts tracing the development of Black communities in Britain, for instance in Liverpool and Butetown, Cardiff (Sinclair, 1993; Costello, 2001; Llwyd, 2005). The most comprehensive reference is provided by Dabydeen *et al.* (2007), who highlight the wide-ranging contribution of Black people to British society. Over the past 20 or so years, there has been a steady growth in educational resources for teaching Black history (see websites). For instance Black History Month, set up in 1987 and observed every October, has the educational goal of redressing perceived distortions and omissions of African and Caribbean contributions to national and global civilisation (**www.black-history-month.co.uk**). There are many stories of Black people who have made significant contributions to Britain's heritage and society (see Table 7.2). Cultural events, such as the Notting Hill Carnival

Table 7.2 Black contributions in British history	
Area	**Examples**
Performing Arts	Black dance; Notting Hill Carnival; actor Ira Aldridge (1807–1867)
Music	Reggae, soul; gospel; the pianist Winifred Atwell (1914–1981); composer Samuel Coleridge-Taylor (1875–1912); the international singer Shirley Bassey (1937–)
Literature	The writers Francis Williams (1702–1770) and Una Marson (1905–1965)
Medicine	Mary Seacole (1805–1881), 'the Black Florence Nightingale'
Politics	Olaudah Equiano (1745–1797), freed slave, author and anti-slavery campaigner; Bernie Grant (1944–2000), first Black councillor and joint first Black MP (along with Diane Abbott and Paul Boateng)
Sport	Walter Tull (1888–1918), footballer and First World War officer; Frank Bruno (1961–), world heavyweight boxing champion; Linford Christie (1960–), world champion sprinter
Religion	Bishop Wilfred Wood (1936–), first Black bishop

(which began in 1964 in response to race riots), convey the vibrancy of multicultural Britain. Teachers should take advantage of events such as the 2012 Olympic Games or the 2014 Commonwealth Games to highlight the rich diversity of British society.

The website **www.100greatblackbritons.com/home.html**, set up because no Black people had featured on the BBC's Greatest Britons poll, provides biographical sketches of major figures that can be used as a starting point for further classroom research. Sources such as oral history, autobiographies, paintings, films and artefacts can begin to illuminate the 'hidden' lives of ordinary Black and Asian people (Marsh, 2005). The British Pathé News website (**www.britishpathe.com**) contains examples of brief films on topic such as:

Jamaicans arriving (1950–1959) – newly-arrived families walking down the gangplank.

Immigrants beat clock (1962) – arrival of West Indian immigrants in Southampton before the new Commonwealth Immigration Act.

East meets West (1945) – Chinese couple adapting to life in Britain.

Schools can also subscribe to **www.britishpathe.com/education/** to access curriculum-specific collections.

Tolerant society?

The commitment to political freedom, and giving refuge to people in need of protection, is part of British identity. In a sixteenth-century parliamentary debate on the subject of accepting refugees, Sir John Woolley argued: 'they are strangers now, we may be strangers hereafter. So let us do as we would be done to' (Arbabzadah, 2007: 15). As Vaclav Havel, the Czech playwright and politician, put it: 'The state is to be judged by how it treats its minorities' (quoted by Williams *et al.*, 2003: 14). Unfortunately, the British historical record is not free from bigotry, racism and prejudice. In medieval times, the English referred to 'cursed forrainers', while in 1597, Elizabeth I decreed that there were too many 'Negroes and blackamoors' in England and set out to deport them all. The Victorians talked about 'blasted furriners', while no-one frowned when a character in Enid Blyton's *The Mystery of the Vanished Prince* (1951) remarked of the dark strangers: 'We're got two at our school. One never cleans his teeth and the other howls if he gets a kick at football' (quoted by Winder, 2004: 348).

The summer of 1948 marks a defining moment in Britain's long story of immigration. For many years, the Jews and the Irish were the prime 'other' targets of abuse. This changed when 492 Black males and one stowaway woman stepped off the *Empire Windrush* – amidst immediate fears that they would 'take' jobs from the locals. Through Britain's history there have been race riots and, at times, appalling treatment of ethnic and religious groups such as the Irish, Chinese and Jews. Hostility has been demonstrated in many forms, ranging from the individual action of a shopkeeper refusing to serve a Black person to national legislation. During the First and Second World Wars, Germans living in Britain suffered trade and movement restrictions. Even Black American troops experienced racism, including a few instances of police prosecution when they associated with white women. Panayi (1994: 109) argues that the

British government was 'fundamentally racist' through the period 1815–1945. Only a few decades ago, it was once acceptable to put up a sign in a boarding house or B&B saying 'No blacks, no Irish, no dogs' (CRE, 2007: 1).

However, there is a danger in overplaying Britain's longstanding prejudices. By and large, Britain has proved to be a tolerant society whose reputation for respecting fundamental human rights has attracted and retained people from all over the world. The post-war influx of migrants has created a new concept of what it means to be British. In recent years, there have been phenomenal increases in the proportion of Eastern European immigrants to Britain – for instance, Slovakians rising by 977 per cent and Lithuanians by 582 per cent (Doward and Pemberton, 2011). While ethnic minority groups make up only 8 per cent of Britain's population, this is expected to rise to 20 per cent by 2051 (Tran, 2010). A recent Citizenship Survey (DCLG, 2009: 33–36) found that 93 per cent of people had strong feelings about being British. Moreover, 68 per cent agreed that it was possible to belong to Britain and maintain a separate religious or cultural identity.

Promoting cultural awareness

Many schools plan an international week to raise pupils' cultural awareness but this could also include British culture. The following questions could be considered when planning a British culture week:

- What do we want to achieve this week?
- How can each area of the curriculum contribute?
- What are the national symbols, figures and landmarks of England, Scotland, Wales and Northern Ireland?
- What do we think of first when this country or people come to mind?
- What stories are in the news about these countries?
- In history, how can we construct a timeline to show the links between the four 'home countries'?
- What events affected people from the whole of the UK (e.g. the First World War) and how can we show this on our timeline?
- In geography, can pupils mark on a map of the UK the location of the cities, towns and natural features? What are the famous natural and human features?
- In Religious Education, what are the major religions? What do they have in common?
- What languages are spoken in the school and local community?
- What works of art, music and food can we share?
- Where could we visit?
- How do the respective tourist boards present the home countries to the wider world?
- What are the traditional stories, legends, myths and poems?
- Who are the famous writers, musicians, poets and artists?

- How will we share outcomes of the week, for instance through a special assembly or website?
- How will we evaluate the week?
- How will we sustain some of the ideas?

One of the assumptions underpinning the UK curricula is that all students should be prepared for life in a multicultural society. Children living in rural parts of the UK as well as the inner-cities and large towns need to know about different lifestyles, values, beliefs and customs. The humanities have a strong responsibility here in providing the most appropriate contexts for teaching pupils about Britain's diverse heritage and multicultural make-up. There are a number of excellent museums, publications and other resources available to teachers. The Moving Here website includes free source material for schools on a wide range of migration projects such as:

- exploring the lives of Victorian immigrants to London and Yorkshire (History);
- using maps and statistics to discover more about birthplace, ethnicity, and net migration (Geography); and
- exploring the faiths of immigrants (Religious Education).

The British Empire and Commonwealth Museum, based in Bristol, provides a range of resources, including workshops on 'suitcase stories' to describe the origins of today's multiracial Britain, and multi-media materials on the subject of migration (**www.empiremuseum.co.uk/index.htm**). The important contribution of such museums is that they help young people and their families, particularly Black and other minority groups, to understand their own sense of self and heritage (Hann, 2004). An exhibition of Sikh art at the Victoria and Albert Museum (V&A) brought thousands of British Sikhs to the museum – 70 per cent of whom had never been to the V&A and 40 per cent of whom had never visited a museum (Hunt, 2002).

The challenges of multicultural education

Multicultural education has its background in the 1960s when African-Caribbean children became a significant presence in primary schools. The UK government first sought to assimilate these children into the British norms, values and mores. There was no inclination to learn about the African-Caribbean culture and the pupils were seen to bring 'problems' that needed to be remedied. In the 1970s political support increased for an integrated model and the promotion of mutual tolerance and equal opportunities. The concept of multicultural education, based on the principle of celebrating diversity, developed in the 1980s. The Rampton Report (1981) highlighted the underachievement of Black children, racism in school and society and low expectations among teachers. By the mid-1980s the 'soft' side of multicultural education was criticised for not addressing structural racial inequalities. The

Swann Report (1985) suggested that the confusion around multicultural education was based upon two dimensions:

- meeting the educational needs of ethnic minority pupils; and
- broadening the education offered to all pupils to reflect the multi-racial nature of British society.

(See **www.educationengland.org.uk/documents/swann/swann06.html**)

The Swann Committee preferred the term 'education for all' rather than 'multicultural education'. It was critical of the tendency to restrict multicultural policies and practices to schools or authorities with ethnic minority pupils, ignoring 'all-white' schools, although the actual presence of such pupils formed the rationale for change. The concept of multiculturalism continues to attract controversy and divide opinion, partly because it is interpreted in different ways – from respect and tolerance for different cultural differences to full integration; from Islamic extremism to the Manchester Gay Pride march (Parekh, 2000; Modood, 2007; Goodman, 2011). It is also tied closely to the human rights agenda, for instance children's rights to celebrate cultural diversity (Swainston, 2001).

There remain concerns that schools are not doing enough to promote pupils' understanding of Britain's multicultural nature and to embed concepts of racial equality within the curriculum (Ofsted, 2005). Primary schools are required under the Race Relations (Amendment) Act (2000) to promote good race relations, equality of opportunity, have a written race equality policy and monitor the impact of policies on pupils, parents and staff from different racial groups.

In providing a multicultural curriculum, schools need to move from what Banks and Banks (2001) describe as a nominal 'contributions' approach (focusing on heroes and holidays) to a transformative and social action agenda, where pupils view life from the perspectives of different ethnic groups and learn to make informed decisions; for instance, how they might reduce prejudice in school or by writing a letter of complaint about adverse media reporting of a minority ethnic group. In the Early Years, practitioners can consider how the 'home corner' might look like from the perspective of someone from a particular ethnic or religious background. A good multicultural curriculum tackles the hard issues of intolerance, prejudice and racism. Knowles and Ridley's (2006) *Another Spanner in the Works* builds on many projects in Cumbria during the 1990s to promote racial equality and social justice in white schools.

Unfortunately, particularly in schools where there are very few ethnic minority pupils, teachers lack knowledge of multicultural education and this does not feature strongly within initial teacher training programmes (Cline *et al.*, 2002). More alarmingly, research (albeit dated) has shown than one in ten postgraduate trainees hold racist views and there is widespread confusion over what is meant by 'a good citizen' (Wilkins, 1999). In the best practice, primary schools that are successful in raising the standards of ethnic minority pupils provide a rich curriculum that draws upon pupils' different cultural experiences (Ofsted, 2002). Fortunately, there are examples of good practices and resources that show the potential of the humanities in addressing the more challenging aspects of multicultural education. For example, Ofsted (2005: 12) reports the following case study:

> In a Year 6 history lesson pupils discussed *Kristallnacht* (Night of Crystal) in 1930s Germany and the concept of prejudice and discrimination against Jews. The class was composed mostly of pupils from Muslim backgrounds. The pupils tried to understand the feelings of children involved in the *Kindertransport*, respecting the symbols of the Jewish religion.

Responding to pupils' diverse needs

Teaching in the twenty-first century requires the knowledge, understanding and skills to respond appropriately to the diverse interests, experiences and needs of learners (see Table 7.3). Over recent years, schools have been charged with promoting an inclusive curriculum so that all pupils can experience success. Inclusion focuses in particular on promoting the achievement of different groups including gifted and talented pupils, newly-arrived children, those from ethnic minority backgrounds, boys and girls, looked-after children, those from the travellers' community and pupils with additional learning needs (Sebba, 1994; Carpenter *et al.*, 1996; Swift, 2005; Richards and Armstrong, 2011). Generally, gifted and talented pupils (between 5–10 per cent of a school's population) are good readers, show mature awareness of current events, like to talk, ask lots of questions, recall things well, and often have unusual hobbies and sometimes struggle to tolerate other children. In some cases, children demonstrate a real passion for subjects such as history or archaeology and teachers can support such interest. For example, they can offer contact details for local clubs, bring in 'expert' speakers, set open-ended challenges, ask 'What if . . .?' questions, and encourage them to be 'intellectually playful' (Eyre, 2006: 267). Research suggests that teachers need to focus on developing pupils' self-regulating skills, such as setting personal goals, time management and planning homework (DCSF, 2008).

TASK

- Choose a group of learners and conduct further research to find out strategies to support their learning in the humanities.

Where in-class support is available, adults can read sources to children and use tape-recordings in advance of the lesson. Visual glossaries of key words are also important. Organisations such as the National Association for Language Development in the Curriculum (NALDIC) provide specific strategies for monolingual practitioners including supporting children at the non-verbal stage through visual clues, puppets and artefacts   (**www.naldic.org.uk/ITTSEAL2/teaching/MonolingualPractitioners.cfm**). It also provides examples of how student teachers might develop inclusive practices while teaching geography and other subjects:

Table 7.3 Meeting the diverse needs of pupils

Group	General strategy	Specific examples
Boys (and girls)	• Use short focused tasks. • Be explicit about expectations • Use humour. • Give and ask for regular feedback. • Focus on problem-solving. • Use practical activities (e.g. drama). • Use ICT regularly and appropriately. • Use mixed gender groups. • Use praise (not just for academic performance).	• Use history detective stories. Tell adventure stories and graphic accounts of historical events, such as the experience of the Great Fire of London; • Follow-up interests, such as the history of football teams founded in the Victorian period e.g. Arsenal; • Make models e.g. castle siege weapons
Special educational needs (additional learning or educational needs)	• Break tasks down into small steps. • Use multi-sensory approaches. • Allocate greater time for completion of work. • Use targeted additional adult support. • Differentiate resources such as textbooks, work-sheets and tasks. • Consider reducing writing demands (e.g. through writing frames).	• Focus on a particular sense such as smell. For example, in RE: *Judaism* – smell of cinnamon, nutmeg and cloves in a spice box; *Hinduism* – smell of warm ghee used in cooking; *Sikhism* – smell of divas and joss sticks burning.
Pupils for whom English is an additional language	• Use a variety of visual prompts including arte-facts, pictures and puppets. • Provide a trained 'buddy' who, wherever possi-ble, speaks the same language as the new arrival. • Provide key vocabulary lists, bilingual dictionar-ies and dual language or picture books.	• Make connections with newly-arrived children's homelands e.g. using maps, food and drink, cultural artefacts, flags, postcards, websites.
Gifted and talented	• Use a variety of questions, especially open-ended ones. • Use differentiated planning – stimulus, resources, tasks, outcome, response. • Use appropriate pace identified in planning. • Set tasks that focus on critical thinking, interpre-tations, reasoning. • Use original, challenging sources. • Provide opportunities for out-of-school links with specialists. • Provide acceleration – working with older pupils for certain subjects.	• Engage with religious metaphors, symbols and allegories. • Let children create their own publications on research topics. • Develop 'Premiership League' subject vocabulary lists. • Provide workshops with historians and geographers.

A student on the Primary PGCE programme set up the sand area in their placement Year One classroom. During the lesson observation a range of pupils from a variety of different backgrounds and a range of first languages were observed playing in the sand. They were creating their own world by making roads for vehicles. During this time the children scooped out holes and used sand to make a hill; they poured water into the hole to make a lake and sticks were used as trees. The children named the roads that they had made and used a watering can to make rain.

The student observing this session noted the sustained nature of the play and the focus and dedication that the pupils showed as their world was created. However, upon further analysis the student was encouraged to see from a geographical perspective how this play also indicated the pupils' knowledge and growing understanding of the world around them.

Source: www.naldic.org.uk/ITTSEAL2/teaching/Geography.cfm.

Classroom displays are a good means of promoting inclusive practice. Many children like to see the countries from where they originate, or where they have relatives, reflected in displays. Photographs, artefacts and postcards from different countries can illustrate diversity in the world of today. It may be possible for schools to work closely with English as an Additional Language (EAL) staff from local authority services to develop induction materials for new arrivals. Such materials should introduce children to the geography of the UK, and geographical enquiry skills, especially where children come from countries where the educational systems put a high priority on the acquisition of knowledge.

Teachers should draw upon the experiences and interests of pupils when responding to their needs. Hence, the experiences of children that have lived overseas can be an advantage in geography lessons. For example, if teaching about the rainforest ecosystem, children from countries such as Colombia, Brazil and the Democratic Republic of Congo will often have personal knowledge and sometimes direct experience of the rainforest. Moreover, most newly-arrived children will have experience of a different climate to that of the UK, as well as different housing, transport and shopping patterns. Teachers need to demonstrate professional judgements in deciding whether to refer to pupils' previous experiences, which could be traumatic and counter-productive.

Developing an inclusive humanities curriculum

An inclusive humanities curriculum makes room for all pupils and is representative of different cultural perspectives. Claire (1996: 10) provides excellent ideas for promoting equality and diversity through the history curriculum (see Table 7.4). She suggests stories and other resources for each major period in history and includes a useful list of famous people hitherto much neglected, including: Black activists, nurses, inventors, scientists, 'people of courage', sportsmen and women, musicians, dancers, writers and politicians.

An inclusive history curriculum has a strong focus on the lives of the 'working class'. The term was first used in the 1820s to describe those who worked in industry, particularly factories; previously they were known as 'the lower orders', 'the masses', or even 'the mob' (Hopkins, 1991: 2). Over recent years, the British working class has gone from 'salt of the earth' to 'scum of the earth', seen as objects of fear and ridicule manifested in the likes of *Little Britain's* Vicky Pollard (Jones, 2011). By studying the

Table 7.4 Opportunities to develop an inclusive history curriculum		
Aspect of inclusion	**Objectives**	**Examples**
Race and ethnicity	• To support the learning, self-esteem and identification with history of Black and ethnic minority children. • To give white children non-European approaches that help them understand the modern world and counteract ignorance and prejudice.	• Topics on 'Moving' or 'Memories'. • Using stories with a strong international dimension such as Margy Knight (1992), *Talking Walls*, Gardiner Maine: Tilbury House Publishers. • Exploring Welsh, Scottish and Irish links for each period such as the Welshman Henry Tudor (Henry VII), Hadrian's Wall (Romans) or Highland Clearances (Victorians).
Gender	• To counter sexism and marginalisation of women's contribution, as part of the education of boys. • To offer girls positive role models and foci for identification to support their interest and motivation.	• A project on mothers and grandmothers. • Links to International Women's History week. • Role of women in particular campaigns, such as anti-slavery movement.
Class	• To make sure that working-class children are able to have some point of entry and identification with the content of history. • To empower children by challenging the view that change has always been the work of the rulers and powerful. • To give children the opportunity to start learning about the difficult and painful path towards democracy.	• Exploring levels of society during Tudor or Victorian times, contrasting rich and poor (homes, leisure, education, health employment). • Studying reasons behind popular protest movements such as Rebecca Riots (Wales), Luddism (England), Chartism (Britain).

Source: Adapted from Claire (1996: 10).

contribution of individuals from working-class backgrounds, pupils can begin to see that the 'movers and shakers' of history are not always the rich and powerful. For instance, the trade unionist Jimmy Reid (1932–2010) is seen by many as a true working-class Scottish hero. The Learning and Teaching Scotland website provides learning resources associated with his life (**www.ltscotland.org.uk**). The daily lives of ordinary people should feature strongly in the primary history curriculum. These are the ancestors of the vast majority of pupils and whatever the theme or historical period, teachers should seek to introduce pupils to 'history from below'. The success of historical reconstruction-style programmes and publications, such as *Edwardian Farm, 1900 House* and *1940s House,* is that they offer believable insight into the lives of ordinary people.

From a religious perspective, an inclusive humanities curriculum develops pupils' knowledge, understanding and tolerance of different faiths. There have been many successful projects in which primary schools have worked closely together to develop pupils' understanding of different faiths (Ackroyd *et al.,* 2003). For instance, the Building Bridges Pendle programme involves primary and secondary schoolchildren reflecting on their own 'Faith or human values', drawing upon specific topics such as 'marriages around the world' (Billings and Holden, 2007; see also (**www. buildingbridgespendle.org.uk**). Another example is a joint project between two charities, Islamic Relief and Tide ~ global learning, which has produced useful resources to guide teachers about shared values among Muslims and non-Muslims (**www.tidec. org/primary-early-years/citizenship-muslim-perspectives**).

However, as Erricker *et al.* (2011) point out, it would be naive to think that simply to inform young people about the differences in religion and culture will be likely to change attitudes, opinions and behaviour for the good. Moreover, for those children living in essentially mono-cultural environments (such as many village schools), their direct experience of different faiths will be very limited. One of the challenges is ensuring that pupils acquire accurate information about different beliefs. Unfortunately, research shows that teachers cannot always rely on published materials. For instance: 'Sikhism tends to receive a superficial treatment focusing on the externals of the religion (e.g. buildings) rather than on its power for transformation in the lives of the individual or its contribution to wider society' (DCSF, 2010a: 5).

This is a significant issue given the limited subject expertise of most primary teachers. In many cases, teachers prepare their own resources and pupils are naturally excited to see their faith or that of their family and friends represented. Resources from faith communities can also prove beneficial. In one primary school, a number of parents from a local Jehovah's Witness community expressed a wish to withdraw their children from RE lessons. The head teacher took time to meet with representatives from the community to explain the school's approach to the subject. As a result, the school developed a trusting relationship with the community, and the school was able to identify aspects of the RE programme that the parents were happy for their children to join and those from which the children would be withdrawn – mainly the celebration of Christmas (DCSF, 2010b: 29).

One of the major challenges for primary teachers is how to promote critical insight among older pupils about religious teachings and practices, such as those relating to marriage, family life and attitudes towards women, which run contrary to established traditions in the UK. This is not confined to aspects of the Islamic faith. There are individual pupils who are brought up within strong minority faith communities, such as Plymouth Brethren, and these voices need to be heard if schools are to be regarded as genuinely inclusive. But as Erricker *et al.* (2011) point out, while inclusivity is essential, it is also controversial. How do teachers treat aspects of a religious faith or ethnic culture that they strongly oppose? Many would find beliefs and practices of religious ethnic minorities as oppressive – especially concerning women and children, trapped within 'mono-religious, mono-cultural' segregated communities (Hasan, 2009). As Wilson (2000) points out, it is easy to utter platitudes about human equality and one religion is as good as another. In reality, issues such as female circumcision are not morally neutral.

There are a number of controversial issues related to the humanities that primary teachers are likely to encounter. Woolley (2010: 4–5) reports that fears among student teachers include teaching about: 'media influence', 'relationships', 'family values', 'antiracist and multicultural education' and 'spirituality and religion'. There are many recommended general approaches when discussing controversial issues. Claire and Holden (2007) mention dramatic and discussion techniques including:

Conscience alley – one child acts as a judge and the rest form an alley of opposing arguments. The judge walks down the alley listening to all the arguments and then reaches a decision.

Thought tracking – a scene from a play/book is 'frozen' and the actors say what they are thinking and the audience is invited to explain their motives at that point in the drama.

Take the power – participants explore how, by entering the scene as a character, they can change the power relationships.

Mantle of the expert – pupils become experts and explore fictional situations.

Listening triads – two people talk about an issue while one listens and prepares a feedback summary of discussion but does not participate.

Envoying –in small groups pupils think of questions, having seen a picture, read a book or in response to another stimulus; these are then recorded on index cards and one pupil visits another group to present its question and to hear its responses before returning to host group to feedback responses.

Questioning the author – devising challenging questions for authors to answer (e.g. Why did you describe XX as YY? Whose views are not represented in the book? What do you think about . . .?)

Resources such as anti-bias persona dolls (Brown, 2001) also help pupils think about people's feelings and challenge discrimination based on a lack of experience or ignorance. The Historical Association provides online materials for planning emotive and controversial issues through the primary school, including case studies (**www. history.org.uk/resources/primary_resource_1140_2.html**). Its TEACH report suggests that from a young age children should explore such questions as:

- Who am I?
- How do I know that it is me?
- What other things make me, apart from how I look?
- What is the same about me and other children?
- What is different about me that makes me who I am?

At Key Stage 2, pupils can explore such controversial issues as slavery, methods of government, conquest and the role of women within the British, European and global contexts.

This chapter has shown that Britain has a long history of cultural diversity. Good humanities teaching should reflect this within an inclusive school ethos. One of the core aims of *all* primary schools should be to promote respect for ethnic and faith minorities: 'It is inconceivable that any pupil currently in school live their lives without meeting, working with, or in some way affecting or being affected by, people from a wide range of different ethnic backgrounds' (Gillborn and Mirza, 2000:6).

SUMMARY

- Being British means different things to different people. The quest for Britishness has occupied the minds of many generations. In recent years, there has been a renewed interest in promoting British values in school and the humanities have a key role to play.

- Through such approaches as projects on names, stories about national figures, role-play, museum visits and visiting speakers, young children can begin to build up a sense of their own identities and the diverse nature of the British society.

- Older pupils in the primary school should engage in discussions about national identities because this can improve their understanding of the challenges facing their own communities and wider contemporary society.

- Good multicultural education goes beyond celebrating diversity. It addresses challenging issues such as racism, bias and intolerance through subjects such as history, geography and religious education.

- There is considerable guidance available to primary teachers to accommodate the diverse needs of pupils. The humanities should be accessible to *all* pupils.

References

Ackroyd, C., Grant, P., Kershaw, J. and Kotler, A. (2003), 'Building Bridges – Making Links: Bradford's Linking Schools Project, 2001–2004, *Race Equality Teaching*, 11–14.

Arbabzadah, N. (2007), (ed.) *From Outside In. Refugees and British Society*, London: Arcadia Books.

Banks, J.A., and Banks, C.A. (2001), *Multicultural Education*, New York: John Wiley.

Barker, I. (2008), 'Do you teach Britishness?' *Times Educational Supplement*, 3 October 2008.

Barrett, M., and Davey, K. (2001), 'English children's sense of national identity and their attachment to national geography', Unpublished paper, Department of Psychology: University of Surrey.

Barrett, M. & Buchanan-Barrow, E. (2002). Children's understanding of society, in Smith, P.K. & Hart, C. (eds.), *Blackwell Handbook of Childhood Social Development*, Oxford: Blackwell, 491–512.

Barrett, M. (2005). 'National identities in children and young people', in Ding, S. & Littleton, K. (eds.), *Children's*

Personal and Social Development, Milton Keynes: The Open University/Blackwell, 181–220.

Billings, A and Holden, A. (2007), *The Burnley Project: Interfaith Interventions and Cohesive Communities*, Lancaster: Lancaster University.

Bradley, I. (2007), *Believing in Britain*, London: IB Tauris.

Brown, B. (2001), *Combating Discrimination: Persona Dolls in Action*, Stoke-on-Trent: Trentham.

Browne, A. (1997), *Changes,* London: Walker.

Carington, B. and Short, G. (1995), 'What Makes a Person British? Children's conceptions of their national culture and identity', *Education Studies,* Vol. 21: 2, 217–238.

Carpenter, B., Ashdown, R., and Bovair, K. (eds) (1996), *Enabling Access*, London: David Fulton.

Catling, S. (2009), 'Thinking of Britain in Children's Geographies', *Primary Geography,* 17–19.

Chave, O. (2011), 'Mapping the British Isles with heart and head', *Primary Geography,* summer 2011, 14–15.

Claire, H. (1996), *Reclaiming our Pasts*, Stoke on Trent: Trentham Books.

Claire, H. and Holden, C. (2007), *The Challenge of Teaching Controversial Issues*, Stoke on Trent: Trentham Books.

Cline, T., de Abreu, G., Fihosy, C., Gray, H., Lambert, H., and Neale, J. (2002), *Minority Ethnic Pupils in Mainly White Schools* Norwich: DfES.

Costello, R.H. (2001), *Black Liverpool: The Early History of Britain's Oldest Black Community 1730–1918,* Liverpool: Picton Press.

CRE (2005), *Citizenship and Belonging: What is Britishness?* London: ETHNOS.

CRE (2007), *A lot done, a lot to do*, London: CRE.

Crick Report (1998), *Education for Citizenship and the Teaching of Democracy in Schools*, London: DfEE.

Dabydeen, D., Gilmore, J., and Jones, C. (eds) (2007), *The Oxford Companion To Black British History*, Oxford: OUP.

Davies, N. (1999), *The Isles,* London: MacMillan.

DCLG (2009), *2007–08 Citizenship Survey Identity and Values Topic Report*, London: DCLG.

DCSF (2008), *What works in improving the educational achievement of gifted and talented pupils? A systematic review of literature,* London: DCSF.

DCSF (2010a), *Materials Used to Teach About World Religions in England*, London: DCSF.

DCSF (2010b), *Religious education in English schools: Non-statutory guidance* 2010, London: DCSF.

Devine, T. and Logue, P. (eds) (2002), *Being Scottish: Personal Reflections on Scottish Identity Today*, Edinburgh: Polygon.

Doward, J. and Pemberton, J. 'Britain's changing ethnic map: how suburbia has been transformed', *The Observer*, 10 April 2011.

Dunkling, L. (1998), *Dictionary of Surnames*, Glasgow: HarperCollins.

Erricker, C., Lowndes, J., and Bellchambers, E. (2011), Primary Religious Education – a New *Approach,* London: Routledge.

Estyn (2001), Y Cwricwlwm Cymreig, *The Welsh dimension of the curriculum in Wales: good practice in teaching and learning*, Cardiff: Estyn.

Eyre, D. (2006), 'Gifted and Talented', in Arthur, J., Grainger, T., and Wray, D. (eds), *Learning to Teach in the Primary School*, London: Routledge.

Ewart, S., Schubotz, D., Abbs, F., Harris, D., Montgomery, L., Moynagh, C., Maguire, G., and Livingstone, S. (2004), *Voices behind the Statistics. Young people's views of sectarianism in Northern Ireland*, London: National Children's Bureau.

Freeman, J. W. (1994), *Discovering Surnames*, Princes Risborough: Shire.

Fryer, P. (1984), *Staying Power*, London: Pluto Press.

Gillborn, D. and Mirza, H. (*2000*), *Educational Inequality: Mapping Race, Class and. Gender*, London: Ofsted.

Goodman, P, (2011), 'It's Time to end the Tory War on Multiculturalism and Engage with Ethnic Minority Communities', in Davis, D., Binley, B., and Baron, J. (eds), *The Future of Conservatism: Values Revisited,* Biteback Publishing.

Groom, N. (2006), *The Union Jack. The Story of the British Flag*, London: Atlantic Books.

Hann, K. (2004), 'In My View. Migration: the search for a better life?' *Primary History*, 6–9.

Hasan, R. (2010), *Multiculturalism: Some Inconvenient Truths*, London: Politico's Publishing.

Hayward, F.H. and Freeman, A. (1919), *The Spiritual Foundations of Reconstruction*, London: King and Son.

Historical Association, *TEACH: A Report from The Historical Association on the Challenges and Opportunities for Teaching Emotive and Controversial History 3–19* available at: **www.history.org.uk/resources/resource_780.html**.

Home Office (2007), *Life in the United Kingdom: A Journey to Citizenship*, London: Home Office.

Hopkins, E. (1991), *Rise and Decline of the English Working Class*, New York: St Martin's Press.

Howard, M. (2011), 'The Killing of St George', *The Guardian*, 23 April 2011.

Hunt, T. (2002), 'Uncovering Britain's multicultural heritage', *The Guardian*, 6 June 2002.

Jenkins, D. (1975), *The British: Their Identity and Their Religion*, London: SCM Press.

Jones, O. (2011), *Chavs. The Demonization of the Working Class*, London: Verso.

Knight, M. (1992), *Talking Walls,* Gardiner Maine: Tilbury House Publishers.

Knowles, E. and Ridley, W. (2006), *Another Spanner in the Works*, Stoke-on-Trent: Trentham Books.

Kumar, K. (2003), *The Making of English National Identity*, Cambridge: Cambridge University Press.

Llwyd, A. (2005), *Cymru Dddu Black Wales: A History*, Llandybïe: Gwasg Dinfewr Press.

Logue, P. (2000), *Being Irish: Personal Reflections on Irish Identity Today*, Dublin: Oak Tree Press.

Marsh, J. (2005), *Black Victorians: Black People in British Art, 1800–1900*, Aldershot: Lund Humphries Publishers Ltd.

Martin, F. (2006), *Teaching Geography in Primary Schools*, Cambridge: Chris Kington Publishing.

Merriman, N. (ed.) (1994), *The Peopling of London*, London: Museum of London.

Modood, T. (2007), *Multiculturalism*, London: Polity.

Muslim Council of Britain (2007), *Towards Greater Understanding Meeting the needs of Muslim pupils in state schools. Information & Guidance for Schools*, available at: **www.mcb.org.uk/**.

Ofsted (2002), *Achievement of Black Caribbean Pupils: Three Successful Primary Schools*, London: Ofsted.

Ofsted (2005), *Race equality in education*, London: Ofsted.

Ofsted (2007), *History in the Balance*, London: Ofsted.

Ofsted (2011), *Geography. Learning to make a world of difference*, London: Ofsted.

Orwell, G. (1947), *English People,* London: Collins.

Panayi, P. (1994), *Immigration, ethnicity and racism in Britain 1815–1945*, Manchester: Manchester University Press.

Parekh, B. (2000), *Rethinking Multiculturalism: Cultural Diversity and Political Theory*, London: Macmillan.

Paxman, J. (1999), *The English*, London: Penguin.

Pierson, J. (2002), *Tackling Social Exclusion*, London: Routledge.

Phillips, R. (2000), 'Culture, Community and Curriculum in Wales' in Lawton, D., Cairns, J., and Gardner, R. (2000), *Education for Citizenship*, London: Continuum, 151–161.

Pugh, G. (2007), *London's Forgotten Children: Thomas Coram and the Foundling Hospital*, Stroud: The History Press.

Rampton Report (1981), *West Indian Children in Our Schools* (Interim Report of the Committee of Inquiry into the Education of Children from Ethnic Minority Group), London: HMSO.

Richards, G. and Armstrong, F. (2011), (eds), *Teaching and Learning in Diverse and Inclusive Classrooms*, London: Routledge.

Sebba, J. (1994), *History for All,* London: David Fulton.

Sinclair, N. (1993), *The Tiger Bay Story*, Cardiff: Butetown History & Arts Centre.

Spencer, N. (2009), 'Measuring British religion', *The Guardian*, 9 June 2009.

Swainston, H. (2001), 'The right to celebrate cultural diversity', *Primary Geography,* October 2001, 25–27.

Swift, D. (2005), *Meeting SEN in the Curriculum: Geography*, London: David Fulton.

The Swann Report (1985), *Education for All.* Report of the Committee of Enquiry into the Education of Children from Ethnic Minority Groups, London: HMSO.

Tran, M. (2010), 'Ethnic minorities to make up 20% of UK population by 2051', *The Guardian*, 13 July 2010.

Visram, R. (2002), *Asians in Britain*, London: Pluto Press.

Ward, P. (2004), *Britishness since 1870*, London: Routledge.

Wiegand, P. (1992), *Places in the Primary School: Knowledge and Understanding of Places at Key Stages 1 and 2*, London: Falmer Press.

Wiegand, P. (2006), *Learning and Teaching with Maps*. London: Routledge.

Williams, C., Evans, N., O'Leary, P. (2003), *A Tolerant Nation? Exploring Ethnic Diversity*, Cardiff: University of Wales Press.

Wilson, J. (2000), *Key Issues in Education and Teaching*, London: Cassell.

Wilkins, C. (1999), 'Making 'Good Citizens': the social and political attitudes of PGCE students, *Oxford Review of Education,* Vol. 25, 1–2, 1999.

Winder, R. (2004), *Bloody Foreigners*, London: Abacus.

Woolley, R. (2010), *Tackling Controversial Issues in the Primary School,* Abingdon: Routledge.

Zephaniah, B. (2000), *Wicked World*, London: Puffin.

Useful Websites

Association for Citizenship Teaching includes many resources including members-only materials on promoting pupils' understanding of identity and diversity issues: **www.teachingcitizenship.org.uk**.

The National Archive, pathways to the past, Black presence: Asian and Black History in Britain 1500–1850: **www.pro.gov.uk/pathways/blackhistory/index.htm**.

The Institute of Race Relations has educational resources: **www.irr.org.uk**.

The Black and Ethnic Minority experience archive: **www. be-me.org/body.asp**.

Black History 4 Schools contains many resources: **http:// blackhistory4schools.com**.

Moving Here explores, records and illustrates why people came to England over the last 200 years and their experiences. It includes many educational resources from local, regional and national archives, libraries and museums: **http://movinghere.org.uk**.

Anti-racist materials form part of the Learning and Teaching Scotland website: **www.ltscotland.org.uk/ supportinglearners/positivelearningenvironments/ inclusionandequality/antiracism**.

Centre for Studies on Inclusive Education: **http://www. csie.org.uk/**

Internet surname database provides free access to the meaning and history of around 50,000 surnames: **www. surnamedb.com**.

The wider world and children's spiritual, moral, social and cultural development

Ninety per cent of the human race is an utter disgrace. The other ten, you would agree, consist of such as you and me.

(Harri Webb, 1983: 27)

Developing a deeper understanding of people and places, and of the need to live in balance with an increasingly fragile environment, is more important than ever in today's world.

Ofsted (2011: 01)

Learning objectives

By the end of this chapter you should be able to:

- recognise the importance of pupils learning about the wider world through the humanities;
- describe the range of approaches and resources for teaching distant places, global history and world religions;
- understand the role that the humanities play in promoting pupils' spiritual, moral, social and cultural development; and
- identify the major challenges linked to teaching about the wider world.

'Us and Them'

In the Western world, there has been a long tradition of separating 'us' from 'others'. This often divides along European and non-European lines, but can also break down to particular 'rivalries' between countries or regions. The ancient Greek word *ethnos* originally meant 'a group of people who live together' but later came to signify the barbarians, the uncultured 'others' that could not speak Greek. Similar concepts are evident in the Hebrew word *goyim* (plural of *goy*, 'non-Israelite') and the Roman distinction between the *populus* of citizens and the *gentes*, comprising those others ruled by nature and local practices. Even within a modern, pluralistic society, the 'others' have been described as the 'side-scenes' in a world show or the 'ungrievables' – such as those killed in a faraway war reported on the world news but soon forgotten (Mikander, 2010). The 'us-and-them-thinking' can extend the 'other' beyond ethnic groups to the poor, women and religious followings. In developing children's understanding of the wider world, one of the key principles is to draw attention to shared concerns across time, place and society. Teachers can build upon children's fascination with different cultures, lands and lifestyles so that they learn tolerance (at least) and respect (at best) for 'others'; however, these are defined.

Why teach about the 'wider world'?

The curriculum throughout the UK requires pupils to develop their knowledge and understanding of the wider world beyond children's direct and immediate experiences. It recognises the importance of pupils learning about Britain in a wider global context (see Table 8.1). This chapter focuses on distant places, global history and world religions.

Table 8.1 KS2 Requirements: the wider world

	England	Northern Ireland	Scotland	Wales
History	Learn about change and continuity in their own area, in Britain and in other parts of the world.	Study change over time – the effects of positive and negative changes in the local area, nationally and globally.	Develop understanding of chronology of key events in Britain, European and world history.	Study life of people and communities in the past in the local area, Wales and the wider world.
Geography	Describe and explain how and why places are similar to and different from other places in the same country and elsewhere in the world.	Learn how we are interdependent with other parts of Europe and the wider world for some of our goods and services.	Develop a sense of place and begin to locate key features within Scotland, the UK, Europe and the wider world.	Study living in other countries (i.e. contrasting localities outside the UK and in the wider world).
Religious Education	Learn about Christianity and at least two of the other principal religions, recognising the impact of religion and belief locally, nationally and globally.	Study relationship with the wider world – an awareness of experiences, lives and cultures of people in the wider world.	Explore the world's major religions and approaches to lives and cultures of people in the wider world.	Study the world religions and respect the diversity between lifestyles, cultures and beliefs.

Sources: DCELLS (2008a, 2008b, 2008c); CCEA (2007); Scottish Government (2009); http://www.education.gov.uk/schools/teachingandlearning/curriculum/primary

The strong rationale for pupils to learn about the wider world includes the following:

- to broaden pupils' cultural, social and political horizons, for instance developing a positive sense of identity and appreciation of the diversity in the world;
- to redress pupils' misconceptions and errors about life in the 'wider world'; and
- to develop pupils' knowledge and understanding of global history and world faiths.

Distant places

In his excellent introductory text, Creswell (2004: 11) suggests that place is 'a way of seeing, knowing and understanding'. While there are common sense ideas of what places are, these are often vague. Most people's experiences of places will naturally be limited to their locality. More distant places tend to be seen in terms of facts and figures (however accurate) rather than as a rich and complicated interplay of people and their environment. When people look at the world as a world of places, they see different things. To think of Afghanistan as a place, in all its richness, is different to thinking of it as a location for terrorists. Yet often places are seen through a narrow lens leading to prejudice and conflict. 'Our place' can become territorial and seen as under threat, requiring the need to exclude people. Place is a complex concept but is very much about social space and how people experience their world wherever they live.

It is important for pupils to draw upon their local knowledge and experiences when discussing places and issues around the world. Through such comparisons, pupils should build up their understanding of how communities are interconnected, and gain an appreciation of the impact that one may have on another. Children in the UK live in one of the wealthiest nations of the world. The Key Stage 2 geography curriculum in England and Wales requires pupils to study a locality in a less prosperous part of the world, in order that children develop a sense of the diversity of people's contexts and lives (DfEE/QCA, 1999; Catling and Willy, 2009).

There are strong arguments for teaching children about distant places beyond their locality. From a young age, children gain experience about various places around the world. Usually, these are indirect experiences gained from the media, games or friends. Often, particular parts of the world are reported upon in negative contexts such as wars, famines, floods, earthquakes or droughts. The danger is that children do not go beyond these images and are left with misleading impressions. Hence, the requirement to study distant places is perhaps one of the most challenging areas of primary geography (Scoffham, 2007).

Reasons for studying distant places

- To build on children's curiosity and early images of places and people.
- To provide a context to explore geographical ideas – similarities and differences, spatial pattern, change and its impact on sustainability – and to use and develop children's enquiry approaches and skills (e.g. map reading and language). ▶

Reasons for studying distant places (*Continued*)

- To foster awareness of the common needs of life (e.g. homes and clothing, food and water, and work and leisure) and to consider why this might be.

- To examine and clarify children's existing awareness and understanding of places, developed via a variety of sources, including television, films, websites, games, stories and family links.

- To address children's ignorance, partiality and bias, which frequently are the basis for their misunderstandings, stereotypes and prejudices about people and places in others parts of the world.

- To develop children's spatial awareness through exploring particular places and their regional, national and global settings.

- To enable children to recognise their interdependence with the rest of the world.

- To develop children's knowledge and understanding of how others live, why places are as they are, and what they might aspire to and become in the future.

- To develop children's appreciation and value the diversity of people, places, environments and cultures around the world; foster tolerance towards others, building positive attitudes to other people both in the UK and around the world.

Source: Adapted from Catling (1995).

BOX 8.1 RESEARCH BRIEFING – CHILDREN'S UNDERSTANDING OF THE WIDER WORLD

The importance of redressing pupils' imbalanced and misconceived ideas and perceptions, such as believing that all people in Africa are very poor, has been widely researched (Catling, 2003; Hirst, 2006; Martin, 2006). For example, Jenner's research (2011) on young children's perceptions of distant places reports that their knowledge before and after teaching about a distant place changes significantly. The post-test information highlighted certain fundamental conclusions, such as pupils' need to be provided with accurate information about ways of life in distant places early in their education in order to avoid stereotyping and forming imbalanced ideas (**www.geography.org.uk/download/ GA_EYPPRRJenner.pdf**). From around the age of three, children identify with categories such as gender and ethnicity. Rutland (1999) found that national prejudice, in-group favouritism or self-stereotyping did not generally develop until around the age of ten.

> **TASK**
>
> - Ask a group of children to draw pictures or say what comes to their mind when they think of Africa, America or another place in the world.

Global history

Global history addresses the deep structural changes that have shaped human experience, including the domestication of animals, the development of agriculture, the Industrial Revolution and the rise of technologies (Crossley, 2008). It is concerned with political themes, such as stability and security, religious and ideological questions about understanding the self and salvation, and the economic problems of subsistence and surplus (Cowen, 2001). All of this might seem too high-brow for schools. However, the study of themes such as Food and Farming, Transport, and Homes and Households, all offer opportunities to explore continuity and change in history. In a class project on the Romans, the following points could be highlighted to illustrate connections to the present:

- concern over international security and border control (Hadrian's Wall; redeployment of troops; coastal forts);
- the rise of technologies (central heating, siege weapons, bridges, fire engines);
- town planning (along grid patterns similar to modern American cities);
- the human interest in cosmetic appearance (findings have included tweezers, nail cleaners, toothpicks, ear scoops, make-up); and
- fast food take-away bars (provided pastries, meats, pies and the equivalent of hamburgers).

The Romans were mass producers, capitalists, civil servants and empire builders, who transformed much of Britain during their 400-year stay. The Roman Empire provided Britain's first multicultural society, drawing upon soldiers and merchants from Spain, North Africa, Gaul, Germany and western Asia. The Roman legacy forms the basis of much of our technology today (Wilkinson, 2000). The extraordinary achievements of ancient peoples, tax even the most sophisticated of modern-day engineers, who have struggled to recreate their building techniques (Barnes *et al.*, 1996).

When planning to study major civilisations it is important for children to see the relevance to their lives. For example, an obvious starting point for a study of ancient Greece is the Olympic Games. The Olympics are far more than a sporting competition held every four years between the countries of the world. They symbolise the optimistic, aspiring side of human nature – a sense of sharing, of open, honest competition, of coming together in a spirit of fraternity, friendship, caring and community (Nichol, 2011). The Olympics are the most powerful of antidotes against bigotry, racism and related persecution and victimisation.

Teachers should highlight the legacy of civilisations, whether through physical forms (e.g. buildings), ideas (e.g. democracy), beliefs (e.g. superstitions), language or customs. Historians have increasingly acknowledged the contribution of non-Western civilisations, such as Iraq, India and Central America, to the modern world (Wood, 1992; Hart-Davis, 2004). Anniversaries, landmarks and traditions are a good lead-in to global history. Teachers could use a two-minute news slot at the start of each day or week to introduce a key event, person or landmark in history or geography commemorated on the day. Global links can also be highlighted through traditions. The truce was established in Ancient Greece in the ninth century BC so that people could travel in safety to participate in or attend the Olympic Games. Today, the Olympic Truce is symbolised by the dove of peace with the traditional Olympic flame in the background.

Older pupils' sense of chronology can be developed by producing a timeline of key turning points in world history. Pupils' research into great discoveries and inventions can focus on the global impact on everyday life. There are many books and websites that detail the stories behind inventions (Dyson and Uhlig, 2001; Harrison, 2003; Behar and Yarham 2007; Challoner, 2009). Human inventiveness can be traced back over thousands of years and the domestic highlights include: soap (2800 BC), central heating (150 BC), fork (1000 AD), buttons (1235), toothbrush (1498), sandwich (1762), canned food (1809), lawnmower (1830), vacuum flask (1892), frozen food (1924), television (1926), microwave oven (1946), post-it note (1973), and personal computer (1975). Each of these had a significant impact on the lives of ordinary people throughout the world. For example, a small bent piece of wire, or the paper clip, has global sales in excess of 100 trillion (Rubino, 2010). Groups of pupils can contribute to a class 'Book of Firsts' by exploring different themes such as food and drink, leisure, transport, medical achievements, technologies, law and order, communication and sport. They can vote for their 'top ten' inventions and discoveries, justifying them in terms of global impact, such as sales or improvements in the quality of life. One school researched, furiously debated and finally voted for:

1. Mobile telephone
2. Internet
3. Computer
4. Television
5. Football
6. Motor car
7. Chocolate
8. Airplane
9. Cinema
10. Camera

Such a list illustrates the importance of the digital age. Homework activities can include finding out the views of parents and neighbours. Pupils' research will reveal surprising findings about when a product was invented – the mobile phone, for example, first appeared in 1947 although it was not popularised until the 1980s. Bill Bryson's (2010) *At Home* provides an excellent tour of how the key discoveries of humankind can be found in the very fabric of the homes in which we live. For example, he traces the history of how salt and pepper appeared on the kitchen table, a story of international bloodshed, suffering and woe. The history of spices and drink is a very large part of world history (Kurlansky, 2003); Standage (2007) shows in his *A History of the World in Six Glasses* how beer, wine, distilled liquor, coffee, tea, and Coca-Cola have shaped the human story.

One of the advantages of considering a global context to history is that it provides teachers with the opportunity to illustrate variation at a particular time in the past. This contributes to understanding historical interpretations. The medieval period (fifth to fifteenth centuries AD), for example, was once regarded as a period of intellectual stagnation. However, from this misunderstood age came a wide range of cultural and technological innovations, including buttons, underwear, trousers, eyeglasses, glazed windows, dining tables, chairs, fireplaces, and clocks (Frugoni, 2001).

The tendency to see history from the Western point of view can ignore the contributions of great civilisations such as the Chinese. Their astonishing list of achievements spans three thousand years and includes:

Agriculture – iron plough, efficient horse harnesses, multi-tube seed drill.

Engineering – water power, suspension bridge, cast iron, deep drilling.

Technology – lacquer (the first plastic), paper, strong beer, wheelbarrow, fishing reel, matches, stirrup, umbrella, chess, brandy, whisky, porcelain, mechanical clock, printing, playing-cards, paper money, paper, spinning-wheel.

Medicine and health – circulation of the blood, diabetes, immunology.

Mathematics – decimal system, a place for zero, decimal fractions.

Magnetism – first compass, earth's magnetic field, dial and pointer devices.

Physical sciences – first law of motion, seismograph, spontaneous combustion.

Transportation – kite, first relief maps, parachute, rudder, masts and sailing.

Sound and music – tuned drums, large tuned bell, research laboratories.

Warfare – crossbow, gunpowder, chemical warfare, grenades, rocket, cannons.

Temple (2007) concludes that one of the greatest untold secrets of history is that more than half of the basic inventions and discoveries upon which the modern world rests come from China.

The most studied global episode in school history lessons is the Second World War, the greatest cataclysm in the modern age. To cite a contemporary cliché and the title of the best-single volume account of the war: *'All Hell Let Loose'* (Hastings, 2011). Grim statistics bear out the physical and psychological burden of mass slaughter: an average of 27,000 people died each day between September 1939 and August 1945; of six million Poles who were killed by the Germans, a third were children; 66 per cent of all deaths in the 1939–45 war were civilians (compared to 5 per cent of deaths in the 1914–18 war); entire communities were executed; up to 16 million non-Jews were victims of Nazi mass murder including gypsies, German communists, Jehovah's Witnesses, the mentally and physically handicapped, the chronically ill and homosexuals (Bourke, 2001). This was a total war. On the home front, the traditional image is one of cheeky Londoners, singing along to Vera Lynn on the radio and a make-do-and-mend attitude. Hylton (2001) reveals another side to the war at home including racism, looting, class tensions and child abuse.

It is too easily forgotten that anti-Semitism was a significant issue in Britain as well as Germany – Jews were accused in the press of being cowards, black-market racketeers, shirkers and 'overstayers in air-raid shelters' (Julius, 2010: 324). Clearly, teachers need to show sensitivity in such matters. Effective use of oral testimony, films, autobiographical accounts, newspapers and diary extracts provide a rounded picture of life. The Second World War as a topic is very well resourced for teachers who, for instance, can draw upon educational packs from the Imperial War Museum and online materials at the National Archives.

World religions

Of the five billion or so people in the world that profess a religion, most are Christians, Muslims or Hindus. Religion is a part of life for around 80 per cent of the world's population with Christianity accounting for 31 per cent of worshippers, Islam 22 per cent and Hinduism 16 per cent (CIRCA, 2008). While Christianity has the most followers, it also has the largest number of denominations. Comparatively speaking, Islam is on the increase and Christianity declining – predicted trends are that well before 2025 Muslims will outnumber Christians as a percentage of the world population.

The rise of Islam and its role in the modern world should interest all teachers. To begin with, Muslims should not be treated as one homogenous group. There are long-standing leadership differences between the Sunnis, who make up about 85 per cent of Muslims, and the Shi'as. However, all Muslims observe the five pillars of Islam:

1. The *Shahada* – reciting the basic statement 'There is no God but Allah, and Muhammad is his messenger'.

2. *Salah* (prayer) – five times a day.

3. *Zakah* (charity) – expected to donate 2.5% of their annual income to the poor.

4. *Sawm* (fasting) – during the month of Ramadan.

5. *Hajj* (pilgrimage) – religious journey to Mecca at least once during a lifetime.

Over recent years, there has been a growth in Islamic self-consciousness. The term 'fundamentalist', borrowed from Christianity, is applied to those Muslims who call for a strict implementation of *sharia* law culminating in the establishment of an Islamic state. Opposition to the Western ways and the perceived corruption of the Muslim society are important. Militant expressions of fundamentalism could be seen in the London bombing attack of 7 July 2005. Thereafter, both the left- and right-wing media, from the *New Statesman* to the *Daily Telegraph*, increasingly referred to 'Londonistan' to anxiously describe the presence of radical Muslims. Rageh Omaar, a British Muslim citizen born in Somalia, describes life in London during the 1990s and early 2000s. He calls for better understanding of the Islamic faith among Muslims as well as non-Muslims, pointing out that both carry damaging preconceptions and stereotypes (Omaar, 2007). Modernist Muslims seek to embrace change while at the same time drawing attention to the Islamic basis for many Western ideas – for instance, democracy being practised in many early Islamic communities (Rippin, 2012). Gillam (1999) reports children's common misconceptions about Islam including its association with violence. She recommends training of RE coordinators and staff, the use of Muslim visitors, limiting the number of religions taught, and calls on teachers to strike a balance between rules and faith in the presentation of Islam.

An understanding of world faiths begins by tracing their history and development. There are many concise, readable and informative books and websites for teachers (National Geographic, 2011; Toropov and Buckles, 2011; for example **www .bbc.co.uk/religion/religions**). Pupils can refer to world maps, charts and timelines to trace the spread of a particular world religion. The Farmington Institute provides concise reports on teaching aspects of different world faiths such as Jewish festivals, resources for Sikhism, ecology and world religions, and exploring the relationship between Christianity and Islam (**www.farmington.ac.uk/**). Most local authorities have well-conceived schemes of work that set out key questions to pose when studying world religions. Typically these might include questions about the founder(s), major festivals, holy scriptures, food, dress, prayer and other religious practices.

Humanism

One of the aims of RE is to broaden children's knowledge about people's values and beliefs. Most pupils in schools in Britain today do not identify very closely, if at all, with a religious community. It is therefore appropriate that RE should include consideration of some of the alternatives to religion that exist in society. Humanists have a strong belief in science and the power of rational thought. Many consider religion to be dangerous and offering false hope (Law, 2011). The British Humanist Association (BHA) would like to see the withdrawal of legislation requiring acts of worship in schools and the introduction of a broad study of belief systems, religious and non-religious, with an emphasis on shared human values (**www.humanism.org.uk/education/ education-policy**). The BHA was influential in the development of the National Framework for RE (QCA, 2004), which recommends the study of secular philosophies such as humanism for all pupils.

Resources for wider world investigations and issues

Teachers have access to a range of resources to support the teaching of the wider world, including artefacts, maps, aerial photographs, stories, reference books, websites, CD-ROMs and poster packs. Legends from non-European cultures can make an important contribution to children's understanding of the diverse human family. Taoist and Buddhist stories, for instance, present a particular slant on animals, while Japanese folk-tales often include bizarre and humorous characters. There are many websites that include overviews of myths and legends from around the world, such as the Scholastic project (**http://teacher.scholastic.com/writewit/mff**).

Digital photographs are among the most common, cheap and easily accessible resources. Whether these are presented in the form of holiday 'snaps', tourist brochures, glossy magazines or commercially produced photo packs, children should learn that they are selective and may not represent everyday life in the distant place. Photographs should be chosen to depict human and natural features. They should represent different aspects of life, such as home, school, work, travel, worship and leisure. Martin (2006) describes how positive attitudes towards people and places can be promoted; she cites examples such as photographs from a Gambian village that show people playing football, selling goods, going to school, having a party and growing vegetables. The important point is for children to make connections and recognise similarities, as well differences in lifestyles.

Many voluntary and non-governmental organisations (NGOs) produce resources to support distant locality and global dimension studies (Drake, 1996). These organisations include: ActionAid; Catholic Agency For Overseas Development (CAFOD); Cyfanfyd, the umbrella network for organizations and individuals involved in Education for Sustainable Development and Global Citizenship (ESDGC) in Wales; Christian Aid; Friends of the Earth; Oxfam; Save the Children; UNICEF (United Nations Children Fund); World Wide Fund for Nature (WWF); Red Cross; and Development Education centres. Their resources are written from a particular context and for a reason, whether to support fundraising or to help change attitudes, challenge stereotypes and break down prejudices.

Many have been produced by education officers and through curriculum projects involving practising teachers. One example is Tide ~ global learning, which is a teachers' network promoting global perspectives, human rights, sustainability and international development. When evaluating such resources it is important to check when materials are published to ensure that dated resources are not used. The quality of the photographs and maps, the language level, the variety of ways in which information is presented, and the usefulness of the activities suggested, also need to be monitored.

All resources have been produced by someone or a team, who in the process will have made decisions over what to include and omit. Teachers can develop pupils' appreciation of *how* resources are published and possible bias, by considering:

Photographs – where the photographer points the camera and what/who might be outside the frame.

Photo packs – inclusion of people from different ages, backgrounds, gender, culture, places, times.

Sketches – how lifelike are these and how do these compare to photographs or films.

News reports – whether broadcasters say that these have been reported under censorship.

Newspaper accounts – comparing different reports of the same event.

Books – choice of illustrations, language, background of author(s).

Websites – reading the 'All about' section for the background of the website.

When planning for teaching about the wider world, resources should be selected to represent different cultures. The history of the Indus Valley Civilisation is one of increasing interest in schools where there is a growing Asian population. Aronovsky (2007) provides a CD-ROM round-up of relevant resources. The history of Benin raises talking points on the slave trade and its eventual abolition (Midwinter, 1994;

Dresser, 2002). While the contribution of William Wilberforce was notable, children could be introduced to the life of Olaudah Equiano. He grew up in Benin, was taken as a slave, won his freedom, and then joined Wilberforce in London to assist in his abolitionist work. Equiano's autobiography describes his early memories of an idyllic existence in Benin (Equiano, 1789/2000). The Historical Association is a good starting point for resources on non-European peoples (**www.history.org.uk**). The British Museum provides reliable background information and educational resources on cultures from around the world.

The lives of famous men and women from different ethnic, social and religious backgrounds should feature in the history curriculum. Publishers have generally responded well to this need and there are now stories on global figures such as Nelson Mandela, Mahatma Gandhi, Martin Luther King, and Maharaja Ranjit, the great Sikh leader. Recognition of the contribution of women on the global stage has improved. Over recent years Mary Seacole (1805–1881) has become a popular figure in stories read to young children (Lynch, 2006; Cooke and Axworthy, 2008; Harrison, 2009). She was one of the most eccentric and charismatic women of her day, dismissed by Florence Nightingale as a brothel-keeping quack but loved by many, including the royal family. She was dubbed a heroine by *The Times* and recently voted the greatest Black Briton in history for her nursing during the Crimean War (Robinson, 2005).

TASK

- Find out about the lives of Mother Teresa, Helen Keller, Rosa Parks, Pocahontas, Mary Wollestonecraft and Maria Montessori. Produce a short presentation for children on the values that these women demonstrated in their lives.

Humanities and spiritual, moral, social and cultural development

Under the terms of the 1988 Education Act, schools in England and Wales are required to promote pupils' spiritual, moral, social and cultural development (SMSC). This is broad-ranging and can include developing children's personal capacities in terms of:

- their enjoyment of life;
- sense of awe, wonder and mystery;
- identity and feelings of self-worth;
- quality of silence and reflection;
- relationships with others; and
- sense of right and wrong.

Spiritual development

Spirituality is difficult to define. Ofsted (1994: 86) suggests that it is concerned with 'aspect of inner life' characterised by reflection and valuing a non-material dimension to life. However, Haigh (1999) rejects the notion that spirituality is only inwards – it is also about what's between people. Spirituality deals with the fundamental questions in life, namely 'Who are we?', 'Where are we going?' and 'What do we value most?' While many people respond to these questions through religious experiences, non-believers can also express their spirituality – for instance in their awe of the natural world, mystery or human achievement. Innermost feelings can be expressed in response to the historical landscape, the forces of nature, music, literature, arts and crafts. Hay and Nye (1998: 18) argue that children's spirituality is 'rooted in universal human awareness' and that it can have religious and non-religious forms of expression. Clearly, spirituality is not the same as being religious. For Haigh (1999), there are characteristics of the spiritually aware child, such as understanding the worth of others, sensitivity, striving to do the right things, and self-knowledge (starting to know personal strengths and weaknesses, feelings and thoughts). Similarly, for Watson and Thompson (2007), there are 'signs of transcendence' such as the experience of hope, altruism, the fact of love, and a sense of wonder at beauty, especially the beauty of nature.

The spiritual side of life is about the force that motivates and sustains people, sometimes referred to as their personality, soul or character (Ofsted, 1994). The Ofsted definition of spiritual development has been criticised for being overly concerned with the individual, rather than concepts such as justice and neighbourly love, while also lacking any generally acceptable criteria (Erricker and Erricker, 2000). More fundamentally, it does not indicate to schools how spiritual development should be addressed. Clearly, creating the appropriate environment in which children feel comfortable about asking questions, discussing issues, and taking responsibilities is key to promoting SMSC. Eaude (2008: 76) discusses small actions in the classroom that can make a difference such as:

- enjoying children's company, celebrating their successes and sharing their pleasures;

- demonstrating how to regulate one's emotions and interact with other people; and

- helping children to appreciate the simple things in life, from a funny incident to a thoughtful comment or action.

When reading stories, children should regularly discuss motives that drive the characters' actions. Through drama, they should rehearse a range of feelings, such as anger, joy, and hope. Roberts (2000) discusses specific examples of how spirituality can be promoted in a practical way across the curriculum. In geography, for instance, pupils can move from local maps to global views to gain a sense of place in the universe. This can include mapping different religious groups and the boundaries that separate them. By studying medieval maps, pupils will see that Jerusalem was the centre of the world and Britain was very much on the edge. This contrasts with the nineteenth-century maps of the British Empire, which denote an Anglo-centric view of the world.

> **REFLECTION**
>
> - Consider what young children's spirituality might look like and how this would be manifested when they study the past.

Moral development

Children's moral development has occupied generations of teachers, parents and governments. It has been foremost in curriculum design since schooling began, with very little change in the basic aims of education – namely to produce wise and good people (Wynne and Ryan, 1993). This was once referred to as 'character formation', based on the twin core values of respect and responsibility. In effect, respect represents the passive element of morality while responsibility is the more active form (Lang *et al.*, 1998).

Lawrence Kohlberg's (1984) theory of children's moral development suggests that children move through three levels: pre-conventional (characterised by reward and punishment), conventional (respect for authority), and post-conventional (forming values and principles). Although Kohlberg did not identify precise age ranges for these stages, pre-conventional reasoning is typical of children in the primary school and can be seen in many adolescents (Schaffer, 1996). The theory has been criticised because it focuses solely on reasoning about moral issues, overlooking the importance of emotions. Moreover, critics point out that people often know more than they say. Recent research supports the view that children act as moral beings in searching for 'truths' derived from social encounters (Doherty and Hughes, 2009). In the first three years, children are capable of showing pro-social behaviours, for example when sharing toys and food. They are able to show empathy in understanding different emotions and act with a selfless concern for others (altruism). Further research shows that from the age of two onwards, young children have feelings of guilt and shame, are aware of standards and how things ought to be and demonstrate a 'moral instinct' (Underwood and Rosen, 2011: 248).

Moral education is concerned then with developing values and principles to guide behaviour. It involves promoting a sense of what is right and wrong, understanding the ethical dilemmas people face and how others should be treated. As Bigger and Brown (1999) point out, policymakers can become obsessed that pupils should be taught 'right' from 'wrong'; the distinction between externally imposed and internally chosen morality is a reappearing theme in the literature on moral education. Teachers may feel uneasy about discussing what is right and wrong in an age of moral relativism. However, it is important to explore why people believe what they do, act in a particular manner and how they know whether something is right or wrong. Philosophy for Children, with its emphasis on promoting questioning (**http://sapere.org.uk**) and other 'thinking skills' approaches, facilitates discussions over moral issues. For instance, one class of ten-year-old children discussed with us 'What is Truth?', the age-old question raised by Pontius Pilate, the Roman governor that crucified Jesus. They considered what might happen if people generally did not tell the truth. They concluded that communication would be almost impossible because each person would have to check everything for themselves. Class discussions might revolve around scenarios, such as whether it is right ever to do the following:

- buy something which you know is stolen;
- keep money that you found in the street;
- throw away litter in a public place; and
- cheat in an examination.

A recent study suggests Britons are becoming less honest than they were a decade ago (Whiteley, 2011). Such studies, reported on websites such as the Economic and Social Data Service, can inform discussions with children and enable them to set their own views within the wider social context. Teachers need to exercise editorial rights, however, given the adult nature of particular questions.

The humanities are rich in opportunities for pupils to consider moral questions. The Citizenship Education Review Group (Deakin *et al.*, 2004) suggests how teachers can promote these opportunities by:

- sharing personal stories and histories;
- building in reflection time;
- instigating discussion of rights and responsibilities;
- coaching in 'why?' and 'how?' questions;
- encouraging a critical response to questions; and
- encouraging pupils to ask questions themselves.

Humanities are concerned with why people live the way they do and the consequences of their actions. For some religious followers, there are 'absolute' moral principles to follow, as laid down in the Qu'ran for Muslims, the Torah for Jews or the golden rule for Christians. Others follow a more liberal line and morality is shaped by secular influences such as humanism. By exploring such choices, children can be led to reflect upon their own morality. In geography, they can consider the rights and responsibilities of individuals and groups within different environments and places, whether on a local, national or global scale. Studies of localities in economically developing countries raise questions about inequalities and social justice. There should always be a moral dimension to issues within the humanities, such as land re-development, the building of a new road or waste management. The views of environmental groups such as Friends of the Earth and Greenpeace could be contrasted with those of multinational companies such as Shell. Through fieldwork pupils can collect, analyse and reflect upon the ethical issues associated with data – for instance, who they select to interview when undertaking a shopping survey, how the results are shared and with whom.

Similarly, the study of historical source material highlights questions of truthfulness. The partial nature of evidence means that understanding how people lived and why they behaved in a particular way is sometimes elusive. The reliability of written, visual and oral sources is often called into question by historians who have their own political, moral, social and religious values. The transient nature of beliefs and values can be illustrated by reading texts from the period under study. The year 2012 marks the bicentennial anniversary of the birth of Charles Dickens. Classics such as *A Christmas Carol* are replete with moral messages concerning charity, goodwill, family, kindliness and humility. More generally, Halstead and Pike (2006) cite examples of moral themes to explore in history such as:

Democracy and human rights – for example, Sparta and Athens in the fifth century BC.

Immigration and diversity – for example, the long line of immigrants dating back to the Iron Age Celts, disproving the notion that Britain's multicultural state is a new phenomenon.

Law and order – for example, the introduction of the modern police force in Victorian times.

The rights of the child – for example, contrasting child poverty in Victorian times and today.

History is littered with philanthropists that donated their wealth to support the less privileged. Their stories can be read to children to illustrate how morality (usually Christian) guided their lives. For instance, Sir Titus Salt (1803–1876) was a nineteenth-century industrialist with a social conscience, who built houses, bathhouses, institutes, hospitals, almshouses and churches, to make up the model village of Saltaire. More than 100,000 were reported to have attended his funeral as a mark of respect for his work. Salts Mill in Bradford is now a world heritage site. (**www.saltsmill.org.uk/**). The relationship between wealth generation and moral obligations can be illustrated with modern-day examples, such as Sir Richard Branson and Bill Gates, the latter providing £750,000 from his personal fortune to fund vaccines for children in Third World countries.

Teachers also have a responsibility to model the values associated with social justice and to help pupils develop an awareness of how it affects their lives. From an early age pupils' develop a keen sense of what is 'fair' and 'unfair'. This can be a starting point for exploring social justice in RE. Any age group can begin by thinking about their own experiences of fairness. They can talk about what 'fair' and 'unfair' mean to them. The teacher might read them stories that demonstrate these two concepts, for further discussion. The work can then be developed into explicitly religious contexts such as:

- reading stories from religion that demonstrate fairness and unfairness;
- studying which religious groups are persecuted or discriminated against today;
- examining the teachings of the world faiths and how we treat others;
- exploring how people of different religious traditions fight for social justice today; and
- examining the lives of religious teachers and figures who fought for social justice.

Pupils should be encouraged to identify their role in promoting social justice in the world today. Teachers can pose questions such as: 'How would they respond if someone discriminated against them?' or 'How would they respond if they witnessed someone abusing someone else?'

Questions relating to the humanities to use during Circle Time

- How does that make you feel? (Seeing your friend crying and unhappy.)

- Why does that happen? (Rubbish around the swings in the playground.)

- What do you think? (Why do you think this teddy has lost one eye?)

- What is your favourite? (What is your favourite place in the school grounds?)

- How does it work? (Religious, geographical, historical artefact.)

- What does it remind you of? (Birthdays, holidays.)

- Can you think of something? (. . . you could do to make the world a better place?)

- Can you remember? (. . . a special day in your life/a time where you helped and comforted somebody?)

Social development

Social education involves pupils learning to work well together and the development of life skills, such as decision-making, coping and communicating. How well children relate to others depends on many factors, including their emotional state. Creating a calm environment contributes towards children's capacity to respond sensibly and regulate feelings such as anger, fear and surprise. Many schools use Circle Time, persona dolls and visits to enhance children's social skills. Circle Time provides a daily structured framework for group discussion which, although used in different ways, focuses on the positives, building team spirit, a sense of belonging and improved self-awareness (see questions to use on next page). It is based upon such principles as respect, inclusion, democracy and choice (Roffey, 2006). Critics argue that improved relationships much depend upon the quality of teachers' reflection on their practice rather than 'gimmicks' (Housego and Burns, 1994). Persona dolls are seen as a 'magical conduit' that enable children to examine how they view those who are different to themselves (Brown. 2001). Children respond to the dolls' stories in a non-threatening climate. Persona dolls have been used internationally by teachers to address sensitive issues – for example, the development of prejudice and racism in young Anglo-Australian children towards Australia's indigenous peoples and cultures (MacNaughton, 2001).

School councils also have the potential to make a difference to children's personal development – in one example pupils worked with a local artist to create murals for the playground, created a school garden, purchased compost and recycling bins, helped to refurbish the toilets and had a say in redesigning the dining hall (DCELLS, 2009). Effective school councils develop pupils' skills in listening, negotiating and democratic decision-making. However, introducing a token council can increase students' scepticism (Alderson, 2000).

There are many opportunities to promote social skills in different contexts within the humanities. In RE, pupils might organise and prepare a special meal for others. In geographical fieldwork, groups can collaborate in sharing resources and when undertaking tasks such as measuring, photographing, interviewing, filming and sketching. During visits, especially residential ones, groups can demonstrate their social skills through their behaviour and attitudes to learning. Most museums, galleries and places of worship provide guidance on what they expect in terms of visiting parties. Talboys (2010) goes so far as to suggest drawing up a contract for pupils to sign: if they keep to it, they can go on the next visit; if they do not, then they are under review. Pupils can demonstrate good social and moral values by knowing and respecting the need for conservation.

History provides many opportunities to promote pupils' personal and social skills. For instance a study of the 1960s offers appropriate opportunities to develop children's knowledge and understanding of tolerance. Many individuals campaigned strongly against racism, especially in the anti-apartheid movement. During the 1950s, Britain was projected as a tolerant and decent society, which extended a welcome to refuges with its 'open door' policy on immigration from the Commonwealth. After 1962, the importance of the Commonwealth faded, and the notion of tolerance was modified by a determination to limit the number of Black immigrants. Despite the goodwill and mutual respect that existed among the different ethnic minority groups, Britain and the wider world experienced widespread racism in the post-war years. Shirley Bassey remembers being called a 'nigger' and 'darkie' to her face while attending primary schools in Cardiff during the 1940s (Hogan, 2008).

Cultural development

The term 'culture' has a broad application, including the arts (e.g. dance, song, and paintings), heritage and particular beliefs. Religion, festivals, foods, and ethical codes all contribute to cultural identity. Sometimes, these cut across national boundaries. Hence, a Muslim may be African, Arab or British. There are many more Jews in America than in Israel and there are different Jewish traditions, such as Orthodox, Reform and secular Jews. In essence, cultural development involves fostering pupils' awareness of beliefs, practices, lifestyles and values in a pluralistic society (Rivett et al., 2007). If one of the fundamental functions of schools is to transmit culture, this should reflect the diversity of a particular society. Hence, pupils need to learn that difference does not equate with inferiority and that other cultures have the same basic rights as their own (see Table 8.2).

Through the humanities, pupils can contribute to their own culture. They can participate and organise local events. For instance, some schools in Cornwall promote children's understanding of Cornish life, culture, history and language through St Piran's Day, Murdoch Day and Trevithick Day. Schools in Wales are expected to develop pupils' awareness of the Welsh dimension to the curriculum (*Y Curiuwlum Cymreig*) to include linguistic, historical, environmental, religious and economic aspects (Estyn, 2001). This is reported to be good in three-quarters of secondary schools (Estyn, 2006). In the best practice, primary and secondary schools make effective use of fieldwork, poetry, local artists, contemporary music, extracurricular activities and community events. Similarly in Northern Ireland and Scotland, schools should seek to promote children's understanding of the respective cultural heritages, discussed further in Chapter 6.

Table 8.2 Opportunities to promote SMSC through humanities

Area	Examples
Social	• Making positive contributions to well-being of others (e.g. by participating in group research projects).
	• Able to take on different roles (e.g. leader, team worker).
	• Making informed decisions.
	• Understanding rights and responsibilities, past and present.
	• Understanding links between home, school and community through visits and fieldwork (community cohesion).
	• Demonstrating enjoyment and excitement (e.g. willingness to explore and question).
	• Negotiating roles and responsibilities.
	• Knowing and understanding how communities function.
	• Listening and responding appropriately to the views of others.
	• Expressing a desire for lifelong learning and leisure interests (e.g. local history, metal detecting, allotments, using museums, rock collecting, membership of choirs).
Cultural	• Knowing one's own cultural traditions and practices.
	• Knowledge of other major cultural traditions.
	• Valuing cultural achievements of individuals and societies (e.g. musicians, artists, Classical Greece, Renaissance).
	• Developing an understanding of local heritage.
	• Showing an awareness of diversity (e.g. different personalities, cultures, habits and practices).
Moral	• Knowing the difference between right and wrong.
	• Knowing, understanding and using the language of morality (e.g. fair, equal, wrong).
	• Promoting positive attitudes (e.g. fostering curiosity and open-mindedness).
	• Desire to persuade others through moral reasoning.
	• Desire to listen to and respect others.
	• Developing shared values (e.g. respect, tolerance, empathy).
	• Understanding ethical issues (e.g. related to sustainable development and environmental education).
	• Informed concern for the world in which we live, for its people and for the natural environment.
	• Understanding the unique value of each individual.
	• Gaining the confidence to cope with setbacks and learn from mistakes.
	• Taking initiative and acting responsibly with consideration for others.
	• Distinguishing between right and wrong (e.g. slavery in history).
	• Showing respect for the environment (e.g. the Countryside Code).
	• Making informed and independent judgements.

Area	Examples
Table 8.2 Opportunities to promote SMSC through humanities (*Continued*)	
Spiritual	• Understanding sacred things and places (e.g. River Ganges). • Experiencing moments of stillness and reflection (e.g. during visits to places of worship or woodlands). • Recognition of contribution of faith in some people's lives. • Reflecting on, considering and celebrating the wonders and mysteries of life. • Discussing the spiritualities of specific religious traditions. • Studying the lives of people who are considered to be 'spiritually enlightened'. • Sustaining self-esteem and confidence. • Understanding and explaining one's own beliefs. • Developing personal views and insights. • Asking questions about the purpose and experiences of life (e.g. times of pain, suffering, beauty, joy, hope). • Responding to religious events.

Challenges when teaching the wider world and SMSC

Promoting SMSC is challenging because teachers lack clarity over what this means in practice. Moreover, there is a debate over how each element relates to each other and to other agendas, such as pupils' personal, social and health education. Moreover, schools have their own particular contexts, and individual children come from different cultural backgrounds. In faith schools, the promotion of moral development may take on a distinctive flavour. Children's morality is likely to be shaped by religious principles – hence they may say that stealing is wrong because the Bible says so. This makes it difficult to ascertain whether the child is less or more morally aware than a child who says stealing is wrong because the thief has not worked for the thing he has stolen (Farrell, 1999). In effect, moral development can be shaped by faith and/or reason. Writers such as Wilson (2000) argue strongly that the approach to moral education must be non-partisan, by which he means based on reason rather than creed or ideology. He calls upon schools to develop a 'moral methodology' through which teachers develop reasoning skills. Such methods include:

• working through an issue logically, using examples and questions at each step;
• use of simulations, videos, role-play;
• oral discussions of moral questions;
• using sources such as newspapers and cartoons to illustrate;
• getting children to make up their own rules; and
• giving children experiences of people unlike themselves (e.g. old people, those from different cultural backgrounds, to enlarge their understanding).

Studying distant places, global history and world religions presents a range of challenges. Pupils can be misguided in their belief that because they have access to a higher standard of living they are superior to those who are less materially well-off and that the poor deserve pity and charity. It is important to avoid sweeping generalisations about a country that can exacerbate stereotyping and present an unbalanced view of life elsewhere. To consider an obvious example, children should not associate pizza purely with Italy. Drawing upon native speakers and resources from different parts of the country, through the Internet, television documentaries, magazines such as *National Geographic* and respective tourist board materials, can contribute to a more balanced understanding of foreign lifestyles. It can also inform debate over how countries are 'packaged' to others around the world.

Teaching about world religions also poses challenges. In Northern Ireland, Barnes (2010) discusses the Inter-Faith Forum's recent claim that exclusively Christian content may be in breach of equality and human rights legislation. He concludes that there should be teaching about world religions, but the multi-faith approach of England and Wales is inappropriate to the Northern Irish educational and cultural context. Ipgrave (1999) highlights the tensions that can exist between the educational and religious interests and values of teachers and pupils, with reference to Muslim children in Leicester. Staff in multi-ethnic schools report difficulties in teaching children about terrorist attacks because they were concerned about dealing with the possible expression of Islamophobia, anti-American feeling and anti-Semitic racism (Madden, 2011). Highlighting the shared messages of holy books is an important means of recognising similarities between great faiths. For instance the Qu'ran and Bible, the holy scriptures of Islam and Christianity respectively, both teach the creation of the world by a single Almighty. The core principle behind both Islam and Christianity is that God should figure strongly in directing people's lives. Although Islam means 'surrender', it has the same origin as *shalom*, the Hebrew word for peace.

Nonetheless, there are aspects of faith that teachers and pupils may find difficult to understand. Many Muslims adhere strictly to the *shari'a* legal code (meaning 'path to the watering hole'). This governs all aspects of life, ranging from politics to personal conduct. Countries such as Saudi Arabia retain strict adherence to *sharia* law – this has had a poor press in the West because of the severity of punishments, such as amputation of the hand for stealing and the possibility of the death penalty for adultery. In reality the details of the law are often more complicated than reported in the media – adultery, for example, has to take place in public and be seen by four reliable witnesses, while it is often forgotten that the New Testament refers to cutting off a hand that sins (Mark 9: 43). The *Jihad* is a concept frequently misunderstood in the Western society. It does not mean a 'holy war' to convert non-believers, a stereotype first put forward by the medieval Crusaders. Rather, *Jihad* means a struggle, usually of a personal nature in attempting to overcome the obstacles that prevent someone from getting closer to God. Jihad can include fighting to restore peace and freedom of worship, but has to be headed by a spiritual leader and judge. Modern Muslim scholars are 'understandably touchy' over the incessant media interest and 'the at-times unsavoury history of *Jihad*' (Jordan, 2006: 30). However, as Winston (2005) points out, Islam is no more a warlike faith than Christianity. A thoughtful study of the wider world should enable teachers to focus on building a shared understanding of what the vast majority of people have in common, such as the desire to live peacefully and amicably.

SUMMARY

- It is important for pupils to learn about the wider world through the humanities. This can develop pupils' knowledge and understanding of distant places, global history and world religions.

- Teachers can access a range of resources relating to the wider world including photographs, websites, stories, maps and ICT sources.

- The humanities have an important role to play in promoting pupils' spiritual, moral, social and cultural development.

- There are challenges to address when teaching about the wider world. These include overcoming misconceptions, stereotypes and bias.

References

Alderson, P. (2000), 'School students' views on school councils and daily life at school', in Children & Society, 14: 121–134.

Aronovsky, I. (2007), *Indus Valley KS2 History Teaching and Resourcing Guide*, HEC History Education Consultancy.

Barnes, L. P. (2010), 'World Religions and the Northern Ireland Curriculum', in Journal of Beliefs and Values: Studies in Religion and Education, Volume 23, Issue 1, 19–32.

Barnes, M., Brightwell, R., Von Hagen, A., Lehner, M. and Page, C. (1996), *Secrets of Lost Empires*, London: BBC Books.

Behar, S. and Yarham, R. (2007), *Great Inventions. 100 inventions that have shaped our world*, Sywell: Igloo.

Bigger, S. and Brown, E. (eds) (1999), *Spiritual, Moral, Social and Cultural Education*, London: David Fulton.

Bourke, J. (2001), *The Second World War*, Oxford: Oxford University Press.

Brown, B. (2001), *Combating discrimination. Persona Dolls in action*, Stoke: Trentham Books.

Bryson, B. (2010), *At Home*, London: Doubleday.

Catling, S. (1995), 'Wide Horizons: The Children's Charter', Primary Geographer 20, 4–6.

Catling, S. (2003), 'Curriculum Contested: Primary Geography and Social Justice', Geography 88,164–210.

Catling, S., and Willy, T. (2009), *Achieving QTS. Teaching Primary Geography*, Exeter: Learning Matters.

CCEA (2007), *Northern Ireland Curriculum Primary*, Belfast: CCEA, available at: **www.nicurriculum.org .uk/docs/key_stages_1_and_2/northern_ireland_ curriculum_primary.pdf**.

Challoner, J. (2009), *1001 Inventions: That Changed the World*, London: Cassell.

CIRCA (2008), *Where We Are Now*, London: Mitchell Beazley.

Cowen, N. (2001), *Global History: A Short Overview*, Cambridge: Polity.

Cooke, T. and Axworthy, A. (2008), *Hoorah for Mary Seacole* (Hopscotch London), Franklin Watts.

Cresswell, T. (2004), *Place a Short Introduction*, Oxford: Blackwell.

Crossley, P.K. (2008), *What is Global History?*, Cambridge: Polity.

DCELLS (2008a), *History in the national curriculum for Wales,* Cardiff: Welsh Assembly Government.

DCELLS (2008b), *Geography in the national curriculum for Wales,* Cardiff: Welsh Assembly Government.

DCELLS (2008c), *National exemplar for religious education for 3 to 19-year-olds in Wales,* Cardiff: Welsh Assembly Government.

DCELLS (2009), *School Councils in Wales; Best Practice*, Cardiff: Welsh Assembly Government.

Deakin Crick R., Coates M., Taylor M., Ritchie S. (2004), 'A systematic review of the impact of citizenship education on the provision of schooling', in: Research Evidence in Education Library. London: EPPI-Centre, Social Science Research Unit, Institute of Education, University of London.

DfEE/QCA (1999), *The National Curriculum for England: Citizenship*, London: HMSO.

Doherty, J. and Hughes, M. (2009), *Child Development*, Harlow: Pearson.

Drake, M. (1996), 'Resources for global understanding' in Steiner, M. (ed.), *Developing the global teacher*, Stoke-on-Trent: Trentham.

Dresser, M. (2002), 'Bristol and the slave trade: a virtual slavery trail for school children and their teachers', in *Primary History*, 32, 32–36.

Dyson, J. and Uhlig, R. (2001), *The Mammoth Book of Great Inventions*, London: Robinson.

Eaude, T. (2008), *Children's Spiritual, Moral, Social and Cultural Development*, Exeter: Learning Matters.

Equiano, O. (1789/2000), *The Life of Olaudah Equiano: Or Gustavus Vassa, the African*, Mineola, NY: Publications.

Erricker, C. and Erricker, J. (2000), *Reconstructing Religious, Spiritual and Moral Education*, London: RoutledegeFalmer.

Estyn (2001), *Y Cwricwlwm Cymreig: The Welsh dimension of the curriculum in Wales: good practice in teaching and learning*, Cardiff: Estyn.

Estyn (2006), *Cwricwlwm Cymreig. Phase 2*, Cardiff: Estyn.

Farrell, M. (1999), *Key Issues for Primary Schools*, London: Routledge.

Frugoni, C. (2001), *Books, Banks and Buttons*, New York: Columbia University Press.

Gillam, K. (1999), 'How can children reflect on Islam when there are misconceptions in the classroom?', available at: farmington@hmc.ox.ac.uk.

Haigh, G. (1999), 'Awe and Wonder', in *TES Primary*, 26 November 1999, 9–12.

Halstead, J.M. and Pike, M.A. (2006), *Citizenship and Moral Education*, London: Routledge.

Hart-Davis, A. (2004), *What the Past Did for Us: A Brief History of Ancient Inventions*, London: BBC Worldwide Books.

Hastings, M. (2011), *All Hell Let Loose*, London: HarperPress.

Hay, D. and Nye, R. (1998), *The Spirit of the Child*, London: Harper Collins.

Harrison, I. (2003), *The Book of Firsts*, London: Cassell.

Harrison, P. (2009), *Mary Seacole? (Who Was)*, London: Wayland.

Hirst, B. (2006), *The impact of global dimension teaching on children's achievements*, Manchester: North West Global Education Network, Manchester Development Project.

Hogan, P. (2008), *Shirley Bassey: Diamond Diva*, London: Harper Collins.

Housego, E. and Burns, C. (1994), 'Are You Sitting Too Comfortably? A Critical Look at "Circle Time" in Primary Classrooms', in *English in Education*, 28: 2, 23–29, Summer 1994.

Hylton, S. (2001), *Their Darkest Hour*, Stroud: Sutton Publishing.

Ipgrave, J. (1999), 'Issues in the Delivery of Religious Education to Muslim Pupils: Perspectives from the Classroom', in *British Journal of Religious Education*, Volume 21, Issue 3, 146–157.

Jenner, S. (2011), 'Young children's perceptions of distant places', Occasional Paper No.5 – Classroom Research (**www.geography.org.uk/download/GA_EYPPRRJenner.pdf**.

Jordan, M. (2006), *In the Name of God*, Stroud: Sutton.

Julius, A. (2010), *Trials of the Diaspora*, Oxford: Oxford University Press.

Kohlberg, L. (1984), *The Psychology of Moral Development: The Naming and Validity of Moral Stages*, San Francisco: Harper & Row.

Kurlansky, M. (2003), *Salt: A World History*, London: Vintage.

Lang, P., Katz, T., and Menzes, S. (1998), *Affective Education: A Comparative View*, London: Blackwell.

Law, S. (2011), *Humanism: A Very Short Introduction*, Oxford: Oxford University Press.

Lynch, E. (2006), *The Life of Mary Seacole*, Heinemann Library

MacNaughton G. (2001), 'Beyond 'Othering': rethinking approaches to teaching young Anglo-Australian children about indigenous Australians', in *Contemporary Issues in Early Childhood*, 2(1), 83–93.

Madden, K. (2011), '9/11 attacks prove a lesson too far', *Times Educational Supplement*, 24 June, 2011,15.

Martin, F. (2006), *Teaching Geography in Primary Schools: Learning How to Live in the World*, Cambridge: Chris Kington.

Midwinter, C. (1994), *Benin: An African Kingdom – Exploring the History, Geography, Culture and Environment of Benin Past and Present,* Godalming: World Wide Fund for Nature.

Mikander, P. (2010), 'World view in Finnish school textbooks – a categorization of us and them?', available at: **http://vefsetur.hi.is/phdsoced/groups**.

National Geographic Society (2011), *Concise History of World Religions: An Illustrated Time Line*, London: National Geographic Society.

Nichol, J. (2011), 'The National Curriculum Review', Primary History, 58, 2–4.

Ofsted (1994), Spiritual, Moral, Social and Cultural Development: An Ofsted Discussion Paper, London: Ofsted.

Ofsted (2011), *Geography: Learning to Make a World of Difference*, London: Ofsted.

Omaar, R. (2007), *Only Half of Me,* London: Penguin.

QCA (2004), *Non-statutory Framework for RE*, London: QCA.

Rippin, A. (2012), *Muslims*, London: Routledge.

Rivett, R., Draycott, P. and Blaylock, L. (2007), *A Teacher's Handbook of Religious Education*, Birmingham: REtoday services.

Roberts, J. (2000), 'Practical ways for developing SMSC across the curriculum', in Best, (ed.) *Education for spiritual, moral, social and cultural development,* London: Continuum, 37–51.

Robinson, J. (2005), *Mary Seacole*, London: Constable and Robinson.

Roffey, S. (2006), *Circle Time for Emotional Literacy*, London; Sage.

Rubino, A. (2010), *Why Didn't I Think of That?: 101 Inventions That Changed the World by Hardly Trying*, Adams Media Corporation.

Rutland, A. (1999), 'The development of national prejudice, in-group favouritism and self-stereotypes in British children', *British Journal of Social Psychology*, Vol. 38:1, 55–70.

Schaffer, H.R. (1996), Social Development; *An Introduction*, Oxford: Blackwell.

Scoffham, S. (2007), 'Please Miss, why are they so poor?', *Primary Geographer 62*, 5–7.

Scottish Government (2009), *A Curriculum for Excellence: Building the Curriculum 4, Skills for learning, skills for life and skills for work*, Edinburgh: Scottish Government.

Standage, T. (2007), *A History of the World in Six Glasses*, London: Atlantic Books.

Talboys, G.K. (2010), *Using Museums as an Educational Resource*, Farnham: Ashgate.

Temple, R. (2007), *The Genius of China*, London: André Deutsch.

Toropov, B. and Buckles, L. (2011), *The Complete Idiot's Guide to World Religions*, Alpha Books.

Underwood, M.K. and Rosen, L.H. (2011), *Social Development*, New York: Guildford Press.

Watson, B. and Thompson, P. (2006), *The Effective Teaching of Religious Education*, London: Longman.

Webb, H. (1983), *Poems and Points*, Llandysul: J.D. Lewis and Sons.

Whiteley, P. (2011), 'Are Britons Getting More Dishonest?', available at **www.esds.ac.uk/news/newsdetail.asp?id=3125**.

Wilkinson, P. (2000), *What the Romans Did For Us*, London: Boxtree.

Wilson, J. (2000), *Key Issues in Education and Teaching*, London: Cassell.

Winston, R. (2005), *The Story of God*, London: Bantam Press.

Wood, M. (1992), *Legacy*, London: BCA.

Wynne, E.A. and Ryan, K. (1993), Reclaiming our Schools; *A handbook on teaching character, academic and discipline*, Columbus Ohio: Merrill Books.

Useful Websites

There are many charities who work overseas to support the poorest and most vulnerable people and their websites include educational resources e.g.

Oxfam Education: **www.oxfam.org.uk/education/**

Action Aid: **www.actionaid.org.uk**

Catholic Overseas Development Agency (CAFOD: **www.cafod.org.uk**

Christian Aid: **www.learn-christianaid.org.uk**

Cyfanfyd: **www.cyfanfyd.org.uk**

Development Education Association (DEA) case studies: **www.globaldimension.org.uk**

Department for International Development (DfID): **www.globaldimension.org.uk**

The British Humanist Association is a national charity working on behalf of non-religious people and includes educational links to toolkits, ideas for assemblies,

humanist discussions of a range of topics studied in school: **www.humanism.org.uk/education/ sacres-and-ascs/humanism-in-the-nffre**

The RE Directory is run by the Culham Institute and provides a very good starting-point for resources: **www.theredirectory.org.uk/index.php**

Teachers in Development Education (Tide ~ Global) is a teachers' network promoting the idea that young people have an entitlement to global learning through engaging with global perspectives, human rights, sustainability and international development: **www.tidec.org/**

Save the Children has a section for teachers including ideas for classroom activities such as Friendship Passport: **www.savethechildren.org.uk**

UNICEF has a major education section including initiatives such as the Rights Respecting Schools Award: **www. unicef.org.uk**

Education for sustainable development and global citizenship

We all live on the same planet, it is our only home, so . . . we used to rotate crops back in the day and, you know, who cares if you're going to make a profit if everybody's too dead or glowing in the dark to be able to purchase anything.

(Michael Berryman, born1948, American actor)

You can never have an impact on society if you have not changed yourself.

(Nelson Mandela, born 1918, former South African President)

Learning objectives

By the end of this chapter you should be able to:

- define the content for Education for Sustainable Development and Global Citizenship (ESDGC);
- reflect upon the concept of the 'global village' and the potential for developing literacy skills;
- identify the links between ESDGC and other curriculum developments;
- recognise the need to integrate ESDGC when planning lessons in the humanities;
- recognise the contribution of the humanities in developing ESDGC within the primary curriculum; and
- describe how the humanities subjects and ESDGC can promote critical thinking skills.

Defining education for sustainable development

Over the past 30 or so years, there has been a shift in the prevailing world view of the environment. Van Petegem and Blieck (2006) trace this movement from a human dominant view to an ecological one; from seeing the world as a story of progress, to one of concern over how ecosystems have been disrupted by modern industrial societies. An important milestone was the setting up of the Brundtland Commission in 1983 by the United Nations (UN) in response to concerns over environmental issues. This was a significant act by the UN General Assembly in formally recognising that environmental problems were global in nature and that it was in the common interest of all nations to establish policies for sustainable development. Although there are many definitions of sustainable development, the one recommended by the Brundtland Report, *Our Common Future*, remains a useful starting point: 'Development that meets the needs of the present without compromising the ability of future generations to meet their own needs' (Brundtland Report, 1987: 4). Ofsted (2008a: 6), in its review of sustainable development in schools, extended this view: 'The goal of sustainable development is to enable all people throughout the world to satisfy their basic needs and enjoy a better quality of life without compromising the quality of life of future generations.'

On current projections humanity will be using two planets' worth of natural resources by 2050 – if those resources have not run out by them – as 'people are turning resources into waste faster than nature can turn waste back into resources' (WWF, 2006: 11). Education for sustainable development means developing understanding of the planet's finite resources and how children and young people can personally play a part in helping make best use of these. The school curriculum should provide opportunities to promote pupils' understanding of sustainability in the stewardship of resources locally, nationally and globally (DfE, 2011).

A guiding principle of sustainable development is to enable all to achieve a better quality of life, and to do so without compromising that ability of future generations to do the same. There are three elements to sustainability: economy, environment and society. If sustainable development was a three legged stool, the legs would represent these three elements of sustainability (see Figure 9.1). When thinking about sustainability of any development all three need to be taken into account because without any one support the stool would collapse.

Wales is one of the few countries in the world to have governmental policy specifically regarding ESDGC and has produced materials aimed at trainee and serving teachers, head teachers and local authority advisers (DCELLS, 2008). Ofsted (2008b) has noted that much work remains to be done as few schools have developed co-ordinated and coherent approaches integrating sustainability throughout the school and curriculum. Work to promote sustainability in schools is supported through the Sustainable Schools website (**www.suschool.org.uk**).

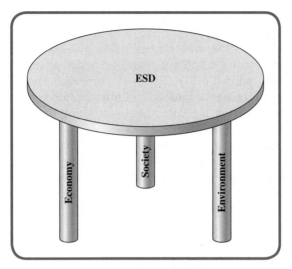

Figure 9.1 Three elements of sustainability.
Source: Martin and Owens, (2010: 6).

Citizenship education

The concept of education for citizenship dates back to the first democratic society of the ancient Greek city-state or *polis*, (root of the word 'politics'), and the duties of citizens to contribute towards the good of society. Their term for the private individual was *idiotes* (idiot), who showed no interest in public affairs. On the other hand, those who demonstrated a cosmopolitan outlook were 'citizens of the world' (derived from the Greek *kosmopolites* – '*cosmos*' or 'world', and *polites*, 'citizen'). Citizenship continues to be seen at local, national and international levels. Social unrest is a salutary reminder of the importance of promoting political literacy so that children are well informed about what is happening in their communities, country and the wider world. Against a background of racial and religious tensions in towns such as Oldham and Bradford in 2001, the promotion of 'community cohesion' or 'living together with differences', has been set as a priority for schools (DCSF, 2007a). In essence, citizenship is about how well people 'get along' in their communities (**www.citizenshipfoundation.org. uk/main/page.php?286**).

The aim is to build stronger ties based on tolerance and mutual respect. This is a global message. When President Obama addressed leaders in Berlin in 2009, he referred to the 'burdens of global citizenship continue to bind us together'. Invoking memories of the Berlin Wall, he added: 'The walls between the countries with the most and those with the least cannot stand. The walls between races and tribes, natives and immigrants, Christians and Muslims and Jews cannot stand'.

The 'Arab Spring' protests, which spread across the Middle East and North Africa in 2011, have brought into sharp focus a worldwide interest in education for democracy.

Smith (2002) discusses how this has been interpreted in different ways (**www.infed.org/biblio/b-dem.htm**). In England, citizenship became a statutory subject on the secondary curriculum in 2002, with a specific unit on local democracy. Citizenship became optional in primary schools, as part of a wider programme with Personal, Social and Health Education (PSHE). The school curriculum should provide opportunities for pupils to appreciate the national cultures, traditions and values of England and the other nations within the UK, while recognising diversity and encouraging responsible citizenship (DfE, 2011).

Citizenship education is not a matter of creating identikit citizens but of empowering children and young people to make informed decisions, show concern for the welfare of others and become productive members of their diverse communities. It is not about telling pupils what to do or believe but rather developing their capacity to make responsible decisions for themselves.

Education for 'a global village'

The term 'global village' was first popularised in 1960 by Herbert Marshall McLuhan (1911–1980), a Canadian educator, philosopher and communications expert. He believed that the world had entered an age of high technology and international communications, through which global events could be experienced simultaneously by everyone, thus apparently 'shrinking' world societies to the scale of a single tribe or village. In particular, he singled out television as the major force for change. The concept of globalisation describes the increasing integration of the world's economic systems by removing trade barriers, quotas and tariffs. The aim is to increase material wealth of multinational corporations through the purchase of uniform products – the 'McDonaldisation' of society. This has led to concern that cultural differences of nations will be eroded (Lechner and Boli, 2012).

McLuhan's vision has proven to be very accurate. The modern world has been described as the 'age of communication'. Consumers in the UK are dealt with by call centres in India, while American companies make products in Asia for European markets. Technology has enabled journeys that once took many weeks to be completed in hours. Mobile phones keep families and communities in contact and supply farmers and businesses all over the world with key market information. Social media has arguably been a major force in bringing down dictatorships in the Middle East and North Africa. Images can be transferred around the world immediately and to graphic effect – the attacks on the Twin Towers in September 2001 are the most obvious example. Colin Powell, former US Secretary of State, pointed out the events of '9/11', the world financial crisis and the dawning of the information age have created unprecedented need to focus on international knowledge and skills. He added that to solve most of America's major problems requires every young person to learn more about other world regions, cultures and languages.

The UN-sponsored website '7 Billion Actions', which provides a range of educational ideas, identifies key global issues such as: poverty and inequality; an ageing population and environmental damage. Global poverty has been falling since the 1980s, perhaps for the first time in history. However, while extreme poverty has been reduced, there are significant regional variations across sub-Saharan Africa and South Asia. Children can consider their definitions of poverty. Besides the lack of necessary resources for basic well-being, such as food, shelter and clothes, poverty extends to: inadequate access to services such as health care and education; lack of voice, power and independence; inability to maintain cultural identity and lack of physical, human, social and environmental assets (World Bank, 2007).

TASK

- Visit the UN website **www.7billionactions.org/data** and explore current global themes. How might you introduce these to children?

In the UK, it has long been recognised that children need to be taught about global issues. In 1939, the Council for Education in World Citizenship (CEWC, now part of the Citizenship Foundation) was established to promote the importance of political and civic engagement within and across national boundaries. In the 1970s and 1980s 'world studies' was highlighted by the Schools Council, a government agency, and other bodies to help pupils understand the interdependence of individuals, groups and nations. Fisher and Hicks (1986) wrote *World Studies 8–13*, which provided practical ideas for teachers on topics such as exploring the neighbourhoods, getting on with others, respecting other worlds and thinking about the world tomorrow. Suggested classroom activities included:

- 'The World in our Town' – making a town trail that draws out links with other countries;
- Ranking news cuttings – ranking nine newspaper cuttings in response to 'You are writing to a pen friend in a distant country; which of these will you enclose to show the world as seen in your country?';
- Compiling a book of questions about the future;
- Listening to the radio news and discussing one item, to be marked on a world map;
- Studying conflicts – pupils observing younger children over a period of time and noting down the causes of any conflicts, how they are resolved and their consequences; comparing these experiences with conflicts in the wider world; and
- Choosing and describing three images that pupils think typically represent a particular country, then discussing the choice with another pair, before negotiating a joint selection.

The World Studies Trust was set up in 1988 to promote young people's social and environmental responsibility in a multicultural society and an interdependent world (**www.globalteacher.org.uk**). Various publications have since been produced including those aimed at trainee and serving teachers to demonstrate how a global perspective could be included in the curriculum (Brown, 1996; Whitaker, 1997; Midwinter, 2005).

There are also a number of recent educational programmes that promote children's understanding of global issues. The American-based Facing the Future charity provides a curriculum spanning 120 countries, with a global perspective on issues such as climate change, population growth, poverty, environmental degradation and sanitation (**www.facingthefuture.org**). The International Primary Curriculum, introduced in 2000, is designed to develop respect for nationalities and cultures around the world (**www.internationalprimarycurriculum.com**). There are also many well-established charities, such as Oxfam, Christian Aid and the International Red Cross and Red Crescent Movement, which provide materials to support the teaching of global perspectives. Many schools contribute to Send a Cow, which provides training, livestock, seeds and long-term support to African farmers (**www.sendacow.org.uk/schools**).

The 'global village' concept has been communicated effectively in the primary school through stories, videos and other interactive resources.

If the World Were a Village

Smith and Armstrong's book *If the World Were a Village* (A&C Black, 2004) conveys global issues clearly to children by providing data on the basis of the world being a village of 100 people. Of these:

- 61 are Asian (20 Chinese), 14 African, 11 European, 9 South American, 5 North American, 0 from Australia.
- 70 are employed, of whom 28 work in agriculture, 28 in services and 14 in industry.
- 63 have inadequate sanitation.
- 60 are always hungry.
- 50 are males.
- 37 have mobile phones.
- 33 are Christians, 20 Muslims, 13 Hindus, 12 non-religious, 6 Buddhists, 14 members of other religions.
- 27 are under 15 years of age.
- 26 are smokers.
- 24 have televisions in their home.
- 18 are unable to read.
- 18 are car owners.
- 16 have Internet access.
- 14 are classified as obese.
- 7 are over 64 year olds.

By the end of a year, one villager would die and two new villagers would be born so thus the population would climb to 101.

Sources www.iftheworldwereavillage.org/index.html; www.100people.org/statistics_ detailed_statistics.php

---

TASK

- Devise different activities to demonstrate visually to pupils the information from *If the World Were a Village*. Try to update these statistics and apply them to your country along the lines of 'If Scotland were a village'.

One Well by Strauss (2007) was published to help pupils value the importance of water in the world by asking them to imagine that all Earth's water came from one source – for instance, from a global village well. For younger ones, books such as *My World, Your World* (Walsh, 2004) introduces the notion that children share similarities and differences around the world: they speak different languages but they all say 'achoo!' when they sneeze. The story *The World Came to My Place Today* (Readman and Roberts, 2004), explains how plants from all over the world affect children's lives. It is inspired by the Eden Project based in Cornwall. Other children's publications by the Project include *The Global Garden* (Petty and Maizels, 2005), which describes where sugar comes from and what a chocolate tree looks like.

Financial literacy

The world financial crisis of the late 2000s, considered to be the worst since the 1930s, reinforces the need for schools to teach financial literacy and develop pupils' appreciation of the moral dimension to finance. Pope John Paul II warned of 'the idolatry of the market' where 'having is more important than being' (cited by Mayo and Nairn, 2009: 230). The global financial crisis presents opportunities for teachers to help pupils understand how the economy works, and why it is such an important force in people's lives. Resources such as the online materials available from the Bank of England (**www.bankofengland.co.uk/education/index.htm**) and the *My Money Primary Toolkit* (DfE, 2009; available at **www.mymoneyonline.org**) provide ideas for promoting financial capability throughout the primary years. In one case study, a Year 5 class considered why Fairtrade was introduced and who the main beneficiaries are, before planning their own Fairtrade picnic, working out the best value per pound. Fairtrade is a good example of how children can demonstrate their global citizenship – there are nearly 500 Fairtrade schools and in 2010, the Fairtrade market in the UK was worth £1.17bn, a 40 per cent increase on 2009 (**www.fairtrade.org.uk/schools**). In 2006, a group of 11- and 12-year-old children launched the Chocolate Challenge Manifesto to press for a fairer deal for cocoa farmers; for a typical £1 bar of chocolate is split as follows:

40.5p goes to the company that actually makes the chocolate.

28p goes to shops.

17.5p goes to the UK taxman.

7p goes to the government in Ghana.

7p goes to the farmers who grow the cocoa in Ghana.

Pupils can be asked to suggest what would be considered fair distribution of income *before* discussing these figures.

Population growth put enormous strain on the global financial market. On 30 October 2011, the 'world's seven billionth baby was born (Coleman, 2011). According to Pearce (2011), despite passing the seven billion mark, the global population birthrate is slowing to the benefit of the environment. Whether driving the economic growth or demanding democracy, young adults are dynamic forces for change in any society and as each society ages, such dynamism is lost.

Media literacy

The mass media touches all aspects of life and occupies significant amounts of professional and personal time. On average, adults spend more than 41 per cent of their day using media, whether the Internet, mobile phones, personal computers, watching television or listening to the radio (Biagi, 2012: 5). Children spend on average almost 45 hours per week with the media (Rideout *et al.*, 2003) – this is more time than is spent with parents (17 hours) or at school (30 hours). McLuhan was rightly concerned about the impact of technology and mass media in replacing individualism with collective identity. The importance of media literacy in the modern age cannot be underestimated. Media literacy is essentially the skills of accessing, understanding and creating communication in various contexts. There are those who argue that children as young as five should learn the 'language' of advertisers so that they are less susceptible to sophisticated campaigns (Asthana, 2009; Buckingham, 2011; Marsh and Larson, 2005). Developments such as Media Smart (**www.mediasmart.org.uk**) have been designed to raise children's awareness of advertising, one of the most powerful global forces that shape our lives. The average child in the UK watches 10,000 adverts a year – in America it can reach 40,000. So-called 'Tweens' (8–12-year-olds) are reported to 'heavily influence' more than $30 billion of their parents' spending, and 80 per cent of all global brands now deploy a 'tween strategy' (**www.globalissues.org/article/237/children-as-consumers**). Brand loyalty can be encouraged from the age of two, and children's 'pester power' influences not only what they want for themselves but also family purchases – from cars, holidays and entertainment to household items. This is part of what Palmer (2006) has described as 'Toxic Childhood'.

There are a number of exciting projects that use media to engage the interests of learners. The National Media Museum, Education Bradford and the British Film Institute (BFI) provide educational resources including materials designed to improve boys' achievement in writing (**www.nationalmediamuseum.org.uk/Educators.aspx**). For older and more able pupils, Oxfam (2006) suggest activities such as comparing media representations of conflicts from around the world and includes appropriate weblinks for newspaper reports from Africa and elsewhere.

Websites such as Google Earth and LiveLocal bring otherwise distant and far-off places directly to us, providing pupils with detailed, if pre-selected images. This access, supported by other primary and secondary sources such as visitors, books, photo packs, artefacts and stories, can help pupils construct more informed ideas about places. One useful resource is First News (**www.firstnews.co.uk/teachers/ks2-3-newspaper-i4**), which engages pupils with more contentious issues in their world.

TASK

- Trawl through the newspapers for a week and compile examples of pictures, headlines, television programmes and other entries that show pupils the relevance of geography, history and RE today.

Environmental literacy

Present-day global economic challenges are compounded by natural disasters, costing billions in reconstruction costs. During 2011, a devastating earthquake and tsunami left 2,000 dead in Japan, famine ravaged northeast Africa and tropical storm 'Irene' caused widespread havoc. The evidence for major climate change, social injustice, war, and economic turmoil is compelling and cannot be dismissed as media hype. The National Aeronautics and Space Administration website acknowledges that the earth's climate has changed throughout history, but graphically depicts the changes in shrinking ice sheets, warming oceans, global temperature rises and extreme events, since the Industrial Revolution (**http://climate.nasa.gov/evidence**). Boyle (2010), a Cambridge professor, suggests that over the past 500 years each century has been marked by a great event, normally occurring within the first two decades – for instance: 1517 (Reformation), 1618 (Thirty Years War), 1914 (First World War). He speculates that 2014 will mark the next great event, triggered by the global financial crisis, which will either result in a new era of poverty and violence or one of global cooperation, marking the end of individual nation states.

Not everyone holds a pessimistic world view. In the United Kingdom, 40 per cent of people believe that global warming is exaggerated and 60 per cent doubt that it is man-made (Lomborg, 2009). It is important to remember that when pupils encounter phrases such as 'environmental change' and 'environmental impact' they are introduced to the positive side of these changes, for instance provision of paths and car parking areas in national parks help the preservation of farmed and wild environment. Sometimes pupils encounter environmental change only in the context of destruction and degradation, for example the impact of flooding and high winds damaging homes and the local infrastructure.

There is a danger that pupils can become unduly frightened over the environment and see little hope for the future. Lomborg (2009) cites the example of an eight-year-old worried about the impact of global warming killing polar bears when, in reality, the global polar bear population has doubled and perhaps even quadrupled over the past half-century. One recent survey showed that half of young children aged 7–11 are anxious about the effects of global warming, often losing sleep because of their concern. However, children are genuinely interested in 'green' issues and can exert powerful influences. According to another survey, six out of ten parents say their children persuade them to be greener ('Children want to learn about the environment, survey finds', *The Guardian*, 20 September 2011). Teachers have a moral and social duty to ensure that pupils are well informed, have the necessary skills and are motivated to understand why and how they can live their lives in more sustainable ways. As Nelson Mandela (1994, cited by DCELLS, 2008: 4) said: 'Education is the most powerful weapon you can use to change the world'.

In order for children to become environmentally literate, among other things, they need to:

- know and appreciate the ecosystems that support human well-being;
- demonstrate care over, and interest, in their environment;
- want to improve their place and act accordingly;
- recognise the links between their environment and the wider world; and
- express viewpoints based on evidence.

Acting sustainably would be second-nature to an environmentally literate person who would live in accord with Mahatma Gandhi's philosophy that the earth provides enough to satisfy every man's need but not every man's greed.

One of the challenges for teachers is conveying to pupils the reality of climate change. Although there are many high-quality resources available, the impact of global warming can seem remote and abstract to adults, let alone pupils. Al Gore (2009) points out that traditional human thinking, based on the rule of reason, inhibits action because people think that as individuals they cannot make much of a difference. Moreover, neuroscientists suggest that part of the brain is programmed to apply limited willpower to solving a problem that persists over decades or centuries. Fortunately, the human conscience serves as a guide in making longer-term decisions based on shared and enduring values. Oxfam supports the use of Philosophy for Children (P4C) for classroom discussions over issues such as climate change, poverty and suffering so that children become critical thinkers about the development process **(www.oxfam.org.uk/education/resources/category.htm?293)**.

As for the human dimensions of natural disasters, Lambert and Swift (2005: 4) say that there is no 'right' way to teach about these but that, in order to help young citizens think rationally about such events, we need to 'call on their geographical thinking in a sustained way'; one-off sequences of lessons representing, for example, the tsunami, with an emphasis on sympathy for the victims, may be inappropriate. They suggest that 'interdependence' is the key geographical concept that guides our choices in how we cover such an event. None of the places affected, directly or indirectly, by the event is isolated. There is a complex web of physical, human and environmental processes that connects us all. The old African proverb 'If you want to go quickly, go alone; if you want to go far, go together' sums up the importance of joined-up thinking by political leaders, multinational companies and environmentalists.

Listening to learners

For head teachers, one of the most important ESDGC messages is to develop opportunities for pupils to have a significant say in seeking to improve their school grounds and immediate environment. The environmental mantra 'think global, act local' has to include children participating fully in decisions affecting their environment.

Article 12 of the United Nations Convention of the Rights of the Child states that children have 'the right to be listened to and taken seriously'. There is overwhelming evidence that children can make sensible contributions to every aspect of school life: management, policy development, publicity, project design, evaluating provision for younger ones, research, campaigning, lobbying, peer representation, advocacy, community relations (Lansdowne, 2001). Because ESDGC cuts across all of these aspects, pupil engagement has to be taken seriously. Young children are able to voice legitimate concerns over global issues. For example, Holden (2007) has shown that pupils as young as seven are already concerned about things they hear in the news such as war and climate change, as well as things they have personal experience of, such as bullying and local issues. Although pupil voice still needs to be developed in schools, beyond the school council forum (O'Kane, 2010), there has been significant progress in society at large. One recent national survey reports that only 5 per cent of children thought that adults 'hardly ever' or 'never' listened to them (Davey, 2010: 7).

Many schools, particularly in Wales, follow the international Eco programme designed to support schools on their sustainable journey. Each school sets up an Eco-Committee, charged with improving the school grounds through 'Environmental Weeks' and other initiatives (**www.eco-schools.org.uk**). Eco-Committees must include: pupils chosen or elected to represent different year groups and the whole school; and a member of staff (the Eco-Coordinator) to support but not lead the committee. The Eco programme covers nine topics: Energy, Water, Biodiversity, School grounds, Healthy living, Transport, Litter, Waste and Global Citizenship. Schools can apply to receive an award at three progressive levels: bronze, silver and the most coveted 'green flag'. This scheme has proved popular with schools across the UK. An evaluation of the Eco programme in Scottish schools found that many primary-aged children derived real benefits from feeling that they could 'make a difference' (Pirrie *et al.*, 2006). Key to transformational change is good leadership, including forging strategic partnerships – for instance, with those schools that have attained the green flag. Many of the schools involved in the Geographical Association's Primary Geography Quality Mark (PGQM) are Eco-Schools (**www.geography.org.uk/eyprimary/primary-qualitymark**). Many schools take part in Walk to School Weeks, Walk on Wednesday, and Park and Stride through projects locally organised or through charities such as Living Streets.

ESDGC and other curriculum developments

The ESDGC agenda should be seen as complementary, rather than additional to, recent key strategies, initiatives and policies affecting primary schools. This can be illustrated with a few brief examples. In England, these include *Excellence and Enjoyment: A Strategy for Primary Schools* (2003), *Every Child Matters* (DfES, 2004), *Social and Emotional Aspects of Learning* or SEAL (DCSF, 2007b) and *Personalised Learning* (DCSF, 2008). ESDGC is an umbrella approach to teaching and learning, which has the potential to tie all these initiatives together.

Every Child Matters (ECM)

ESDGC is an integral part of the principles embodied in ECM introduced to ensure that all children succeed in reaching five broad outcomes: staying safe, being healthy, enjoying and achieving, making a contribution and avoiding poverty (DfES, 2003). As Catling (2007: 15) observes, 'the government sees the five ECM outcomes as almost providing a blueprint for child-centred sustainable development'. The Coalition government, elected in 2010, found it necessary to clarify its support for the principles of ECM when it dropped the phrase 'Every Child Matters' in favour of 'Help children achieve more'. It still remains unclear whether the change in terminology and funding signals a shift in policy. Nonetheless, examples of how humanities subjects and ESDGC can contribute to the five ECM outcomes are outlined in Table 9.1.

Table 9.1 ESDGC and ECM	
ECM outcomes	**How humanities and ESDGC can contribute**
Be healthy	Teaches pupils to recognise the distinction between needs and wants as part of their understanding of what constitutes a healthy lifestyle. Understanding physical, mental and emotional health is an integral part of understanding the key concept of quality of life.
Stay safe	Pupils learn about health and safety issues, risk assessments and the use of common sense when working in the outdoor environments. Pupils debate what counts as anti-social behaviour in the context of their interactions with the environment.
Enjoy and achieve	Pupils gain a great sense of achievement when they are involved in decision-making processes that relate to their real-world experiences and concerns. When these are used as curriculum examples pupils' motivation levels, and therefore achievement, are potentially much greater.
Make a positive contribution to society	It is action orientated. Action in school can have a positive impact on the local community, and the local community can make a positive contribution through active involvement in school projects.
Achieve economic well-being	It encourages pupils to consider the distribution of resources, both locally and globally. Through topics such as energy, travel and food they develop an understanding of how to use resources wisely. The skills, knowledge and understanding developed through ESDGC are those required to be active and responsible global citizens.

Source: Adapted from Martin and Owens (2010: 10).

Environmental well-being and outdoor learning

Pupils' environmental well-being can be promoted through ESDGC (Catling, 2007; Collins and Foley, 2008; DfES, 2006). Environmental well-being concerns peoples' state of happiness and contentment within their environment, natural and built, and is underpinned by the concept of care (Noddings, 2005). One survey of 10–11-year-olds in the UK reports that many have a surprisingly good grasp of environmental issues. They gain such understanding by exploring outdoors, although this is being constrained by restrictions on access. This means that children are losing their connection with their natural environment, to the detriment of their well-being (Thomas and Thompson, 2004; Louv, 2008). Schools have moral and social responsibilities in the unsettled world to equip pupils with the life skills so that they become active and effective citizens, with a role to play and a difference to make (Catling and Willy, 2009). For instance, young children can be encouraged to think about recycling through sorting activities (Photo 9.2).

In terms of making use of the outdoor environment, there are promising signs with initiatives such as the Royal Horticultural Society's Campaign for School Gardening (**http://apps.rhs.org.uk/schoolgardening/default.aspa**), which aims to support schools to create and actively use a school garden. The Co-operative Green Schools Revolution is another exciting development designed to develop pupils' understanding of particular themes – energy, water and healthy living – and provides teachers with a wide range of resources (for 5–16-year-olds) to this end (**www.co-operative. coop/green-schools-revolution**).

Forest Schools

The Forest School programme, which originated in Scandinavia, is a good example of how pupils can grow in their awareness of sustainability issues. The philosophy of Forest Schools is to encourage and inspire individuals of any age through positive outdoor experiences. It has been described by Knight (2009) as an inspirational process that offers children regular opportunities to achieve and develop confidence through hands-on learning in a woodland environment. The Forest School model involves participants journeying by foot (if possible) to a local woodland environment to learn outdoors on a regular sustained basis (Photo 9.1). It is a long-term child-led educational process that promotes, observes and explicitly supports the social, emotional and physical development of children in an outdoor, preferably woodland, environment. Forest Schools use the woods and forests as a means to build independence and self-esteem in pupils. Topics include the natural environment, for example the role of trees in society, the complex ecosystem supported by a wilderness, and recognition of specific plants and animals.

Developing children's caring for the environment requires active engagement (Martin and Owens, 2008). Nursery children can begin to develop positive attitudes by:

- taking resources out and putting them away carefully, discussing why this helps, what they learn about care and what others should do;
- showing responsibility with adults for looking after particular areas in the nursery to see that everything is in order and is being cared for;

- walking around the nursery outdoor area periodically to see what is there and to talk about how plants grow, the needs of mini-beasts, birds and other creatures, to check the fencing, to see that paths are looked after, to check for litter or fallen leaves; and

- observing whether something seems 'shabby' and in need of repair and painting – they can discuss who would do this, and how to improve the look and use of the resources and area.

Source: Catling (2009: 97).

Through such activities, young children learn about environmental care and concern, using observation and discussion and appreciating who helps to keep places clean and tidy. They can record what they see and hear, and discuss what care for the environment is and why people think it is important. They can consider when it is important to tidy up and when and why some things may be left untidy, such as a wild area in the grounds or if individuals leave off part way through an activity and come back to it later. Case studies of schools in Wales can be viewed at the NGFL Wales website (**www.ngfl-cymru.org.uk**).

Personalised learning

The phrase 'personalised learning' was introduced by the Blair government in 2004, based on learning style theory and the principle that it is possible to tailor teaching to the needs of different pupils rather than a 'one size fits all' philosophy. It aims to enable all children and young people, whatever their starting point, to fulfil their potential as learners (DfES, 2007). At a fundamental level, teachers need to learn about children as individuals and what makes them who they are: their families, homes, language, beliefs, customs, hobbies, fears, hopes and interests. Such knowledge should inform

Photo 9.1 Forest School. *Source:* S. Hughes.

Photo 9.2 Children sorting out rubbish with the help of a puppet 'Eco-Ed'. *Source:* S. Hughes.

planning, teaching and assessment. Personalised learning requires personalised care – making space for children to be unique (Glazzard *et al.*, 2010).

In reality, no teacher can offer a bespoke educational programme for each individual in the class. Moreover, critics suggest that too much is made of accommodating pupils' preferred learning styles with scant evidence of this making any significant difference to raising standards (Coffield *et al.*, 2004). Nonetheless, there are projects in the humanities in which teachers assert that creating different opportunities and contexts for learning improves the quality of pupils' responses. In one example, a Year 6 class spent a day considering whether the Earth is precious. They looked at the Earth on a small scale to appreciate its variety of landscapes and environments and were asked to design a small community of the future using modern technologies, including renewable energy sources. They considered Mick Inkpen and Nick Butterworth's (2010) *A Wonderful Earth*, which introduces the idea that, despite their intelligence, human beings are in the process of ruining the Earth but it is not too late to turn things around (**www.geography.org.uk**).

Children's holiday experiences are a very good opportunity for teachers and parents to personalise learning in the humanities. Postcards, family photographs, artefacts, clothes and stories from different towns and countries can be collected, displayed and discussed. Teachers can highlight similarities and contrasts between different environments, peoples and climates.

Social and Emotional Aspects of Learning (SEAL)

Recent neurological research highlights how learning is more longlasting when it appeals to both the affective and cognitive sides of the brain (Smith, 2002; Sousa, 2009). The SEAL programme aims to develop the qualities and skills that promote positive behaviour and effective learning. It focuses on five social and emotional aspects of learning: self-awareness, managing feelings, motivation, empathy and social skills. For the Early Years, the Social and Emotional Aspects of Development (SEAD) programme has been devised to promote effective interaction with children and their parents/carers (**www.birthtofive.org.uk/sead.aspx**). Successful ESDGC rests on good personal and social development. Care is not only a core value of ESDGC, for instance caring for self, others and the environment, but also a core value of the humanities. For instance, in Religious Education and geography pupils learn to care for the environment and the world around them. In history, pupils are encouraged to develop empathy with people in the past, for instance child refugees during the Second World War.

Planning to integrate ESDGC

ESDGC is integral to the curricula throughout the UK (see Table 9.2). It should feature across the curriculum and not be confined to particular subjects. School leaders need to see ESDGC holistically by making connections between teaching, learning

Table 9.2 ESDGC concepts	
ESDGC concept *(title used in Wales)*	**Definition of concept**
1. Citizenship and stewardship *(choices and making decisions)*	Gaining the skills, knowledge and understanding to become informed, global citizens, recognising that we all have rights and responsibilities to participate in decision-making and that everyone should have a say in what happens in the future.
2. Interdependence *(the natural environment)*	Understanding that people, places and environments are all interrelated at local and global levels, and that decisions taken in one place have repercussions elsewhere.
3. Needs and rights of future generations *(wealth and poverty)*	Knowing about human rights and learning how to lead lives that consider the rights and needs of others, and that what we do now has implications for what life will be like in the future.
4. Diversity *(Identity and culture)*	Understanding the importance and value of diversity in our lives – culturally, socially, economically and biologically.
5. Quality of life *(health)*	Recognising that for development to be sustainable it must benefit people in an equitable way and improve the welfare of all people.
6. Sustainable change *(consumption and waste)*	Understanding that there is a limit to the way the world can develop and that consequences of unsustainable growth are increased poverty and degradation of the environment.
7. Uncertainty and precaution *(climate change)*	Recognising that we are learning all the time and we should adopt a cautious approach to the welfare of the planet as our actions may have unforeseen consequences.

Source: Adapted from Holland Report (1987); DCELLS (2008).

and other areas of school life, such as energy and waste management. The potential benefits can include:

- reduced operating costs;
- improved environmental impacts; and
- raised environmental awareness and responsibility of staff, learners and employers.

Planning ESDGC should be based on the key concepts identified by the Holland Report (1998) and these are illustrated with reference to a history topic, teaching about the 1960s (see Table 9.3). The National Curriculum suggests that ESDGC will

Table 9.3 Opportunities to promote ESDGC through a 1960s history study

Main concept	Possible talking points
Interdependence	• Trade links from major ports in Wales, Scotland, Ireland, England, etc. • Transport and communication (e.g. railways – the introduction of the 'Beeching Plan'). • Legacies of industrialisation – the disfigurement of the landscape.
Citizenship and stewardship	• The first motorways opened in 1958/9 (M6/M1). By 1969, 600 miles of motorways had been built. Consider the impact on lifestyle and landscape. More cars on the roads. More cars meant more roads. Each mile of motorway takes nearly 10 hectares (100,000 square metres) of land and damages ecology and environment. Road building also has an impact on animal life. • People did not travel as far as today and made fewer journeys.
Needs and rights	• Basic needs (and wants) could be discussed in the context of immigrants. • Civil rights movement of the 1960s. • Campaign for equal play for women. • Contribution of figures such as Martin Luther King, and make links to US President Obama.
Diversity	• Case-studies (e.g. Tiger Bay, Wales) and the values of mutual tolerance and respect that were fostered in the 1960s.
Sustainable change	• Increased traffic on roads brought more congestion, and better controls were needed (e.g. traffic wardens, one-way systems, speed limits, etc.). • Clean Air Act (1956) attempted to end smog. • Controversial development of nuclear power stations. • Consider the work of Friends of the Earth UK, founded in 1970.
Quality of life	• Status and treatments of non-whites in Britain, South Africa and America. • Global protests – the Vietnam War, Flower Power movements, anti-nuclear protests. • Lyrics of Bob Dylan, Beatles and other musicians.
Uncertainty and precaution	• Consider planning of housing developments such as high-rise flats and prefabs. • Compare transport systems in the 1960s and today: the decline in railways and trams; the development of motorways and hovercraft.
Values and perceptions	• Consider experiences of racial prejudice by immigrants in the 1960s (e.g. the colour bar in the renting of houses). • Euphoria of winning the World Cup (1966).

Source: Based on Grigg and Stevens (2010).

help pupils in developing confidence and responsibility and making the most of their abilities. It will also prepare them to play an active role as citizens and develop good relationships by promoting respect for differences between people.

History

Environmental histories of Britain show clearly than Britons have transformed, exploited, abused and cherished their surroundings for thousands of years (Simmons, 2001; Pryor, 2011). History contributes to pupils' understanding of ESDGC by developing their understanding of how working and living conditions affected people's health in the past. Pupils can research how different past societies managed their natural environments, while archaeology enables pupils to find out about key concepts such as consumption and waste.

Examples of how history can promote ESDGC can be seen in Table 9.3 Pupils can explore differences and similarities between historical events, people, places, cultures and environments through time, and the interconnectedness and interdependence of our world's history. Older pupils should explore themes such as prejudice, conflict and oppression and relate historical examples to contemporary events and experiences. For example, pupils could explore the significance of Rosa Parks' gesture in the wider civil rights movement (Claire, 2006).

Pupils can consider how past societies have exchanged goods, balanced the needs of competing groups and managed their resources, especially during post-industrial times. The social and environmental impact of the Industrial Revolution (since the 1780s), the development of the railway system and more latterly the rise of the motor car, are all relevant research topics. When comparing where food and materials originated in the past, pupils develop their knowledge and understanding of sustainability and finite resources. Local history provides opportunities for teachers to illustrate national and global themes, such as the rise and fall of the coalmining industry. In one Welsh school, Key Stage 2 pupils visited an exhibition on the transatlantic slave trade in Penrhyn Castle as part of their study of historical and present-day links between a north Wales quarry and Jamaica (DCELLS, 2008).

Religious education

There are many opportunities during RE to promote ESDGC. Pupils should understand the influence of belief, values and traditions on individuals, societies, communities and cultures. They should discover and experience the wealth and variety of religious traditions, and how these are expressed through practices and customs such as worship, literature, drama, dance, music and art. They should also reflect on their own beliefs, values and practices and be encouraged to develop respect, tolerance and empathy for the beliefs and practices of other people. The values promoted by the great traditions of Christianity, Islam, Hinduism, Judaism, Buddhism and Sikhism stress the importance of humankind's responsibilities in serving as good stewards of the planet.

Values of the Six Great Religions

Do not cut trees because they remove pollution

Hinduism (Rig Veda, 6: 48: 17)

Then the Lord God took the man and put him in the garden of Eden to tend and keep it

Christianity (Genesis 2: 15, New King James Version)

Do not dump waste in any place from which it could be scattered by the wind or spread by flooding

Judaism (Maimonides' Mishneh Torah)

The world is beautiful and verdant, and verily God, be He exalted, has made you His stewards in it, and He sees how you acquit yourselves

Islam (Hadith of sound authority, related by Muslim on the authority of Abu Sa'id al-Khudri)

(Cited by Gore, 2009: 308–309).

RE can promote pupils' awareness and importance of being carers or stewards of the earth when they explore different religions' approaches to the environment, natural world and economic growth. Examples of possible ways RE can promote ESDGC can be seen in Table 9.4. There are opportunities within RE for pupils to explore citizenship issues – for instance, justice, equality, care for others and for the planet, and peace and conflict, from different perspectives.

Geography

The key geographical concepts of space, place, scale and interdependence, and knowledge and understanding of physical and human processes, all relate to sustainable development and global citizenship. Geography is a good lens through which to focus an interdisciplinary approach to ESDGC because it involves learning about the world in everyday contexts and at different scales, demands participative and enquiry-led skills, and takes an interconnected view of local and global events (Martin and Owens, 2010). Geography is essential to developing children's environmental awareness, so they may act as responsible local and global citizens. Good primary geography raises questions about how societies function and the potential environmental, social and technological challenges ahead. It serves to illustrate global interconnectedness and interdependence. The following extract shows how a student teacher introduced the topic of fair trading to a group of primary school children:

> During a recent school experience I introduced the topic to the group by giving them some facts about our mystery topic and the children were invited to touch the banana in a black feely bag. When some suggestions had been offered, a child

Table 9.4 How RE can contribute to the delivery of ESDGC

Main concept	Possible talking points
Interdependence	<ul><li>Moral decision-making activities.</li><li>Look at the contents of a shopping bag and labels on clothing to see how much these basic items link to other parts of the world. Link this to the concept of '*tawhid*' (the oneness of God) in Islam, or the Buddhist and Hindu concepts of oneness and interdependence of the universe.</li><li>Consider the similarities and differences between themselves and the children the study.</li></ul>
Citizenship and stewardship	<ul><li>Analysis of the media, (e.g. BBC's *Newsround* programme), looking for values and perceptions underlying selection and presentation of news items.</li><li>Participating in community environmental projects.</li><li>Exploring their own identity through affirmation exercises and learning about family life in various religious communities in the UK and wider world.</li><li>Finding out about the work of charitable organisations linked to religious traditions such as Christian Aid.</li><li>Looking at and responding to the arts in particular religions.</li></ul>
Needs and rights	<ul><li>Examining the laws and teachings of specific religious traditions and what they reveal about how humankind is viewed.</li><li>Exploring how people's religious responsibilities can be integrated with life in the UK and the issues this might raise.</li></ul>
Diversity	<ul><li>Learning about the similarities and differences between world religions and the diversity within them.</li><li>Studying case studies of families from different cultures living in the UK and how religion shapes their lives, their beliefs and way of life.</li><li>Appreciation of the variety and achievements and ways of overcoming adversity.</li><li>Moral education – exploring teachings on prejudice and the dangers raised by this.</li></ul>
Sustainable change	<ul><li>Developing a sense of awe and wonder at the natural world.</li><li>Discovering the various teachings on looking after animals and the environment in different religious traditions.</li><li>Exploring the consequences of action in relation to the future of the planet.</li><li>Listening to stories that challenge the acquisition of wealth as the source of happiness.</li><li>Guided meditation on the beauty and wonder of the earth.</li><li>Learning to treasure and value what you have.</li><li>Listening to each other's experiences and opinions with respect.</li></ul>

Main concept	Possible talking points
Quality of life (social justice)	• Studying the lives of individuals – some great religious leaders who, inspired by faith, sought to bring justice and equality to the world: Gandhi, Martin Luther King, Guru Gobind Singh, etc. • Examining religious discrimination in the past and the present. • Considering rights and responsibilities within the religious traditions. • Exploring concepts of power and authority.
Uncertainty and precaution (conflict resolution)	• Exploring classroom conflicts and the various ways in which they might be resolved in circle time. • Listening to people from other faiths and expressing thoughts and feelings. • Asking questions to clarify misunderstandings about faith, traditions and learn from some of the stories in faith traditions about ways to resolve conflict and overcome hatred. • Developing empathy with children from other cultures with different ethnicity, and learning how to appreciate diversity.
Values and perceptions	• Examining religious teachings and texts to identify and discuss the values that underpin them. • Having conversations with members of different faith traditions about what is important to them. • Identifying and developing their own beliefs. • Exploring how religious beliefs informs perceptions of the world and how to live within it.

Table 9.4 (*Continued*)

Source: Adapted from *McCreery et al. (*2008: 74).

took out the fruit, which was to be our focus for four weeks. During that time we discussed jobs and who should earn more and why. We sequenced these jobs and discussed each. We had debates from shippers and growers etc. We learned about the monies involved and we discussed fair trading. The children then thought of their own questions to research and did so through the Internet Wibdeco site, and books.

(Primary PGCE trainee)

Source: DCELLS (2008: 25).

Education for global citizenship through geographical contexts provides opportunities for pupils to take informed, responsible action. It addresses diversity and identity issues and enables pupils to develop investigative skills (see Table 9.5.)

Table 9.5 Activities to promote ESDGC and geography skills

- Observing and asking questions: Where is it? What is it like? How did it get like this? How is it changing? What might happen next? What do I think about it?
- Noting similarities and differences – way of life in contrasting countries.
- Recognising the importance of the environment.
- Using out-of-classroom learning – visits, surveys, etc.
- Discussing how people across the world are linked (interdependent) – food, clothes, fuel, environment etc. (globingo – activity).
- Taking part in international school partnerships and links and using them to explore opinions and responses to issues such as climate change and trade (**www.britishcouncil.org.uk/comenius**).
- Holding role-plays and debates about sustainable development and global issues.
- Playing stimulation games on food and farming, global trading and comparing issues of fair trade, free trade, unfair trade.
- Exploring economic, social and environmental aspects of issues affecting their communities.
- Discussing the importance of the environment, people's effect on environment, caring for environment.
- Exploring global warming and climate change impact.

Humanities, ESDGC and thinking skills

One of the aims of ESDGC is to promote pupils' creative and critical thinking skills. These include the ability to select relevant information, weigh up opposing arguments, consider alternatives, read between the lines, reach informed conclusions and present a point of view in a structured, clear and well-reasoned way. Cottrell (2011: 2) highlights the ability to reflect sceptically, meaning bringing in 'an element of polite doubt' to discussions. Pupils need to recognise the importance of gathering good evidence to underpin arguments. Bell and Morse (2003) argue that children should not be cheated on issues surrounding sustainability. For example, they should not conclude that everything man-made is destructive and damaging. Huckle (1990) pointed out that while it is valuable for children to make a real contribution to their environment, there is a danger that they can end up seeing everything natural – trees, plants, animals, birds – as good, and all human activity as corrupting and polluting. Children should not limit their view of nature as something to be protected from people.

Through first-hand experiences, children can see what works well – for example, caring for gardens and pets, using water, energy and other resources wisely, and understanding that waste can be recycled and not just 'dumped' (Scoffham and Dorman 2007). In philosophical discussions, pupils can consider what kind of world they would like to grow up in – what kind of neighbourhood they would like, how they think the school grounds could be improved. When Richard Gerver took over as headteacher of the Grange Primary School (Derbyshire), he asked his staff what kind of people they wanted the children to be at the end of their journey at school. One of the creative outcomes was a commitment to three-dimensional real-life, applied learning. They established Grangeton, the children's own real town, with its elected council, environmental team, counsellors, café, healthy-eating shops, craft shop, museum and media centre (Gerver, 2010; **www.grange. derbyshire.sch.uk/grangeton1b.htm**).

The current school vision is based on 'living, learning and laughing' (**www.grangeton. com**). Establishing and sharing a vision is essential to creating a desired future. As Fisher (2004: 11) notes, 'imagination can be used to serve evil ends so it needs to be informed by values' (in this case, the values that underpin ESDGC and the key concepts). Imagination can lead to false belief so it needs to be tempered by critical thinking, reasoning and judgements.

BOX 9.1 RESEARCH BRIEFING – THINKING SKILLS

Teaching and developing pupils' thinking skills within primary education has been extensively researched (Gardner, 1993; Goleman, 1995; McGuinness, 1999; Claxton, 2002; Adey and Shayer, 2002; Wegerif, 2002; Coffield *et al.*, 2004). There is debate over whether thinking skills are transferable or subject-specific (Winch *et al.*, 2010) and there are many different approaches. For instance, Philosophy 4 Children (P4C) focuses on developing reasoning skills (Worley, 2010). It began in America in the 1970s when Matthew Lipman, a professor in New Jersey, was dismayed at the muddled thinking among educated people when discussing the Vietnam War. Small research studies have since shown improvements in pupils' critical reasoning, speaking, behaviour, listening and concentration as a result of having one P4C hour a week during the year (Lightfoot, 2011; see also **www.thinkingeducation. co.uk/p4c.htm**). As Fisher (2004) states, the unique value of P4C is that it is the only-well researched thinking approach that focuses specifically on developing questioning, and in particular the kinds of questioning that enable pupils to think and act with philosophical intelligence. There are many examples of pupils raising profound questions during P4C sessions, including a desire among one group of Year 3 and Year pupils to discuss God (see **www.teachingthinking.net/thinking/web%20resources/robert_fisher_ talkingtothink.htm**).

An analysis of thinking skills that develop through geographical enquiry is shown in Table 9.6.

TABLE **9.6** DEVELOPING THINKING SKILLS THROUGH GEOGRAPHY

Skill	Suggested activities
Information processing skills	• Extract information about views of different people from newspaper article and photograph. • Extract evidence to support arguments from different perspectives from the Internet, other photos and brochures. • Use information from globes, maps, atlases.
Reasoning skills	• Develop arguments, supported by evidence, from point of view of tourists, tour operators, explorers, environmentalists, shipping companies, scientists, wildlife. • Weigh arguments.
Enquiry skills	• Identify issues – express in own words. • Identify and investigate key questions using geographical skills and concepts: Where is it taking place? What is the place like? How could we get there?
Creative thinking skills	• Use imagination to see issues from different perspectives.
Evaluation skills	• Consider what is important. • Understand the need to reach a consensus in a group, to show tolerance and compromise. • Class debate, followed by the need to reach a point of view. • Evaluate tour company's video for bias.

Source: Mackintosh (2005) in Cooper *et al.* (2006).

Conclusion

This chapter has shown the importance of promoting a global perspective through the humanities. The Cambridge Primary Review (Alexander, 2010) identifies the empowering of local, national and global citizenship as one of the fundamental aims of primary schools in the twenty-first century. Teachers need to encourage pupils to take increasing responsibility in their classes and schools, to grow in their understanding of human rights, the importance of democratic engagement, the resolution of conflict and the fragile nature of the planet. The Review also recognises another aim, namely to promote interdependence and sustainability so that children move on from understanding to positive action in order that they can make a difference to their worlds.

SUMMARY

- Education for Sustainable Development (ESD) is concerned with developing pupils' knowledge, skills and values to participate in decisions about how to improve the quality of life now without damaging the planet for the future.

- Education for Global Citizenship (EGC) focuses on the global forces that shape people's lives. It aims to equip children and young people so that they can participate in decision-making, both locally and globally, which promotes a more equitable and sustainable world.

- The humanities have an important contribution in supporting ESGDC in the primary curriculum.

- There is a need to integrate ESDGC when planning lessons in the humanities. ESDGC should not be confined to geography lessons.

- Pupils' creative and critical thinking skills can be promoted through ESDGC. Teachers should make good use of real-life contexts and a range of resources, including the immediate environment and current news stories to engage pupils.

References

Adey, P. and Shayer, M. (2002), *Learning Intelligence,* Buckingham: Open University Press.

Alexander, R.J. (ed.) (2010), *Children, their World, their Education*, London: Routledge.

Asthana, A. (2009), 'Primary schools need to make children 'media savvy', *The Observer*, 22 November 2009.

Bell, S. and Morse, S. (2003), *Measuring Sustainability Learning From Doing Learning By Doing*, London: Earthscan Publications Ltd.

Biagi, S. (2012), *Media Impact: An Introduction to Mass Media, 2013 Update*, Boston MA: Wadsworth.

Boyle, N. (2010), *2014 – How to survive the next world crisis,* London: Continuum.

Brown, M. (ed.) (1996), *Our World, Our Rights: teaching about rights and responsibilities in the primary classroom*, London: Amnesty International.

Bruntland, G. (1987), *Our Common Future*: The World Commission on Environment and Development, Oxford: Oxford University Press.

Buckingham, D. (2011), *The Material Child*, Cambridge: Polity Press.

Catling, S. (2007), 'ECM6 = environmental well-being?' in *Primary Geographer*, 63, 5–8.

Catling, S. and Willy, T. (2009), *Achieving QTS: Teaching Primary Geography,* Exeter: Learning Matters.

Claire, H. (2006), 'How should we remember Rosa Parks?', *Primary History*, 43, 18–20.

Claxton, G. (2002), *Building Learning Power: Helping Young People Become Better Learners*, Bristol: TLO Limited.

Coffield, F., Moseley, D., Hall, E. and Ecclestone, K. (2004), *Should we be using learning styles. What research has to say to practice*, London: Learning Skills and Development Agency.

Coleman, J. (2011), 'World's 'seven billionth baby is born' in *The Guardian*, 30 October 2011 **www.guardian.co.uk/environment/series/ crowded-planet-population+world/philippines.**

Collins, J. and Foley, P. (2008), *Promoting children's well-being: Policy and practice*, Bristol: Policy Press.

Cottrell, S. (2011), *Critical Thinking Skills*, New York: Palgrave.

Cooper, H., Rowley, C. and Asquith, S. (2006) *Geography 3–11: A Guide for Teachers*. London: David Fulton.

Davey, C. (2010), *Children's participation in decision-making. A Summary Report on progress made up to 2010*, London: National Participation Forum.

DCELLS (2008), *Education for Sustainable Development and Global Citizenship: Information for teacher trainees and new teachers in Wales*, Cardiff: Welsh Assembly Government.

DCSF (2007a), *Guidance on the Duty to Promote Community Cohesion*, Nottingham: DCSF.

DCSF (2007b), *Social and Emotional Aspects of Learning (SEAL)*, Nottingham: DSCF.

DCSF (2008), *Personalised Learning – A Practical Guide*, Nottingham: DCSF.

DfE (2009), *My Money Primary Toolkit*, London: DfE.

DfE (2011), *The Framework for the National Curriculum. A report by the Expert Panel for the National Curriculum review*, London: DfE.

DfES (2003), *Excellent and Enjoyment: A Strategy for Primary Schools*, London: DfES.

DfES (2004), *Every Child Matters: Change for Children*, London: DfES.

DfES (2006), *Guidance on the Extended Schools Initiative and the provision of preschool childcare*, London: DfES.

DfES (2007), *PNS: Pedagogy and personalisation*. London: DfES.

Fisher R. (2004), *Teaching Thinking: Philosophical Enquiry in the Classroom*, London: Continuum.

Fisher, S. and Hicks, F. (1986), *World Studies 8–13*, Edinburgh: Oliver and Boyd.

Gardner H. (1993), *Multiple Intelligences: The theory in practice*, New York: Basic Books.

Gerver, R. (2010), *Creating Tomorrow's Schools Today*, London: Continuum Books.

Glazzard, J., Hughes, A., Netherwood, A., Neve, L., Stokoe, J. (2010), *Achieving QTS – Teaching Primary Special Educational Needs*, Exeter: Learning Matters.

Goleman, D. (1995), *Emotional Intelligence*, New York: Bantam.

Gore, A. (2009), *Our Choice: A Plan to Solve the Climate Crisis*, London: Bloomsbury.

Grigg, R. and Stevens, C. (2010), *Everyday Life in Wales in the 1960s*, Aberystwyth: Canolfan Astudiaethau Addysg.

Holden, C. (2007), 'Young people's concerns', in Hicks, D. and Holden, C. (eds), *Teaching the Global Dimension: Key principles and effective practice*. Abingdon: Routledge.

Holland, G. (1998) *A Report to DfEE/QCA on Education for Sustainable Development in the Schools Sector* from the Panel for Education for Sustainable Development, available at: **www.defra.gov.uk/environment/sustainable/educpanel/1998ar/ann4.htm**.

Huckle, J. (1990), 'Environmental education: Teaching for a sustainable future', in Dufour, D., *The new social curriculum*, Cambridge: Cambridge University Press.

Inkpen, M. and Butterworth, N. (2010), *A Wonderful Earth*, London: O Books.

Knight, S. (2009), *Forest School and Outdoor Learning in the Early Years*, London: SAGE Publications Ltd.

Landsowne, G. (2001), *Promoting Children's Participation in Democratic Decision Making*, Florence: UNICEF Innoceti Research Centre.

Lambert, D. and Swift, D. (2005), 'GeoVision: past, present and future', *Teaching Geography*, 30 (1), 4–7.

Lechner, F.J. and Boli, J. (eds) (2012), *The Globalization Reader*, London: Wiley-Blackwell.

Lightfoot, L. (2011), 'Time to take the won't out of Kant', TES pro, 30 September, No 3, 4–7.

Lomborg, B. (2009), 'Scared silly over climate change', *The Guardian*, 15 June 2009.

Louv, R. (2008), *Last child in the woods: saving our children from natural-deficit disorder*, New York: Algonquin Books.

Mackintosh, M. (2005), 'Talking about "the last wilderness"', *Primary Geography*, Spring (56) 32.

Marsh, J. and Larson, J. (2005), *Making Literacy Real*, London: Sage.

Martin, F. and Owens, P. (2008), *Caring for our world: A practical guide to ESD for ages 4–8*, Sheffield: Geographical Association.

Martin, F. and Owens, P. (2010), 'Children making sense of their place in the world, 'in Scoffham, S (ed.),

Primary Geography Handbook, Sheffield: Geographical Association.

Mayo, E. and Nairn, A. (2009), *Consumer Business: How big businesses are grooming our children for profits,* London: Constable & Robinson.

McGuinness, C. (1999), *From Thinking Skills to thinking classrooms: a review and evaluation of approaches for developing pupils' thinking.* London: DfEE, (Research Report RR115).

McCreery, E., Palmer, S., and Voiels, V. (2008), *Teaching Religious Education,* Exeter: Learning Matters.

Midwinter, C. (2005), *Global Perspectives in the National Curriculum: Guidance for KS 1 and 2*, London: Development Education Association.

Noddings, N. (2005), *The Challenge to Care in Schools*, New York: Teachers' College Press.

Ofsted (2008a), *Schools and Sustainability: A climate for change*, London: Ofsted.

Ofsted (2008b), *Learning Outside the Classroom*, London: Ofsted.

O'Kane, K. (2010) *Research to develop more inclusive and representative models of pupil participation in Wales*, Cardiff: Welsh Assembly Government.

Oxfam (2006), *Education for Global Citizenship: A Guide for Schools,* London: Oxfam.

Palmer, S. (2006), *Toxic Childhood: How the modern world is damaging our children and what we can do about it*, London: Orion Books.

Pearce, F. (2011), 'The population crash will kill our economy – good news for the planet', *The Guardian*, 26 October 2011.

Petty, K. and Maizels, J. (2005), *The Global Garden*, London: Eden Project Book.

Pirrie, A. Elliot, D., McConnell, F. and Wilkinson, J. (2006), *Evaluation of Eco Schools Scotland*, Glasgow: SCRE Centre.

Pryor, F. (2011), *The Making of the British Landscape: How We Have Transformed the Land, from Prehistory to Today*, London: Penguin.

Readman, J. and Roberts, L. (2004), *The World Came To My Place Today*, London: Eden Project Book.

Rideout, V.J., Vandewater, E.A. and Wartella, E.A. (2003), 'Zero to six: Electronic media in the lives of infants,

toddlers, and preschoolers', The Henry J Kaiser Family Foundation: Children's Digital Media Centers.

Scoffham, S. and Dorman, P. (2007), 'Multiple perspectives, profound understandings', *Primary Geographer*, 64, 31–3.

Simmons, I.G. (2001), *An Environmental History of Great Britain: From 10,000 Years Ago to the Present* , Edinburgh: Edinburgh University Press.

Smith, A. (2002), *The Brain's Behind It*, Stafford: Network Education Press.

Smith, D. and Armstrong, S. (2004), *If the World Were a Village*, London: A & C Black.

Sousa, D. (2009), *How the Gifted Brain Learns*, London: SAGE publications.

Strauss, R. (2007), *One Well: The Story of Water on Earth*, London: A&C Black.

Swift, D. (2005), 'Linking lives through disaster and recovery', *Teaching Geography* 30 (2), 78–81.

Thomas, G. And Thompson, G. (2004), *A Child's Place: why environment matters to children,* London: Demos/Green Alliance.

Van Petegem, P. and Blieck, A. (2006), 'The environmental worldview of children: a cross-cultural perspective', in *Environmental Education Research*, Vol. 12, No. 5, November 2006, 625–635.

Walsh, M. (2004), *My World, Your World,* London: Corgi Childrens.

Wegerif, R. (2002), *Literature review in thinking skills, technology and learning*, available at: **www. nestafuturelab.org**.

Winch, C., Johnson, S., and Siegel, H. (2010), *Teaching Thinking Skills (Key Debates in Educational Policy)*, London: Continuum.

Whitaker, P. (1997), *Primary Schools and the Future: Celebration, Challenges and Choices,* Buckingham: Open University Press.

World Bank (2007), *Collins Atlas of Global Issues*, London: Collins.

Worley, P. (2010), *The If Machine: Philosophical Enquiry in the Classroom*, London: Continuum.

WWF (2006), *Living Planet Report 2006*, available at: **www.panda.org/news_facts/publications/living_planet_report/index.cfm**.

Useful Websites

Association for Citizenship Teaching includes many resources including members-only materials on promoting pupils' understanding of identity and diversity issues: **www.teachingcitizenship.org.uk**.

The Citizenship Foundation is an independent charity that aims to encourage and enable individuals to engage in democratic society: **www.citizenshipfoundation.org.uk**.

The Eco Schools Scheme is an international award programme that guides schools on their sustainable journey: **www.eco-schools.org.uk**.

Learning and Teaching Scotland. Sustainable development education advice and resources : **www.ltscotland.org.uk/sustainabledevelopment/index.asp**.

Geography Teaching Today. Follow links for 'KS1–3 courses' and 'Primary geography and ESD' for online CPD and supporting resources. Thinking education: **www.thinkingeducation.co.uk/p4c.htm**.

10 Progression and assessment in the humanities

We are all easily misled by the 'halo effect' of neatly presented written work or socially skilled children's conversation into thinking that a particular pupil's understanding is greater than it in fact is. Perhaps we also tend to focus too readily on what children cannot do rather than on what they can.

(Wiegand,1997: 267)

It is ironic that . . . at the dawn of the twenty-first (century), at the same time as we are becoming aware that a key feature of children's learning is that it is situated in activity and social practice, governments are requiring national curricula and universal measures of individual achievement.

(Carr, 2001: 19)

Learning objectives

By the end of the chapter you should be able to:

- define and explain the important role of assessment in humanities;
- distinguish between the different types of assessment and identify their key elements;
- describe the characteristics of pupils' progression in primary humanities; and
- value monitoring, reporting and recording children's learning in humanities.

Introduction

Assessment is not straightforward but it matters. Put simply, well-conceived and timely assessment can significantly improve learning (Black *et al.*, 2003; Hattie, 2009). On the other hand, assessment can create confusion, mistrust and sap pupils' confidence.

This chapter clarifies what is meant by assessment in its various forms, how teachers can support pupils' progression and the implications for teaching primary humanities. In a climate of accountability, educationalists and governments are eager to measure performance and the 'value-added' by schools (Black and Wiliam, 1998; Clarke 2005; Briggs *et al.*, 2008). Among the key messages emerging from the recent literature on assessment is the need for teachers to draw more on the views of pupils themselves, work closely with parents and to integrate assessment within their everyday teaching. Research suggests that teachers need to work smarter and not harder, for instance by thinking carefully about their questioning skills, how and when they give feedback, and the extent to which they empower pupils to assess their own performance and that of others. Despite considerable research and government investment, concerns remain over teachers' practical knowledge of assessment. Watkins *et al.* (2007: 141) call for 'reclaiming assessment to promote effective learning' because there is too much assessment of performance leading to distortion of roles and purposes.

The role and purposes of assessment

Assessment is the collective term applied to the methods used to find out what pupils know, understand and can do; it also measures the level pupils achieve or attain in specific standards, for instance mapping skills, chronology or knowledge of world religions. In general, assessment serves to:

- check teaching objectives against learning outcomes;
- discover what pupils know, understand and can do;
- inform pupils, parents and others about progress in learning;
- support pupils when devising personal targets;
- evaluate teacher effectiveness and performance;
- recognise and plan for pupils' learning needs;
- measure pupil attainment against different benchmarks, such as 'level descriptors'; and
- motivate teachers and pupils.

Assessment can take a formative role in shaping everyday learning and teaching. It can also serve summative purposes by indicating the level of pupil attainment. Some writers propose a third type of assessment – 'Assessment *as* Learning', which focuses on supporting pupils to reflect on *how* they learn (Jacques and Hyland, 2007; Briggs *et al.* 2008; Webster, 2010).

Evidence about the current state of assessment in primary humanities can be found in recent inspection reports and surveys by subject associations and bodies such as the National Foundation for Educational Research (NFER). In England, recent Ofsted reports suggest that the assessment picture in primary humanities is weak. In history, there is little rigorous assessment of pupils' performance and teachers are not always clear about the standards expected; as a consequence, pupils' progress is 'faltering'

(Ofsted, 2007: 5). Too many schools pay insufficient attention to constructive feedback in geography (Ofsted, 2008; Ofsted, 2011) while assessment in Religious Education is poor because teachers are unclear about what constitutes progression (Ofsted, 2010). In the light of these comments it is important to develop a good practical working knowledge of assessment in the humanities at the earliest opportunity.

Assessment for Learning (AfL)

AfL is an approach to assessment based on 10 underlying principles recommended by the Assessment Reform Group (2002), namely that assessment:

1. is part of effective planning;
2. focuses on how students learn;
3. is central to classroom practice;
4. is a key professional skill;
5. is sensitive and constructive;
6. fosters motivation;
7. promotes understanding of goals and criteria;
8. helps learners know how to improve;
9. develops the capacity for self assessment; and
10. recognises all educational achievement.

Central to AfL is the belief that all pupils can make progress. Teachers are expected to give feedback and receive feedback from pupils on a daily basis.

Pupils themselves are involved in the process of assessment and learning through reflecting on their own progress and responding to feedback. Each time a lesson is taught, teachers assess what the children have achieved relative to the objectives of the lesson; for example, whether pupils are able to sequence events in a chronological order. The teacher then acts on this by planning the next lesson to take account of how well the children achieved the objective. AfL has received government backing throughout the UK on the basis that it works well (DfES, 2007; Daugherty Review, 2004; DCELLS, 2010). Pupils' scores in national tests and examinations have improved along with their capacity to learn how to learn.

Starting with the pupils: elicitation

An elicitation activity might form the starting point to initiate a humanities topic (see Figure 10.1). When providing their responses pupils might note, using a traffic-lights system, their confidence in their knowledge and understanding about the topic. Teachers need to probe beyond such quick forms of assessment by encouraging pupils to explain their responses. These can then inform future planning.

During a history topic, children might be asked to identify where they consider they are misunderstanding the ideas, skills or content they are studying. Common

To initiate the study of a locality in Botswana, the teacher gave each of the six groups in his Year 4 class a large cut-out letter from the word B-O-T-S-W-A-N-A. He asked the groups to write or draw what they knew about Botswana. This was a 15-minute activity, which he followed up by asking the children to list questions that they wanted to use in their enquiry. After the lesson, the teacher reviewed the children's ideas about Botswana and examined the questions they had listed. From this first activity, he became aware of misconceptions, misunderstandings and misinformation that he felt needed to be addressed. He adjusted his plan to engage the children in identifying some core information about Botswana before returning to the questions, which he wanted the children to reconsider and revise, as well as group and then organize into priorities for their enquiry.

Figure 10.1 Assessing through elicitation in geography.

K (Know)	W (Want)	H (How)	L (Learn)
What do you know about World War 2?	What do you want to know about World War 2?	How have you learnt about World War 2?	What have you learnt about World War 2?
• It took place during the twentieth century. • Many people were killed. • Many cities were bombed. • Children had to move to the country.	• When was World War 2? • Why did children have to move to the country? • What did they eat during World War 2?	• Using reference books. • Using the BBC website. • Asking my relatives. • Visiting the museum.	• World War 2 happened between 1939 and 1945. • Children were moved to the country to be safe. They were called evacuees. • Food was rationed during World War 2.

Figure 10.2 Example of a completed KWHL grid.

problems can be highlighted and teaching adjusted, perhaps through some whole-class or group teaching or by providing time for children who understand to work together with those in need of support. Many teachers provide structure through the form of KW(H)L grids: where pupils identify what they *Know* about a topic, what they *Want* to find out, *How* they will do so and what they have *Learnt* (see Figure 10.2). It is good practice for teachers to model the process, for instance by linking questions in the 'W' column to the learning intention.

Table 10.1   Examples of WILF, WALT and TIB in humanities

	History	Geography	RE
WILF (What I'm Looking For ...)	to sequence photographs correctly on a timeline.	to write a letter to complain about the traffic outside school.	to use correct words to label features inside a church.
WALT (What Are We Looking To ...)	sequence the photographs on a timeline.	write a formal letter to complain about an issue.	know the correct names of features inside a church.
TIB (This Is Because ...)	this will help you describe how things have changed over time.	you can use this information in a role-play – meeting of a local council.	you will be able to use these names to describe the church.

Sharing learning objectives

Sharing clear and appropriate learning objectives or intended learning outcomes provides structure to lessons. In many schools, older pupils themselves record learning objectives in their books and use them as a basis for assessing their progress during the lesson. Some schools use strategies advocated by Clarke (2001) and others, such as WILF (What I'm looking for?), WALT (What are we learning today?) and TIB (This is because) to share learning intentions with pupils (see Table 10.1).

There are times when teachers decide not to share the learning objectives with the class and instead encourage suggestions as to what these could have been at the end of the session. Moreover, to develop pupils' understanding of the learning purposes they should have experiences in setting their own goals rather than always work towards teaching intentions.

It is common practice to note within lesson plans that children's prior knowledge and understanding will be reviewed at the outset. This diagnostic approach can provide useful information and questions such as 'Who can tell me what we did in our last geography lesson?' or 'Can anyone show us how to ...?', which creates a link between teacher assessment and subsequent pupil learning (Wragg and Brown, 2001).

Effective questioning

Questioning is an essential skill in teaching and learning. However, research indicates that teachers need to improve their questioning skills. They spend too much time asking low-level recall questions that do not challenge pupils (Skinner, 2010). It has been estimated that teachers of five years' experience have probably asked a quarter of a million questions while even student teachers, who spend ten weeks in school teaching half a timetable, may well ask up to 10,000 questions (Wragg and Brown, 2001). Teachers need to ask fewer and better questions. During a typical lesson a teacher will ask questions to: seek information, clarify pupils' understanding, encourage thinking, engage attention and to further their own insights into pupils' development. According to Black *et al.* (2002), a question is asked every 72 seconds while 38 per cent of questions are answered by the teachers themselves. Moreover, teachers do not give enough time for pupils to think about the questions: most teachers only wait around a seconds for an answer, whereas if this was extended to three seconds or more, the quality of learning would improve.

Effective questioning is characterised when teachers keep questions short, use pupils' responses, distribute questions around the class and model appropriate language. The overall quality of questions will be measured by their impact on learning; whether, for instance it gives teachers a better insight into where pupils are in their understanding and how this can be sustained. The point of wait time and other strategies is to motivate pupils, free them from the 'teacher-has-the-right-and-only-answer' syndrome and create a genuinely inquisitive environment (see Figure 10.3).

Questions have been classified in different ways. Most famously, Bloom (cited by Wragg and Brown, 2001) proposed a taxonomy of questions from simple memory recall through basic understanding to higher-level questions demanding analysis, evaluation or synthesis. Teachers need to support pupils in moving from descriptive

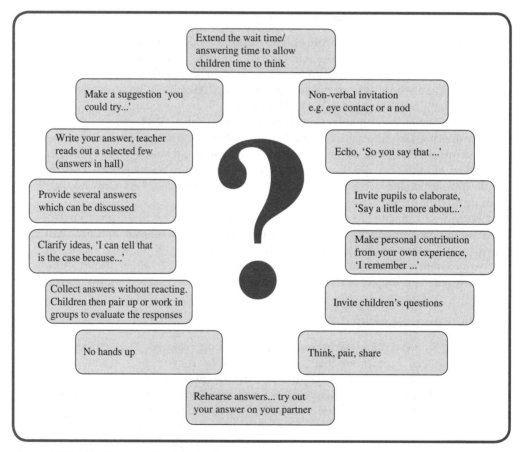

Figure 10.3 Effective questioning strategies. *Source:* CCEA (2008:72; see also Clarke, 2003).

questions (what? where? when? who?) to ask more challenging questions (why? how? so what?). They should model asking a range of questions. In geographical enquiries, Roberts (1996) suggests the use of closed, framed and negotiated questions. The closed form are concerned with the recall of particular information, the framed type involve activities that make pupils ask questions, while negotiated questions arise when pupils decide what they want to investigate under the guidance of the teacher.

Rephrasing questions can improve the quality of discussion; for instance, the question, 'Is there equal access to safe drinking water in the world?' can become open-ended: 'Why is there not equal access to safe drinking water in the world?' where the given situation is the basis for the question and not the question itself. Useful stems for open-ended questions include:

- *How can we be sure that . . .?* (people do not want wind farms in the valley)?
- *What is the same and what is different . . .?* (between our neighbourhood and the area of Lesotho that we investigated)?
- *How do you know . . .?* (what children would most like to change in the playground)?
- *How would you explain . . .?* (the amount of litter we found on the beach)?
- *What does that tell us about . . .?* (how and where we use energy in school)?
- *What is right/wrong with . . .?* (saying that fair trade is always a good thing)?
- *What reasons can you give for . . .?* (people parking where they should not)?
- *Why did you . . .?* (choose the questions about access to clean water for all)?
- *How might you . . .?* (find out what people would like to see replace the empty shop)?
- *Why do you think . . .?* (it will be better if the shanty town is rebuilt)?
- *Why have you proposed that . . .?* (the pedestrian area needs to be less cluttered for disabled people)?

(*Source*: Adapted from Catling, 2009: 159, and QCA
www.qcda.gov.uk/assessment/3871.aspx).

For pupils, asking questions is a means of exploring their physical and natural worlds. They come to understand historical events, the character of places and why people believe and act the way they do. As Johnston *et al.* (2007) point out, however, children's level of curiosity is directly related to their temperament, experience, environment and social constraints. Pupils are more likely to ask questions when they work within stimulating contexts and feel that their participation is valued.

TASK

- Undertake a small-scale piece of classroom research on questioning in the humanities. Select a series of geography/history or RE lessons to observe or ask an assistant to take notes on your own questioning – reflect on the findings and what they reveal about your questioning.

Providing feedback

The purpose of feedback is to help children identify their strengths and areas to develop by setting future targets. It is essential when giving feedback on pupils' work to make it relevant, meaningful and directly related to the learning intention and specific assessment criteria (Catling, 2009). For instance, when assessing pupils' ability to locate a point on a map using four-figure grid references, their skill in giving the correct references is the focus. If an intention is met, feedback should praise this; if not, it should show how the child can meet it. Pupils should be encouraged to work through problems and situations on their own or with peers and to become more self-reliant and responsible for their own learning and progression. Feedback can be written on the work while sitting alongside pupils. However, discussion with individual pupils is more effective and enduring than written feedback (Catling and Willy, 2009). Such dialogue encourages children to be more confident in asking questions to aid their own learning (Owen and Ryan, 2001).

Teacher assessment can be immediate through verbal praise and individual or collective feedback, or written after the lesson has finished. Either way, it is important always to remember what pupils are expected to know, understand and do and then reflect on whether these expectations have been met. Learners need to know which aspects of their work are successful, and what they need to improve. One approach is to use 'two or three stars and a wish'. The teacher or the pupils or peer identifies these subject-specific aspects of the work that are effective (the stars), and identifies one particular detail that needs to be improved (the wish). The pupil then acts on the 'wish' as soon as the comment is received. Younger or less experienced pupils might find it useful to use two rather than three stars. It is important that each 'star' is clearly written and linked to developed success criteria. Pupils should act on the 'wish' if the feedback is to become formative (see Figure 10.4).

Marking

Marking provides a record for the child to refer to and should be a reward and guide system, providing positive comments on the work and their attainment and stating specific targets and actions for improvements. When giving feedback about a piece of work in the humanities, it is important that this is subject or topic specific. However, it is appropriate to comment on the quality of language, graphics or other form of presentation where this is pertinent to effective communication of the geographical or historical information and understanding. Too often, marking within the humanities does not include sufficient focus on subject-specific details (Ofsted, 2011).

The marking of pupils' work during and after lessons needs to be thorough and constructive, and returned in good time. Feedback that enables pupils to make further progress by understanding more clearly what needs to be done can enhance motivations and self-confidence. For example, receiving a low mark for the imaginative quality of a piece of written work, for example a newspaper article on a local geographical issue, without any guidance on how the work could have been improved, will dishearten. Constructive and helpful guidance on how a better piece of work could have been produced, however, will help stimulate further progress.

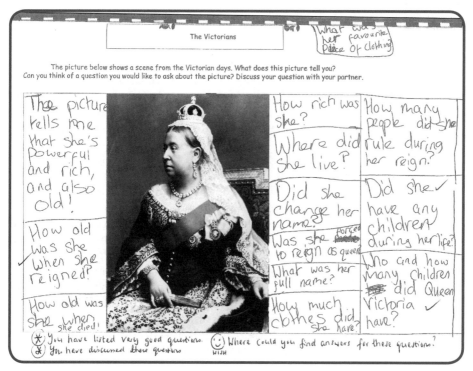

Figure 10.4 Example of 'two stars and a wish'.

Self assessment

Self assessment is a process that involves children reflecting upon what they have done and making some assessment of what they think they have achieved (Hoodless *et al.*, 2009; Webster, 2010). Self and peer assessment can be encouraged among young children through the use of simple visual and verbal instructions. For older children the use of written checklists or reminders on the wall serves to focus their attention on whether they have completed the tasks required. A 'yes/no' or 'tick/cross' entry would keep this manageable and provide children with the beginning of self-review prior to handing in work (Briggs *et al.*, 2008).

Pupils will improve most when they understand what they are trying to achieve. In some cases learning objectives may be tailored to individual children in the form of personalised targets. These may include:

- What did you find difficult about learning to . . .?
- What are you very pleased with about learning to . . .?
- Can anyone remember what we were trying to learn today?
- What new thing have you learnt today that you didn't know before?
- What do you think you need to do next to improve your learning about . . .?
- If you told someone else what this lesson was about, what would you say?

When self assessment involves pupils setting their own targets from feedback on their work – and once practised in it – this becomes a highly effective form of assessment (Kerry, 2002). Children carrying out self assessment become more reflective and realistic about their work, gaining the confidence to admit when they do not understand something and seeking help to address this. They begin to recognise possible gaps and weaknesses and consider effective forms of addressing these. Clarke (2005) and Pollard *et al.* (2009) both believe that children should be empowered to unlock their own knowledge and become reflective learners, hence the need to be aware of, and ideally understand, the assessment process. To be able to do this, pupils should be provided with a learning criterion so that they can use it to figure out how far along they are in meeting the skills and concepts identified.

However, self assessment for pupils needs to be kept simple and manageable. For the youngest children it may be conducted using a more informal style of self assessment, where they use a visual cue to help them to reflect on their learning within a lesson such as a thumbs up, middle or down sign or including a smiley or sad face in their work book to show how much of the objective they feel they understood (Webster, 2010). Such simple techniques need to be followed up with questioning so that children can show or explain their learning (Photo 10.1). For older children it can be appropriate to invite them to note what they feel they have learnt to say, what they feel they need to focus on and what they want to learn in a topic or from one lesson to the next. Through this approach children are encouraged to identify not only their strengths but also areas for development, which can be translated into targets. For self assessment to be effective the teacher has a key role to play ensuring that the children are continuously made aware of the learning objectives.

Photo 10.1 Example of self assessment in geography. *Source:* S. Hughes.

Peer assessment

Peer assessment involves pupils reviewing the work of each other. This is not simply swapping work and giving feedback, but is a process where the children need to be trained into understanding the criteria that the work is based on so that they have the ability to recognise features within it. Through undertaking peer assessment and learning how to give reflective but critical feedback, the children actively learn the skills needed to become competent learners within a subject (Weavers *et al.*, 2008).

However, as Briggs *et al.* (2008) suggest, children need to be comfortable with self assessment before being introduced to peer assessment so that they can understand that the process is more important than the outcome. Peer assessment encourages children to recognise the learning intention and the reason why they are learning through discussion, so clarifying their own understanding as well as assessing the work of their peers. It can be most supportive when children are not sure whose work it is that they are commenting on. However, if this is not possible it is wise to ensure that they mark different children's work each time, avoiding opportunities to be competitive (Scoffham, 2010). Ofsted (2008) reports that peer assessment has had a positive impact on children's geographical learning and understanding.

> In one school, pupils assessed each other's work against clear descriptions of levels and grades. This helped them to understand the quality of their own work better; good diagnostic marking also contributed to this. Pupils recorded their results on a progress chart and indicated with an arrow whether they had improved, remained the same or fallen. They also noted specific targets. All pupils were very clear about the process and how to achieve their geography-focused targets.
>
> *(Ofsted, 2008: 3)*

Summative and ipsative assessment

Summative assessment is also known as Assessment of Learning (AOL). This assessment gives teachers a snapshot of a child's achievement at a particular time. It is a particularly useful assessment for reporting to parents, governors and local authorities, for instance informing annual reports. The most obvious example is England's Statutory Assessment Tests (SATs) in the core subjects of English, mathematics and science. In the non-core subjects, schools must provide parents with brief details of their children's achievements in each subject or area of learning. As Chapter 11 notes, it is good practice for schools to assemble portfolios of pupils' work, individually and collectively, to illustrate attainment in history, geography and RE. Such evidence can then inform reporting to parents, teachers during the next phase of education, inspectors and other audiences.

The prime objective of assessment is to support learning. Black and Wiliam (1998) have argued that assessment that does not do this is not assessment but a form of testing. This has often proved controversial. Historically, testing has served as an educational and social filter, most famously as a means of recruiting to the medieval Chinese civil service. Critics maintain that high-stake testing has squeezed out the humanities, de-motivated pupils and teachers and not resulted in marked improvements in learning (Guest and Lee, 2008). Assessment should help motivate pupils and enhance well-being.

How children feel about their learning is a key factor in their success. Children's motivation and self-esteem are very vulnerable and responsive to the processes and outcomes of assessment. Both can be enhanced by assessment, but all too often they are damaged, often unintentionally. The effects of assessment practice on children's motivation and self-esteem need to be continually borne in mind. Whenever teachers are engaged with assessment, they should be reflecting upon purposes and principles, as well as the impact of their practice on children's motivation and self-esteem.

Ipsative (from the Latin *ipse*, 'of the self') assessment is widely supported by educationalists. For instance, Claxton *et al.* (2011) call for students to be given more opportunities to reflect on, talk about or write about themselves as learners. To raise students' self-awareness, they recommend the use of learning logs, digital records of personal best moments taken by students themselves, self-report questionnaires and personal testimonies. Similarly, Carr (2001) advocates a 'learning story' approach to assessment based on 4 Ds:

- Describing episodes of achievement;
- Discussing children's assessment and their learning with other staff, the children and with families;
- Documenting learning and assessment; and
- Deciding what to do next.

Rather than adults adopting the assessor role for most of the time, Carr(2001) supports activities that provide their own assessment, such as jigsaws, constructing buildings, writing a name and being included in play. These writers adopt a credit rather than a deficit model of assessment. Their emphasis is thinking about assessment along divergent rather than convergent lines.

Recording and reporting humanities learning

Records of learning provide information to be passed to the next teacher and across key stages, for example at transfer from primary to secondary school. They also inform reports to parents. Reports should focus on positive outcomes of children's historical, geographical and religious learning and should indicate areas for development. The latter might be identified by learning targets that have been agreed by the child and the teacher. An additional record might be the child's self-evaluation of learning, completed at the end of each unit or the year. From a young age, children should contribute to their own record-keeping, for example in choosing work that they are particularly proud of and which represents a milestone in their learning journey. Various record-sheet formats are in use within the humanities (Lomas *et al.* 1996). Recording should be minimal – just enough to have a feel for the progress of pupils and enough to write a useful report and to assess where the future emphasis might need to be placed.

Progression and assessment

In order to provide evidence for progression, children's starting points need to be clearly recorded. In the Early Years, this will draw upon baseline assessment records informed by observations and information shared by parents and other settings at times of transfer. Observations should contribute to a picture of children's development in each area of learning. For children to progress in their learning, they need to build upon their existing knowledge, skills and understanding in a systematic manner (Hayes, 2010). However, any assessment should recognise the unpredictability of children's development; a 'staircase' model does not reflect the uneven nature of learning. For this reason, Carr (2001) advocates narrative approaches in the Early Years, drawing upon exemplars rather than performance indicators. Claxton *et al.* (2011) refer to the importance of building learning power by fostering three dimensions of progress:

Strength – more and better use of learning skills and tools.

Breadth – applying knowledge and skills in different contexts.

Depth – more subtle, sophisticated learning.

Hence pupils need to exercise their 'learning muscles' more often, in more contexts and more skilfully so that questioning, considering alternatives, and comparing should become 'second nature'. A unit from the Northern Ireland Curriculum, 'The World Around Us', serves to illustrate progression in the context of the humanities (see Table 10.2).

Table 10.2 Progression within 'The World Around Us'	
FROM **By the end of Key Stage 1**	**TO** **By the end of Key Stage 2**
Make first-hand observations and collect primary data.	Examine and collect real data and samples from the 'World Around'.
Identify similarities and differences.	Investigate similarities and differences, patterns and changes.
Use everyday language to communicate ideas.	Use increasingly precise subject-specific vocabulary, notation and symbols.
Handle, recognise and describe objects and places from first-hand experience or from secondary, traditional and electronic ICT sources.	Locate, analyse and use secondary sources such as maps, photographs, written accounts and digital images; research topics using traditional and electronic sources.
Develop a sense of place using maps to locate places learned about by sequencing events and objects on a time line in chronological order.	Locate all places studied in atlases and maps; use resources such as atlases, maps and electronic sources to identify and describe places and environments investigated; develop a sense of change over time and how that past has affected the present.
Use traditional and electronic resources to record and present information.	Record, analyse and present using a range of appropriate means, including ICT.

Source: Adapted from CCEA (2007:55). Northern Ireland Curriculum, Primary.

The evidence of progression in assessment should be developed informally in different contexts because written work alone may give a distorted impression. Teachers should draw upon a range of work to demonstrate progression, for instance tape-recordings of speaking and listening skills, artwork and performances.

Progression in history

Successive Ofsted reports have noted that in many primary schools planning for progression in the humanities is not as effective as it should be (Ofsted, 2000; Ofsted, 2004; Ofsted, 2007). In history, for instance, the focus for much of the planning and the teaching is on pockets of knowledge at basic levels. Thus, the notion that pupils can progress and do better over time in history is not well established (Ofsted, 2007). The result is that pupils have insufficient opportunities to develop their historical skills, or to gain a more secure understanding of the past.

Progression in history is characterised by pupils asking and answering more complex questions, making links between different historical periods, people and events, handling abstract concepts, engaging with a range of interpretations and deploying analytical skills. Progression in history is not as simply hierarchical as the National Curriculum may suggest. However, a synopsis of the broad progression within the National Curriculum in England is shown in Table 10.3. Some of the best evidence for progress is when pupils are 'doing history' – genuine investigations and enquiry rather than measuring assessment pieces lacking a context.

Progression in geography

The Geographical Association are among those that provide guidance to assist teachers in planning for progression in areas such as map work, fieldwork and geographical vocabulary. Martin (2006) suggests the kind of language that children might use to demonstrate increasing understanding of geographical concepts. Hence, in a project on rivers, pupils might:

Name and identify – stream, water, sand, stones, sea, rocks.

Describe – trickling, splashing, crashing, rushing, rippling.

Locate – up there in the hills, down here by the sea.

Question – What is it doing? Why does it do that? Where is it going?

Explain – The stream is full at the moment because it is raining.

Hypothesise – What if we do this, let's try …

Predict – The water will move pebbles, if we make the slope [of the river] steeper then . . .

Evaluate, judge – beautiful, exciting, interesting.

From describing the main features of where they live, children begin to compare and contrast places, identify patterns and how places are changing, recognise the impact of processes, gain growing awareness of responsibilities to care for places and appreciate the diversity of environments. Table 10.4 illustrates progression in geography.

Table 10.3 Progression in history

Understanding	Nursery—Reception	Key Stage 1	Key Stage 2
Area of Study	• Family • Locality • Artefacts • Events • Perspectives	• Lives and lifestyles of people in the recent past. • Famous people and events from the more distant past. • Use variety of sources.	• Four specified dimensions: *local, national, Europe, global.* • Coherence within a period: *impact of personalities and events of everyday lives of men, women, children.*
Concepts (e.g. chronology, time; cause/effect; motive; similarity/difference):	• Sequence objects; talk and answer questions about changes over time.	• Sequence events and objects; use time vocabulary to identify differences, give reasons for cause, effects, motives.	• Sequence using appropriate periods. • Use vocabulary of time measurements to identify characteristics of periods. • Using specific characteristics, explain changes.
Historical interpretations		• Identify different ways in which the past is represented.	• Identify different ways in which the past has been represented and subsequently interpreted.
Historical enquiry	• Ask questions to gain information about why things happen and how things work (e.g. family, locality, objects).	• Ask and answer questions about a greater range of sources (e.g. pictures, photographs, eye-witness accounts, ICT).	• Select and record sources relevant to a focused enquiry (e.g. additional sources: documents, printed sources, music, sites, records).
Skills in organising and communicating information	Recall in talking.	Increased means of recall (e.g. writing, drawing, ICT).	• Select information; use historical vocabulary.

Source: Adapted from Lomas (2011).

Table 10.4 Assessing progress in geography

Assessing progress in geography		Names of pupils:			Year:	
Level	Enquiry and skills	Places	Space: Patterns and processes	Environmental impact and sustainability	Comment
1	Pupils use resources that are given to them, and their own observations, to ask and respond to questions about places and environments.	… show their knowledge, skills and understanding in studies at a local scale.	… recognise and make observations about physical and human features of localities.	… express their views on features of the environment of a locality.	
2	Pupils carry out simple tasks and select information using resources as above. They use this information and their own observation to help them ask and respond to questions about places and environments. They begin to use appropriate geographical vocabulary.	… show their knowledge, skills and understanding in studies at a local scale. They show an awareness of places beyond their own locality.	… describe physical and human features of places, and recognise and make observations about those features that give places their character.	… express views on the environment of a locality and recognise how people affect the environment.	
3	Pupils use skills and sources of evidence to respond to a range of geographical questions, and develop the use of appropriate vocabulary to communicate their findings.	… show their knowledge, skills and understanding in studies at a local scale. They are aware that different places may have both similar and different characteristics. They offer reasons for some of their observations and for their views and judgements about places.	… describe and compare the physical and human features of different localities and offer explanations for the locations of some of those features.	… offer reasons for some of their observations and for their views and judgements about environments. They recognise how people seek to improve and sustain environments.	

Table 10.4 Assessing progress in geography (*Continued*)

Assessing progress in geography	Names of pupils:		Year:	
Level	Enquiry and skills	Places	Space: Patterns and processes	Environmental impact and sustainability	Comment
4	Drawing on their knowledge and understanding, pupils suggest suitable geographical questions, and use a range of geographical skills from KS 2 PoS to help them investigate places and environments. They use primary and secondary sources of evidence in their investigations and communicate their findings using appropriate vocabulary.	... show their knowledge, skills and understanding in studies of a range of places and environments at more than one scale and in different parts of the world.	... begin to recognise and describe geographical patterns and to appreciate the importance of wider geographical location in understanding places. They recognise and describe physical and human processes. They begin to understand how these can change the features of places, and how these changes affect the lives and activities of people living there.	... understand how people can both improve and damage the environment. They explain their own views and the views that other people hold about an environmental change.	
5	Drawing on their knowledge and understanding, they select and use appropriate skills and ways of presenting information from the KS2 PoS to help them investigate places and environments. They select information and sources of evidence, suggest plausible conclusions to their investigations and present their findings both graphically and in writing.	... show their knowledge, skills and understanding in studies of a range of places and environments at more than one scale and in different parts of the world. They recognise some of the links and relationships that make places dependent on each other.	... describe and begin to explain geographical patterns and physical and human processes. They describe how these processes can lead to similarities and differences in the environments of different places and in the lives of people who live there.	... suggest explanations for the ways in which human activities cause changes to the environment and the different views people hold about them. They recognise how people try to manage environments sustainably. They explain their own views and begin to suggest further relevant geographical questions and issues.	

Source: Catling and Willy (2009: 197).

Progression in RE

Pupils' acquisition of religious knowledge, understanding, skills and values is a developmental and incremental process. Official guidance suggests that pupils' progress in RE can be monitored using 'levels' of achievement. In the QCA National Framework, for example, Level 1 describes the earliest level of pupils' understanding as they begin RE in school:

Level 1

Children use some religious words and phrases to recognise and name features of religious life and practice. They can retell religious stories and recognise symbols, and other verbal and visual forms of religious expression.

(QCA, 2004: 36)

By the time they reach the age of 11, most pupils are expected to progress to the following:

Level 4

Children use a developing vocabulary to describe and show understanding of sources, practices, beliefs, ideas, feelings and experiences. They make links between them, and describe the impact of religion on people's lives. They suggest meanings for a range of forms of religious expression.

(QCA, 2004: 36)

Therefore, it is important that suitable challenges are planned following assessment activities for pupils to deepen, widen and extend their understanding. Too often in RE lessons, pupils are given the same kind of activities over and over again, resulting in a very narrow or superficial RE curriculum, which restricts pupils' development (McCreery *et al.*, 2008).

It is much more difficult to assess pupils' skills, knowledge and understanding of matters relating to learning 'from' religion rather than learning 'about' religion. While assessing 'learning about religion' requires the teacher to consider what the pupils know about religion, 'learning from religion' requires the teacher to look at how pupils reflect, interpret, respond imaginatively and discuss a variety of religious concepts (Webster, 2010). Assessing these skills requires a more sensitive approach, because measuring emotions and opinions is subjective. A strong religious faith may be interpreted by a non-specialist as an extreme religious view and therefore inappropriately judged. According to McCreery *et al.* (2008), religious commitment and beliefs should not be assessed. Rather the focus should be on pupils' acquisition of knowledge and skills, the development of conceptual understanding and how well pupils relates to others.

Fowler (1995) suggests the following model of faith development:

Stage 0 – 'Primal or Undifferentiated' faith (birth to two years), is characterised by an early learning of the safety of their environment (i.e. warm, safe and secure vs. hurt, neglect and abuse).

Stage 1 – 'Intuitive-Projective' faith (ages three to seven), is characterised when children follow the beliefs of parents/carers. Children tend to imagine or fantasise about angels or other religious figures in stories as characters in fairy tales

Stage 2 – 'Mythic-Literal' faith is when children tend to respond to religious stories and rituals literally, rather than symbolically

Stage 3 – 'Synthetic-Conventional' faith (arising in adolescence; aged 12 to adulthood) is characterised by conformity to religious authority and the development of a personal identity. Individuals tend to have conformist acceptance of a belief with little self-reflection on examination of these beliefs. Most people remain at this level.

Stage 4 – 'Individual-Reflective' begins a radical shift from dependence on others' spiritual beliefs to development of their own.

Stages 5 and 6 – these relate to individuals that become more tolerant of others' points of view, consider serving others and begin to search for universal values such as justice and unconditional love.

Fowler's stage theory has been criticised for its over-reliance on Piaget, suspect methodology and distortion of faith (Heywood, 2004). However, it has a powerful message in conveying the notion of human development as based on experience rather than age.

Using the level descriptors

Day-to-day formative assessment should contribute towards end-of-phase summative views. For geography and history, the National Curriculum for England and Wales provides level descriptions as a basis for making judgements about pupil performance at the end of key stages. Level descriptions describe the subject knowledge, skills and understanding that children working at that level should be demonstrating. The nature of humanities learning is such that pupils will not develop a skill in isolation. For instance, pupils carrying out an enquiry into changes in their local area will be using a range of geographical skills and studying different physical or human processes. Similarly, pupils who are learning about an overseas locality may be developing their map work, and photograph interpretation skills as well as enhancing their ability to use the Internet and ICT packages as sources of information (DCELLS: 2008).

In England, the majority of children are expected to work between Levels 1 and 3, achieving a Level 2 at the end of Key Stage 1. At Key Stage 2 the majority of the children are expected to work between Levels 2 and 5 and attain a Level 4 at the end of the key stage. In using level descriptions at the end of key stages, it is necessary for teachers to judge the description that 'best fits' the children's performance. When deciding on a particular level description, careful consideration needs to be given to the adjacent levels so that the 'best fit' is achieved. It is also important that judgements about level descriptions are based upon a representative sample of each child's work.

As RE is not part of the National Curriculum, there are no statutory level descriptions, but locally agreed syllabi often include guidance on expectations for end of key stage attainment. Over a period of time a portfolio of evidence can be collated to provide an accurate overview of what each child knows and understands. Such evidence can include pictures, reports, observational jottings, video recordings and extracts from workbooks. Evidence of learning in RE can be shown through:

- art work (laminate windows – creating a stained glass window);
- concept mapping;
- labelling;
- dance (a themed dance – a taste of traditional India (e.g. Jathiswaram);
- demonstrations of religious practice;
- diagrams, tables and religious maps;
- drama (persona dolls – five Ks of Sikhism);
- the Godly play (Christianity – **www.godplay.org.uk**);
- drawings, pictures, photographs;
- games;
- lyrics to a song (writing or reflecting);
- musical composition;
- modelling – bring items from home;
- observing a child/group to see what they are discussing and doing;
- one-to-one discussion about an issue;
- presentations;
- questioning specific children;
- quizzes and tests;
- recounting;
- poetry; and
- stories.

Pupils' work in classroom displays is also a good way of celebrating their achievements.

BOX 10.1 RESEARCH BRIEFING – TRACKING PROGRESS

The importance of tracking pupils' progress in subject-specific skills, knowledge and concepts has been widely researched (Black and Wiliam, 1998; Weeden, 2005: Clarke, 2005). Tracking enables coordinators to gain a clearer picture of how the subject is performing in the school in readiness for a school inspection or to inform colleagues. For example, in geography, Storey's research (2002) focused on gathering children's assessment of place information from postcards and email communication. All the children approached their geographical tasks with increased skill and confidence in the classroom and through fieldwork. Pupils used correct geographical terms and discussed geographical issues, often in tasks for other subjects (See: Occasional Paper No.2 – 'Best Practice in Raising Achievement', Register of Research in *Primary Geography*, (2002: 85–94) **www. geography.org.uk**, which can also be read online via the British Education Index).

Assessment in the Early Years

Over recent years, establishing agreement over appropriate assessment practices in the Early Years has proved something of a holy grail. In England, for instance, Early Years' practitioners have seen numerous changes in government guidance (DCSF, 2008; Tickell Review, 2011). The Assessment and Reporting Arrangements (ARA) contain guidance on the Early Years Foundation Stage (EYFS) Profile (DfE, 2011). This is a way of summarising each child's development and learning, for most children at the end of the Reception Year in school. The Early Years Foundation Stage Profile handbook provides additional information and guidance. The Profile is based on practitioners' ongoing observations and assessments in all six areas of learning, which are set out in the revised statutory framework for the Early Years Foundation Stage.

Central to good practice in the Early Years is involving children in active or dynamic learning. This does not necessarily mean moving around. Ferre Laevers clarifies 'involvement' as follows:

> Involvement means that there is intense mental activity, that a person is func-tioning at the very limits of his or her capabilities, with an energy flow that comes from intrinsic sources. One couldn't think of any condition more favour-able to real development. If we want deep level learning, we cannot do without involvement.

> *(HMIE, 2006: 5)*

Observation

The importance of observation as an assessment strategy, particularly for young children, is widely endorsed across the UK (Hobart and Frankel, 2004; Curtis and Carter, 2000; Barber and Paul-Smith, 2010; Palaiologou, 2012). Put simply, observation is the practice of looking at and listening to children to check how they are developing, what they like doing and what they are learning through their play and the experiences on offer.

Many local authorities provide informative online guidance for teachers on observational strategies. These include:

- informal arrangements when practitioners record on post-it notes anything of *significance*, such as explaining something in a new way or doing something for the first time;
- regular timed observations with a specific focus, such as transitions;
- making field notes on group interactions; and
- tracking a particular child over a sustained period and observations of how well or often areas of the classroom or outdoor area are being used.

The central government also provides guidance on observations, informing assessment across areas of learning (DCSF, 2008; CCEA, 2008; DCELLS, 2008). The Westminster government (DCSF, 2008) advocates a 'Look, Listen and Note' approach (see Figure 10.5).

Place

	Development matters	Look, listen and note	Effective practice	Planning and resourcing
Birth–11 months	■ Explore the space around them through movements of hands and feet and by rolling.	■ The movements that young babies make as they find out about their environment.	■ Encourage young babies' movements through your interactions, for example, touching their fingers and toes and showing delight at their kicking and waving.	■ Provide spaces that give young babies different views of their surroundings, such as a soft play area, with different levels to explore.
8–20 months	■ Love to be outdoors and closely observe what animals, people and vehicles do.	■ How babies explore space, objects and features of the environment.	■ Draw attention to things in different areas that stimulate interest, such as a patterned surface.	■ Display and talk about photographs of babies' favourite places.
16–26 months	■ Are curious about the environment.	■ Responses to sights, sounds and smells in the environment and what they like about playing outdoors.	■ Encourage young children to explore puddles, trees and surfaces such as grass, concrete or pebbles.	■ Develop use of the outdoors so that young children can investigate features, for example, a mound, a path or a wall.
22–36 months	■ Enjoy playing with small-world models such as a farm, a garage, or a train track.	■ The things children say about their environment.	■ Tell stories about places and journeys, for example, *Whatever Next!* by Jill Murphy.	■ Provide story and information books about places, such as a zoo or the beach, to build on visits to real places.
30–50 months	■ Show an interest in the world in which they live. ■ Comment and ask questions about where they live and the natural world.	■ Children's interest in things they see while out for a walk. ■ The questions children ask about features of the built environment, such as road signs.	■ Arouse awareness of features of the environment in the setting and immediate local area, for example, make visits to shops or a park. ■ Introduce vocabulary to enable children to talk about their observations and to ask questions.	■ Plan time for visits to the local area. ■ Provide play maps and small-world equipment for children to create their own environments.

Figure 10.5 The 'Look, listen and note' approach. *Source:* DCSF, (2008: 87).

Observers can look out for how children show their understanding of time, for example by using phrases such as 'It's nearly home time', and how well they recall significant events in their lives. When assessing toddlers' understanding of place, observers should note their readiness to point out things and their response to local walks and places that interest them.

Key considerations include deciding what *needs* to be observed and what should be recorded, avoiding the danger of amassing mountains of post-it notes. Effective observers must have good concentration, must not be easily confused or sidetracked, are conscious of their own biases and take the matter seriously. McLeod (2008) cites research that shows significant discrepancies when two observers watched the behaviour of children, particularly when value judgements are involved. To assist teachers' observational skills, Laevers has devised a five-point scale that measures both children's well-being and involvement (see Table 10.5).

Unless children are operating at the higher levels, learning will be limited. However, even a low level of well-being or involvement can become a learning opportunity that can result in higher levels.

Table 10.5 Laevers' scale to measure children's involvement

Level	Involvement	Signals
1	Extremely low	Activity is simple, repetitive and passive. The child seems absent and displays no energy. They may stare into space or look around to see what others are doing.
2	Low	Frequently interrupted activity. The child will be engaged in the activity for some of the time they are observed, but there will be moments of non-activity when they will stare into space, or be distracted by what is going on around.
3	Moderate	Mainly continuous activity. The child is busy with the activity but at a fairly routine level and there are few signs of real involvement. They make some progress with what they are doing but don't show much energy and concentration and can be easily distracted.
4	High	Continuous activity with intense moments. The child's activity has intense moments and at all times they seem involved. They are not easily distracted.
5	Extremely high	The child shows continuous and intense activity revealing the greatest involvement. They are concentrated, creative, energetic and persistent throughout nearly all the observed period.

Source: Laevers and Heylen (2004).

To build up a picture of how well each is doing, observations should be supplemented with other sources and approaches, such as video and audio recordings, children's drawings and paintings and information from parents. There needs to be a regular two-way dialogue between family and setting; for instance, in order to understand potential cultural differences and plan together children's next steps. Moreover, parents/carers should be involved in reviewing their children's achievements, including those demonstrated at home. Effective home-school partnerships have an important bearing on children's development. Hattie (2009) singles out the aspirations, encouragement and expectations parents transmit to their children as the strongest 'home' factors bearing on achievement in school, rather than family structure, home surroundings or interest in homework.

SUMMARY

- Assessment informs teachers about the effectiveness of their own teaching as well as the progress of children.

- There are two main types of assessment: formative assessment and summative assessment.

- Within the humanities a variety of assessment strategies should be used, including marking of written work, observations of children and pupil self assessment.

- Planning for progression in the development of pupils' knowledge and skills is essential. Generally, pupils progress in the humanities when they show greater independence and depth of learning. They develop a more sophisticated level of research skills in gathering, interpreting and presenting information.

- Record-keeping systems need to be manageable and efficient but contain sufficient subject attainment information for purposes such as reporting.

References

Assessment Reform Group (2002), *Assessment for Learning: 10 Principles*, London: Assessment Reform Group.

Barber, J. and Paul-Smith, S. (2010), *Early Years Observation and Planning in practice*, Salisbury: Practical Pre-School Books.

Black, P. and Wiliam, D. (1998), *Inside the Black Box*, London: Kings College London.

Black, P., Harrison, C., Lee, C., Marshall, B. and Wiliam, D. (2002), *Working inside the Black Box*, Department of Education and Professional Studies, London: King's College.

Black, P., Harrison, C., Lee, C., Marshall, B. & Wiliam, D. (2003), *Assessment for learning: putting it into practice*. Buckingham, UK: Open University Press.

Briggs, M., Woodfield, A., Martin, C. and Swatton, P. (2008), *Assessment for Learning and Teaching*, Exeter: Learning Matters.

Carr, M. (2001), *Assessment in Early Childhood Settings: Learning Stories*, London: Sage.

Catling, S. and Willy, T. (2009), *Achieving QTS, Teaching Primary Geography*, Exeter: Learning Matters.

CCEA (2007), *Northern Ireland Curriculum Primary*, Belfast: CCEA, available at: **www.nicurriculum.org. uk/docs/key_stages_1_and_2/northern_ireland_ curriculum_primary.pdf**.

CCEA (2008), *Learning Through Play at Key Stage 1*, Belfast: CCEA.

Claxton, G., Chambers, M., Powell, G., and Lucas, B. (2011), *The Learning Powered School*, Bristol: TLO Ltd.

Clarke, S. (2001), *Unlocking Formative Assessment*, London: Hodder & Stoughton.

Clarke, S. (2003), *Enriching Feedback. Oral and written feedback from teachers and children,* London: Hodder & Stoughton.

Clarke, S. (2005), *Formative Assessment in the Secondary Classroom*, London: Hodder & Stoughton.

Curtis, D. and Carter, M. (2000), *The Art of Awareness*, St Paul: Redleaf.

Daugherty, R. *et al.* (2004), *Learning Pathways through Statutory Assessment; Key Stages 2 and 3. Final Report of the Daugherty Assessment Review Group*, Cardiff: WAG.

DCELLS (2008), *Making the most of learning: Implementing the revised curriculum*, Cardiff: Welsh Assembly Government.

DCELLS (2010), *How to develop thinking and assessment for learning in the classroom*, Cardiff: Welsh Assembly Government.

DCSF (2008), *Practice Guidance for the Early Years Foundation Stage*, London: DCSF.

DfE (2011), *Assessment and reporting arrangements Early Years Foundation Stage*, London: DfES.

DfES (2007), *The Report of the Teaching and Learning in 2020 Review*, London: DfES.

Fowler, J.W. (1995), *Stages of Faith: The Psychology of Human Development and the Quest for Meaning*, New York: HarperOne.

Guest, G. and Lee, J. (2008), 'Current assessment practice. Driving or supporting practice?', in Harnett, P. (ed.), *Understanding Primary Education*, London: Routledge, 71–105.

Hattie, J. (2009), *Visible Learning*, London: Routledge.

Hayes, D. (2010), *Encyclopedia of Primary Education*, London: David Fulton Publishers.

Heywood, D. (2004), *Divine Revelation and Human Learning*. Aldershot: Ashgate.

HMIE (2006), *HMIE Early Years Good Practice,* Edinburgh: Scottish Government, available at: www. educationscotland.gov.uk/inspectionandreview

Hobart, C. and Frankel, J. (2004), *A Practical Guide to Child Observation and Assessment*, Cheltenham: Stanley Thornes.

Hoodless, P., McCreey, E., Bowen, P., Bermingham, S. (2009), *Teaching Humanities in Primary Schools*, Exeter: Learning Matters.

Kerry, T. (2002), *Learning Objectives, Task Setting and Differentiation*, Cheltenham: Nelson Thornes.

Jacques, K. and Hyland, R. (eds) (2007), *Professional Studies: Primary and Early Years*, Exeter: Learning Matters.

Johnston, J. Haolcha, J., and Chater, M. (2007), *Developing Teaching Skills in the Primary School*, Maidenhead: Open University Press.

Laevers, F. and Heylen, L. (2004), *Involvement of Teacher and Children Style: Insights from an International Study on Experiential Education*, Leuven: Leuven University Press.

Lomas, T., Burke, C., Cordingly, D. and McKenzie, K. (1996), *Planning Primary History*, London: Murray.

Lomas, T. (2011), 'Monitoring, Recording, Assessment and Reporting', in *Primary History* 57, 36.

Martin, F. (2006), *'Everyday Geography' in Primary Geographer*, Autumn 2006, 4–7.

McCreery, E., Palmer, S., and Voiels, V. (2008), *Teaching Religious Education*. Exeter: Learning Matters.

McLeod, A. (2008), *Listening to Children*, London: Jessica Kingsley.

Ofsted (2000), *Primary Subject Report: Religious Education 1999–2000*, London: Ofsted.

Ofsted (2004), *Ofsted Subject Reports 2002/03: Geography*, London: Ofsted.

Ofsted (2007), *History in the Balance. History in English Schools 2003–2007*, London: Ofsted.

Ofsted (2008), *Geography in Schools: Changing Practice*, London: Ofsted.

Ofsted (2010), *Transforming Religious Education*, London: Ofsted.

Ofsted (2011), *Geography: Learning to Make a World of Difference*, London: Ofsted.

Owen, D. and Ryan, A. (2001), *Teaching Geography 3–11*, London: Continuum.

Palaiologou, I. (2012), *Child Observation for the Early Years*, Exeter: Learning Matters.

Pollard, A., Anderson, J. and Maddock, M. (2009), *Reflective Teaching: Evidence-informed Professional Practice*, London: Continuum International Publishing Group.

QCA (2004), *Religious education, the non-statutory National Framework*, London: QCA.

Roberts, M. (1996), 'Teaching styles and strategies', in Kent, A., Lambert, D., Naish, M., and Slater, F. (eds), *Geography in Education: Viewpoints on Teaching and Learning*, Cambridge: Cambridge University Press.

Scoffham, S. (ed.) (2010), *Primary geography handbook*, Sheffield: Geographical Association.

Skinner, D. (2010), *Effective Teaching and Learning in Practice*, London: Continuum.

Tickell Review (2011), *The Early Years: Foundations for life, health and learning – an independent report on the Early Years Foundation Stage to her majesty government* (www.education.gov.uk).

Storey, S. (2002), 'Occasional Paper No.2 – Best Practice in Raising Achievement, Register of Research' in *Primary Geography*, (2002: 85–94), (www.geography.org.uk).

Watkins, C., Carnell, E and Lodge, C. (2007), *Effective Teaching in Classrooms*, London: Paul Chapman.

Weavers, G., Keogh, B. and Naylor, S. (2008), *Made You Look – Made You Think – Made you Talk*, Cheshire: Millgate House Publications.

Webster, M. (2010), *Creative Approaches to Teaching Primary RE*, Harlow: Pearson Education Ltd.

Weeden, P. (2005), 'Feedback in the Geography Classroom; *Developing the Use of Assessment for Learning*', in Teaching Geography, 30(3): 161–163.

Weeden, P. and Lambert, D. (2006), *Geography Inside the Black Box: Assessment for learning in the geography classroom*, London: NFER-Nelson.

Wiegand, P. (1997), 'Principles of pupil assessment', in Tilbury, D. and Williams, M. *Teaching and Learning Geography*, London: Routledge.

Wragg, C. and Brown, G. (2001), *Questioning in Primary School*, London: Routledge.

Useful Websites

Nuffield Primary History Project developed a range of approaches and techniques for 'doing' history with children: www.history.org.uk/resources/primary_resources_129.html.

The Department for Education includes a wide range of assessment materials: http://education.gov.uk/vocabularies/educationtermsandtags/731.

Education Scotland provides guidance for Scottish schools on assessment matters: www.educationscotland.gov.uk/learningteachingandassessment/.

Practical guidance on assessment for learning in Northern Ireland is available for each phase of schooling, for example for the Foundation Stage at: www.nicurriculum.org.uk/foundation_stage/assessment/assessment_for_learning.asp.

For Wales, guidance on thinking skills and assessment for learning is available at: wales.gov.uk/topics/educationandskills/schoolshome/curriculuminwales/thinkingandassessmentforlearning/.

Rubrics – Assessment as Learning: http://edtech.kennesaw.edu/intech/rubrics.htm.

Staffordshire Learning Net Geography website: http://www.sln.org.uk/geography/primary.htm.

11 Humanities and professional development

It may be said of teaching more than of other callings that the training is never complete; the equipment in art and scholarship gained at college merely provides a foundation for methods of investigation which should occupy the teacher all his life.

(Findlay, 1911: 181)

The quality of an education system cannot exceed the quality of its teachers.

(Barber and Mourshed, 2007: 19)

Learning objectives

By the end of this chapter you should be able to:

- define professional development and its various models;
- recognise the importance of reflective practice in the humanities;
- understand the importance of working with other professionals; and
- describe the role and responsibilities of a humanities subject leader.

Background

J.J. Findlay, Professor of Education at Manchester University, believed in the concept of lifelong learning for teachers. He justified their long holidays on the grounds that this was the time for them to attend summer schools, travel, join scientific societies and pursue hobbies, so that their own minds were broadened and refreshed from the 'nervous fatigue induced by active work in the classroom' (Findlay, 1911: 181). Teacher development has progressed significantly over the past hundred years. Modern teachers are less isolated, better qualified and more supported than previous generations. In the UK, all teachers have a responsibility to be engaged in effective, sustained and relevant professional development. It is essential to school improvement (Borko, 2004).

Professional development is defined as 'reflective activity designed to improve an individual's attributes, knowledge, understanding and skills' (TDA, 2008: 4). A focus on self-improvement is an acknowledgement that teachers matter – they are the most significant operational cost to schools and they are the most decisive factor influencing pupil progress. The ultimate aim of all professional development is to improve teaching and learning. In recent years, the drive for workforce reforms has brought in a 'new professionalism' with an emphasis on links between performance management, continuing professional development (CPD) and school improvement (Walker *et al.*, 2011).

In England, since 2012 one single set of professional standards apply to teachers through the different stages of their career. However, a recent survey reveals that only 44 per cent of primary teachers use professional standards as a basis to determine their professional development needs (NFER, 2011).

Chartered teacher status, introduced in Scotland in 2003 and revised in 2008, provides opportunities for outstanding teachers to receive additional salary for leading learning beyond their own classes. Several subject bodies offer teachers the opportunity to obtain chartered status. For instance, the Royal Geographical Society with the Institute of British Geographers (RGS-IBG) supports the Chartered Geographer (Teacher) scheme. Membership indicates:

- a commitment to promoting learning and to raising geography standards in schools and the wider community;
- an awareness of recent developments in the subject, its delivery in schools and the importance of good practice;
- personal commitment to self-evaluation and development;
- the maintenance of an ongoing programme of CPD; and
- ability to identify future CPD requirements and embed them to improve teaching and learning.

Those who become a Chartered Geographer (Teacher) are required to complete 35 hours of professional development each year. Moreover, most other professions, including law, medicine and social work, follow a licence to practise system that requires practitioners to complete particular training and/or a set number of hours of professional development. This is also the case for the teaching profession in many other countries. This can range from 12 hours per year in Latvia to 166 hours in the Netherlands (Wilson *et al.*, 2006). But a licence scheme, opposed by many teachers' unions, would prove costly and would need to have a clear impact on improving the quality of learning and teaching. Guskey (2000) argues that professional development evaluation should focus on measuring its impact in terms of changes in teachers' knowledge, skills, attitudes and beliefs *before* considering the impact on learners.

Unfortunately, CPD within the humanities subjects has suffered for a number of reasons, including a lack of priority, falling some way behind literacy and numeracy (Ofsted, 2005). In one survey, in a third of primary schools visited by Ofsted (2006), there had been little or no recent CPD within the subject being inspected. This was

BOX 11.1 RESEARCH BRIEFING – IMPACT OF CPD

American research shows that professional development can have a significant impact on teacher effectiveness—often as much as an extra six months of pupil progress per year (Saunders *et al.*, 2009). Similarly in the UK, there is strong evidence that what teachers learn through professional networks can make a difference to school improvement by widening teachers' access to a range of resources, ideas and support (Pedder and Opter, 2011). The TDA (2008) has produced useful guidance to assist schools in evaluating the impact of CPD on teaching and learning experiences, stressing the importance of agreed success criteria, timetables, regular review and cost-benefit analysis. However, a recent survey suggests that there is little indication that current CPD is 'having an impact on raising standards or narrowing the achievement gap' (Pedder *et al.*, 2008: 44). In Scotland, the impact of CPD on teachers' classroom practices and the subsequent effect on pupils has not been well researched (Wilson *et al.*, 2006).

partly attributed to a lack of specialist subject expertise, which meant that managers were failing to pick up important subject-related issues. In a more recent overview of primary history teaching, Ofsted (2011) reports that there was not enough subject-specific expertise or professional development to help teachers to be clearer about the standards expected in the subject and to improve their understanding of progression in historical thinking.

Models of CPD

There are a number of theories about teacher development that describe distinctive phases characterised by the level of experience, competence and dispositions (Fessler and Ingram, 2003). Each phase in the journey from beginner to expert practitioner brings its own professional development needs and represents a transition from a personal focus on survival, to task and impact. However, the specific needs have not been well defined by research (Wilson *et al.*, 2006). Broadly speaking, these should cover areas such as subject knowledge and understanding, teaching and assessment, and management (people, resources and the curriculum).

CPD is often defined by teachers conservatively and limited to workshops, seminars and 'in-service' training (INSET) designed to update subject knowledge and improve their understanding of pedagogy. This training model generally involves an 'expert' delivering a body of 'new' material. Typically a local authority adviser or consultant might provide content related to a set agenda, such as promoting thinking skills in the humanities or teaching world faiths. While there are opportunities for teachers to discuss ideas, the framework is often instructional. Moreover, as much as two-thirds of all professional development is 'passive learning'– sitting and listening to a presentation (House of Commons Select Committee, 2010).

No one model of CPD has been shown to be the most effective. However, research has generally supported partnerships between individual teachers, schools and universities based on negotiated needs (Wilson *et al.*, 2006). The characteristics of effective CPD include:

- a clear focus on pupil learning;
- teachers are involved in identifying their needs;
- use of coaching and mentoring;
- observation, feedback and collaborative working; and
- providing opportunities for research and reflective practice.

Good CPD requires school leaders to provide time for staff to discuss and reflect on their learning (Ofsted, 2010). A professional development culture is essential to the creation of learning organisations (Banks and Shelton Mayes, 2001). Teachers have access to various sources of professional development indicated in Figure 11.1.

Drawing upon a Scottish context, Kennedy (2005) describes alternative models of CPD (see Table 11.1). CPD activity needs to focus on long-term sustained gains and linking theory with practice. There are indications that the emphasis for CPD in the UK has shifted from a focus on teachers' individual needs to meeting systemic needs (Bolam, 2000; McMahon, 1999; Jones, 2011; O'Brien, 2011). In Scotland, Donaldson (2010) recommends more local team-based CPD rather than set-piece events, a blend of tailored individual development and school improvement, and evaluating more closely the intended impact on learning.

The 'award-bearing' and 'action research' models have widespread support within academic circles. Much of this was pioneered through the work of Lawrence Stenhouse

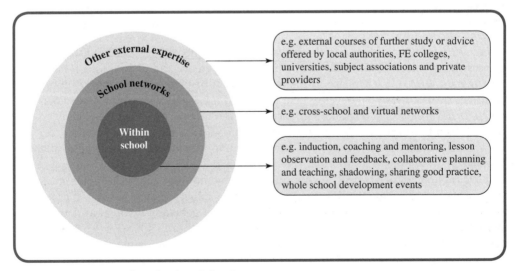

Figure 11.1 Sources of professional development.

Table 11.1 Models of CPD

Model	Characteristics
Training	Attendance at a course; teachers generally passive.
Award-bearing	Often university-provided modules or courses leading to some form of accreditation and award of diploma, certificate or Masters qualification.
Deficit	Addresses aspects of underperformance.
Cascade	Individual teachers attend a course and then disseminate findings to colleagues.
Standards-based	Teachers demonstrate through professional actions how they have met particular standards or competencies, as with the Chartered Teacher programme.
Coaching/Mentoring	Personalised learning, often on one-to-one basis within school context; coaching is sometimes seen as more skills based over a shorter period of time than the longer-term novice/expert relationship of mentoring; both are based on professional dialogue and support.
Community of practice	Involves more than two people collaborating as 'equals', for instance when teachers work with colleagues from other schools as networks of professional practice or within their own school as professional learning communities.
Action Research	Teachers working as researchers critically reflecting on their everyday teaching and learning experiences with a view to improving these.
Transformative	Combining ideas from other models to make a difference.

Source: Adapted from Kennedy (2005).

(Stenhouse, 1975). More recently, the Geographical Association (GA) publicised classroom research on its website – examples include researching the development of four-year-olds' geographical concepts through a year and exploring children's environmental attitudes and values. The Geographical Association has also supported the setting up of a Register of Research in Primary Geography. This provides a database of research activity within the subject and is aimed at undergraduate and postgraduate students, teacher trainers, academics, newly-qualified teachers and experienced coordinators (**www.geography.org.uk/eyprimary/ primaryresearch**).

With an increasing emphasis on cost-effectiveness, school leaders are under pressure to ensure that professional development provides value for money and stands up to scrutiny. For instance, there has been much talk in recent years about the importance of teachers responding to different learning styles (visual, auditory and kinaesthetic) and there is no doubt that creative approaches to teaching have injected greater enthusiasm and fun into the classroom. But the starting point has to be 'what works'? – Adey (2007: 361), for example, argues that there is no evidence in peer-reviewed academic journals for the efficacy of labelling children with a supposed learning style. Moreover, one leading scientist has dismissed as 'nonsense' the view that pupils prefer to receive information either by sight, sound or touch, and is thus critical of wasting valuable time and resources (cited by Henry, 2007). Yet there are a plethora of CPD courses pushing 'inspirational' and 'innovative' learning styles, despite the conceptual and practical difficulties (Franklin, 2006; Watkins *et al.*, 2007). Learning style theory has influenced government policies in recent years, including its 'personalised learning' agenda and the publication of official support materials in the humanities (for example, see DfES, 2002a and 2002b). The domino-effect is that once such a development becomes educational orthodoxy, publications and CPD courses follow without too much thought about challenging its rationale. Moreover, as Alexander (2010: 505) points out, there is a real danger that CPD becomes 'policy-informed', subject to passing fads rather than research based, and thereby fails to meet the needs of teachers, particularly more advanced practitioners.

Research also shows that when teachers work together over at least one term (but more usually two or three terms), this increases their confidence and commitment in making a difference to pupils' learning (**www.curee-paccts.com**). The most effective CPD occurs when senior managers are committed to using it as a key driver for school improvement. This would include a commitment to making necessary changes to timetables or school development plans. Otherwise there is a danger that the enthusiasm associated with attending a course becomes short-lived and the opportunity is missed to exploit its full potential.

Reflective practitioners

Underpinning the rationale behind most CPD models is the concept of teachers becoming reflective practitioners (Pollard *et al.*, 2008; Paige-Smith and Craft, 2011). This has become the dominant discourse in teacher education over recent years. A case in point is the stance taken by the General Teaching Council for Northern Ireland (GTCNI), which has consistently rejected attempts to adopt a reductionist approach to professional development. Instead, through its *Teaching: the Reflective Profession* (GTCNI, 2007) it acknowledges the organic nature of professional knowledge and advocates seeing competences holistically, trusting the professional judgements of teachers and setting education within a framework of values. Being reflective requires a self-critical attitude, a commitment to high standards and persistence in striving to achieve goals.

The concept of reflective practice is generally attributed to the work of the American John Dewey (1859–1952), who explored the actions involved in learning new skills.

He contrasted 'routine action', characterised by tradition, habit and following authority, with a much more dynamic, fluid and socially aware 'reflective action'. His ideas
were developed by Donald Schön (1930–1997), who argued that professionals learn
most effectively when they are encouraged to think carefully about what they do, when
they are doing it. His complementary concepts of 'reflection-in-action' (while teaching) and 'reflection-on-action' (after teaching) are now central to teaching (Schön,
1983). Pollard and his colleagues (2008) have since popularised reflective and reflex-
ive (experience-based) practice in *Reflective Teaching*, their 600-page core handbook
for school-based professional development.

Table 11.2 illustrates the four related characteristics of reflective teaching. The
reflective model sits comfortably with those that work within the humanities field
(Kent, 2000; Rudge (2007); Jackson, 2004). By nature, historians, geographers and
students of religion are reflective individuals. They are continually reviewing evidence,
comparing viewpoints and seeking to improve our understanding of human behaviour: people's motives, hopes, anxieties, beliefs and actions. The humanities offer a
model for teachers that wish to become reflective practitioners.

Action research

One of the outcomes of reflective practice is the construction of new knowledge and
perspectives on teaching. The everyday routine of teachers involves a cycle of planning,
acting, observing and evaluating. When this is framed within an action (teacher-led)

Table 11.2 Characteristics of reflective practice and the humanities

Characteristics	Examples
Active concern with aims and consequences, as well as with means and technical efficiency.	Challenging taken-for-granted ideas; speaking out about policies, procedures and established beliefs.
Cyclical process, in which teachers monitor, evaluate and revise their own practice continuously.	Planning; providing; doing; analysing evidence; making judgements; taking decisions.
Competence in methods of evidence-based classroom enquiry.	Reviewing existing research; gathering new evidence by collecting data; observing; analysing findings; evaluating impact.
Attitudes of open-mindedness, responsibility and wholeheartedness.	Listening to 'both sides'; challenging prejudices; asking open-ended, 'difficult' questions; taking moral stances; showing commitment and perseverance.

Source: Adapted from Pollard *et al.*, (2008).

research model, such activities become more systematic than normal, focusing on a particular issue over an extended period of time. There is no shortage of guidance for teachers conducting their own 'living enquiries' (Wicks *et al.*, 2008; McNiff and Whitehead, 2005; Mills, 2010). Plymouth University provides clear advice on conducting action research in education and specific guidelines on research tools (**www. edu.plymouth.ac.uk/resined/actionresearch/arhome.htm**).

With action research, teachers deliberately try out something new ('action') and reflect on what happens ('research'), focusing on how improvements can occur (see Figure 11.2), although critics have argued that there is often more action and little research. The starting point for action research might be a hunch, question, a priority within the school development plan, or a stimulus from an in-service training event. Examples of starting points in the humanities might include:

- Observations that pupils are not asking enough open-ended questions in their RE lessons and exploring why this might be.
- Following attendance at a CPD event, introducing, monitoring and evaluating a new initiative (e.g. impact of using thinking hats in promoting creative thinking skills in geography).
- Posing a question: 'If I focus on developing pupils' understanding of historical interpretations, will this transfer to the playground?'

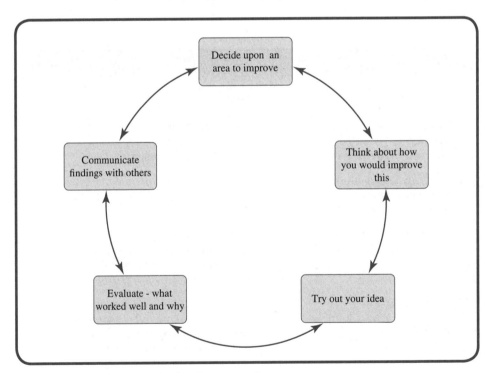

Figure 11.2 A simple model of action research.

Action research projects within the humanities can be read in publications such as the *British Journal of Religious Education*, and organisations such as the Warwick Religions and Education Research Unit (**www2.warwick.ac.uk/fac/soc/wie/research/wreru**). The Nuffield Primary History Project supported action research and its materials are now hosted by the Historical Association (**www.history.org.uk/index.php**).

There are a number of general websites that teachers can draw upon to keep up-to-date with latest research. The Teaching and Learning Research Programme provides research digests and 'tasters' (**www.tlrp.org/pa**) while the Centre for the Use of Research and Evidence in Education (CUREE) (**www.curee-paccts.com**) produces various resources to keep teachers informed. The Teaching and Learning Academy resources, formerly supported through the General Teaching Council, include research summaries and presentations (**www.tla.ac.uk**). Education Scotland (Learning and Teaching Scotland) provides research round-ups, bi-monthly digests that collate and summarise national and international educational research, and statistical reports (**www.ltscotland.org.uk/aboutlts/whatwedo/research**). In Northern Ireland, the Department of Education (DE) provides research briefings and reports (**www.deni.gov.uk**).

Professional development within school

Over recent years teachers and colleagues within schools have been encouraged to work closely together to raise standards. The concept of a professional learning community (PLC) links pupils' achievement to teachers' professional development. An effective PLC is defined as having 'the capacity to promote and sustain the learning of all professionals in the school community with the collective purpose of enhancing pupil learning' (Bolam *et al.*, 2005: iii). To build capacity requires teamwork and a willingness to make change in an 'open classroom' culture (Southworth, 2000; Hustler *et al.*, 2003). Eight characteristics of effective PLCs have been identified:

- shared values and vision;
- collective responsibility for pupils' learning;
- collaboration focused on learning – individual and collective professional learning;
- reflective professional enquiry;
- openness,
- networks and partnerships;
- inclusive membership; and
- mutual trust, respect and support.

Source: Bolam *et al.* (2005: iii)

The rationale behind PLCs is that when teachers work collaboratively the quality of learning and teaching improves. PLC activities are evidence based, for example action research projects, case analysis and lesson observations, with a focus on a particular skill or concept such as enquiry or chronology in primary history.

Lesson observations

There are many general proformas available for use when observing sessions. Most schools will follow an agreed format and procedure that will include the observer and observed agreeing upon:

Focus – e.g. a skill, concept, theme, resource, group of learners.

Style of observation – e.g. observer acting as participant, 'fly on the wall', systematic or more open-ended.

Duration – e.g. whole session, introduction, plenary.

Location – e.g. school grounds, library, ICT suite, museum.

Level – e.g. general history lesson, specific detail of a geography session, level of pastoral support to a particular group.

Means of recording and evaluating – e.g. field notes, video, time log, sociograms (mapping relationships between pupils/teacher).

Such lesson observations in the humanities are not common because priorities have tended to be given to literacy and numeracy. Observational notes should include judgements (rather than descriptive detail) about the following:

- standards seen (whether generally below, in line with, or above National Curriculum or other expectations);
- quality of learning (pupils' responses); and
- quality of teaching.

Clearly, the context of any observation is critical – particularly, the nature of pupils' learning needs and their prior learning. The following prompts could be used for observational purposes, but these need to be tailored to the circumstance; for instance, observing a group of four-year-olds in a role play area is quite different from eleven-year-olds undertaking historical research in an ICT suite.

Prompts to use when observing lessons/sessions

Below are some suggested prompts for session observations (not all of these would be appropriate for every observation):

The teacher/practitioner

- Does the teacher demonstrate good up-to-date subject knowledge?
- Do adults hold high expectations of all pupils?
- Do plans show clear objectives? Are these history-, geography- or RE-specific?
- Does the planning take into account the different needs of pupils?
- How well does the teacher draw upon pupils' own experiences, cultural backgrounds and religious beliefs?

- Does the session include a range of teaching approaches and resources to sustain interest?
- Do adults model good subject-specific language?
- Is behaviour well managed?
- Are there good working relationships within the class?
- Are learning support assistants deployed effectively?
- Are the activities sufficiently challenging?
- Is the pace of the lesson appropriate?
- How well does the teacher use illustrations, questions and gestures?
- Are opportunities well taken to make links to the locality?
- How well does the teacher set the material in a wider (regional, national or global) context?
- How well does the teacher provide feedback on pupils' progress?
- Do adults encourage pupils to ask questions and follow lines of inquiry?
- Are links made to homework if appropriate?

The pupils

- What have pupils learnt (in the humanities) by the end of the lesson that they didn't know or couldn't do at the start?
- What progress have particular groups of pupils made during the session (e.g. boys, girls, more able and talented, those with special educational needs)?
- How well do pupils develop their communication, literacy, numeracy and ICT skills?
- Are pupils motivated, engaged and enthusiastic?
- How well do pupils show independence in learning?
- How well do pupils know what they have to do to improve their work?
- What standards have the pupils demonstrated in the session in terms of knowledge, skills, attitudes and values?
- How do their oral responses compare to their written work?

School networks

Internationally, there is growing interest in developing schools as learning organisations and in ways for schools to share their expertise and experience more systematically (OECD, 2005). One of the core principles behind the introduction of the School Effectiveness Framework in Wales is recognition that large scale change can only occur if all professionals work collaboratively and in partnership (DCELLS, 2008; Harris,

2010). In effect, this requires good communication, problem-solving and leadership skills across partners.

The importance of schools working alongside each other is not a new idea but it remains a concern in the humanities despite the excellent leadership by professional bodies such as the Geographical Association. Ofsted (2008) calls upon local authorities to take a more proactive role in setting up networks, for example in order to share and develop good practice in geography. However, local authorities themselves have suffered considerable financial constraints over recent years and courses on primary humanities are not well funded. Moreover, one of the challenges is a lack of enthusiastic, able and knowledgeable subject leaders to initiate or contribute to such networks; for instance, Ofsted (2008) reports that leadership and management of geography are good in only a minority of primary schools. Further, those who do show promise are sometimes quickly 'promoted' to manage a core subject or given other responsibilities. However, networks of professional practice have much to offer primary teachers. They extend their professional frames of reference, and through informed discussion with others teachers challenge beliefs, customs and taken-for-granted practices.

There are examples of very effective networks in primary humanities. For instance, the GA's government-sponsored Action Plan for Geography (2006–11) provided CPD opportunities for 5,000 teachers, the appointment of Primary Champions, the introduction of Geography Quality Marks to recognise good practice and the setting up of regional networks (Geographical Association, 2011). An online professional community has also been established and includes more than a 1,000 members (**http:// geographychampions.ning.com**).

Other external expertise

A major review shows the important role of external specialists, including universities, in supporting teacher research especially in relation to such matters as data analysis, conducting interviews and devising questionnaires and other research tools (Bell *et al.*, 2010). If schools are serious about CPD, then they need to engage with external expertise on a regular basis. Such externality can sharpen understanding by offering a broader context to challenge complacency. Many universities and other organisations offer accredited and non-accredited courses within the humanities. The Culham Institute, for instance, provides booster courses for teaching RE (**www.teacher.co.uk**). One of the difficulties for busy teachers, however, is navigating the maze of CPD. It is not surprising, therefore, that a recent independent report in England has called for the setting up of regionally based CPD 'clearing houses', described as 'one-stop centres where schools can access quality-assured programmes that address the complete range of their training and development needs' (Gray, 2005: 3). There are CPD registers that teachers can access. For example, the TDA hosts a national database of CPD activities with details of courses, costs and providers (**https://cpdsearch.tda.gov.uk**) – a search for 'history' reveals a wide range of CPD opportunities including Masters level courses, conferences and free publications.

Throughout the UK there are professional bodies within the humanities field that offer resources, teaching ideas and opportunities for further professional development. In England, the subject resource networks (SRNs) provide subject-specific initial teacher training (ITT) materials (see Table 11.3).

Education (Citizenship, History, RE) MA

Institute of Education, University of London

£4,900 (full-time, Home/EU); £2,450 (part-time, Home/EU)

Teaching Black and Asian History

Wiltshire History Conference

Creative Education

£270+VAT

Being a Subject Leader in History

Historical Association

no cost

Exciting Cross-curricular History in KS1 and KS2

Creative Education

£219+VAT

Developing Diversity Through History

Kirklees Children and Young People Service, Learning

Standard rate: £155.00 Kirklees; £165.00 Non Kirklees

Mathematical History for Primary Schools

BEAM Education

£185+VAT   *https://cpdsearch.tda.gov.uk*

The websites of these professional bodies are excellent starting points for research. The Council for Subject Associations, created in 2006, attempts to provide a single voice for subject members. It also includes useful classroom materials – for instance, on promoting community cohesion through history, geography and RE – and free downloads of Primary Project Boxes on topics such as Our Wider World, Our Changing World and Our Future World (**www.subjectassociation.org.uk/index.php**).

REFLECTION

• Consider your own professional needs within the humanities. What can you do to address these?

Good subject coordinators also establish links with local networks such as history societies, archaeology clubs, curators and neighbourhood ramblers' associations. Unfortunately the economic climate over recent years has affected the provision of libraries, museums, heritage centres and other potential networks. For example, thousands of archaeologists have either lost their jobs or found new work impossible when old contracts have been terminated: 'The cuts are set to change the face of British archaeology as they threaten to do to every other part of British life' (Durrani and Faulkner, 2011: 1124).

Table 11.3 Professional bodies associated with the humanities

Subject	Professional bodies and other useful links	Details
History	The Historical Association: www.history.org.uk.	Articles, resources, online CPD materials, sections for primary and secondary schools.
	The Nuffield Primary History Project: www.primaryhistory.org/.	The Nuffield Primary History Project provides support for teaching history in primary schools.
	History Initial Teacher Training: www.historyitt.org.uk.	Materials organised in units, resources and activities.
Geography	Geographical Association: www.geography.org.uk.	Lesson ideas, resources, reading lists, web links, and 'Think Pieces'.
	Royal Geographic Society: www.rgs.org/OurWork/Schools/Schools.htm.	Founded in 1830, the schools and education section provides activities, advice, resources and training opportunities.
	National Geographic: www.nationalgeographic.com.	Publishes award-winning magazine (since 1888) and website includes education section with multimedia resources and fun activities for 'kids'.
Religious Education	The National Association of RE Teachers: www.natre.org.uk/.	Publishes the journal REsource, offers CPD opportunities, teaching materials and guidance on religious visitors to schools.
	Better RE: http://betterre.reonline.org.uk/index.php.	Provides advice, support and encouragement for RE teachers, advisers and other professionals seeking to raise standards in RE teaching and learning.
Citizenship	Citizenship Education: www.citized.info.	Sections for student teachers, teacher, mentors and tutors.

The inspectorate bodies for the UK contain examples of 'state-of-the-nation' reports and surveys, which are important sources to inform discussion with colleagues, as illustrated in the following example of excellent subject leaderships in history:

> What was particularly exciting was the enquiry-based approach that underpinned history teaching and was the result of a well-researched project undertaken by the coordinator. Following an audit of strengths and areas of development in history, the coordinator enlisted the help of the local authority adviser for primary

history to train all the staff in progression in skills in primary history. At the same time she read widely about teaching and learning in history, consulting materials produced by the Historical Association and by the Nuffield Primary History Project, as well as Ofsted's 2007 history report, *History in the Balance*. She also consulted a local primary Advanced Skills Teacher for history. As a direct outcome of this school-based research project, all the staff, teachers and teaching assistants, were trained how to develop pupils' skills through an enquiry-based approach to teaching and learning in history. This took place over a series of twilight training sessions.

At the time of the visit, the revised approach had been in place for just over a year. Careful monitoring of classroom practice and the rigorous assessment procedures introduced by the coordinator showed that the training had had a direct impact on improving pupils' achievement. Self-help and commitment had led to exciting teaching, as well as enthusiastic and engaged pupils who were making excellent progress.

Source: Ofsted (2011: 42–43).

TASK

• Consider this case study. What makes this practice excellent?

Some local authorities provide excellent websites to support subject leaders and teachers in the humanities including forums, resources, web links, exemplar plans and case studies of good practice. For instance, Staffordshire, Lancashire and Hertfordshire local authorities all provide a range of materials on whole-school issues such as tracking subject-specific skills (see Figure 11.3):

www.sln.org.uk/geography/primary.htm.

www.thegrid.org.uk/learning/geography/ks1-2/assessment/index.shtml.

www.lancsngfl.ac.uk/curriculum.

The Internet and other technologies are essential to the development of professional practice. Leach (2003) points out that they have not only made the workplace more efficient but have transformed the nature of work itself by creating new knowledge and skills. Teachers can gain fresh insight into how pupils interact with each other through technologies. For instance, in Religious Education the Building E-Bridges Project linked children from primary schools in the multicultural city of Leicester in the English Midlands with children from East Sussex. The pupils asked themselves questions about their different daily life experiences and their religious backgrounds. They were able to combine a dialogue of life with a dialogue of faiths (McKenna *et al.*, 2008).

The Internet remains a major source for professional networking as well as social interaction. Professional networking sites such as Xing and LinkedIn have seen exponential membership growth with millions of members worldwide. There are a

History – Progression of Skills					
Skill	**Level 1**	**Level 2**	**Level 3**	**Level 4**	**Level 5**
Chronology	Show their emerging knowledge and understanding of the past by recognising the distinction between past & present. Place a few events and objects in order by using common phrases to show the passing of time, e.g. *old, new/young, days & months*.	Show their developing knowledge and understanding of the past by recognising the distinction between present & past by: Placing a few objects and events in order. Using common words and phrases about the passing of time (*before, after, a long time ago, past…*)	Show their increasing knowledge and understanding of the past by using specialist dates and terms and by placing topics studied into different periods. *Century, decade, Roman, Egyptian, BCE, AD…*	Show their understanding of chronology by sequencing events and periods through the use of appropriate terms relating to the passing of time. Identify where periods studied fit into a chronological framework.	Develop their understanding of a chronological framework through studying different periods, using appropriate vocabulary when describing the passing of time.
Events, people and changes	To tell the difference between past and present in their own and other people's lives.	Recognise that their own lives are different from the lives of people in the past by describing some of the topics, events and people they have studied.	Be able to describe some of the main events, people and periods they have studied. Recognise some of the similarities and differences between these periods. Begin to suggest causes and consequences of the main events and changes.	Show their knowledge and understanding of local, national and international history by describing some of the main events, people and periods they have studied. Describe the characteristic features of past societies and periods to identify change and continuity within and across different periods. Identify some of the causes and consequences of the main events and changes.	Show their knowledge and understanding of local, national and international history by describing events, people and some features of past societies and periods in the context of their developing chronological framework. Begin to recognise and describe the nature and extent of diversity, change and continuity and suggest relationships between causes.
Interpretation		To begin to understand the reasons why people in the past acted as they did from a range of sources (pictures, plays, films, written accounts, songs, museum displays, stories).	Identify some of the different ways in which the past can be represented through *artists' pictures, museum displays, written sources…*	Identify and describe different ways in which the past has been interpreted.	Suggest some reasons for different interpretations of the past. Begin to recognise why some events, people and changes might be judged as more historically significant than others.
Enquiry	Use sources to answer simple questions about the past.	Answer questions about the past through observing and handling a range of sources, such as objects, pictures, people talking about their past, buildings, written sources.	Use sources to make detailed observations, finding answers to questions about the past.	Use sources as a basis for research from which they will begin to use information as evidence to test hypotheses.	Investigate historical problems and issues using a range of sources and begin to ask their own questions. Begin to evaluate sources to establish evidence for particular enquiries.
Communication	To show what they know, understand in different ways, such as speaking, role-play and drawing	To show what they know and understand about the past in different ways, such as speaking, role-play, drawing and writing.	To show what they know and understand in different ways, such as speaking, role-play, drawing and writing. When doing this they should use specialist terms like *settlement, invasion* and vocabulary linked to chronology.	Begin to produce structured work, making use of appropriate dates and terms.	Select and deploy information and make appropriate use of historical terminology to support and structure their work.

Figure 11.3 Example of a tracking sheet in history. *Source*: Lancashire Grid for Learning, (Lancashire County Council at: www.lancsngfl.ac.uk/curriculum/).

growing number of online professional communities including those hosted by newspapers such as the *Times Educational Supplement* and *The Guardian*. The Geographical Association Network **http://geographical.ning.com**) has more than 2,000 members and includes forums, blogs, videos and groups. The Expansive Education Network (**www.expansiveeducationnet**) offers schools the opportunity to work closely with other schools on projects broadly relating to thinking skills, facilitated by universities offering action research seminars to inform practice.

Teachers, let alone pupils, should not assume that information on the Internet is accurate, up-to-date, clear or relevant. Most web pages are not reviewed or edited by professional editors or publishers. There is a common perception that if something appears in print, then it must be true. There is much advice on evaluating websites available in universities and libraries. It is important to question websites, rather than simply absorb information provided, and prompt cards can be prepared for older pupils and colleagues:

Authorship– is this website an established voice?

Purpose – what does the website set out to do?

Currency – is the website up to date?

Evidence – check at least three sources that support what is said (triangulation of evidence is standard research practice).

Research on world faiths and some of the lesser-known religions is particularly liable to bias and misinformation. All of the major world faiths have authorised websites. One of the most informative websites is the Ontario-based Religious Tolerance multi-faith group (**www.religioustolerance.org**), while the BBC usually provides reliable information to accompany its programmes; for instance, the BBC2 series *Around the World in 80 Faiths* (**www.bbc.co.uk/programmes/b00glqx9**). The BBC and its regional websites offer concise information on the humanities for primary teachers (**www.bbc.co.uk/learning**). Education Scotland brings together materials from Learning and Teaching Scotland (LTS), HM Inspectorate of Education (HMIE) and other bodies (**www.educationscotland.gov.uk**).

The role and responsibilities of the humanities subject leaders

The role of the subject leader is to act as a point of contact for colleagues, offering support and leadership with the view of raising standards and improving the quality of learning and teaching. This brings a range of specific responsibilities including:

- to act as consultant by keeping up to date with the latest documents, learning methodologies and courses available;
- to oversee and ensure continuity and progression in humanities through the school;
- to audit, allocate and update resources;
- to liaise with the assessment coordinator about assessment procedures for humanities;
- to ensure that the Humanities Policy and guidelines are regularly reviewed and updated; and
- to advise on and provide for staff development as required.

Good overviews of subject leadership in the humanities are provided by the Falmer Press Subject Leader handbooks for history (Davies and Redmond, 1998), geography (Halocha, 1998) and Religious Education (Bastide, 1998). They are still relevant a decade or so after publication. Subject leaders need to be outward looking, always seeking to capitalise on CPD opportunities, anniversaries and events such as Celebrating RE, a month-long celebration of RE organised by the RE Council for England and Wales (**www.celebratingre.org/index.php/about**). Once allocated curriculum responsibilities, it is useful for subject leaders to undertake a self-evaluation exercise. It is also wise to maintain a detailed record to keep track of the various responsibilities. Most subject leaders use a lever-arch file divided into sections (see Figure 11.4).

It is important for subject leaders to offer a clear, evidence-based view on how well older pupils are doing in history, geography and RE, irrespective of whether these subjects are taught separately or through a cross-curricular approach. Similarly in the Foundation Stage, there should be evidence to support judgements on children's progress since entry to the school in their knowledge and understanding of the world.

TASK

- If applicable, refer to Table 11.4 and indicate how well your subject leadership is progressing.

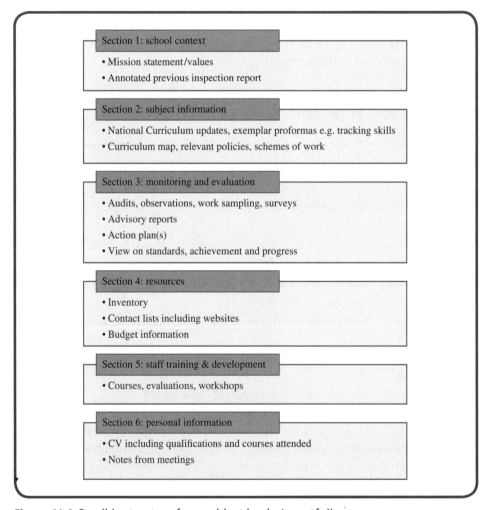

Section 1: school context

- Mission statement/values
- Annotated previous inspection report

Section 2: subject information

- National Curriculum updates, exemplar proformas e.g. tracking skills
- Curriculum map, relevant policies, schemes of work

Section 3: monitoring and evaluation

- Audits, observations, work sampling, surveys
- Advisory reports
- Action plan(s)
- View on standards, achievement and progress

Section 4: resources

- Inventory
- Contact lists including websites
- Budget information

Section 5: staff training & development

- Courses, evaluations, workshops

Section 6: personal information

- CV including qualifications and courses attended
- Notes from meetings

Figure 11.4 Possible structure for a subject leader's portfolio.

Table 11.4 Self-evaluation of subject leader responsibilities.			
Responsibility	**HS**	**GG**	**RE**
Complete using the following scale: 1 = well established; 2 = recently introduced; 3 = yet to begin *Documentation*			
I ensure that curriculum documentation is accessible for all staff including teacher assistants.			
I distribute to staff relevant catalogues, newsletters, information from subject associations.			
I keep parents and governors informed of subject developments.			
The curriculum policies are in place and reviewed regularly.			
The school's long-term plans or maps are in place for humanities.			
Short-term planning includes provision for different groups (e.g. SEN and gifted and talented).			
Teaching, learning and assessment			
I have provided a 'model' lesson to colleagues.			
I undertake session observations.			
I undertake a scrutiny of pupils' work.			
I have surveyed pupils' views about the subjects.			
I have surveyed teachers' views about the subjects.			
I undertake other monitoring activities (e.g. displays).			
I keep a whole-school portfolio of work to show progression in pupils' subject-specific skills.			
Training and development			
I lead staff training.			
We have invited in external speakers.			
We have links with other schools (e.g. twinned with a school in mainland Europe).			
Resources			
I evaluate resources against best-value-for-money principles.			
I ensure that the resources are well organised and audited each year.			
We have an allocated budget for the humanities.			

(Continued)

Table 11.4 (Continued)			
Responsibility	HS	GG	RE
Leadership			
The humanities have featured on the School Improvement Plan over the past 3 years.			
We have set priorities for the humanities that have allocated costs and agreed timetables for evaluation.			
I am a strong advocate for the humanities (e.g. in team meetings, providing material for the website, through displays).			
I have good links with other schools, local authority advisers, and local university subject departments.			
We have good links with local museums, galleries, national park rangers and ministers.			

Resources

Subject leaders need to demonstrate a good awareness of the resources available within the humanities including: publishers, artefact suppliers, websites, education packs, maps, globes, atlases, large format books, timelines, aerial photographs, historical pictures and replica costume suppliers. University libraries provide access to a good range of e-journals such as those listed below:

BBC History Magazine
The Historian
History Today
Primary History
History of Education
National Geographic
Primary Geography
RE Today
REsource
British Journal of Religious Education
British Educational Research Journal
British Journal of Special Education

Times Educational Supplement

Junior Education

Infant Projects

One of the most time-consuming but necessary duties of a subject leader is resource management. Resources need to be monitored for quality, range and interest. Inventories should consider what needs to be bought, replaced or even discarded. When considering library stock, some older history books should be retained for discussions about historical interpretations.

Monitoring and evaluation

The main responsibility of subject leaders is to have a secure view on standards in the school and how these might be raised. This requires monitoring, supporting and motivating other teachers and setting targets for professional development and improvement. Without monitoring it is difficult to evaluate the impact of any subject action plan. However, effective monitoring needs a shared understanding among staff of its purposes and the intended use made of outcomes. Many schools have a schedule for monitoring subjects and senior leaders will undertake separate monitoring in relation to performance management duties. In reality, many humanities subject leaders do not have time or the opportunity to undertake regular lesson monitoring (Halocha, 1998). Given such constraints, they inevitably draw upon other monitoring strategies such as reviews of pupils' books or discussions with pupils. However, in more recent years a renewed interest in cross-curricular provision has the prospect of opening up more opportunities to observe history, geography and RE within integrated contexts (see Table 11.5).

Table 11.5 Examples of whole-school monitoring activities for a subject leader in humanities.

Strategy	Examples of questions
Talk with pupils	How knowlegeable are pupils about their own area? Do they know where they live?
	How well do they know national stories and landmarks?
	How well can older ones use an atlas or globe?
	How good are pupils' independent research skills?
Work samples	How often is work sampled? Why? What are the outcomes? Who does the sampling? What happens afterwards?
Monitor displays	What profile do the humanities have on the wall and other displays? Do the displays include questions, sources, pupils' work, points for reflection, timelines, artefacts, maps? Do they reflect local, national and global dimensions?

(Continued)

Table 11.5 (*Continued*)

Strategy	Examples of questions
External contacts	How well do we make use of parental interests and expertise? For example, do we borrow family artefacts or invite in grandparents to share memories?
	Do we inform parents of humanities events such as visits, exhibitions or anniversaries?
	How well do we use local historians and ministers?
Teachers' planning and evaluations	How much time is devoted to history, geography and RE?
	If integrated, how is the right breadth and balance retained?
	Do plans cover curriculum requirements? Is enough attention given to more challenging areas such as historical interpretations?
	Do teachers show how humanities contribute to development of literacy, numeracy, ICT and thinking skills?
Analyse data	How many pupils are attaining expected National Curriculum levels? What is the trend over time?
Teachers' records	Do teachers keep annotated examples of pupils' work in the humanities?
Pupils' reports	Do these include subject-specific comments for humanities and targets for improvement?
Pupils' evaluation	Are pupils encouraged to review their work and comment on the work of others?
Audit use of resources	Are there enough 'local' sources, globes, maps, atlases, artefacts, ICT, books, copies of historical sources such as census returns, costumes, props, role-play areas? How are these resources stored and managed?
	Does the school library have good examples of up-to-date reference books in humanities?
	Have we a list of recommended websites for each year group?

It is rare for humanities coordinators to have designated time to monitor the teaching of colleagues but it is more common for them to sample pupils' work and review teachers' planning.

When reviewing pupils' work

Examples of questions relating to scrutiny of pupils' work

- How high are standards? Are standards in line with National Curriculum expectations/levels for the appropriate age?

- Is there a sufficient range of work in terms of curriculum requirements?
- Is there evidence of pupils making good progress over time?
- Are there any noticeable differences in the work of boys/girls, ethnic minority groups?
- How well do pupils with SEN make progress towards meeting the targets set for them?
- Does the evidence of work completed indicate that sufficient time is given to this subject?
- What is the balance of work across attainment targets? Is this appropriate?
- What is the depth of study?
- Does the choice of work encourage progression by building on skills previously taught?
- Is subject vocabulary being encouraged?
- Is there evidence for promoting thinking skills?
- Are pupils encouraged to think and use their own ideas?
- How much work is copied?
- Is work differentiated for abilities and age ranges?
- Does the work reveal low-level tasks such as colouring worksheets or is there evidence of challenging tasks including research?
- What is the quality of pupils' communication and presentation?
- Are they recording their work in a variety of formats, such as tables, graphs, and using ICT?
- What does the sample reveal about the quality of marking?
- Are comments subject-specific (e.g. 'You have done well to explain why the Romans invaded Britain') or do they focus too much on general language issues?
- If the humanities work is recorded in 'topic' books, is there evidence of progression in skills, the acquisition of knowledge and conceptual understanding?
- Is the quantity of recorded work reasonable for the time period, and age of pupils?
- Are comments positive, constructive and regular?
- Is there any evidence of self-marking or peer assessment?
- Do pupils indicate their progress against learning objectives?

With children in Nursery and Reception, over the year it should be possible to build up a portfolio of evidence to demonstrate their achievements in all areas of experience. Work scrutiny should be treated in a flexible manner, and its nature will vary according to the purpose of the activity: for example, this could be to target examples of good practice or to track the progress of particular pupils. It is sometimes more productive to focus on particular years, or ability groups such as the more able and talented, or individual teachers such as those who are newly-qualified or new to the school. At times, there may be a need to scan the work of the whole class, especially when the focus is linked to a whole-school issue such as marking or presentation. During inspections, it is customary practice among inspectors to choose the work of one higher, one lower, and one average-attaining pupil.

Strategic direction

Good subject leadership requires vision and a commitment to spreading best practice. This has been highlighted by Ofsted's (2012) recent subject-specific guidance on outstanding subject provision.

> Practice in the subject consistently reflects the highest aspirations for pupils and expectations of staff. Best practice is spread effectively in a drive for continuous improvement. Teaching in the subject is likely to be outstanding and together with a rich curriculum, which is highly relevant to pupils' needs, it contributes to outstanding learning and achievement or, in exceptional circumstances, achievement that is good and rapidly improving. Thoughtful and wide-ranging promotion of the pupils' spiritual, moral, social and cultural development in the subject enables them to thrive. Consequently, pupils and groups of pupils have excellent experiences in the subject, ensuring they are very well equipped for the next stage of their education, training or employment.
>
> *Ofsted (2012:7).*

Yet a recent survey commissioned by the Training and Development Agency reports that there is widespread absence of a strategic approach to CPD in schools (Pedder *et al.*, 2008). It often lacks clear planning and tends to be reactive. It is short-sighted and self-defeating to wait for a school inspection to determine how well pupils are doing. A well-established culture of self-evaluation would be manifested when teachers, as well as senior leaders, regularly discuss pupils' attainment, achievement and progress across the curriculum, including the humanities:

Attainment – how well pupils do in comparison to others, measured for instance in terms of benchmarks such as National Curriculum level descriptors.

Achievement – how well pupils do in relation to their individual capabilities.

Progress – the 'value added' in terms of how far pupils have developed over a period of time, for instance across a key stage or year group.

Staff meetings, led by the humanities coordinator, can focus on questions such as:

- Do we have a clear action plan(s) for the humanities? Are priorities widely known, monitored and evaluated?
- How often does history, geography or RE feature on meeting agendas?

Objectives Key Actions	Outcomes and/or success criteria	Actions	Dates	Responsible Person(s)	Resources	Monitoring/ Evaluation (How, by whom and how often?)
To develop the use of self and peer assessment with regards to geographical knowledge, skills and understanding.	Topic books will show evidence of self and peer assessment with regards to geographical knowledge, skills and understanding, as appropriate for the year group.	Children will assess their own geographical knowledge, skills and understanding, as well as that of their peers, at appropriate points throughtout the year depending on the nature of the topic.	Use of self and peer assessment will be ongoing throughout the year. Geography Co-ordinator to scrutinise topic books during the work sampling staff meeting in the spring term.	Class teachers and Geography Co-ordinator	Time during the extended work sampling staff meeting to allow the Geography co-ordinator to gather evidence.	Geography Co-ordinator to scrutinise topic books during the work sampling staff meeting in the spring term.
To use geography topics where appropriate to continue to develop a topic-based approach, providing a cohesive and meaningful learning experience for all pupils across the school.	Topic-based planning will ensure the children learn in a cross-curricular and meaningful way. Their geographical knowledge and understanding will be enhanced through art, literacy, science and other activities, both in and outdoors.	Teachers will plan in their Key Stages, or with their year group partners as appropriate, to create topic-based long-term and medium-term plans, with one-term or half-term topic having a geographical theme. They will then use these to inform their weekly planning.	Long-term and medium-term planning for the autumn term w/c 27/06/11. Weekly planning ongoing throughout the year.	Class teachers	Time to allow the Geography co-ordinator to sample planning.	Geography Co-ordinator to sample medium-term planning from both Key Stages to ensure that one-term or half-term topic has a geographical theme and encompasses a range of cross-curricular activities.
To improve the children's learning experiences and understanding of geography by ensuring topic boxes contain up-to-date and relevant resources.	Topic boxes will contain resources that will enhance teaching and learning, including DVDs and CD Roms.	Following consultation with teachers in both Key Stages, the Geography Co-ordinator will purchase resources that will assist the teachers in their delivery of exciting and interactive geography-themed sessions.	Geography Co-ordinator to invite teachers to request resources they feel would support teaching and learning during their autumn-term topics on the training day. Further discussions to take place throughout the year at the beginning of each term.	Geography Co-ordinator	£100 to purchase various resources, including DVDs and CD Roms.	Geography Co-ordinator to check teachers have the resources they need to deliver their topics effectively on a termly basis.

Figure 11.5 Geography action plan. *Source:* http://www.thomasmoreprimary.org.uk/pgf/doc/doc0002981tmp-00-4lGeography2011-12.pdf

- How well do we as a staff appreciate the role of the humanities in contributing to higher standards across the curriculum, especially in literacy, numeracy and ICT?

Subject leaders should begin by identifying the needs for the school and these may arise from an internal audit, inspection report or advisory visit – for instance, to develop pupils' mapping skills or historical enquiry. CPD then needs to feature on the school improvement plan with clear priorities established. Good action plans include clear objectives, success indicators, sufficient resources, a realistic timescale and allocated responsibilities (see Figure 11.5). A short-hand guide is to answer the basic questions of who, when, where, how and why. Ofsted (2001) reports that the most effective action plans focus on improving one of a number of issues: levels of attainment and rate of pupils' progress; the challenge and pace of teaching; leadership, with a particular emphasis on raising standards and the quality and range of learning opportunities; planning and organisation of lessons; and pupils' behaviour, attitudes and work habits.

REFLECTION

- Consider the extract from a primary school's action plan for geography and reflect on its quality.

The pace of change in society and technology over the past 30 or so years makes the CPD needs of schools difficult to predict. However, it seems likely that in the future schools will need to respond to:

- an ethnically and socially diverse society;
- the need for a digitally literate and numerate workforce;
- flexible learners who are able to adapt, solve problems and reason; and
- a sharper focus on sustainability and the responsibility of individuals to care for the environment.

The humanities are well placed to provide the curriculum contexts for schools to address these priorities.

SUMMARY

- Continuing professional development (CPD) is an ongoing commitment from teachers to update their knowledge and skills.

- CPD can take various formats, including in-house staff training, attendance at conferences and pursuing accredited courses. CPD can operate within the school context. Observing colleagues teach can form the basis of professional dialogue about pupils' standards and progress, as well as aspects of teaching the humanities.

- Increasingly schools are expected to work as part of networks of professional practice. This can include collaborating with other schools along with external experts such as museum curators, local authority advisers and members of the community.

- Although CPD opportunities within primary humanities are more limited than the core subject areas of literacy and numeracy, the humanities are well represented by professional bodies such as the Geographical Association. These provide resources, forums and opportunities for further professional development.

- Subject leaders have a range of responsibilities including supporting colleagues and the management of whole-school matters such as tracking pupils' progress by reviewing work and setting a strategic lead in the humanities. The major focus should always be on pupils' achievement and how standards can be improved.

References

Adey, P. (2007), 'What next? CPD and the Whole School', in Dillon, J. and Maguire, M. (eds), *Becoming a Teacher. Issues in Secondary Teaching*, Maidenhead: Open University Press, 357–366.

Alexander, R.J. (ed) (2010), *Children, their World, their Education*, London: Routledge.

Banks, F. and Shelton Mayes, A. (eds) (2001), *Early Professional Development for Teachers*, London: David Fulton.

Barber, M. and Mourshed, M. (2007), *How the World's Best Performing School Systems Came Out On Top*, McKinsey and Company.

Bastide, D. (1998), *Coordinating Religious Education Across the Primary School*, London: David Fulton

Bell, M., Cordingley, P., Isham., C. and Davis, R. (2010), 'Report of Professional Practitioner Use of Research Review: Practitioner engagement in and/or with research',

Coventry: CUREE, GTCE, LSIS & NTRP. Available at: **www. curee-paccts.com/node/2303**.

Bolam, R., McMahon, A., Stoll, L., Thomas, S., Wallace, M., Greenwood, A., Hawkey, K., Ingram, M., and Atkinson, A. (2005), *Creating and Sustaining Effective Professional Learning Communities*, University of Bristol, available at: **www.education.gov.uk/publications/ eOrderingDownload/RR637-2.pdf**

Bolam, R. (2000), 'Emerging policy trends: Some implications for continuing professional development', Journal of In-service Education 26(2): 267–280.

Borko, H. (2004), 'Professional Development and Teacher Learning: Mapping the Terrain', *Educational Researcher*, vol. 33: 8, 3–15.

Davies, J. and Redmond, J. (1998), *Coordinating History Across the Primary School*, London: David Fulton.

DCELLS (2008), *School Effectiveness Framework Building effective learning communities together*, Cardiff: Welsh Assembly Government.

DfES (2002a), *Key Stage 3. Learning styles and writing in religious education*, Nottingham: DfES.

DfES (2002b), *Key Stage 3. Learning styles and writing in geography*, Nottingham: DfES

Donaldson, G. (2010), Teaching Scotland's Future, Edinburgh: Scottish Government.

Durrani, N. and Faulkner, N. (2011), 'Archaeology', *Whitaker's Alamac 2012*, 121–1124.

Fessler, R. and Ingram, R. (2003), 'The teacher career cycle revisited: new realities, new responses' in Davies, B. and West-Burnham, J. (eds) (2003), *Handbook of Educational Leadership and Management*, Harlow: Pearson, 584–590.

Findlay, J.J. (1911), *The School*, London: Williams & Norgate.

Franklin, S. (2006), 'VAKing our learning styles', *Education 3–13*, 34 (1), 81–87.

Geographical Association (2011), *The Action Plan for Geography 2006–2011 Final Report and Evaluation*, London: Geographical Association.

GTCNI (2007), *Teaching: the Reflective Profession*, Belfast: General Teaching Council for Northern Ireland.

Gray, S.L. (2005), *An Enquiry Into Continuing Professional Development for Teachers*.

Guskey, T. R. (2000), *Evaluating professional development*, Thousand Oaks, CA: Corwin Press, Inc.

Halocha, J. (1998), *Coordinating Geography Across the Primary School*, London: David Fulton

Harris, A. (2010), 'Leading System Transformation', keynote speech presented at the International Congress for School Effectiveness and School Improvement (ICSEI).

Henry, J. (2007), 'Professor pans "learning style" teaching method', *The Telegraph*, 29 July 2007.

House of Commons Select Committee for Children, Schools and Families (2010), *Training of Teachers*, London: House of Commons.

Hustler, D., McNamara, O., Jarvis, J., Londra, M., Campbell, A. and Howson, J. (2003), Teachers' Perspectives of Continuing Professional Development, DfES.

Jackson, R. (2004), *Rethinking Religious Education and Plurality: Issues in Diversity and Pedagogy*, London: Routledge.

Jones, K. (2011), 'Central, local and individual continuing professional development (CPD), priorities: changing policies of CPD in Wales', Professional Development in Education, Vol: 37: 5, November, 759–776.

Kent, A. (ed.) (2000), *Reflective Practice in Geography Teaching*, London: Paul Chapman.

Kennedy, A. (2005), *Models of continuing professional development: a framework for analysis.* Journal of In-Service Education, 31 (2), 235–250.

Leach, J. (2003), 'Teaching's Long Revolution; from ivory towers to networked communities of practice', in Banks, F. and Mayes, A.S. (eds) (2003), 'Early Professional Development for Teachers', London: David Fulton, 379–394.

McKennah, U., Ipgrave, J., and Jackson, R. (2008), *Inter Faith Dialogue by Email in Primary Schools*, New York: REDCo.

McMahon, A. (1999), 'Promoting Continuing Professional Development for Teachers: an achievable target for school leaders?', in Bush, T., Bell, L., Bolam, R., Glatter, R. and Ribbins, P. (eds), Re-defining Educational Management, London: Paul Chapman Publishing.

McNiff, J. and Whitehead, J. (2005), *Action Research for Teachers: a Practical Guide*, London: David Fulton.

Mills, G.E. (2010), *Action Research: A Guide for the Teacher Researcher*, Harlow: Pearson.

NFER (2011), *NFER Teacher Voice Omnibus February 2011 Survey*, NFER.

O'Brien, J. (2011), 'Continuing professional development for Scottish teachers: tensions in policy and practice', Professional Development in Education, Vol: 37: 5, November, 777–792.

OECD (2005), *Attracting, Developing and Retaining Effective Teachers*, Directorate for Education.

Ofsted (2001), *Action Planning for School Improvement*, London: Ofsted.

Ofsted (2005), *The national literacy and numeracy strategies and the primary curriculum*, London: Ofsted.

Ofsted (2006), *The logical chain: continuing professional development in effective schools*, London: Ofsted.

Ofsted (2008), *Geography in schools: changing practice*, London: Ofsted.

Ofsted (2009), Guidance on making judgements during subject survey visits to schools, London: Ofsted.

Ofsted (2010), Good professional development in schools. How does leadership contribute? London: Ofsted.

Ofsted (2011), *History for all*, London: Ofsted.

Ofsted (2012), *Generic grade descriptors and supplementary subject-specific guidance for inspectors making judgements during visits to schools,* London: Ofsted.

Paige-Smith, A. and Craft, A. (2011), *Developing Reflective Practice in the Early Years*, Maidenhead: Open University Press.

Pedder, D. and Opter, V. (2011), 'Are we realising the full potential of teachers' professional learning in schools in England?', in Professional Development in Education, Vol: 37: 5, November, 741–758.

Pedder, D., Storey, A., and Opfer, V. (2008), *Schools and continuing professional development (CPD), in England – State of the Nation research project (T34718)*, Training and Development Agency for Schools.

Pollard, A., Anderson, J., Maddock, M., Swaffield, S., Warin, J., and Warwick, P. (2008), 3rd edn, *Reflective Teaching*, London: Continuum.

Rudge, L. (2007), Using Research in Religious Education to Develop Reflective Practice, available from **www.re-net. ac.uk**.

Saunders, W. M., Goldenberg, C. N., and Gallimore, R., (2009), 'Increasing achievement by focusing grade level teams on improving classroom learning: A Prospective, Quasi-experimental Study of Title 1 Schools', *American Educational Research Journal*, 46 (4), 1006–1033.

Schon, D.A. (1983), *The Reflective Practitioner: How professionals think in action*. London: Temple Smith.

Southworth, G, (2000), 'How Primary Schools Learn', *Research Papers in Education*, Vol 15, No 3.

Stenhouse, L. (1975), *An Introduction to Curriculum Research and Development,* London, Heinemann.

TDA (2008), *Continuing professional development guidance (CPD)*, London: TDA.

Walker, M., Jeffer, J., Hart, R., Lord, P., and Kinder, K. (2011), *Making the links between teachers' professional standards, induction, performance management and continuing professional development*, London: DfE.

Watkins, C., Carnell, E., and Lodge, C. (2007), *Effective Learning in Classrooms*, London: Sage.

Wicks, P.G., Reason, P. and Bradbury, H. (2008), 'Living inquiry: personal, political and philosophical groundings for action research practice', in Reason, P., and Bradbury, H. (eds), The Sage Handbook of Action Research, 2nd edn., Abingdon: Routledge.

Wilson, V., Hall, J., Davidson, J. and Lewin, J. (2006), Developing Teachers: A Review of Early Professional Development, Glasgow: General Teaching Council Scotland.

Useful Websites

Geographical Association offers online CPD opportunities: **www.geography.org.uk/cpdevents/onlinecpd**.

British Educational Research Association provides details of conferences, publications and research news: **www.bera.ac.uk**.

Department for Education's TRIPS research digests can be viewed at: **www.education.gov.uk/schools/ toolsandinitiatives/tripsresearchdigests**.

Centre for the use of Research and Evidence in Education: **www.curee.co.uk**.

NCSL – National College for School Leadership: **www.ncsl.org.uk**.

Evidence for Policy and Practice Information and Co-ordination Centre (EPPI): **http://eppi.ioe.ac.uk**.

Web-based guides to using history, geography and RE have been published by Becta and are available at the

Department for Education: **www.education.gov.uk/ publications/standard/publicationDetail/Page1/15075**.

Skein (meaning 'reflect' in Norwegian) provides information on CPD networks: **www.skein.org.uk**.

Scotland's Journey to Excellence website features various CPD materials: **www.journeytoexcellence.org.uk/ resourcesandcpd/cpdresources.asp**.

CPD Find website provides opportunity for Scottish teachers to search for CPD opportunities: **www. ltscotland.org.uk/cpdfind/index.asp**.

Probationary Teacher website for those in Scotland: **www. probationerteacherscotland.org.uk/home/home.aspx**.

CPD Scotland: **www.cpdscotland.org.uk**. Department of Education Northern Ireland link for CPD: **www. deni.gov.uk/index/teachers_pg/4-teachers- professionaldevelopment_pg.htm**.

The General Teaching Council for Northern Ireland's Access to Research Resources for Teachers (ARRT) Space: **http://arrts.gtcni.org.uk/gtcni**

Index

ALSO WRITTEN BY
RUSSELL GRIGG

ISBN: 9781405873420

In this book for trainee or newly qualified primary teachers, Russell Grigg explores outstanding practice from all angles. From how researchers and inspectors define high-quality teaching to developing a personal teaching philosophy, the book also includes detailed guidance on creative teaching and learning, knowledge and understanding of the curriculum, lesson planning and assessment.

For further information or to view other textbooks within Education, please visit:
www.pearsoned.co.uk/educationcat